WHODUNIT?

WHODUNIT?

A Guide to Crime, Suspense and Spy Fiction

HRF Keating

VAN NOSTRAND REINHOLD COMPANY

NEW YORK   CINCINNATI   TORONTO   LONDON   MELBOURNE

Compilation Copyright © 1982 by H.R.F. Keating
Text and design Copyright © 1982 by Shuckburgh Reynolds Ltd
except:
Page 56 to 60 Text Copyright © 1982 by Jessica Mann
Page 104 to 106 Text Copyright © 1982 by Eric Ambler

Library of Congress Catalog Card Number 82-8616
ISBN 0-442-25438-5

Typesetting by SX Composing, Rayleigh, Essex
Printed and bound in Spain by Printer Industria Grafica SA
D.L. B. 5077-1982

Published in the United States in 1982
by Van Nostrand Reinhold Company Inc.
135 West 50th Street
New York, NY 10020, U.S.A.

Van Nostrand Reinhold Publishing
1410 Birchmount Road,
Scarborough, Ontario M1P 2E7, Canada

Conceived and designed by Shuckburgh Reynolds Ltd,
8 Northumberland Place,
London W2 5BS, England

Design by Roger Pring
Assistant designer: Dinah Lone
Illustrations by Rene Eyre, Safu-Marie Gilbert,
Carole Johnson, Dinah Lone, David Mallott,
Sheilagh Noble, Andrew Popkiewicz and Roger Pring
Picture research by Linda Proud and Elly Trelawny

Library of Congress Cataloging in Publication Data
Main entry under title:
Whodunit?: guide to crime, suspense, and spy fiction.
Includes index.
    1. Detective and mystery stories, English—History
and criticism.   2. Detective and mystery stories,
American—History and criticism.   3. Crime and
criminals in literature.   4. Spy stories—History and
criticism.   5. Fiction—Authorship.   I. Keating,
H. R. F. (Henry Reymond Fitzwalter), 1926-
PR830.D4W44   1982   823'.0872'09   82-8616
ISBN 0-442-25438-5   AACR2

Picture sources. Numerals refer to page numbers (abbr. *t*, top; *b*, bottom; *r*, right; *l*, left.)

Godfrey Argent: 123, 205, 284; Associated Press: 135t, 156; BBC Hulton Picture Library: 22, 144r, 160, 227; BBC Photo Archive: 57, 258, 274, 281, 300, 307b; Jerry Bauer: 92; Cindy Bellinger: 184; John Bingham: 122; Camera Press: 240; Jonathan Cape Ltd: 82 (Rhoda Nathans), 97 (Jerry Bauer), 158 (Horst Tappe), 197; Cassell Ltd: 172; Chatto & Windus Ltd: 112 (Peter Hampshire); William Collins & Co Ltd: 87, 119, 170, 179, 180, 186; Constable and Co Ltd: 236r; Richard Coomber: 248; Corgi Books: 255b; Daily Express: 254; Doubleday Inc: 232b (Stephen R Dujack); E.P. Dutton Inc: 210 (Michael Pressman); Eyre Methuen Ltd: 243t; Faber & Faber Ltd: 85 (Jerry Bauer); Adrian Flowers (London): 99; Fontana Books: 48, 203 (Hal Boucher); Mark Gerson: 113, 163; Fay Godwin: 161b; Victor Gollancz Ltd: 115, 144l, 187 (Fay Godwin); 220t; Granada Television: 264; Peter Haining: 36, 38, 53, 250, 269, 294; Hamish Hamilton Ltd: 200; Harrap & Co Ltd: 175; John

Patrick Hart: 244t; A M Heath Ltd: 114, 126; Heinemann Ltd: 132, 193, 209; Reginald Hill: 266; Hodder & Stoughton Ltd: 139, 143, 150, 154, 165b, 166, 167, 185 (Crown Copyright) 199t, 214 (Tara Heinemann), 232t (Mark Gerson); Hutchinson Ltd: 201l, 222, 144b; Little Brown & Co: 178 (Diana Gilbert); Michael Joseph Ltd: 146, 181, 183; Dorothy Prentiss Macdonald: 202; Stanley Mackenzie Collection: 27, 28, 47, 52, 286, 304; Macmillan Ltd: 131, 206 (Jerry Bauer), 198, 201r (Mark Mason); Mansell Collection: 238; Gladys Mitchell: 211; National Film Archive: 64, 76, 77, 252b, 256, 260, 262, 276r, 277, 279t, 280b, 287, 288, 292, 295, 297, 299t, 301l, 303r, 304b, 308t; National Portrait Gallery: 21, 141, 151, 242l; Pan Books Ltd: 236l (Celeste Parsons); Penguin Books Ltd: 10, 50, 129, 165t, 215; Roger Pring: 313; Douglas Rutherford: 226; S.R. Archive: 135b, 174, 194, 195, 199b, 220b, 229, 233, 285b; Sidgwick & Jackson Ltd: 217; Julian Symons: 234 (Wyndham Lewis); Thames T.V.: 305; University of Virginia Library: 7; Hillary Waugh: 270; Kathy Waugh: 243b; Weidenfeld and Nicolson Ltd: 106, 162 (Mark Gerson), 242r (Dee Wambaugh)

Contents

Foreword

I would like to take this opportunity to thank, warmly as I can, first the distinguished writers who contributed to this book their hardly-won knowledge in the sections "How I Write My Books" and "Crime Fiction and Its Categories" as well as Professor Philip Graham who contributed the chapter "Why People Read Crime Fiction". Secondly I would like to acknowledge with much gratitude my collaborators in the biographical-critical section, "Writers and Their Books: A Consumers' Guide" who garnered facts by the hundred as well as giving their opinions, fruit of long experience, Dorothy B. Hughes, the noted American crime critic (and splendid author), Melvyn Barnes, Chief Librarian of the London borough of Westminster (and crime connoisseur) and Reginald Hill, until recently Senior Lecturer in English Literature at Doncaster College of Education (and a dab hand at the detective novel). Their work and wisdom will, I am sure, be of enormous use to anyone interested in crime, suspense or spy fiction and particularly to anyone considering embarking on writing in this field.

H.R.F.K.

Right **Edgar Allan Poe,** *the "Godfather" of crime literature and author of the first detective story,* The Murders in the Rue Morgue.

Introduction

W HAT EXACTLY IS CRIME WRITING, the subject of this book? It is, in fact, something notoriously hard to embrace in any one definition. Hence, indeed, the rather clumsy title of the book. But, however wiggly the line has to be that includes whatever it is within it, one thing is clear: there is something to ensnare. Crime writing (or mystery fiction, or suspense writing) exists. People want to read its products as such, some perhaps preferring one of its manifestations, others another, some all of them.

Is there any way we can say what it is that they like, even if as is most probably the case they don't know themselves exactly where the limits come? Perhaps there is. The many-headed hybrid, as I see it, can be said roughly to be fiction that is written primarily as entertainment and has as its subject some form of crime, crime taken in its widest possible meaning.

Crime writing is fiction that puts the reader first, not the writer. The novel pure is written because the novelist wants to say something and is prepared to use whatever devices he or she thinks necessary to induce readers to absorb that something: the crime writer, whether knowing it or not, sets out simply to hold readers and only afterwards to greater or lesser degree tells them something.

That's entertainment. But why is it crime entertainment? There is, I think, no satisfyingly inherent reason. There is no organic link between entertainment, which is the method crime writers use, and crime, which is their subject. It just happens that criminal acts grip the imagination.

They do so because we all of us feel to some extent the fetters of society. We have to live in clumps. To do so we have to have rules. We have to drive on the left, except of course where we have to drive on the right. Arbitrary regulations are necessary. But where we would all like to drive is straight down the middle of the broad highway. We want to break the laws that we know we must have. And from the earliest times there have been people doing that on our behalf, sitting cross-legged under a palm tree telling stories of crimes. Crime stories, originally, where the criminal, the law's defier, was hero; but soon a counter-current must have set in. We, sitting round equally cross-legged, wanted equal reassurance that the law breakers were not going to break us. Hence the guardian of the law, the detective, one head of the hybrid.

So crime writing exists. And, thank goodness, crime readers. And I believe that there is a special system of linkage between them. That crime writers when they set out to write a book sign a special sort of contract, on invisible paper. Invisible as paper, but visible actually in various other ways – in the word 'Death' or 'Inspector' or 'Affair' or 'Caper' in their title, in perhaps the particular publisher they go to, in the covers that get put on their books. In some or all of these ways they say to their potential readers "I promise to look after you first, to entertain you, and to do so with a story that has some form of crime as its nub (and perhaps I'm going to slip you a Mickey Finn of a message, but you won't know)".

And there are a good many crime writers who do favour the Mickey Finn. Because to say that crime fiction is entertainment fiction primarily is not to belittle it. It is not necessarily only a huddle of sideshows round the great circus of the Novel. Some of its manifestations are as dazzling, as well written, as good as any but the very greatest acts in the central show-ring. Indeed, they sometimes shade into the novel proper (Definitions, too, are laws that can be broken). For, when you come down to it, the crime novels that are memorable, a handful of breath-taking plot ideas apart, are the plain products of fine minds at work just as are those mainstream novels that time has picked out from the welter.

So entertainment can embrace the agonies. Crime novels can be about the most terrible and horrible human activities and, provided their authors intend to make them first books to be read and only second books to say something, they can fulfil that invisible-paper contract. This means – let us not claim too much – that the very greatest heights of fiction cannot be scaled by our mountaineers. There has to be introduced into the crime novel at the last a flaw, a concession to the mere need to delight in what is being read, or to be deliciously frightened by it. But, except for this, the crime novel can do every bit as much as its lauded senior.

There are, too, we should realize, levels of seriousness in the layers upon layers that are crime fiction. At the top it can, though naturally it rarely does, deal in fiction's terms with the greatest issues, whether they be what the West should do in face of opposition and penetration by an enemy or at a more intimate level whether it is justified to take a life. But, a step down from this, crime fiction can deal in the same way with lesser issues, with the role of the police in modern society, with some particular scandal, with some ecological outrage.

But seriousness is not a necessary ingredient of the best writing in the field, praise be. Entertainment fiction can be merely entertaining and still be very good. If half crime fiction shows us the face of violence, the other half shows us the spreading hips of cosiness. For every Le Carré there is an Agatha Christie. For every megaton bomb threat to New York there is a visit to the time-sealed world of the Victorians. For every can't-put-it-down there is a laugh-aloud (or, combining crime and humour being a particularly difficult art, there are at least a handful of laughter-makers). For every story that excites us and caters to the violent and the law-breaker within there is a story that soothes and reassures with its assertion that there is a final justice above.

Indeed, for every exploration that uses the crime story there are a dozen crime stories that do their work simply by filling out to the last corner and not a millimetre further some well-established and well-liked formula. And such books should not be despised. One of the social benefits of crime fiction is to provide escape from this vale of tears. Let me quote one unknown reader of Agatha Christie (who was not, on analysis altogether a formula writer) on what her books meant at a time of distress in London in the wartime black-out days: "I had never been away from home before, and I was lonely and depressed beyond anything I can describe. The one thing that made it endurable, going back to that awful little dark room in the evenings, was knowing that my Agatha Christies were waiting for me." To most of us formula crime fiction does less than that. It brings perhaps only a cigarette satisfaction. Still, that is a true pleasure if not a lasting one, and no official health warnings are needed.

But if crime fiction for its readers means either excitement or the warmth of cosiness, to its writers it must look different. To them it is a struggle between the tumultuous facts of the world they see and the need to present their readers with what will excite or delight them, and added to that for some there is a desire within the confines of crime to do what the pure novelist does.

Indeed, the problem that faces all writers of fiction, the wrestling match between the art form and the life sprawl, is perhaps at its keenest in crime fiction, where the facts are always extremely pertinent, where many of them are well known to the readers whom the books are designed to attract, where the brute details of an incident or series of incidents might seem to be almost indistinguishable from the airy nothings that are to take place first in the writer's head and then, via those black signs on the white paper, in the reader's head.

But are the brute details really so similar to the eventual fiction? I think we
continued on page 12

Crime fact and crime fiction

Fortunately for police forces everywhere the adage "truth is stranger than fiction" does not apply in the crime field. Compare the two sequences below. To the left is apparently an account of the investigation of a murder (in rather unusual, but not impossible circumstances) by Supt. Pibble. However, it is in fact the bare bones of a novel, The Glass-Sided Ants' Nest (originally Skin Deep in U.K.) *by Peter Dickinson, with Pibble as hero and a theme behind it—that of the Ideal and the Real. To the right is a factual account of a real Superintendent, named Lestrade, investigating a murder in the same circumstances as those of* The Glass-Sided Ants' Nest.

9 a.m.	Pibble proceeding to scene, swift self-portrait	*Not relevant*
9.15	Pibble at local police station, exposition of set-up (1 page), a left-handed killer	*Lestrade told circumstances, including that killer was left-handed (several pages needed)*
9.45	Pibble at scene (2 pages), quick mention of police photographer, extensive mention of bizarreness of murder	*Lestrade at scene, contact with scene-of-crimes officer, supervision of photographer, fingerprint man. Their preliminary observations (several pages)*
10 a.m.	Pibble examines body (1 paragraph) mention of police surgeon	*Examination of body and consulatation with police surgeon (several pages)*
10.15	Mention of clue of two-headed penny (placed here for best emphasis)	*(Two-headed penny already dealt with at 9.15 briefing)*
10.30	Interview with Dr Ku (mostly description of ultra-light room for contrast purposes, with 1 page on social relationship), Pibble-Dr Ku	*Interview with Dr Ku (several pages of question and answer)*
11.15	Quick mention of second set of house-to-house interviews being set up, mention of earlier set	*Lestrade gives detailed instructions on second set of house-to-house interviews and refers in detail to results of earlier set*
12 noon	Pibble (after a short rumination on the use of baby carriages to assert position in life) sees first outside witness (Mrs Caine), longish description of her preparing lunch and (uncharacteristically) cutting herself on can-opener	*Lestrade might elect to see Mrs Caine before witnesses in house, though unlikely. Detailed account of her answers; no mention of accident with can-opener (even though this is a valuable clue)*
12.15	Arrival of Group Captain Caine and long passage on Pibble's immediate hatred and fear of him	*Group Captain joins interview, some question and answer on factual matters*
12.30	Pibble telephones to check "facts" he has been told	*Lestrade telephones to check facts he has been told*
12.45	General interviews with whole Ku tribe (8 pages) but little factual questioning, more painting in details of tribal life in London attics	*General interview with all inhabitants of house (many pages), strictly concerned with whereabouts at time of crime*

1.15	Search of Ku sleeping quarters (used to make tribe-in-attic situation more credible)	*Search of Ku sleeping quarters, detectives report largely negative findings*
1.45	Forensic staff summoned back to investigate newly-discovered bowl of blood	*Forensic staff, probably still at scene, set on to bowl of blood*
1.55	Pibble meets fellow officer, Supt Rickard, finds he had affair with Mrs Caine	*Lestrade consults Supt Rickard on Caine's climbing skills, hears of affair*
2 p.m.	Pibble lunches, muses (8 pages)	*Lestrade "off duty" for refreshments (3 word mention)*
2.45	Pibble interviews estate agent (true and inflated property values) and short mention of possible sale of terrace of houses including murder house	*Lestrade interviews estate agent. Value of property and possible sale*
3 p.m.	Pibble interviews Group Captain Caine's mistress. The paintings in the pub, their idealistic treatment, some pointers to his motive, a portrait of him as a cheap idealist	*Lestrade interviews suspect's mistress for alibi confirmation. Pointers to his motive*
3.30	Second interview with Dr Ku, a roof prowler revealed by incidental complaints from neighbours (4 pages)	*Second interview with Dr Ku (some 8 pages needed). Incidental information about roof prowler (2 sentences)*
4 p.m.	Pibble a prey to doubts, revisits Mrs Caine more or less to comfort himself (clues to murderer planted)	*Unauthorized respite for Lestrade of visit to Mrs Caine (no mention)*
4.30-6.30	Interviews with other tribespeople in house (half-sentence "took two hours")	*Detailed interviews with other possible suspects (up to 50 pages)*
6 p.m.	One of the interviews at some length (6 pages) (to sow red herring)	
7 p.m.	Pibble eats supper (comment on poor food disguised as good)	*Lestrade "off", refreshments*
8 p.m.	Pibble attends drumming ceremony, a climactic, horror-tinged scene	*Lestrade at drumming ceremony (marginal usefulness)*
9 p.m.	Pibble leaving house, notices roof climber, turns police searchlight on, causes climber to fall	*Chance discovery of potential intruder and accidental death*
9.01	Pibble recognizes body as . . . and realizes this person was left-handed, a vital clue	*Lestrade recognizes . . . is the killer*
Next day	Pibble, knocked out, in delirium, goes over the clues in the case, receives information about builder of terrace, a final ironical note	*Lestrade by chance in hospital, no progress*
Ensuing weeks		*Gathering and checking out confirmatory evidence. Inquest on. . . . Inquest on murdered man, possible verdict "Murdered by . . ."*

should be careful to note that they are not. Take a real crime as it would happen in the world of brute facts and then a crime, apparently similar, as it needs to be put into words to affect readers. Note from any newspaper account what actually happens when a murder is committed, and then go through a murder story, even a police procedural novel, and write down what the author has actually told you. The two accounts will be substantially different.

This is not to say that facts corresponding to the facts of a real crime case, or of real espionage activity, cannot be put into crime fiction. They can be indeed. But they must first be taken into an author's mind, into his subconscious, and then, transformed there into fiction-facts, they will powerfully aid his story. I cite a clutch of spy writers in evidence, Len Deighton, John Le Carré, Gavin Lyall. Their books seem crammed with facts; but the facts urge on the story, give opportunities for their created characters to show themselves to us.

Or, let me point out something about the most famous crime stories of all, the Sherlock Holmes tales. How often in them are we told something as a fact by the great man (for instance that it is possible to tell in which direction a bicycle has been ridden by the overlapping of its tyre marks), to hear immediately poor, dear Dr Watson cry "Remarkable" and to race on then with the story convinced we have learnt a gritty, incontrovertible fact from the world we daily experience with our five senses. And yet, as is now quite well-known, you cannot tell about a bicycle's direction from which tyre-track covers which. But while we lived in the world of "The Priory School" this unfact was a fact, a fiction-fact.

Yet one of the great assets of the modern crime novel is precisely to bring to readers' minds the facts of the contemporary scene. It is a development in the history of crime fiction which its practitioners are right to be proud of. So how do we square this with a denunciation of facts-from-the-world intruding into the crime writer's pages? We do it, as I have already hinted, by remembering that these facts fail of their desired effect, which is at the least to make readers think, if they are presented out of the context of their fictional story. If, in short, they are raw gobbets swimming on the surface of the stew of a work of crime fiction instead of pieces of nourishing meat cooked

The turning points of crime, suspense and spy fiction *On this and the following pages are listed the books that can be said to have marked the start of new directions up to the year 1970.*

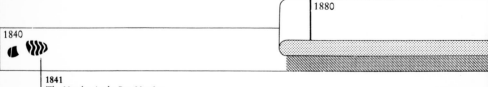

1880

1840

1841
The Murders in the Rue Morgue
Edgar Allan Poe
The first detective story

together with everything else in the pot.

But using and pointing up the facts of the contemporary scene is not the only way that crime fiction can affect the lives of crime readers. For all that the ignorant still are apt to think of the art as being only flamboyant detectives solving puzzles already solved by the author among characters of cardboard, in fact the crime novel parted company from the rich mainstream novel only fairly briefly and it did once and now does again much that the mainstream novel does. The two were one when Dickens wrote *Edwin Drood*; the two are all but one (that duty to entertain first intervening) when Patricia Highsmith writes any one of her books today.

Indeed, it can be said that the detective story, that branch only of crime fiction, after its birth in the wake of the all-sweeping Sherlock Holmes, died, or at least became fairly moribund, about half a century later, but that dead it has proved to be, like a dead virus, an excellent carrier for immunising the body politic. This is a metaphor which can be applied, too, to the modern spy tale where the process happened much more quickly. In very little time the revival that began with James Bond had reached its half-life and the then dead form began to be used to do other things than merely tell tales of espionage derring-do. Read Le Carré, McCarry, Anthony Price, a dozen others.

Even in what seems today on the surface a simple whodunit this process of immunisation of the reader can take place. There are, of course, a fair number of true simple whodunits still being written which do not attempt this, written and eagerly read. But those that one feels to be the leading-edge of the crime-writing art do much more now than set a puzzle and solve it. They often have a parallel movement to the outward story, a theme pivoting exactly on the plot at best, which does such things as move a reader through a consideration of man and his environment (Peter Dickinson's *The Poison Oracle*, 1974) or a consideration of the very pattern of life (James McClure's *The Blood of An Englishman*, 1980), to produce just two instances that occur to me. The crime novel today can, while entertaining its readers first, handle almost any subject, even the paradoxical one of dying as in P. D. James's *The Black Tower* (1975).

This is not to say, of course, that all crime novels reach the high levels of fiction, even when they attempt it. But some attempt and succeed, and many

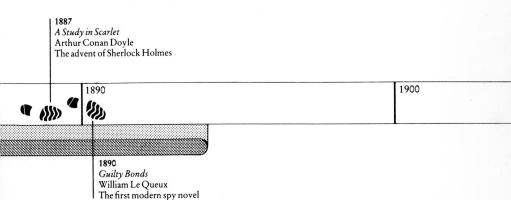

1887
A Study in Scarlet
Arthur Conan Doyle
The advent of Sherlock Holmes

1890   1900

1890
Guilty Bonds
William Le Queux
The first modern spy novel

others find that the description of a crime, of any sort, proves an excellent forcing-ground for the examination of character. It is surely the prime function of the novel to take human motives and in an ever purer fire to burn away the layers of dross until a skeleton of truth is revealed. And what better furnace than crime for this process? Than the holding of human specimens in the intense fires that follow the taking of a life? What better device than the suspense novelists' way of putting a person into crisis and seeing what happens, as in the novels of Dick Francis, of Francis Clifford, of Dorothy B. Hughes, to take but three examples?

Yet attempts to do within the genre of the crime novel more than a certain amount of what the pure novel does are, it must be admitted, fraught with danger. That duty to the reader to entertain, that having, in Raymond Chandler's celebrated words, a man come in the door with a gun every so often, can be too much neglected. The need to allow a flaw into an otherwise pure art form, which is perhaps a condition of crime fiction, can be sacrificed. Even credibility, which is something almost always necessary if readers are to be kept underneath the surface of the fast-flowing stream that is a crime novel, may on occasion be risked. Not every crime egg hatches a swan. Geese are to be found honking about in the field. Yet achievement is at the edge. It is the writers who risk much, and from time to time lose, who push forward a genre to yet greater and greater achievements.

But the need to entertain, to put the reader first, does give to crime novels a whole bag of goodies that the literary novel often goes without. Not all crime novels have each one of these goodies but most have their share.

There is, to begin with, that dear old reader-gripper, the puzzle. It's crude; it's elementary; but, by heavens, it works. Put before any human a mystery or a riddle that tantalisingly hints at a solution, and almost every one of them jumps. A "teaser" headline in a newspaper or an instant puzzle on a hoarding, which of us can resist them?

So it is with almost all crime books, not just the most obvious example, the old "whodunit". They set before the reader a mystery, and the reader, nine times out of ten, probably more, will stay head down until the end is reached and the answer revealed (and the one out of the ten who doesn't is usually the one who cheats by turning to the last page half-way through). But, note,

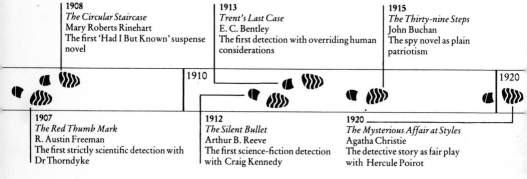

1908	1913	1915
The Circular Staircase	*Trent's Last Case*	*The Thirty-nine Steps*
Mary Roberts Rinehart	E. C. Bentley	John Buchan
The first 'Had I But Known' suspense novel	The first detection with overriding human considerations	The spy novel as plain patriotism

1907	1912	1920
The Red Thumb Mark	*The Silent Bullet*	*The Mysterious Affair at Styles*
R. Austin Freeman	Arthur B. Reeve	Agatha Christie
The first strictly scientific detection with Dr Thorndyke	The first science-fiction detection with Craig Kennedy	The detective story as fair play with Hercule Poirot

puzzle is something more than a mere reader-gripping device: it asserts, too, the primacy of the rational. Write a murder puzzle that is going to be solved, and you imply that the human brain is capable of solving all the myriad puzzles the world presents us with. Perhaps it isn't, but we need the reassurance of the possibility.

In the same way because the majority of crime novels have happy endings, sometimes only happy endings of a sort, they imply that we, too, will have a happy ending, that, however it looks in the horrid world, justice will eventually be done. And, again, this is something that applies to more than the obvious example of the sort of mystery novel that concludes, as did many of those of that British stalwart of old, John Rhodes, "and he was duly hanged". The spy novel that has its hero come out of it all alive implies survival for us all. The happy ending, however muted, however disguised, however sweet-and-sour, is more or less mandatory in crime fiction because of that contract with the reader "We will entertain, nothing too ultimately terrible". But for whatever literary reasons the happy ending is there it answers, too, a strong psychological need.

Crime novels of every sort show almost always (exceptions prove the rule) the hunted squeezing home at last or the goodie hunter getting his man. And here is another asset that crime writing has: it ministers to what Dickens once spoke of as that "passion for hunting something deeply implanted in the human breast". In doing so it often appeals as well to our need to see what our fellow humans can do, to what heights some of us can reach, the need that sends us crowding in to the circus or surrounding in India some yogi buried airless underground for days and days. We need heroes, of all sorts: crime fiction provides them.

We have, too, a curious delight in physical action, something that crime heroes frequently are called on to exhibit. And whether we are achieving physical feats ourselves, be it only hitting the golf ball right, or experiencing them vicariously with James Bond, fighter and deadly shot, we enjoy them deeply. As, too, we, many of us, perhaps secretly all of us, enjoy physical violence. I believe that experiencing this violence through a character in a crime novel does, to some extent at least, quieten the need in us to commit actual violence, be it only to smash up some inoffensive object. And, more,

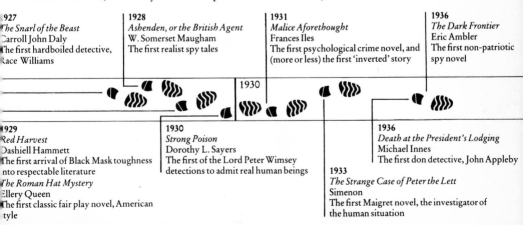

1927	1928	1931	1936
The Snarl of the Beast	*Ashenden, or the British Agent*	*Malice Aforethought*	*The Dark Frontier*
Carroll John Daly	W. Somerset Maugham	Frances Iles	Eric Ambler
The first hardboiled detective, Race Williams	The first realist spy tales	The first psychological crime novel, and (more or less) the first 'inverted' story	The first non-patriotic spy novel

1930

1929	1930	1936
Red Harvest	*Strong Poison*	*Death at the President's Lodging*
Dashiell Hammett	Dorothy L. Sayers	Michael Innes
The first arrival of Black Mask toughness into respectable literature	The first of the Lord Peter Wimsey detections to admit real human beings	The first don detective, John Appleby
The Roman Hat Mystery		1933
Ellery Queen		*The Strange Case of Peter the Lett*
The first classic fair play novel, American style		Simenon
		The first Maigret novel, the investigator of the human situation

reading about violence in a truly written work of fiction helps us to face the horror of it in the real world. In the perspective of the pages, we are enabled, to a greater degree or a smaller, to put violence into the whole perspective of life.

Linked almost inevitably to violence is sex. And the same considerations apply, I believe. Firstly we can in the crime pages often vicariously live some of those sexual impulses which the rigidities of society usually forbid us. Secondly the description of sexual acts in crime novels, the more coolly explicit the better, enables us to come to terms with this dark and powerful instinct within us, to realize as well sometimes if we are young or inexperienced that other people have the same odd and disquieting notions as ourselves.

If vicarious sexual experience is one asset of crime fiction, at what might seem the very opposite pole is beauty of form. Not all suspense novels, of course, have a particularly noticeable and effective form, but the whodunits most certainly do. Think of Agatha Christie's *Ten Little Niggers* (or Indians) or, as it's sometimes called *And Then There Were None* (1939), of how each murder in it clicks neatly into place against that nursery rhyme. And, more, how the whole book has its marked shape, beginning with the tiny hints of murder to come, swelling to the complexities of the crimes, diminishing to that marvellous point where there is only one more murder left to commit on that cut-off island. Few of its readers will have consciously said as they laid the book down at last "Ah, what beauty of form". But almost all will have felt an indefinable extra of pleasure.

They will have got too, Agatha Christie being Agatha Christie, a much more obvious and easily appreciated pleasure from the sheer storyline of the book, and this is a quality that Dame Agatha shares with almost every writer in the field. Because of the need to entertain, crime novels must rely strongly, much more strongly than mainstream novels, on the hawser-tug of a good story, its power to whizz a reader on from page to page.

And here some of the devices that may seem piffling and crude come into their own. We have the device of what might be called the riddle series, whereby a skilled author puts in front of a reader first in the very opening words some little question that promises an answer and then just before that

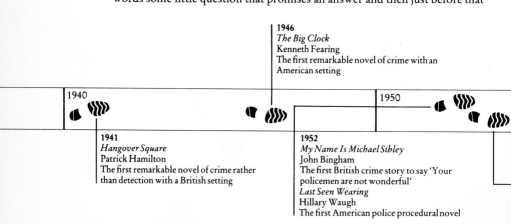

1946
The Big Clock
Kenneth Fearing
The first remarkable novel of crime with an American setting

1940

1950

1941
Hangover Square
Patrick Hamilton
The first remarkable novel of crime rather than detection with a British setting

1952
My Name Is Michael Sibley
John Bingham
The first British crime story to say 'Your policemen are not wonderful'
Last Seen Wearing
Hillary Waugh
The first American police procedural novel

answer comes puts another question, so through a whole series of petty riddles lures on and on the captive audience, keeps their heads for ever under the surface of the stream of fiction. Or we have in the sub-genre of the gothic novel, and sometimes elsewhere, that wonderful female gift of putting such a weight of emotion behind a heroine – what I call First Person Singular Feminine writing – that we do not balk for an instant at her plunging into that inevitable terror-haunted house, we do not laugh by so much as a titter when she exclaims "Had I but known . . .", any more than in another neck of the woods we object when the sternly masculine sleuth says "I cannot tell you who until I have absolute proof".

Story sweeps us past such crudities, which are in fact its means. And in crime fiction story is at its strongest. Nowhere more so, indeed, than in a particular sort of fiction in which the crime genre holds some notable examples. I refer to the Tale as opposed to the story or novel. Stories and novels are written for a purpose: the Tale is written for its own sake, an account of a marvel. Some, perhaps most, of the Sherlock Holmes stories are of this sort and marvellously (pun designed) affecting they are. It is because they appeal not to our everyday ingenuity or interest but to something deeper in us, to our fundamental hopes and fears. This is a huge advantage some crime fiction has, and perhaps most crime fiction has some small share of it.

What appeals to that which is buried in our subconscious appeals with enormous pull, and here, somewhat paradoxically, lies the tremendous attraction of that figure who might seem to be only a brightly coloured counter in the airy game of the puzzle story, the Great Detective. The Great Detective, discovered in a huge stroke of imagination by Edgar Allan Poe, father of the crime story (if it perhaps also acknowledges many other older ancestors), is nothing less than a figure of myth, an archetype. He is more than a mere thinking machine (those that are just this are lesser detectives). He is a being capable of fusing the ratiocinative side of the mind and the intuitive. He deduces, and he also leaps to conclusions which make connections between the apparently unconnectable. And he does this for us, for us as we face life. He observes the trifles and infers what can be inferred from them, but he also announces that here is "a three-pipe problem" and wraps

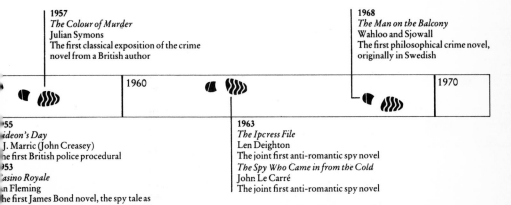

1957
The Colour of Murder
Julian Symons
The first classical exposition of the crime
novel from a British author

1968
The Man on the Balcony
Wahloo and Sjowall
The first philosophical crime novel,
originally in Swedish

1960

1970

⁎55
ideon's Day
J. Marric (John Creasey)
he first British police procedural
⁎53
asino Royale
n Fleming
he first James Bond novel, the spy tale as
n

1963
The Ipcress File
Len Deighton
The joint first anti-romantic spy novel
The Spy Who Came in from the Cold
John Le Carré
The joint first anti-romantic spy novel

himself in a dream world until its solution emerges. He is a hero we can attach ourselves to. He is a digger into the depths who shows us to ourselves.

He shows us to ourselves. He is one of the benefits to mankind – I put it strongly, but it is a strong benefit for all its intangibility – that crime fiction brings. Another, at a similar level but perhaps not so deeply penetrating of the psyche, is crime fiction's assertion that Good wins. Most crime stories, as we have seen, end on this note. A goodie triumphs. It may seem obvious. It may seem against the run of the world. But it asserts for readers that the Good does triumph, and in this way it adds subtly but on a large scale to the necessary quantum of optimism in the world. If murder is the flouting of our general will to survive, the fictional apprehension of the murderer is a countering to that wrong.

On a still lesser plane crime writing today is a notable source of straightforward social comment and criticism. Indeed, a head count will show that there are a good many more crime books of this sort currently published than there are plain mystery puzzles. But crime can deal, too, with matters of more general import than the day-to-day ills of society. It can at its most ambitious, as we have seen, deal with the great complexities that affright the human mind. It may in doing so only repeat what novelists, and playwrights and poets, have done before. But we need to have these things said to us again and again, in, if you like, the most present tense. And crime fiction is especially suited to this: to putting the things that have to be said in their most up-to-the-minute guise.

And, finally, take note of the way in which crime fiction carries out its share of the novelist's task. It does not work openly. It does not, as the master novelists do, say "Hear me" and risk closed ears. It says instead "Read me". It pledges entertainment, and it provides it too. But, in doing so, often and often it teaches its readers, subtly and secretly, and thus perhaps more effectively. It makes maps for them. It shows them for a little what some of the great mess of life really looks like. Crime fiction earns its keep.

H. R. F. Keating

CRIME FICTION
AND ITS CATEGORIES

A Pre-history

by Reginald Hill

CRIME HAS FEATURED IN LITERATURE since Cain and Abel but this does not mean there has to be a literature of crime and still less crime fiction in the contemporary sense. This is a relatively recent phenomenon and could not begin to exist till society had made a significant lurch in the direction of the modern, which is to say when it started to be scientific rather than superstitious, bourgeois rather than aristocratic, urban rather than pastoral, and capitalist rather than Christian.

Such a direction was becoming clear early in the eighteenth century and its literary first-fruit was the novel with its stress on psychological and social realism. The Age of Reason was on its way, though it might with equal justice have been called the Age of Acquisitive Individualism. For every rationalist philosopher, the age produced a thousand pickpockets and pirates, highwaymen and whores, whom moderately reasonable men usually feared, occasionally feted and were always fascinated by. The literature of crime which appears early in the century, providing a pre-history of true crime-fiction which does not appear till the next, reflects both this interest and this ambiguity.

In terms of fiction, the most significant strand in this new literature of crime was the picaresque tale, that loose, episodic, usually autobiographical account of the adventures and tricks of a wandering *picaro* or rogue. Its most important English manifestation hitherto had been Thomas Nashe's *The Unfortunate Traveller* (1594), though translations of the principal native Spanish examples of the genre were popular throughout the seventeenth century.

But still more popular in the sense of being available to the widest audience were those accounts of crime fact provided in broadside ballads and chapbooks. The new age was also the age of information and soon this wide fascination with sensational crime was being catered for by the developing popular press. Instant criminal biography, in its simplest form merely a pamphlet describing in outraged and sensational terms the latest gory crime, was another popular journalistic product, and later it was expanded with a full and rapidly conventionalised biographical apparatus.

Left **Daniel Defoe,** *whose many books about crime and criminals ranged from pure biography to pure fiction and frequently fell somewhere in between.* Opposite **A public hanging in England** *This engraving of 1823 shows a woman selling copies of a pamphlet containing songs and an account of the misdeeds of the hanged man.*

There was no shortage of material for even the idlest hack. Eight times a year the City of London and County of Middlesex Sessions Papers were published, which gave reports, often verbatim, of the latest trials. Better still, on the morning after an execution the Ordinary, or Chaplain, of Newgate would publish his own account of the condemned man's last hours. With their concentration on the struggle for the man's soul rather than on the causes of his crime (usually conventionally catalogued as drink, bad company and Sabbath-breaking), these accounts can sound banal and tedious to the modern ear, but they were immensely popular.

Upmarket, the taste had long faded for those awful-waring stories of the fate of top people, the native version of which, *A Mirror For Magistrates* (1559), had remained a best seller throughout Elizabeth's reign, but the working classes were much more conservative and their love of the lurid was still accompanied by a fondness for the exemplary tale, and a medieval optimism that, with God's help, murder would out. It is the erosion of this optimism both by the secularization of society and by a vast increase in the incidence of crime that helps pave the way for the novel of detection. But at the start of the century, the public's trust was mainly in Providence, and criminal biographies were to some extent morality plays with real people and real blood.

It is this which gives them their peculiar flavour, peculiar that is to the modern palate which can find them moralizingly sucrose and sensationally bland. What was needed was a writer skilful enough to bring other qualities to bear, able to straddle the gulf between fact and fiction, journalism and literature. One was on his way.

Defoe (1660-1731) was that unusual thing in literature, a jack of all trades who became a master of many. A thorough-going professional journalist, he had a sharp nose for the commercially viable. In particular, he recognized the new market demand for "truth" and set about providing it even when he had to invent it. Nowhere is this process clearer than in his dealings with criminal biography.

Piracy was a peculiarly fascinating crime for all kinds of reasons and one of Defoe's most popular biographical works was *A General History of The*

Jack Sheppard, *the thief, escapologist and public hero, whose "own story" was almost certainly written, and embellished, by Defoe.*

Pyrates (1724 and 1728) which recounts the lives of thirty or so real-life villains and also, without distinction, or at least one purely fictitious character. Earlier, in *The King of Pirates* (1719), he had already "fictionalized" one of the real pirates, Captain Avery, by composing two alleged letters from the captain, setting the record straight on points where previous "unreliable" biographies had misrepresented him!

Defoe used a similar technique in the case of Jack Sheppard, a notorious thief who became something of a public hero through his feats of escapology from the death-cells of the New Prison and of Newgate. In 1724, after this last escape and while sheppard was still at large, Defoe published a pamphlet containing the usual conventional short biography. Later the same year after the thief's recapture, there appeared another account of his crimes and escapes, allegedly composed by Sheppard himself as he awaited execution, but almost certainly written by Defoe. This particular kind of "realism" which deliberately blurs the line between fact and invention is a significant feature of crime-fiction from the nineteen century on. Defoe was such a master of these authenticating stratagems that in some cases it was more than a century before the full extent of his creative involvement was realized.

Other criminal biographies of real people include one of Jonathan Wild, the Thief-Taker, himself taken and executed in 1725. Unlike Sheppard who became a folk-hero, Wild was an object of universal hatred, mainly because he duped both criminals and law-abiding citizens alike. This conventional biography makes interesting reading alongside Fielding's fictionalized and satiric life, published in 1743.

The Six Notorious Street Robbers (1726) gives interesting details of criminal ingenuity and techniques, a feature which remains popular in certain kinds of modern crime-fiction. And in *A Narrative of the Proceedings in France, for Discovering and Detecting the Murderers of the English Gentlemen, September 21, 1723* (1724), the title of which tells all, we find alongside the usual sensational details of crime a more than usually graphic account of the efforts put into tracking down the killers, including for the first time in my experience, that old stand-by of interrogation technique, the claim that the accomplice in the next room has cracked and revealed all.

Defoe's obsession with authenticity makes him naturally incline to the first person narrative form in most of those works which underpin his reputation as the first great novelist. Many of his narrators are rogues and criminals and we frequently find united those two strands of criminal litera-ture already mentioned, the exemplary biography and picaresque tale.

Captain Singleton (1720) is the story of a kidnapped child who grows up to be a sailor, mutineer, pirate, explorer, and finally repents his roguery without giving up his gains which he settles down to enjoy in England. *Colonel jacque* (or *Jack*) (1722) is also a waif who grows up into bad company and wicked ways. His title is not a military rank, but merely a means of differentiation from two other Jacks. He is an amiable rogue, in some ways very much in the *picaro* tradition, but in others he is a very modern character, having an uncertainty of purpose and capacity for self-doubt (not the same as self-reproach) unusual in Defoe's heroes in their prime. His roguery is put down, to start with at least, to his disadvantaged circumstances and the sharp prick of necessity. In the story of his adventures, Defoe displays one of his finest narrative skills, his ability to depict men existing on their nerves, under constant threat of pursuit and capture. Nor does he restrict this skill, which must be the envy of many a modern flaccid thriller writer, to the depiction of men only for we find it used to tremendous effect in his two great whore-biographies, *Moll Flanders* (1722) and *Roxana* (1724).

The tradition from which these derive, like that of the male rogue, is both comic and moral-didactic. And if the heroine's criminal adventurous range is relatively limited, her comic opportunist range is compensatingly broad. Of the two books, *Moll Flanders* is far richer in comedy, though to tell the truth Moll is much more of a criminal than a whore. The narrative is loosely strung together on picaresque lines, Moll's scrapes and japes are interlarded with social and moral reflection, and she ends up at seventy, rich, respectable and reformed.

Roxana, though it has some surface similarities, is really a very different kind of work. The structure of the book is more elaborate than is usual with Defoe, who generally lets the autobiographical form itself dictate the shape. A French girl, she is brought up in England by her Huguenot parents who marry her off at fifteen. Her husband spends Roxana's dowry, sells his own business, and then abandons his wife and five children.

Now, in an age when the only advice such an admirer of the sex as Pope could give to unemancipated women was to be good-natured, the only choice for most of them was either to rely on the generosity of men, or prey on their stupidity and lust. Roxana assisted by her maid, Amy, dumps the children on their aunt, and sets out on a career as a high class whore. In the latter part of the novel, her past begins to threaten her, with Amy's discovery that Toxana's eldest daughter, Susan, abandoned all those years ago, is working in the kitchen of her Kensington home. Roxana does not wish to admit the relationship, at first for reasons of conscience, but later because, after marrying a Dutch merchant, she fears the power that Susan would have over her and the effect a full picture of her past would have on her husband. Susan meanwhile has begun to suspect the relationship and begins a long pursuit of her mother. Amy threatens to get rid of the danger by murdering the girl. Roxana is horrified, but almost as horrified by the prospect of being confronted by her daughter.

The tension of pursuit, evasion, threat of discovery and threat of murder, builds up to a degree which anticipates the central dynamic of an important section of detective and thriller fiction. There lacks, however, either the denouement of the former or the action climax of the latter mode. The novel ends abruptly. Susan has probably (though it is never made explicit) been murdered, and Roxana says that after a few years of prosperity, she and Amy met with disasters which she sees as a punishment for the injury they both did to Susan. So the moral-didactic element prevails to the end, but the large step taken in the direction of much that is important in modern crime literature should not be ignored. Defoe is not a crime-writer in the modern sense, but as a writer on criminal matters, his importance and influence can hardly be overstressed.

After Defoe, novelists experimenting with their new-found powers explore a vast variety of techniques and topics. Crime figures of course, but not largely enough to merit special attention except perhaps in the novels of Smollett (1721-1771) where the picaresque tradition gets its liveliest British airing. *The Adventures of Ferdinand Count Fathom* (1753) is notable for having as its "hero" a thorough-going villain with little of the *picaro's* saving amiability. It also contains elements of the Gothic, the late eighteenth century taste for which can at the same time be linked with the lust after sensationalism catered for in much criminal biography and with that longing for evidence of the supernatural which is a reaction against the age's secular spirit.

Horace Walpole's *The Castle of Otranto* (1764) is the first purely gothic novel in English, and the genre is developed in works such as Beckford's *Vathek* (1786), Lewis's *The Monk* (1795), Mrs Radcliffe's *The Mysteries of Udolpho* (1794), and Maturin's *Melmoth the Wanderer* (1829). None of these is, properly speaking, a work of crime fiction. Their aim, even when naturalistic explanations are provided for apparently supernatural events, is simply to terrify. But they all contain crimes and they are the ancestors of the modern American "Gothic" genre in which a heroine in a remote situation finds herself threatened by dangers which are usually explained in conventional criminal terms.

But let us end where many historians of crime fiction begin. The political philosopher, William Godwin's *The Adventures of Caleb Williams* (1794) is frequently pointed to as the only true begetter of the classical crime novel. Certainly the plot, baldly stated, shows many generic resemblances. Williams suspects that his master, Falkland, has murdered a neighbour and framed one of his tenants by planting evidence. Falkland, fearing Williams' suspicions, fires him, frames him for theft, and thereafter systematically uses his wealth and influence to pursue and persecute him, despite all his efforts at evasion by flight and disguise. Finally Williams publicly accuses him, and Falkland confesses and dies.

The book's technical composition is interesting and relevant too. Godwin, knowing the situation he wished his hero to have reached in the latter part of the story, worked backwards to devise a logical route to this point. But though the technique bears some resemblance to that used by those crime-writers for whom the puzzle is all, Godwin's purpose was very different, and as exemplary in its way as that of *A Mirror for Magistrates*. He wants to demonstrate his thesis that man, born free and capable of perfect happiness if only he follows the dictates of pure reason, is corrupted and deflected by society's institutions, in particular those of the law which places men in a false relation to each other.

Now, this is revolutionary stuff and the crime novel, certainly the detective story, is essentially conservative. The Age of Reason has not killed God but merely retired him. The detective is His agent, and pure reason will lead him to the solution of crimes, not to the dissolution of society. Detective stories may help to expiate guilt, as W. H. Auden suggests. They will never imply, as does *Caleb Williams*, that there is a way back into the Garden without paying off some divine landlord's arrears.

But it may be more than a pleasant irony that *Caleb Williams* is so often cited as the ancestor of a genre whose great absolute, The Law, it sets out to attack. This is simply one among many apparent contradictions that we find in the move from the literature of crime to the genre of crime-fiction. Perhaps they stem from the contradictory nature of crime itself. It is disgusting, it is fascinating; we find it incomprehensible, we feel the same impulses; we want the criminal to be caught, we want him to escape; he is a monster, he is a hero; he should be treated, he should be shot. There is no space here to discuss these ambivalences, but the paradox of *Caleb Williams* is not unique in a pre-history which begins with an author, Defoe, who must have come very close to losing the ability to distinguish between truth and fiction, and ends with another, Poe, whose ratiocinative stories are set among tales of the most extraordinary and irrational Gothic horror.

One last irony: the first signposts on the road to "crime-fiction" are biographies of criminals who can be at the same time exemplars of the certainty of divine wrath and popular heroes. The last signpost is the autobiography of a criminal whose "repentance" helped him to escape at least earthly retribution and who became a popular legend as a detective. François Eugene Vidocq in his *Memoires* (1828-1829) describes how from being a convicted criminal he moved by way of employment as a police informant to his appointment as *Chef de la Sûreté*. His "real-life" adventures often sound more unlikely than Defoe's fictions, but his influence on early nineteenth-century crime-writing was immense.

The movement from the literature of crime to genre "crime-fiction" is broadly a movement from the criminal as hero to the detective as hero. And this process is encapsulated in the life, and in the literature, of this one man. He confirms that the new myth of law and order has taken over from the old myth of divine providence. The stage is set for the appearance of the most popular, most prevalent and, apparently, most permanent literary genre ever known to mankind.

Reginald Hill is the author of many crime novels and was formerly Senior Lecturer in the English Department of Doncaster College of Education, Yorkshire.

The Godfather and the Father

by H.R.F. Keating

YOU CAN EITHER say that crime stories have always been with us, told as soon as the bonds of society began to irk and told still today, or you can say that crime writing began with Edgar Allan Poe, experienced a hiatus of some forty years and then flowered once and for all with the arrival of Conan Doyle's Sherlock Holmes in the pages of the *Strand* magazine. And, certainly, it is very possible that we would not talk today about crime fiction as a separate, recognizable genre had it not been for the phenomenal success of those Holmes stories.

So I call Conan Doyle the Father of Crime Literature and Poe the Godfather. In three, four or five tales (depending on what importance you attach to the fourth and fifth) Poe laid down most of the basics of mystery writing. He seized on a dozen disparate elements, ranging from Voltaire's story of clue-following, *Zadig*, to the antics of his contemporary police investigators, and in a few strokes of lightning fused them into something definable and coherent. He was a genius (or perhaps the nineteenth-century American critic James Russell Lowell is right in saying he was "three-fifths genius and two-fifths sheer fudge"). However, whatever rating you give him, as he poured out in his short life fine poetry and sentimental rubbish, marvellous tales and some shame-making bits of facetiousness, as he struggled as a magazine editor of considerable achievement, as he dashed off a textbook on the fashionable study of shells, conchology, he has and will for ever have this blazing act to his credit.

The full extent of that discovery of the deep delight of following an unravelling is recorded elsewhere in these pages (under Poe in the "Consumer's Guide" and under his creation, Le Chevalier Auguste Dupin, in "The People of Crime"), but it should be pointed out here that Poe also was a notable contributor to the river of gothic writing that parallelled the stream-that-became-a-river of strict crime writing and in the end flowed together with it. Indeed, not the least of Poe's achievements was, in *The Murders in the Rue Morgue*, to anticipate this coming together by giving us a story in which the methodical and the macabre mingled to splendid effect.

It should be added, too, that in such asides as "Who has not a hundred times found himself committing a vile or silly action, for no other reason than because he knows he should *not*?" (from his story *The Black Cat*) he laid down guidelines for as modern a suspense writer as Patricia Highsmith. The great French poet Baudelaire used of Poe's stories words that could equally well be applied to hers: that in them we see "absurdity installing itself in the intellect, and ruling there with crushing logic". Nor was it for nothing that another suspense writer of as much modernity, Ruth Rendell, took as the title of one of her most compelling books the last five words of this fragment of Poe's poetry

> . . . the cloud that took the form
> (When the rest of heaven was blue)
> Of a demon in my view.

Yet, remarkable and compelling as Poe's linked discoveries were, they did not at once produce that spawn of imitators which forms the first stage of a new literary genre. This honour, despite the intervention of a solitary masterwork, Wilkie Collins' *The Moonstone* in 1877, was to go to Conan Doyle in 1891 when Holmes made his first proper impact (with a nod of acknowledgement to J. M. Stoddart, editor of the American *Lippincott's Monthly Magazine*, for picking on the otherwise largely neglected *A Study in Scarlet* and commissioning *The Sign of Four*, a book that kept Holmes in the forefront of his creator's mind until the *Strand* magazine became a receptive

> made some warm friends. I am on a historical novel now "The White Company," which I think will be better than Micah.
>
> With kindest regards
>
> Yours very truly
>
> A Conan Doyle.

> Bush Villa
> Southsea
> March 14th /90
>
> Dear Hemingsley
>
> Many thanks for your note. I have forwarded a copy of "The Sign of Four" for Mr Palmer. Lippincott is so little read as yet that the story is fresh to the public. Yet I should never have thought of using it as a serial had I not had several unsolicited requests from different papers. So I thought I might as well extend it. No other offer in the Birmingham district. I think the intermediate syndicate may very well be dispensed with in transactions between author and editor.
>
> Saw Longmans yesterday. The Polestar was sold right out in a day. They are now reprinting, and no doubt your copy will reach you then. "Mysteries & Adventures" is a pirated edition of tales written years ago in London Society — some of them when I was little more than a boy. It is rough on me having these youthful effusions brought out in this catch penny fashion, but I have no legal redress. The less reviewed or read they are the better. So glad you liked Micah. He has

The gradual rise of Sherlock Holmes
Conan Doyle wrote this letter to the Literary Editor of the Birmingham Daily Times *in March 1890. His second Holmes story,* The Sign of Four, *had appeared in* Lippincott's Monthly *in the United States in February of that year. It was eventually serialized in three English provincial newspapers. The third story,* A Scandal in Bohemia, *appeared in the* Strand *magazine in July 1891 and only then, with the appearance of a new story each month, did Holmes' popularity soar.*

seedbed for the astonishing growth).

Why was there this forty year gap between Poe's invention and Doyle's exploitation? Partly it was because of the very novelty of what Poe had done. "Invent that which is new, even if it be made of pine from your own yard," the American poet William Carlos Williams has said writing about Poe, "and there's none to know what you have done"; and, after all, it was not until 1856, seven years after Poe's death, that the word "detective" was used of anyone outside the police.

Partly, too, the gap was because Poe, for all his genius, omitted one vital ingredient in the formula. He failed to make Le Chevalier Dupin much of a person. He failed to give him enough substance for us to sympathize with. Beyond his one set of illustrative qualities (fascinating though these are), we learn scarcely a thing about him. In the *Rue Morgue* we are just told that "Le Bon once rendered me a service for which I am not ungrateful" (no more than that half-hint) and in *The Purloined Letter* we learn that Dupin and the Minister had had some ambiguous encounter in the past. That is almost all. Compare this to the rich mine of Holmes' character, to all that we know about him and to the way that all the contradictions in him hang marvellously together. This is why the Holmes stories took off in the extraordinary way they did, and why Poe's hero never became a living myth.

The Ghost of Sherlock Holmes, *a song by Richard Morton and H. C. Barry,
appeared in 1894. In 1893 Doyle had killed off Holmes at the Reichenbach Falls.
Popular demand was such that Doyle was forced to resurrect his hero.*

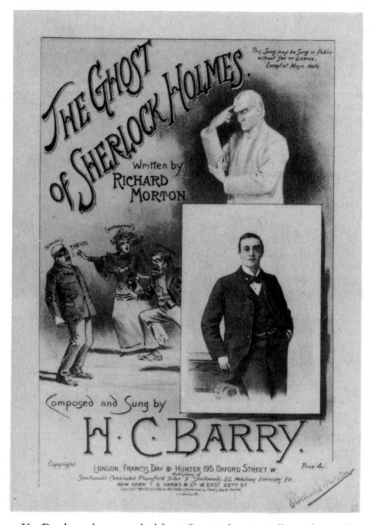

Yet Doyle took a great deal from Poe, and was usually ready to acknowledge the debt. He said once that the writer of tales of detection "sees the
footmarks of Poe always in front of him. He is happy if he ever finds the
means of breaking away and striking out on some little side-track of his
own." And this debt goes not only for the detection in Doyle's stories but
also for the element of the extraordinary that plays as important, if less often
recognized, a part in them.

Nor is Doyle's debt confined to such obvious (but always transmuted)
borrowings as the smoking-out of a concealed document taken from *The
Purloined Letter* for *A Scandal in Bohemia*. A little delving will show, for
instance, that Doyle's story *The Engineer's Thumb* is (although it is also
itself) Poe's *The Pit and the Pendulum*. The room-sized hydraulic press of
the former, in which the young engineer is trapped, is very much the pit with
its walls "seemingly of stone masonry – very smooth, slimy and cold" but in
fact of "iron or some other metal, in huge plates" where Poe's hero awakes to

find himself. Each protagonist, too, has a last-moment escape, and it is Doyle's engineer who says that, were it not for his severed thumb, "all that has passed during those dreadful hours might have been an evil dream."

But *The Engineer's Thumb* is more than the simple romantic yarn it seems on the surface. Doyle in telling it was reaching, probably unconscious of what he was doing, into the lower depths of his mind. He was telling a tale twining with symbolism, as, more obviously, was Poe. The pit and the press are both locked rooms, prisons, however, not just for bodies but for minds. They represent men shut up in their own worlds, their own personalities. The engineer had spent, as well, most of two years alone in his office without a client coming, and in his story it is through the agency of the Great Detective that his prison is located and destroyed, a strongly symbolic action. The Great Detective is more, much more, than a mere solver of interesting crimes. he is a powerful mythic figure (which is in large part why detective literature flourished).

The Great Detective, as brought into being by Edgar Allan Poe, as definitively established by Conan Doyle, is a being capable, as ordinary mortals are not, of escaping from the trap of his own personality. Most of us live in the prison, or the locked room, of rules we have made up for ourselves and dare not break. We are the plodding police officer, Doyle's Inspector Lestrade, the Prefect G--- of Poe's stories. We can apply to a problem only the procedures we have always applied, can bring to it only our ordinary selves. The Great Detective brings something more.

He has the ability to leave his own personality and to enter into those of others. "An identification of the (opponent) reasoner's intellect with his own," says Dupin's friend, understanding at last. Dr Watson speaks of Holmes' ability to vary "his expression, his manner, his very soul" in adopting disguises. G. K. Chesterton's Father Brown says "When I'm quite sure I feel like a murderer, of course I know who he is." Agatha Christie's Miss Marple in *Sleeping Murder* feels positively ill placing herself in the murderer's shoes.

The process whereby the Great Detective breaks out of the prison of his own personality is a mingling of the rational and the intuitive. Dupin is just that combination of reason and imagination which Poe in his literary essays frequently praised. He is a poet and a mathematician. He can arrive at what seems to be a discovery, something altogether new, by making this combination. (Think of the hiding-place of the purloined letter). "All novel conceptions are merely unusual combinations," Poe said in writing about Fancy (the reasoning faculty) and Imagination (the intuitive). That ability Dupin passed down to his many successors, first among them Holmes. Holmes the reasoner we see in plenty, but we also watch him, enfolded in a cloud of tobacco smoke letting his intuition work in silence, as, equally smoke-wreathed Simenon's Maigret does in his turn.

Thus the Great Detectives rise to an originality that puts the plodding police, and the plodding reader, to shame. Thus they can enter a scene where, with murder done, it seems that society has reverted to utter turmoil, and, by at last pointing the finger at the sole criminal they restore to us our serenity.

H. R. F. Keating is crime books critic of The Times, *London, and author of* Sherlock Holmes, the Man and His World *and* Murder Must Appetize, *a study of Golden Age detective stories.*

The English Detective Story

Robert Barnard

IN THE EARLY 1920s the British were recovering from a war in which three-quarters of a million of their young men died. Recriminations were replacing patriotic euphoria, and the unemployed ex-army salesman was a familiar sight in the streets. But for most people the overwhelming desire was to put those four years behind them. There were innumerable musical shows to go to, both home-grown and transatlantic. Nigel Playfair was reviving Restoration comedies with Edith Evans at the Lyric; Noel Coward, with *Hay Fever,* was proving that the comedy of manners was not dead. And for reading matter there were Christie, Sayers, and a whole host of lesser names who make up what we today call the Golden Age of the detective story.

One should not take the comparison between the classic crime story and the comedy of manners too far, but the parallels are striking. In 1660 in Britain the metropolitan upper class had just been through two gruelling decades: their king had been executed, their estates sequestered, they themselves had been reduced to risible or pathetic hangers-on at continental courts. Through Restoration comedy they built a new wall around themselves, to keep out the realities of the changed world: they created an artificial world of aristocratic elegance, where their standards ruled, where their wit and taste were exalted, where the rude outsider could be ejected from the charmed circle.

In 1920 the English middle classes had seen empires crumble, new Bolshevik republics established, Labour parties flourishing, a whole battalion of middle-class standards collapse. They suspected, like the Restoration nobility, that their world was gone for ever, and they took refuge in a form of literature that was hedged with rules and conventions, that flourished on stereotyped situations and characters, that looked back to a period of stability, a period where class distinctions were easily defined and generally accepted. In the detective story, too, the outsider could be cast out of the charmed circle. Permanently. By murder, or by judicial execution. The detective story was a way of saying that the dykes had not given way.

Which is not to be taken for a criticism. The golden age crime writers created an artificial world, and critics who complain that Sayers and Christie are stereotyped and dated have missed the point as surely as the modern teenager who reads a fifty-year-old Christie as if it were written yesterday has got it. *The Murder of Roger Ackroyd* is not dated, it is dateless.

This highly artificial product, created partly as an escape from an intolerable reality, had the effect of highlighting one aspect of great appeal in the traditional detective story. This was a contract between author and reader that the latter would be entertained (not necessarily excited, but entertained) by the presentation of a problem that appealed to his intellect. The author promised to present the problem in a fair way, and the reader, if he was to be entertained at all, was bound to keep his mind working to spot the clues and wrestle with their significance. If the reader guessed the solution he was pleased with himself; if he did not he was pleased with the author. In neither case was the author the loser.

It was, like Restoration drama, a literary form abounding in rules, conventions, imperatives, prohibitions. These were wittily formulated by Ronald Knox in 1929 into a Decalogue. Some of the Commandments seem designed to mark the detective story off from other (by implication lesser) popular literary forms: "No Chinaman must figure in the story" distinguishes it from the cheap thriller; "Not more than one secret room or passage is allowable" prevents contamination from the Gothic. But most of the others (for example "The detective must not light on any clues which are not instantly produced for the inspections of the reader", or "No accident must ever help the

I

THE CRIMINAL must be someone mentioned in the early part of the story, but must not be anyone whose thoughts the reader has been allowed to follow.

II

ALL SUPERNATURAL or preternatural agencies are ruled out as a matter of course.

III

NOT MORE THAN ONE secret room or passage is allowable.

IV

NO HITHERTO UNDISCOVERED poisons may be used, nor any appliance which will need a long scientific explanation at the end.

V

NO CHINAMAN must figure in the story.

VI

NO ACCIDENT must ever help the detective, nor must he ever have an unaccountable intuition which proves to be right.

VII

THE DETECTIVE must not himself commit the crime.

VIII

THE DETECTIVE must not light on any clues which are not instantly produced for the inspection of the reader.

IX

THE STUPID FRIEND of the detective, the Watson, must not conceal any thoughts which pass through his mind; his intelligence must be slightly, but very slightly, below that of the average reader.

X

TWIN BROTHERS, and doubles generally, must not appear unless we have been duly prepared for them.

Ronald Knox's Decalogue *appeared in the Preface to* Best Detective Stories of 1928-29 *which Knox edited. Though a few of the rules are frivolous, most were intended to ensure "fair play" in the construction of an entertaining puzzle.*

detective, nor must he ever have an unaccountable intuition which proves to be right") affirm the logical rigour which should be maintained, and amplify that part of the contract between author and reader which enjoins "fair play". The term itself, with its overtones of gentlemanliness, is one more indication of the conservativeness of the form. The sort of fuss that arose over whether or not the solution of *Roger Ackroyd* was "foul" seems to us absurd. But it may, on consideration, seem endearing as well. One cannot, sadly, imagine any popular writer today engendering any sort of even marginally ethical debate.

What the classic English detective story essentially was can be more easily described than defined. When one thinks of likely or essential ingredients one could name: a country house or rural village; a corpse; a closed circle of suspects; an extended family group; a surprise solution. These conjure up the sort of book well enough, but there are many oddities and exceptions. Christie began with a country house party (*Mysterious Affair at Styles*) but it was not a setting she was particularly happy with, and Dorothy Sayers only uses it once; Sayers often forswears the surprise solution, and once forswears the corpse; Sayers and Allingham are as happy in London as in the country; Allingham often edges her books in the direction of the thriller by using a basic chase formula.

Of the writers whom we now think of as the big four, Agatha Christie was the first to publish (*Styles* was set in the war, and came out in 1920), and to judge by sales she is the one most triumphantly to survive. We think of her as an English village writer, but in fact her production is very varied: she liked to alternate her home settings with international excursions, and (like any country gentlewoman) took the occasional trip to London.

Her hold on the reader was due, to my mind, to her productivity, her consistency, her narrative skill, and her clear-eyed concentration on problem, on reader deception. In her heyday (say 1925-1950) she usually produced two, sometimes three titles a year. There is not a dud among them, except for the odd thriller or inferior short story collection. If the characterization is basic, the writing lacklustre, the story-telling on the other hand is superb, brilliantly organized around the need to present a problem and to

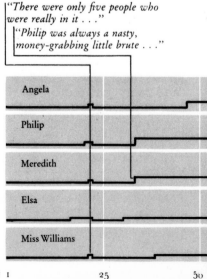

Suspicion quotient *of the suspects in a classic English detective story. Agatha Christie's* Five Little Pigs *(1943) has a closed circle of five suspects and the narrative follows an oft-repeated pattern: the guilty suspect, Elsa Greer, falls under some suspicion near the beginning, but is effectively dismissed as a possible culprit until shortly before the end. Meanwhile the suspiciousness of the other potential murderers see-saws up and down, and is always above that of the murderer.*

page 1   25   50

"The Big Four" *writers of classic English detective stories (*left to right*): Agatha Christie, Margery Allingham, Ngaio Marsh, Dorothy L. Sayers.*

both conceal and facilitate its solution. The clues are always there, though not always presented as clues, and Christie showed her understanding of the average reader in the way she used everyday objects as clues – things he could relate to as he could not to the intricacies of railway timetables, or some erudite piece of scholarship.

The reader loved Christie, above all, for the panache of her solutions. *Styles* used a "Yes he did, no he didn't, yes he did" formula (repeated later in *Murder at the Vicarage*) and later books break every convention and code of honour by incriminating the romantic interest, the narrator, a child, the whole cast list, the detective and so on. And yet in spite of this, the reader always felt that Christie played fair: like the traditional arrested burglar he could always say "It's a fair cop, governor".

Her construction of her stories must have been highly abstract – she worked rather like a mathematician evolving a brain-teaser. It is in this

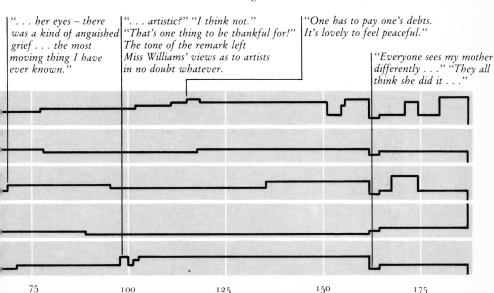

". . . her eyes – there was a kind of anguished grief . . . the most moving thing I have ever known."

". . . artistic?" "I think not." "That's one thing to be thankful for!" The tone of the remark left Miss Williams' views as to artists in no doubt whatever.

"One has to pay one's debts. It's lovely to feel peaceful."

"Everyone sees my mother differently . . ." "They all think she did it . . ."

abstract ingenuity that much of her strength lies, and she decisively tipped the balance away from character and setting, and back towards the supremacy of plot. She understood better than any that popular literature demands story, that it must force the reader to get through just one more chapter before putting the light out.

Dorothy Sayers was a much more intellectual, perhaps a much more intelligent woman than Christie. In the earlier novels she was intelligent enough not to let this show. We note her perceptive treatment of young men physically or mentally shattered by war, of women enforced by the slaughter of war to a life of spinsterhood, even on occasion of intellectuals, usually ridiculed in crime stories. We also note that her intelligence failed her a little when confronted with Bolsheviks, Jews or admirers of D. H. Lawrence – but we all have our limitations of sympathy.

The novels Sayers wrote in the first years of her brief career as crime writer were brilliant and varied. Very often they were not whodunits so much as "How did hes", and the way Sayers rang changes on the basic formula yet kept up suspense to the end is a testimony to her lively mind and story-telling talents. Her characterization is sharp, and she is very good on the shabby, the failures, the commonplace – the second-raters whose moral obtuseness just might shade off into sheer evil. Snobbish she may be, but she has an eye for sheer upper-crust nastiness, notably in the Duchess of Denver.

Each story has shape, but a different shape, and the oeuvre is united by the powerful myth-figure of Lord Peter Wimsey – nonchalant aristocrat, effete man of action, athlete-scholar. Lord Peter is absurd, perhaps, to modern tastes, but television adaptations have suggested that we can still relate to this nobleman with the common touch, the man who can eat pig's trotters with a reformed burglar and only draws the line at the pushy middle-classes.

It is difficult to avoid the conclusion that Sayers fell victim to her own ingenuity and intellectual pretensions. This can be illustrated from one of the 'thirties novels (by no means the dullest) *Have His Carcase* (1932). The solution to the puzzle hangs on a perfectly brilliant use of a simple piece of knowledge – the effects of the disease haemophilia. Christie would have revelled in such a reader-deceiver – she would have surrounded it with one or two double-edged clues from her drawer containing everyday objects, and hey-presto the trick would make a book. Sayers, on the other hand, keeps the trick for the very end, naturally, but to get to it we have to plod through acres of dreary alibi-busting, false identities and (worst of all) code-breaking. It is unbearably heavy, though not as totally unreadable and exhausting as *Five Red Herrings* (1931).

By the time of *Gaudy Night* (1935) and *Busman's Honeymoon* (1937) she was writing discursive conversation pieces with as she called it "detective interruptions". For all her proclaimed high critical ideals for the detective story, it is clear that she gave it up because she no longer believed in it.

There was always a danger that Margery Allingham might follow in Sayers' footsteps. Her detective, Albert Campion, began as a straight crib of Wimsey, though with typical zany cheek, the desire to go that crucial one step further, she declared to a fellow crime writer that "his destiny was to inherit the British throne", and that he was based on the then Duke of York (later George VI). Again, in the late 'thirties a foolish critic wrote that "to Albert Campion has fallen the honour of being the first detective to feature in a story which is also by any standard a distinguished novel". When a crime critic says something like that you can be sure the book under review is a dreary middle-of-the-road, middle-of-the-brow sort of piece, and indeed *Dancers in Mourning* (1937) is one of Allingham's dullest books.

But though, sadly, she took that review as the greatest compliment her books had ever received, she climbed back up from the slippery slope that that kind of attitude leads to. She did not try to write competent novels for the middle-classes, but she brought to the traditions of the popular crime story a quirky imagination, a zest and a truly Dickensian gift for creating and utilizing grotesques. *More Work for the Undertaker* (1948) is her best work of this kind: it has a marvellous sense of place, and the family of decaying intellectuals is both funny, alarming and touching, in the manner of the great Victorian.

The Tiger in the Smoke (1952) is her best work in the chase genre: the villain genuinely attractive and terrifying (she is usually good with young thugs), and the atmosphere of London in a pea-souper brilliantly caught. Agatha Christie rightly paid tribute to the variety of Allingham's production: "Everything she writes has a definitive shape . . . each book has its own separate and distinctive background."

This is true, and the character of her work changed a good deal during her career. There are the early high-spirited romps (fiendishly difficult to bring off, because effort is so immediately visible). Then there are more serious works in the late 'thirties, some of which escape ponderousness. Then the complete mastery of the 'forties and 'fifties, in which her eye for absurdity, as well as her feeling for evil, are given full rein.

She did dull work, as well as first-rate work, throughout her career, for she was essentially an erratic writer. But *Police at the Funeral* (1931), *Hide My Eyes* (U.S. *Tether's End*, 1958) and *The China Governess* (1962) as well as the two just named, are brilliant, nourishing works. She proved that the crime story could be a work of art without ponderousness, pretension, or aping the middle-brow novel. Only Ruth Rendell, in our own time, has done work that one would think of mentioning in the same breath.

Ngaio Marsh began her career with a murder game in a country house-party (*A Man Lay Dead*, 1934), and continued it with the one where the stage gun that should be loaded with blanks has real bullets in (*Enter A Murderer*, 1935). A suspicion of cliché, in fact, hangs over much of Marsh's production.

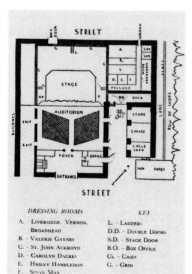

DRESSING ROOMS

A. - Liversidge. Vernon. Broadhead
B. - Valerie Gaynes
C. - St. John Ackroyd
D. - Carolyn Dacres
E. - Hailey Hambleton
F. - Susan Max

KEY

L. - Ladders
D.D. - Double Doors
S.D. - Stage Door
B.O. - Box Office
Cs. - Cases
G. - Grid

Vintage Murder *(1937) by Ngaio Marsh included a ground floor plan of the Theatre Royal, Middleton, New Zealand where the manager was murdered by being hit on the head with a bottle of champagne. Many classic detective stories included plans or maps.*

She is wonderfully readable, she brings off some kinds of thing enormously well, but she is no trail-blazer, and at times her determination to follow in other people's footsteps becomes just a little tedious.

The country house murder is her forte, or at least the kind she does most often: as late as 1972 she was serving up the one where a house-party is snowed up on Dartmoor with only ex-convicts for servants. She gets away from this stereotype now and then, notably with the odd occult murder, the odd New Zealand murder (which mostly prove that patriotism is not enough) and, best of all, the theatre murder. A touch of backstage releases Miss Marsh's inhibitions most wonderfully. There is no danger there of those embarrassing displays of Edwardian snobbery when Alleyn (her detective)'s gentlemanly origins are revealed: just a collection of egos competing for attention, which almost always makes for a good read.

The puzzle in Marsh is meticulously worked out, though it sometimes lacks the brilliant sleight-of-hand of Christie's inter-war production. But where Christie relaxed the meticulous plotting in her later books, Marsh has retained all her care and fairness. The danger is that she plots so carefully and ingeniously that the investigation of the minutiae and the final explanations may become a heavy-handed working over of boring details. And if there is about Alleyn a touch of stiffness, as of a gentleman from Trollope who doesn't quite know what he is doing in a detective story or in the twentieth century, nevertheless he dates wonderfully less than most of the other Golden Age detectives.

When did the traditional whodunit die? It didn't, of course, for readers – any glance at railway bookstalls will tell that. All the writers I have talked about are still triumphantly read, and many others such as John Dickson Carr, Freeman Wills Croft and Anthony Berkeley are read by devotees and enjoy spasmodic revival.

But for writers? Critics keep telling us it is dead, but in fact probably half the crime books published today still stick broadly to the classic formula. At least half of Ruth Rendell's production, more than half of P. D. James' (to name the most obvious successors of the big four I have talked about) adhere to the classic mould, have detectives that are recognizable successors of those towering twenties figures. What writers have learned is that the formula is adaptable, that it will take more realism, more humour, a wider class range, more psychological depth than the Golden Age writers used. But the basic formula is still very much alive and useful. The whodunit is not dead. It is hardly even dozing.

Robert Barnard is Professor of English Literature at Tromso University, Norway, and author of A Talent to Deceive, An Appreciation of Agatha Christie *as well as of novels of detection.*

THE American Detective Story

by Julian Symons

IN A PURELY HISTORICAL SENSE, the American detective story could be said to begin in the late nineteenth century with the work of Anna Katharine Green, succeeded by the tales of mystery and terror written by Mary Roberts Rinehart. They were succeeded in the twenties by S. S. Van Dine, the first American crime writer regarded as intellectually reputable, and Van Dine by the early work of Ellery Queen, from *The Roman Hat Mystery* (1929) onwards. But these were all Americans who looked towards Europe: specifically *American* stories, tales that no European could have written, were born in the pulp magazines.

The pulps got their name from the fact that they were printed on wood pulp, which gave the contents an appropriately coarse, grainy appearance. They were seven by ten inches in size, with gaudy covers showing a scene of violent action, and they contained around 120 pages of short stories, with occasional extracts from novels.

Black Mask *Dashiell Hammett, Raymond Chandler and many others wrote stories for* Black Mask *before moving on to full-length novels.*

Left **Thrilling Detective** *Stories by Carroll John Daly featuring Race Williams, the first of the hard-boiled dicks, appeared in* Thrilling Detective, Dime Detective *and others.*

Right **"The Big Three"** *writers of the American crime story (left to right): Dashiell Hammett, Ross Macdonald, Raymond Chandler.*

The pulps began to appear in World War I, but became popular early in the twenties, so that by the end of the decade there were two hundred separate pulp magazines on the bookstands. Many had a short life, but a few achieved legendary fame – *Black Mask* primarily, *Dime Detective, Thrilling Detective* and *Detective Story Magazine* in much lesser degrees. *Black Mask* survived into the fifties, the other magazines died or changed character earlier than that.

The pulps were born out of disillusionment with the increasing corruption of American social life and a feeling of disillusionment enhanced by the unhappy effects of Prohibition in big cities. They were killed by the emergence of TV. Many of the TV cops are true heirs of the pulp magazine detectives.

The first of the private eyes or hard-boiled dicks was Race Williams, the creation of a former movie projectionist named Carroll John Daly. Williams appeared in 1923, and was developed in later stories. He slept always with a loaded gun in his hand, used the gun often, speedily, and with intent to kill (he once shot a gangster five times before the other man could squeeze the trigger of his own revolver), and thought nothing of throwing a corpse down to the ground seventeen stories below. ("It may be brutal and all that, but why beat around a stiff?")

Williams was a caricature of the private eye as he developed in the hands of better writers, among whom Frederick Nebel, Raoul Whitfield, Frank Gruber, Lester Dent and George Harmon Coxe should be named. Erle Stanley Gardner wrote for the pulps in the early twenties, before his first novel appeared, and in the forties writers including John D. MacDonald and William Campbell Gault came through the pulps to book publication. Of the three most notable practitioners of the American crime story, Dashiell Hammett, Raymond Chandler and Ross Macdonald, only the last did not come to early prominence through the pulp magazines.

This kind of American crime story made a complete break with the European tradition. The detective was utterly unlike Poirot, Lord Peter Wimsey or Mr Campion, and bore no resemblance to their American counterparts, Philo Vance and Ellery Queen. Whether he was named Race

Williams, Steve Midnight, or Big Red Brennan, he was a tough man of action, not always entirely honest, a man who sometimes went to bed with one of the attractive but unreliable women with whom he became involved.

Two of the things that fascinated early readers of Hammett's *The Maltese Falcon* (1930) were an uncertainty throughout the book about Sam Spade's honesty, and his bedding of Brigid O'Shaughnessy. Spade and O'Shaughnessy broke the pattern of totally honest investigator and virtuous heroine for good.

Within a few years the best pulp writers graduated to book publication. Hammett's *Red Harvest* and *The Dain Curse* (both 1929) and *The Maltese Falcon* had all appeared in *Black Mask* prior to the book publication dates given above. Raymond Chandler wrote a number of stories for the pulps before emerging to fame in 1939 with *The Big Sleep*. In all, Hammett wrote only five novels, *The Glass Key* (1931) and *The Thin Man* (1934) being the others, but it is on these books, rather than the many short stories in which the central character is the short, fattish private eye called the Continental Op, that his fame rests.

Red Harvest is the only Continental Op novel, a book so full of violence that it is hard to discover the number of murders. Yet the violence is never indulged in for its own sake, it does not exclude some brilliant characterization, in particular of the chief woman character Dinah Brand, and the atmosphere of Poisonville is convincingly similar to that of many American towns in the period, where the police worked hand in hand with the gangsters. Hammett developed his talent, so that in his masterpiece *The Glass Key* the violence is well under control, and is not used casually, the plotting is as cunning as in Agatha Christie, and the characterization is handled with the utmost skill and assurance. The book is also a serious novel, one that does not suffer by comparison with anything written in the thirties by dos Passos, Faulkner or Hemingway. After the amusing but relatively trivial *The Thin Man*, however, Hammett wrote no more novels.

Raymond Chandler wrote seven novels, after cutting his teeth on the pulp stories. His reputation, like Hammett's, rests on the novels, of which *The Little Sister* (1949) and *The Long Goodbye* (1953) are the best, in part because they are the most clearly plotted. Chandler came late in life to the crime story, and brought to it a literary quality unknown to most of the pulp writers. He had a great feeling for the sound and value of words, and the wisecracks that stud his books are remarkable for the smoothness with which they run, as well as for the fact that they make one laugh. In the later books he took care with every paragraph, every phrase, and his pains were rewarded.

At the centre of all the stories is his detective Philip Marlowe, about whom opinions differ. For Chandler himself, Marlowe gave meaning to the stories. Through the landscape of Southern California, with its characteristic fauna of brutal or incompetent policemen, vicious gang bosses, unfeeling millionaires, and the brightly enamelled fast-talking ladies who accompanied them as wives, mistresses or family, moved Marlowe who had to be, as Chandler said, "a complete man and a common man, and . . . to use a rather weathered phrase, a man of honour". In this grubby world the detective "is the hero, he is everything".

For some readers this apotheosis of Marlowe makes him the most admirable, as he is certainly the most amusing, of private eyes. For others it shows a sentimentality which reduces the reality not only of the detective himself, but of the world in which he moves.

As a writer Chandler succeeded Hammett, and acknowledged a debt to him. Ross Macdonald belongs to a later generation, and has both built on, and moved away from, the influence of his elders. His early books, published under his own name of Kenneth Millar, owe a good deal to Hammett, although *Blue City* (1947) is marked by strikingly individual turns of phrase.

A change to the name of John Ross Macdonald (the "John" was later dropped to avoid confusion with John D. MacDonald) marked the introduction of the detective Lew Archer. *The Way Some People Die* (1951), *The Ivory Grin* (1952) and *The Barbarous Coast* (1956) offer portraits of Southern California as vivid as anything in Chandler, but there is too much gun play and at times the wisecracks seem forced. The voice is individual, but sometimes the stories are not. Macdonald was looking for a story "roughly shaped on my own early life, transformed and simplified into a kind of legend", and found it in *The Galton Case* (1959).

Since then he has exploited many variations on this theme, so that the solution of the recent crimes which occur early in a book is always found to lie somewhere in the past. In accordance with this changed approach, Archer has become more a catalyst than a character. He is in one aspect a kind of father confessor to whom people talk, in another the figure whose appearance makes things happen.

On the appearance of *The Goodbye Look* (1969) Macdonald was greeted by the American press, not simply as a mystery writer but as a major American novelist. He himself has said that he goes on writing the same novel. This is much too modest, but it is true that his persistent belief in the importance of the past enters each book, quite often along with such current interests as ecology, which motivates in part *The Underground Man* (1971) and *Sleeping Beauty* (1973). Something of the zest in his early books is missing in these very accomplished novels (as he has said, "a writer in his fifties will not recapture the blaze of youth"), but he has worked steadily and successfully to a total achievement which makes a statement of his own beliefs about the nature of personality and the shape of society.

Macdonald has had no direct followers, but there are several recent writers whose work has been generally influenced by the three major figures. Robert B. Parker's entertaining Spenser stories offer a lighter version of the Marlovian original, Roger L. Simon's *The Big Fix* introduced a Jewish detective named Moses Wine, Joseph Hansen's Dave Brandstetter is a homosexual detective who keeps us up to date with the gay scene.

The American crime story has moved also in another, less desirable direction. The work of Mickey Spillane makes its appeal to the human desire for power and domination. Spillane, whose early work also appeared in the pulps, offers a hero who takes pleasure in shooting a murderess in the stomach, and burns another woman to death. "Heroes" like Don Pendleton's Mack Bolan ("His buddies in Vietnam had called him 'The Executioner'") and Frank Scarpetta's Philip Magellan who deliberately rubs shreds of broken glass into the "villain's" face until "it didn't look like a human face at all" are two of several who carry on this unlovely inheritance of the pulp tradition.

There are other, more agreeable, writers who do not belong to the Hammett-Chandler-Macdonald line of descent. Among them are W. R. Burnett, who wrote a series of very efficient realistic crime stories, including *Little Caesar* (1929) and *The Asphalt Jungle* (1949), James M. Cain who never repeated as a crime writer the success of *The Postman Always Rings Twice* (1934), William P. McGivern, and John D. MacDonald, whose Travis McGee stories have a wide following.

It would be hard to overstate the importance of the American crime story's origins in pulp fiction. Many of those original pulp fictioneers were bad writers: yet the urgency of their story-telling, the need for action and for harsh, sharp dialogue – the American language as it is actually spoken – remains in the work of authors like Ed McBain and George V. Higgins, who may have read very few pulp magazines.

Of course there are writers who have not been influenced by the pulps, like Patricia Highsmith, and the two ladies who write orthodox detective stories under the name of Emma Lathen, yet even they perhaps owe an indirect debt

Hard-boiled dicks *All of the American private eyes have tough exteriors and are well-skilled at delivering a punch. Some, such as Mickey Spillane's Mike Hammer, are unremittingly hard-boiled. Others reveal a soft centre at times and occasionally pull their punches. The leading private eyes are here rated 1 to 10 for "hard-boiledness".*

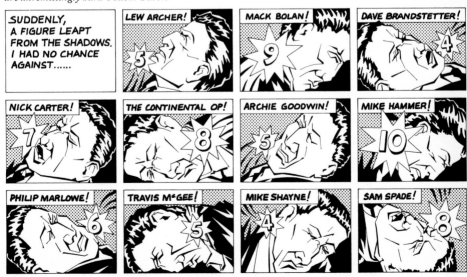

to those mostly crude pioneers who broke away so violently from European models. So also does Ross Thomas, whose stories about varieties of American corruption, like *The Porkchoppers* (1972), *If You Can't Be Good* (1973) and *Chinaman's Chance* (1978) explore political and social evils more directly than Hammett and Chandler ever did. Thomas also often blends adventure with crime, in a way personal to himself.

The rules of the game in the American crime story, the concepts that mark it out from English and European counterparts, are an approach that is generally nearer to realism both in conveying the social scene and in details of police work (although there are exceptions, like the Swedish Martin Beck novels), and a highly demotic use of language.

The language in most English crime stories is that used by the middle class, "BBC English" not only in grammatical usages, but in its vocabulary. A typical American crime story will use much racier speech, belonging far less to a particular class, language that reflects the variety of nationalities and forms of speech in the United States.

Julian Symons is the author of Bloody Murder, A History from the Detective Story to the Crime Novel *(*Mortal Consequences *in U.S.) as well as of numerous crime novels. He was crime books reviewer for the Sunday Times, London, for ten years and is President of the Detection Club.*

Right **The reader and the detective story** *The position of the reader varies from one form of detective story to another. In Conan Doyle's Sherlock Holmes stories (1) the reader and Dr Watson together form an audience which simply observes the master-detective at work. In classic detective stories (2) the reader joins the detective onstage, inspects the clues, and, like the detective, tries to identify the murderer. In hard-boiled private-eye stories (3) the relationship between reader, detective and events is essentially the same; however, realism is added and the reader becomes more interested in the character of the detective, identifies with him to a greater extent and shows correspondingly less interest in the puzzle element of the story. Police procedurals (4) lift the reader into the world of policemen and show him how police forces work; again he is onstage, but more interested in the milieu than in the puzzle.*

The American Police Procedural

by Hillary Waugh

TO UNDERSTAND THE POLICE PROCEDURAL detective story, it is necessary to relate it to the types of detective stories which preceded it, to view the similarities and differences.

The police procedural represents the second major change in the nature of the detective story since it achieved its puzzle form with the advent of the classical school in the 1920s.

The progenitor of the classical school was the incomparable Sherlock Holmes. While it is true that Conan Doyle got the inspiration for Holmes from Poe's Auguste Dupin, the dominant personality of Holmes so swept the field that all the fictional detectives who followed were created in his image. Born were such semblances as Hercule Poirot, Philo Vance, Ellery Queen, Charlie Chan, Lord Peter Wimsey and Nero Wolfe, to name a few. Like Holmes, they were, essentially, detached from and disdainful of the local constabulary. Like Holmes they were intellectual giants, standing head and shoulders above their fellows – except for the villain! As Holmes had to have a Moriarty to challenge him, so the classical detective had to face a gifted murderer in order to exhibit his skill.

In one important way, the classical detective story differed from the Holmes tales. Whereas, when Sherlock Holmes was on the trail, the reader stood at Watson's side, watching the Great Man operate, the writers of the classical school moved the reader onstage and, giving him all the clues available to the detective, let him try to beat the detective to the solution.

It was this development which made the detective story what it is today, an entity, complete and fulfilled. This feature has been the hallmark of the detective story ever since, no matter what form it takes.

The first trend away from the classical tale in America began in the late twenties and is known as the private-eye, or hard-boiled school. The best

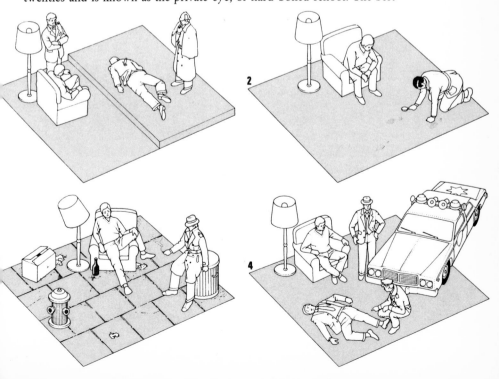

known representatives of this new approach to crime writing were Dashiell Hammett and Raymond Chandler and their stated purpose was to take murder out of the bishop's rose garden – the milieu of the classical detective tale – and put it down in the gutter where real murders took place. This attempt to bring realism to crime writing resulted in stories about seamy characters in seamy backgrounds. The detectives came down from the aeries of the classical school and became working stiffs, hiring themselves out as private investigators.

While these tales had a greater element of realism in them to begin with, unreality soon set in as the hard-boiled school degenerated into the sex-and-sadism school wherein the heroes lived on Scotch whisky but never got drunk, were forever knocked unconscious without getting a headache, and encountered a female population consisting of nothing but oversexed blondes.

The second and latest change in the detective tale in America was the rise of the police procedural, stories in which professional policemen, using police resources and police methods, are the ones who solve the crimes.

While Lawrence Treat's *V as in Victim*, published in 1945, is acknowledged to be the first such novel, it did not establish a trend. In fact, the next such effort was my own *Last Seen Wearing . . .* which, though written in 1950, did not appear until 1952. In the interim, *Dragnet* became a hit radio show and it was so soon thereafter that the police procedural developed and flourished that it may well be claimed that if there is a father of the American police procedural, *Dragnet* is it. While it is true that no police procedural writer I have talked to points to *Dragnet* as his inspiration (most not having written their first procedurals until well after *Dragnet*'s demise), it seems inevitable that the potential of the police station background was first brought to their attention by Joe Friday and company.

How does the police procedural differ from the classical and private-eye forms? The differences are many.

First of all, the procedural thrusts the detective into the middle of a working police force, full of rules and regulations. Instead of bypassing the police, as did its predecessors, the procedural takes the reader inside the department and shows how it operates. These are stories not just about policemen, but about the world of the policeman. Police Inspector Charlie Chan doesn't belong. (There are no police.) Nor does Inspector Maigret. (There are police, but Maigret remains his own man.) When we speak of police procedurals, we are talking about the 87th Precinct books of Ed McBain, about the Elizabeth Linington-Dell Shannon-Lesley Egan, Glendale and Los Angeles police novels.

The thrust is toward the police instead of away from the police and the shift is radical. The classical and private-eye novels have more in common with each other than either has with the procedural. Let us see why.

In the classical mystery, the only way to challenge the giant intellect of the detective was to create a villain of comparable genius who could devise the most elaborate of schemes in order to get away with murder. In reality, most murders are spur-of-the-moment crimes and even those that are planned betray little intelligence on the part of the killer. The procedural writer is at a disadvantage here. He cannot challenge his readers in this manner.

Another advantage to those who wrote the non-procedurals, was the trick of having the hero detective – classical or private-eye – keep all the threads of the mystery in his own head. Not only did this keep the reader in the dark, it made the detective a target of the villain, which is good for suspense. In the procedural, this can't be done. In the police department, all resources and

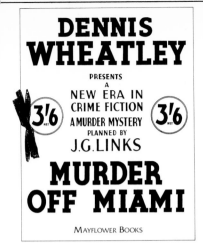

DENNIS WHEATLEY

PRESENTS
A
NEW ERA IN
CRIME FICTION
A MURDER MYSTERY
PLANNED BY
J.G. LINKS

3/6 NET 3/6 NET

MURDER OFF MIAMI

MAYFLOWER BOOKS

Murder Off Miami *(1936, reprinted 1980) is a fictional dossier rather than a novel. The reader is presented with the statements, letters and clues (cigarette stub, lock of hair, etc.) that were available to the police, and invited to solve a murder mystery. The reader gains a small degree of insight into police procedure, but the book and its sequel,* Who Killed Roger Prentice? *(1937, reprinted 1980) belong in the classic tradition where the puzzle is paramount.*

information are pooled. You can't be a loner in a team operation.

One of the real restrictions on the procedural writer is that he has to research police procedure. He has to learn what can and can't be done in real life. Where other writers could talk about fingerprints on guns, wrapping prints in handkerchiefs for protection, and determining the state of mind of a murder victim by the expression on his dead face, the procedural writer can't. He has to know that a print from a gun is a near impossibility, that handkerchiefs smudge, they don't protect, that the best that can be said of a dead man's expression is that he has no expression.

Does this make for reality? Is the police procedural what it appears to be, a *real* picture of the way crimes are solved?

The answer is *no*.

Consider murders in general. Most are done in such a state of emotion and for such personal reasons that the police know within five minutes who did the killing and have a fair idea as to why. Arresting and booking the "alleged perpetrator" is a simple thing. (What happens to him thereafter is another story, and out of their bailiwick. Their job has been done.)

One cannot, however, write up that kind of murder – not as a mystery. There's no mystery. There's no suspense. There's no story.

The kind of murder, therefore, that a writer has to invent and fictionalize, has to be one of the very few – perhaps one in twenty – cases where the number of suspects exceeds one, the motives are numerous or uncertain, and the finger of suspicion points to a variety of capable parties.

If an author is writing a police procedural that takes place in a small town, he's talking about the murder of the century. Except that, if he's reasonably prolific, these once in a century murderers are happening in his small town twice to three times a year. This is hardly realism.

Suppose, instead, the police procedural deals with a large city where there are hundreds of homicides in a year (latest figures for New York City are 1,800). Now it's conceivable that a single homicide detective might get two tough cases in a year. But there's another problem with presenting reality.

The real-life detective does not do his detecting *à la* Sherlock Holmes. He may observe the way Holmes observed: he may well put the pieces of a puzzle together the way Holmes put them together, but this is not the way most real-life crimes are solved. Solutions don't, in most cases, come as the result of ratiocination – not by the exercise of Hercule Poirot's little grey cells, but by the accumulation of information. Dozens of people are questioned – hundreds are questioned – and, bit by bit, pieces of information are gathered which, ultimately, reveal what happened.

That's the hard way.

The easy way is to have the information brought in. Ask a chief of detectives how cases are solved and he won't answer, "Clues", he'll answer, "Informants". It is an adage that a detective is only as good as his informants and the adage is true.

To the mystery story writer, this poses certain problems. The nature of the genre doesn't permit a tough case to be solved by someone coming into police headquarters, telling the detectives who did it and giving them the evidence. That's not the way mystery stories are told. It's not the way any story is told.

But it happens to be the way of the world. So the mystery story writer must make changes in the tale, eliminate the informant and have the detective track down that information through diligence and sweat. But such a tale is no more "real" than the classical ones. Reality and detective stories cannot co-exist. The art of the story must distort the truth.

Now let's consider the hero of the police procedural as opposed to his classical and private-eye counterparts.

Whereas the hero detectives of the classical and private-eye schools were unique individuals, overshadowing the others in the case, the policeman in the procedural has to be shown as a man of ordinary abilities. He can't drink a quart of Scotch without getting drunk, he can't get hit on the head without suffering a concussion. He isn't swarmed over by beautiful blondes because that's not the fate of real policemen and, besides, he's probably a family man. Nor can he heroically invade the villain's stronghold to rescue the damsel in distress. It's the SWAT team that does that. As for collecting evidence and putting clues together, it's a collaborative effort involving such resources as the photo lab, the medical examiner's office, ballistics, latent prints, emergency service, the crime lab and, sometimes, hundreds of other detectives.

This results in one of the great differences that separate the procedural from the other two forms of the detective story. The classical and private-eye novels pit a hero detective against a dangerous and evil genius while everyone else stands helplessly by. In the procedural, there is a villain, but he is not a genius. And against him, what is there? First off, there are two detectives devoting full time to the job of tracking him down. Behind them, at their beck and call, are all the resources of the police, medical and legal systems of the community. It's Mutt against Jeff, the champ against the novice, the sword against the stick. Who's going to want to watch a match like that?

This poses a particular challenge to the writer of the procedural. It is not enough that he must research police departments and criminalistics and learn what can and cannot be done, both legally and scientifically, he must overcome the handicaps mentioned above. He must create excitement out of the unexciting. He must make the mundane interesting. He must extract suspense from the routine.

Hillary Waugh has written more than 30 crime novels, including Last Seen Wearing *widely regarded as a masterpiece of suspense fiction and a pioneer police procedural. He is a past President of the Mystery Writers of America.*

The British Police Procedural

by Michael Gilbert

Inspector Lestrade *characteristically stands in the background fingering his chin while Sherlock Holmes interrogates a witness.*

T HE BRITISH POLICEMAN made his entrance on to the stage of the detective story at an early date; but he played no more than a walking-on part. In the Sherlock Holmes stories Lestrade and his confrères at the Yard had the job of acting what, in music hall terms, would be called the "feed". Their job was to demonstrate the superior skill of Holmes. They earned a lot of kicks and a few grudging ha'pence. "Three undetected murders in one year won't do, Lestrade. But you handled the Molesey mystery with less than your usual – that's to say you handled it fairly well."

This was not a state of affairs which could last indefinitely. Common sense was bound to assert itself sooner or later. I tackled this point in the introduction which I wrote to a reissue of one of the classics of the police procedural *The Lonely Magdalen* (1940) by Henry Wade.

"When detective story writers started to shy away from the talented amateur, with his odd personal habits, who solved problems by the application of intellect alone, and appeared to possess a formula which enabled him to succeed in detection without really trying, it was inevitable that they should turn to the police story. They knew that murderers, in real life, were caught by policemen. They suspected – and a little research soon proved – that policemen did not catch murderers by taking thought. They caught them by taking statements."

Perhaps the main reason why most early detective stories featured a talented amateur – and many still do – was that the writers, were themselves amateurs, and experienced a certain diffidence in describing a professional operation. They knew very little of what went on behind the blue lamp. Almost the only source of information generally available to them was the reminiscences of retired C.I.D. officers, which dealt sketchily with routine and promoted their hero almost to the position of the amateur they despised.

The logical answer to this difficulty would seem to be that the police procedural, meaning the story which not only deals realistically with police work but gives the principal parts to members of the police force, should be written either by policemen themselves or at least by authors whose calling brings them into close touch with police work.

Henry Wade, mentioned above, was, in real life, Sir Henry Aubrey Fletcher, Bt., of Brill. He was Lord Lieutenant of Buckinghamshire and busy for much of his life with police business. His son was a Metropolitan magistrate. In Britain the Crime Writers Association counts amongst its current members three serving policemen, one of whom sometimes appears at its meetings wearing his Murder Squad tie, a police woman, the editor of

The Police Review, and two police public relations officers. (To complete the role of those who have a direct connection with crime, the Association used also to have a safe-cracker among its members, but lack of success at his profession led to his being expelled for non-payment of his dues.)

While agreeing that these professionals should have the edge, with their knowledge of practice and personalities, it has to be admitted that the amateur, standing on the outside, has often produced better results. Incomparable stories about the army were written by Rudyard Kipling who had very bad eyesight and would not have known one end of a rifle from the other. Equally it has to be admitted that to date the classic series of British police procedurals has come from the pen of John Creasey who had no direct connection with the Force.

This brings us to the heart of the matter.

Creasey may not have been a professional policeman, but he was a completely professional writer. One can feel no doubt, as one reads the Gideon saga, that he had friends in the police who were willing to keep him informed of every aspect of organization and procedure. What no-one who is not a policeman can be certain about is whether he was equally correct and realistic about the atmosphere and feeling behind the face of routine. It is a difference which merits consideration.

In one of her best known books, *The Nine Tailors* (1934), Dorothy L. Sayers made campanology, or the ringing of church bells, the pivotal theme of her story, which centred round a church in a remote East Anglian village. So well, and so thoroughly, did she do her homework that most readers assumed that the book must have been based on practical experience. However, in a letter written shortly before her death, she dispelled this illusion. She said, "Technicalities can be 'got up' as counsel 'gets up' a brief. I read up bell-ringing. But I was brought up in the Fens, and I doubt whether any amount of reading would give one the feel of those windswept agricultural flats if one had never seen anything but mountains."

Apply this to the police procedural and the quandary becomes apparent. Can anyone who does not combine the story-telling ability of a Kipling with the fortuitous circumstance that he happens himself to be a policeman, really give us the true impression, the feel, of police work; the sweat and the frustration, the blind loyalty inside the service and the social difficulties outside it, the occasional successes, the ever-present problem of public

Five categories of detective story *as identified by Barzun & Taylor. Two are very common: the Normal, such as Agatha Christie's* Sleeping Murder; *and the Police Routine, exemplified by Ed McBain's 87th Precinct stories. The Inverted, where the reader knows who the murderer is, as in Francis Iles'* Malice Aforethought, *is less common and comes close to the straight novel. Michael Innes'* There Came Both Wind and Snow *and Agatha Christie's* The Murder of Roger Ackroyd *are respectively examples of the rarer Autobiographical type, in which the narrator is a prime suspect, and the mysterious Acroidal stories.*

British police procedural writers (l to r):
*John Wainwright, Roger Busby, Jonathan Ross,
Laurence Henderson,
John Creasey, Jack Scott,
Bill Knox.*

relations? One feels that if Zola had worn a blue helmet he could have done it.

Is this pitching the problem too high? It has to be borne in mind that the writer who embarks on a police procedural is doing more than merely changing the background of his story. *He is shifting his view-point.*

In their *Catalogue of Crime* Barzun & Taylor divide the detective story into five varieties. Normal; Inverted; Police Routine; Autobiographical and Acroidal. The last two of these types are rare (and you will search the largest dictionaries in vain for a definition of acroidal; when the meaning of the word does occur to you, you will appreciate it all the more). The first three varieties encompass the options commonly open to the writer. In the Normal, the story is viewed from the outside. A murder is committed. The reader watches the detective making his careful way among the clues and the suspects and arriving finally at a solution. The reader may, as a technical exercise, attempt to anticipate the solution for himself. But he does so from the outside. He is what A. A. Milne, in a stage play dealing with a murder, called "the fourth wall".

In the inverted story, some of the best of which were written by Anthony Berkeley Cox, under the pseudonym of Francis Iles, the matter is viewed through the eye of the murderer himself. We help him to make his plans and are involved with his hopes and fears. It is perhaps the closest that the crime story comes to the straight novel.

In the police procedural our viewpoint has shifted once more. We are inside the story, but in a different sense. We are not the murderer, and we are certainly not members of the public. Indeed one sometimes has the feeling that in a murder investigation the police have two adversaries to contend with: the criminal; and the great British public, who first confuse the issue by trampling on footprints and concealing clues, and then, when the police have arrested the murderer and have persuaded the Director of Public Prosecutions that they have a case which will stand up in Court, become members of the jury, all too willing to be beguiled by silver-tongued counsel for the defence. In a true-life murder story it might be said that a quarter of the difficulty is identifying and charging the murderer; three-quarters of it is securing a conviction. Many policemen would put these proportions even higher.

"If you want to know what a murder story really is," said a member of C.I.D., now happily retired and, like Sherlock Holmes, keeping bees, "I'll tell you. It's a few hundred statements, a few hours interrogating the man you're going to charge, with a cup of cold coffee in one hand and Judges' Rules in the other, a day in Court having your character torn to pieces by defending counsel, and a fifty-fifty chance of success."

There may be some exaggeration in this, but if it is even broadly truthful, the final question for the writer is, how do I get it on to paper without myself committing the ultimate crime: the crime of being dull?

The answer must lie in the policemen and policewomen. This time they are the real people. Their home-life may be as important as their professional life, a point well brought out by Creasey. It is their hopes and fears, not the hopes and fears of the murderer that are in the forefront of the story. Their motives may be more fundamental to the working out of the plot than the motives of the suspects which form the staple of the normal detective story.

This would not be an easy book to write but it would be something eminently worth doing; to concentrate, not on the murder which was the ostensible reason for the book, but on the fascinating, infuriating, vital job of the professionals whose job it is to catch the murderer. With this in mind might I end with a concrete suggestion? If you have not already done so, read a book written some twenty years ago by Edwin Brock, called *The Little White God*. It is not, in the usual sense of the word, a police procedural, but it was written by a young policeman, and written from the heart, and it did give to this reader at least, a real impression of what policemen think about themselves and their work.

Edwin Brock is a poet. Maybe it needed a poet to do it.

Michael Gilbert has been a prolific author of crime novels and short stories since 1947, including the Petrella police procedurals. He is a partner in a Lincoln's Inn firm of solicitors.

The Short Story

by Eleanor Sullivan

T HE INESCAPABLE TRUTH is that the detective story began its career as a short story.

"The Murders in the Rue Morgue" and Edgar Allan Poe's four subsequent tales published betwen 1841 and 1845 laid down the general principles of the detective story for ever. They gave us our first fictional detective, Chevalier C. Auguste Dupin, our first armchair detection, our first locked-room mystery, and our first puzzle story with a code. They established the convention by which the brilliant intelligence of the detective is made to shine even more brightly by the comparative dullness of a friend-narrator. And they employed such precedent-setting devices as false clues left by the villain, ballistics, and the most unlikely solution being the most obvious and correct.

For forty years after the publication of these stories, there was a shift to a melodramatic type of detective story with a strong element of adventure added to the plot structure. Then Arthur Conan Doyle, with the great Sherlock Holmes, brought a reversion of emphasis to the analytical and deductive school founded by Poe.

Memorial to R. Austin Freeman *This was erected at Gravesend in 1979, 36 years after Freeman's death, a testimony to the enduring appeal of Dr Thorndyke.*

From 1894 to 1907, there was a trend from the "whodunit" to the "howdunit" with the medical and scientific mystery and detection of R. Austin Freeman's Dr John Thorndyke and others, and also to the fictional criminal as protagonist (Melville Davisson Post's Randolph Mason, E. W. Hornung's A. J. Raffles, Maurice Leblanc's Arsène Lupin).

The following decade marked the birth of the "Had-I-But-Known" school attributed to Mary Roberts Rinehart, the first stage of the psychological period (the "whydunit"), and the beginning of naturalism – especially in characterization – that originated with the stories of E. C. Bentley.

The twenties launched the hardboiled detective and the Golden Age of mystery-fiction writers in both Europe and America – Agatha Christie, Ellery Queen, Erle Stanley Gardner, Georges Simenon, Dashiell Hammett, Dorothy L. Sayers, John Dickson Carr, Margery Allingham, and many others who give truth to the following statement by Howard Haycraft, author of *Murder for Pleasure,* the most comprehensive survey of detective fiction up to its revised publication in 1968.

"The short story has often been called the perfect and ideal form of expression for detective fiction. However that may be, it has surely been the most influential. Think of the authors and detective characters that have survived from an earlier day to the present: almost without exception, they have flourished in the shorter medium."

The Strand Magazine, *August 1901*
(left) *and June 1929. The first issue*
appeared in January 1891 and in July of
that year the magazine published the first
Sherlock Holmes short story. The Strand
Magazine continued publication,
presenting crime and other fiction, until
March 1950.

The suspense and psychological story flourished and grew. The war and post-war years saw not only the emergence of the espionage thriller but they reflected a realization that murder has to do with human emotion and deserves serious treatment. And now, as we enter the eighties, the relaxing morality, the widespread lust for money, and the rise in crime and violence on the neighbourhood and international levels provide boundless inspiration for the thoughtful mystery writer.

"A trend," Ellery Queen (Frederic Dannay) has said, "doesn't really start with the writer, a trend starts with the world."

Conan Doyle to Roald Dahl, G. K. Chesterton to Leslie Charteris, Jacques Futrelle to Dick Francis, Craig Rice to Ruth Rendell, the trends continue, each writer defining and investing them with a unique vision of his or her own. Come the 150th anniversary of the detective story in 1991, one wonders what will be jogging the imagination of mystery writers – and readers.

In his assessment of the mystery and detective short in the *35th Annual Best Detective Stories of the Year,* the editor, Edward D. Hoch, himself one of the most prolific and ingenious practitioners of the detective short story, commented, "If the number of new stories and anthologies showed a decline (in 1981), the quality remained remarkably high . . . The trend away from detection toward the crime-suspense story seems to have slackened just a bit."

Frederic Dannay as Editor-in-Chief of *Ellery Queen's Mystery Magazine (EQMM)*, and I have noted that the best stories we receive naturally reflect the changing times. With rare exceptions the stories being written in the classic and hardboiled traditions are poor imitations.

"Critics to the contrary," Mr Dannay says, "we respect Poe's original form and all its later variations; but we are always changing and adapting and innovating and experimenting – to keep the genre alive and healthy and contemporary."

In the past nine years, of the six authors to have been awarded Edgars by the Mystery Writers of America for stories published in *EQMM* three were the authors' first professional fiction. A hearty indication that new writers bring a freshness to their work that appeals to the most discerning readers and that professional is professional even if it's the first time around.

When one talked of the rules of the detective story, Monsignor Ronald Knox said, it was not in the sense in which poetry has rules but in the sense in which cricket has rules. But as someone else said, were the detective story

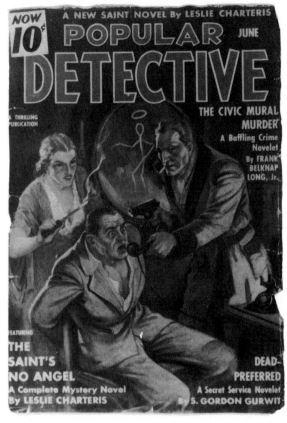

Popular Detective, *June 1938. One of the 200 or so pulp magazines which flourished in the United States during the 1920s and 1930s,* Popular Detective *published several short stories each month and often included a full-length novel.*

only a puzzle there would be no need to make it a book (or, it would follow, a story). It must entertain as well as perplex.

The aspiring mystery writer should never lose sight of the fact that the main requirements are to entertain and to surprise. Anglia Television has been entertaining and surprising us for several seasons now with short stories excellently adapted for their half-hour TV series, *Tales of the Unexpected.* The British-based weekly series is introduced by a narrator telling us that a wise man learns to trust only in lies and to expect only the unexpected. That takes care of your story endings nicely. But what of your beginnings? To her students of speech, Dorothy Sarnoff, founder of the New York-based Speech Dynamics, says, "Begin with the unexpected – an attention-getter." In other words, keep your audience at the edge of their seats from the first sentence to the last.

Stanley Ellin, whose "Specialty of the House" is a classic made the following comment in *Writing Suspense and Mystery Fiction*: "A mystery story is a short prose fiction that is, in some way, concerned with crime. It's as vague and all inclusive as that. And if your definition departs from the above, if it glitters with fine-sounding technicalities and criminous terminology, you will please write on the blackboard one thousand times: *I was completely out of touch with what mystery magazine editors wanted. . . .* It can be anything you want to make of it as long as it has some concern with a crime."

At this point let me make a stab at defining the difference between a straight detective story and a crime-suspense story. In the former the crime is the means and the detection is the end. In the latter, the crime should serve as danger and revelation to at least one major character – perpetrator and/or victim and/or witness.

I can't tell anyone how to write a raving good story, but I can say what it takes to recognize one. An editor tries to be Everyreader, to divine if he or she is turning those pages quickly out of interest or out of impatience, to anticipate and distinguish between the possibility of a happily puzzled and an unhappily puzzled frown, to watch for strong characterization, plausible motives, fair play, and originality, and to pick up on that strangest of all crimes, plagiarism. It's not as much fun day to day as you might imagine, but the prospect is always there of finding a wonderful new story by a new writer or a wonderful new story from a regular or not so regular contributor.

What *isn't* a mystery story besides one that isn't in some way concerned with a crime? Well, except very rarely, it isn't supernatural and it isn't horror. Now and then there's a story of such originality and impact you risk it with readers as the exception that may prove the rule and even start a trend. It happens. Other writers, sparked by the story's special quality, are moved to write another story trying a similar approach. Readers are held, other writers are alerted, and the road takes a turn.

Thinking a bit less grandiosely, where do writers usually get their ideas? How do they approach a story? Let several speak:

William Bankier said in an interview in *EQMM*:

"I do a lot of people-watching. More than one story has come out of a stranger who has behaved in a way that started me imagining. I don't keep a notebook, but I do scribble down ideas on bar mats, serviettes, and flyleaves of paperbacks and toss them behind my typewriter when I get home. There's more material there than I'll ever be able to develop."

In *The Rebecca Notebook* Daphne du Maurier wrote:

"I would sit in a café in Paris or listen to the conversation of my dear French friend Fernande Yvon when she was chatting to her fellow coun-tryfolk, and something observed, something said, would sink into the hidden places of my mind, and later a story would form itself."

Robert Twohy told *EQMM*:

"The best way for me is to start with a sentence and see if it leads to another. If it does, I push further – maybe something will spark. If so, I get interested and keep going, and then something comes alive and things start to happen. I follow along, eager to find out what the next scene will be.

"Things get in a real tangle and I don't know how it can ever get straightened out, but that's not my worry yet, it's the worry of the actors in the turgid drama. My job is just to keep an eye on them, follow them along. In short, once the actors have some reality I let them do their thing. If I try to manipulate them or order them around, they'll turn into plastic figures. If they do have any reality, they'll know what to do – if not, they're not worth a story anyway.

"Later, when the adventure is over, comes my job of shaping up the story, shifting things around, sticking in support props where they're needed, wiring sections together, and hanging a decoration here and there. But that's for later. At the start, stepping back and letting things go their own way is the M.O. that for me is the most rewarding."

There are certain themes and moods that tend to repeat themselves in most writers' work. The quandary of divided loyalties in Graham Greene, the nightmare New York world of Cornell Woolrich, Brian Garfield's vigilant-ism, Julian Symons' masks. The wonder is how such writers can take similar ideas or settings and work them through any number of stories, each one unique and satisfying. This is, incidentally, another proven way to develop a faithful readership – by associating your name in the reader's mind with a certain kind of story.

Why should a writer sit down and write a short story when he or she might spend that same amount of time more lucratively by adding another chapter to a book-in-progress or another scene to a play-in-progress? Quicker gratification perhaps. Or the realization that payment need not necessarily stop with the initial payment for the story. It might be anthologized many times over, adding nicely to the income and enhancing the reputation. It may be picked up for television or for the stage or the movies.

Agatha Christie's "Witness for the Prosecution" was a short story before it was made into a stage play and then a film. Mrs Belloc Lowndes published her classic *The Lodger* (1913) originally as a short story two years earlier.

But chances are that the writer giving time to the short story is doing it out of love. Many writers who tell me regretfully they can no longer afford to write short stories keep coming back to them in spite of their decision because of the joy they take in the form.

I'm not sure why the short story can be such a pleasure to write. There is purity in distilling action and mood, of course, and a challenge to construct-ing a plot – a word with special significance for a writer in our field! – that can be confined to a limited number of pages.

In his Introduction to the Jack Ritchie collection, *A New Leaf and Other Stories*, Donald E. Westlake said of Ritchie, "He knows, maybe better than anybody else currently at work in the area, that a short story needs emphasis on both words – it should be a story and it should also be short."

"Victor Hugo put about 30,000 words into *Les Miserables* delineating the history, structure, and whatnot of the Paris sewers," says Jack Ritchie succinctly. "Now if I'd been in his shoes I could have described the sewers in two paragraphs. Maybe one. *Les Miserables* itself would have become a novelet. Possibly even a pamphlet."

The mystery short story is over 140 years old. The quality has not diminished. On the contrary, it's stable, glowing, and growing under the dancing attendance of the many numbers who love it – writers, editors, and readers who know what good, as well as bad, is.

Eleanor Sullivan succeeded Ellery Queen as Editor of Ellery Queen's Mystery Magazine, the foremost journal for crime short stories.

The Suspense Novel

by Jessica Mann

WHEN THE EDITOR OF THIS VOLUME ASKED ME to write about suspense fiction, we both knew what he meant; but I can only define it by negatives. Suspense novels are not necessarily, though they may be, detective novels. That is, they are not stories whose main purpose is to answer the question "Who did it?" or "How did he do it?" Dorothy L. Sayers wrote that "The detective story does not, and by hypothesis, never can, attain the loftiest level of literary achievement. Though it deals with the most desperate effects of rage, jealousy and revenge it rarely touches upon the heights and depths of human passion. It presents us only with the *fait accompli*, and looks upon death and mutilation with a dispassionate eye." The writer of a suspense novel casts his dispassionate eye as much upon the passion, as upon the deed it produced. He refuses to accept the limitation upon his power to cause cathartic emotion, and while he may not always manage it, hopes to give his reader something more than a pleasantly intellectual stimulation. Yet this distinction is becoming increasingly blurred. Many modern writers of novels whose plots can be expressed purely as detective stories hope to touch the heights and depths of human passion as well. Many of P. D. James's books are examples of this.

Suspense novels are not, though they may be, thrillers. That is, they need not recount a succession of dramatic events, nor need they conform to Stanley Ellin's distinction between mysteries and thrillers, when he pointed out that in the mystery the crime takes place at the beginning, whereas in the thriller, if there is a crime at all, it is more likely to take place at the end. Yet many a dramatically exciting book could be described as a suspense novel or as a thriller. Stanley Ellin's own; or Anthony Price's; or Eric Ambler's books, which he calls thrillers himself; his own definition for the thriller is "An extension of the fairy tale; it is melodrama so embellished as to create the illusion that the story being told, however unlikely, could be true." Not all thrillers are "suspense novels", then; but many suspense novels are thrillers.

Suspense novels are not, though they may be, mysteries; for often the reader learns very early in the story who did what, and how, and even why, so that the tension results from the manner in which an expected conclusion is achieved. Francis Iles, who first pointed out in 1930 that the detective story was likely to become a puzzle of character, rather than a puzzle of time, place, motive and opportunity, wrote an early example of this type of book in *Malice Aforethought* (1931), whose first paragraph tells us that Dr Bickleigh will murder his wife.

Suspense novels are not even necessarily about crime, whether committed or contemplated, though it is true that most include some form of law-breaking or misdeed. But the English Celia Fremlin, for instance, or the American Ursula Curtiss, frequently write about menaces that are undefined, and unrealized.

How then can we distinguish "suspense novels" from any other fiction? For there can be few novels of any kind that are successful if not suspenseful, whether the uncertainty to be resolved is "Will the boy get the girl?" or "Will he end up President?" I think the difference resides in the intention of the author and the expectation of the reader. The suspense novelist's aim is to engage both the intellectual curiosity provoked by a detective story, and the emotional involvement achieved by a novel. The additional pleasure of the actual story, the procession of events each consequential upon the last, is something that "novels" do not always share with good suspense fiction. For novels can be read without the reader particularly caring what happens next, and the novelist and critic Arnold Bennett thought that "what holds you in a fine novel is not the story, but the originality and interestingness of the

Hywel Bennett as Dr Bickleigh *in the BBC dramatization of Francis Iles'* Malice Aforethought, *televised in 1978.*

author's mind and vision, which reveal themselves in every page". In fact, Bennett believed that few books improved as they proceeded; most became progressively more boring. He was contrasting novels with adventure stories, in which it was the story, and what happened at the end, that was interesting, and not the author's mind and vision. If these words were true when they were written in 1927, they are not true now. In Eric Ambler's words: "Few thrillers depend now for their interest on mere narrative. What holds you in a good thriller is what holds you in any other good novel, the originality and interestingness of the author's mind and vision. Not to read through any novel once you have started it is proof that it has failed with you."

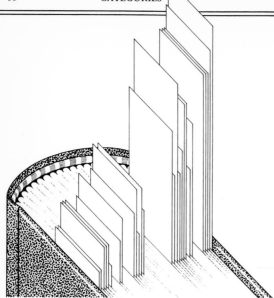

Left **The pattern of suspense** *An analysis of Margaret Millar's* How Like An Angel; *the height of the bookmarks indicates the level of suspense engendered by individual passages. Suspense builds gradually as the novel progresses. (cf. The Pattern of the Thriller, p. 62)*

Right **Detection and suspense novels compared** *In a detective story a murder occurs at the beginning and the action concerns the detection of the murderer. A murder, with a known culprit, may be just an event in a suspense story. The reason for it may be revealed as the story progresses.*

Arnold Bennett's comments were made at a time when critics drew a distinction between a novel and a "tale". The tale was about events and appealed only to the intellect, as though it were a crossword puzzle or a word game. To enjoy such books was regarded by literary pundits as deplorable if not actually vicious. The novel concentrated on psychological and social reality, and its object was to touch the emotions and enlighten the imagination. If such a distinction did really exist, the contemporary suspense novelist is determined to destroy it.

When Wilkie Collins wrote what T. S. Eliot, with hindsight, called the first, longest and best detective story, *The Moonstone* (1868), he did not suppose himself to be writing something that differed in kind from his own earlier work, or from the books of his contemporaries. The classification and sub-division into categories has come much later, and it is a pastime of critics, not writers. Modern writers of what we loosely call suspense novels probably seldom consciously differentiate their work either from mystery fiction, or from mainstream fiction, except in trying to achieve the vivacity, verisimilitude and enthrallment that Wilkie Collins was aiming for in 1868. It is the publisher, not the writer, who decrees that Patricia Highsmith's work is called "suspense fiction" in the United States, and treated as, simply, fiction, in France. It is the publisher and literary editor who decide that novels with crime as their theme shall be published and reviewed in crime lists, unless they are by Graham Greene.

But whether or not they assent to such categorization of their work, authors of what we have come to call suspense fiction do share an interest in the dangerous limits of human experience, endurance, excess, and perhaps above all, in the extent of human duplicity. As Julian Symons says, "If you want to show the violence that lives behind the bland faces most of us present to the world, what better vehicle can you have than the crime novel?"

Most of Julian Symons' own crime novels have had detective plots, but all have revealed an individual, sardonic eye focussed on the emptiness as well as the violence behind his characters' bland faces. He strips them naked; and this is another feature of the best suspense novels. Their characters are shown as fully rounded people, their motives revealed not simply for their crimes, but for their whole lives. There are critics who resent what they see as amateur attempts at psychological understanding. "It cannot improve a genre to drain out its essence, fill the void with second-hand soul searching and arty verbal tricks, and pretend that the result is at once the classic article

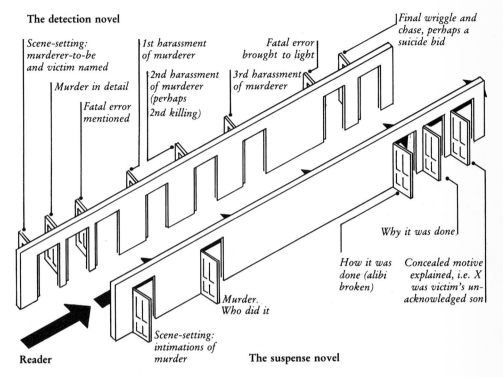

The detection novel

Scene-setting: murderer-to-be and victim named

Murder in detail

Fatal error mentioned

1st harassment of murderer

2nd harassment of murderer (perhaps 2nd killing)

Fatal error brought to light

3rd harassment of murderer

Final wriggle and chase, perhaps a suicide bid

Why it was done

How it was done (alibi broken)

Concealed motive explained, i.e. X was victim's un-acknowledged son

Murder. Who did it

Scene-setting: intimations of murder

Reader

The suspense novel

and something loftier", complains Jacques Barzun, the historian and co-author of *A Catalogue of Crime*; there has been an abandonment of science and reason. For enthusiasts the injection of realism, and of psychological understanding, has been one of the enriching features of the modern crime and suspense novel, even though it means that there is now a pervasive pessimism about suspense fiction that is very different from the cheerful conclusion implicit in the traditional crime story, that everything can some-how, eventually, be put right. Right, that is, by the standards of an ordered society whose members accept its values.

The well known authors in "the golden age" of crime fiction, between the two world wars, had no doubt that it was desirable for society's rules to be observed, and this conservatism is implicit in all they wrote. The best contemporary suspense writers give a completely different impression. Neither law nor law-enforcers are necessarily admirable, and a general disobedience of laws and regulations seems to be common among both criminals and authority; indeed, those in authority are frequently criminals, without any value judgement being made of their behaviour. In crime stories, the police are often corrupt; in spy stories, there is no perceptible moral distinction to be drawn between the behaviour of the "good guys" and the bad ones. Even the psychological, domestic dramas are often now about anarchy, about people who seem to be part of society while inhabiting the psyches of outlaws. A writer like Simenon at least uses the framework of conventional society – Maigret is a policeman, after all. But Maigret, like his author, refrains from judging others. For Patricia Highsmith, the anarchist is presented without even the channel of Maigret's worldly viewpoint. She explores not so much guilt, as lack of guilt. This is particularly evident in the

four books she has written about Tom Ripley, a free spirit untrammelled by
any altruistic scruples. Commentators often describe him as a psychopath,
that is, a person suffering from mental illness. But the fascination of Ripley
both to his creator and to his readers, is that he is not mad, unless it is mad to
be totally self centred. Tom Ripley's own good is his only good.

Highsmith believes that only criminals are free; but also that we are all
criminals, to a greater or lesser extent. It is much more common though, for
criminals in suspense novels to be demonstrably deranged. Those of Ruth
Rendell, for example, have their peculiarities traced in approved psychological style, to childhood experiences and deprivations, and often their misdeeds are sparked off when a precarious equilibrium is accidentally destroyed. In *A Demon in My View* (1976), Arthur Johnson has learnt to control
his murderous urges by strangling a dressmaker's dummy, and only when
the dummy is burnt as the guy on a Guy Fawkes Night bonfire, is he unable
to resist human necks. Ruth Rendell casts a coldly observant eye on the life of
contemporary middle class England. Half her books are detective stories
with a recurring pair of policemen, the others novels in which the development of the characters is as interesting as the crimes; and the causes of the
crimes in society and in the individual are of as much concern as their
detection. Julian Symons spoke of the violence behind the bland face. In
Ruth Rendell's books, the bland faces mask obsession and neurosis.

Suspense novels often have an undertone of unease, of nebulous threats.
This is perhaps especially common in those about domestic life, by such
writers as Ruth Rendell herself, or Celia Fremlin. The effect of such atmospheric writing can be powerful, though it is easy for books of this kind to be
little more than what Jacques Barzun called a mongrel form, "stories of
anxiety which cater for the contemporary wish to feel vaguely disturbed".
But at its best this atmosphere of menace immensely enhances a story, as can
be seen in the novels of Margaret Millar, most of whose books are set in
California, in particularly well realized surroundings.

The late P. M. Hubbard was a writer regarded by many critics as supreme
in conveying threats through atmosphere. His books are often as much love
stories as murder stories, and the suspense lies in the development of the
personal relationships against a subtly drawn background that is at once
beautiful and sinister. But it is easy to fail in the attempt to write a novel in
which the fear is everpresent but undefined. Too many books are nothing but
lists of vague fears and frustrated passions, and the term "suspense novel"
falls into disrepute when it is used for them. In such stories, the action centres
on someone (usually a female character) the reader can imagine being, with
whose fears he (or usually she) can identify. Other writers aim to "give the
reader fear" as Geoffrey Household once said, but it is fear for another, for a
hunted hero quite unlike most readers. Household's heroes, like those in
another kind of suspense novel by Dick Francis, are loners driven by peculiar
and personal obsessions.

I have mentioned few, of many possible examples of suspense novelists.
But the varieties of suspenseful fiction are endless, and almost all the writers
mentioned in this volume could plausibly have been included in the category.

Jessica Mann is the author of novels of suspense and of Deadlier Than the
Male, *a critical study of women crime writers. She is a reviewer for British*
Book News *and the* Times Literary Supplement.

The Thriller

by Jerry Palmer

WHEN ERSKINE CHILDERS PUBLISHED *The Riddle of the Sands* in 1903, it was difficult to say what kind of a novel it was – except that it was an immensely successful novel. Was it a yachting novel? Most of the first third is about sailing. Was it a political novel? Politicians were certainly influenced by it, and when Childers entered the Navy in 1914 his first assignment was to draw up a contingency plan based on the novel. Was it a spy novel? Not only is it about spying, but the Foreign Office man is even called Carruthers! Nowadays it is clearly a spy novel – the first, properly speaking. But in 1903 things were by no means so clear, for most of the modern fictional "formulae" were far from established.

The exception was what subsequently became the classic English detective story – the "school of Mayhem Parva" – which was firmly and durably established by the success of Sherlock Holmes; and *The Riddle of the Sands* looked like a very different kind of novel, for it was more about action and a feel for wide open spaces, and far less about deductive reasoning and collecting evidence: at the time it must have reminded people more of Robert Louis Stevenson than of Conan Doyle. Subsequently, one of the best of Childers' successors, John Buchan, coined a good label for this writing: "shockers". Nowadays they are usually called "thrillers", but in either case the label is accurate, for it is a type of novel which intends to arouse one predominant emotion: the excitement of suspense.

The detective story is easily identifiable, because despite the ingenuity of writers who prevent the reader from guessing "Whodunit", it has only one plot, basically: the solution of a mystery, usually murder. The thriller has a greater variety: on the one hand, it contains stories very similar to the detective novel, based on the solution of a mystery – Buchan's *Thirty Nine Steps* (1915), or Sapper's *Return of Bulldog Drummond* (1932); at the other extreme, pure pursuit and evasion stories, like Geoffrey Household's superb *Rogue Male* (1939) (the prototype of these is R. L. Stevenson's *Kidnapped*, 1886); and in between, the sequences of violent episodes with a little deduction that constitute many of Sax Rohmer's Fu Manchu novels.

In short, thrillers are a more loosely organized body of literature than the detective story, with its golden rules and puzzle-like structure. Yet, at the same time, there are clear affinities between them, as Buchan's *Thirty Nine Steps* indicates: the story starts with the mystery of Scudder's death and his coded notebook, and finishes when it is elucidated and his murderers caught at the house with the 39 steps; on the other hand, the emphasis in the story is not only on the assessment of evidence and its interpretation in order to solve a mystery, but just as much upon the actions taken: Hannay's disguises and adventures. In the words of one young man to whom he tells a garbled version of his story: "By God! It is all pure Rider Haggard and Conan Doyle" – adventure and detection mixed.

Certain generalizations can be made about the English thriller up to the beginning of World War II. The prime focus of these stories is action, and the heroes are correspondingly such as to be plausible in these contexts: rugged outdoor types who despise weedy intellectuals and other pallid urbanites – a certain arrogance about the bulk of humanity is commonplace. Contempt for intellectuals does not preclude a high valuation of intelligence – since deduction and strategy are essential for their survival, let alone success – but it is a practical intelligence, devoid of any speculation which might taint the moral certainties essential for unequivocal loyalty.

Their values are what might be expected in the time and place: absolute conviction in the superiority of the white races, especially the British, coupled with contempt if not downright hatred for "inferior races" – blacks,

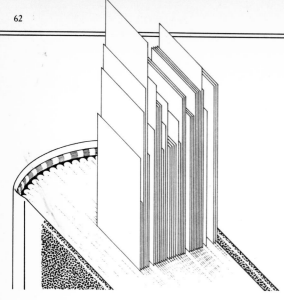

The pattern of the thriller *An analysis of Dick Francis' Whip Hand: the height of the bookmarks indicates the level of tension conveyed by individual passages. After many pages of scene-setting, tension mounts and remains almost constant.*

Balkans and especially Jews. All have servants from whom they expect a degree of intelligent dedication which strikes us today as a trifle optimistic given their wages and the disgustingly patronizing tone of voice in which they are usually addressed. Certain actions – lounging, for instance – while normal in the hero and his friends are positively Bolshevik when performed by a servant.

This class and racial chauvinism is most pronounced in Dornford Yates – who seemed to think that World War I was caused by the collective German cad aspiring to usurp the place of the collective British gentleman. Buchan's imperialist experience in Lord Milner's South African administration imbued him with a sense of the white man's and the black man's rightful and different places, though Davie Crawfurd admires Prester John for his personal strength and charisma; and there are plenty of throwaway anti-Semitic lines in his books. One is not entirely surprised, in Rohmer's *The Drums of Fu Manchu* (1939), to find Nayland Smith defending Mussolini and Hitler from the Oriental doctor, who has decided that the Fascist dictators must be prevented from starting a world war.

In the mid-thirties Raymond Chandler and Dashiell Hammett decided to put murder back where it belonged – with "the people of the mean streets". If their novels are very clearly detective stories, they are also action stories, and in them the distance between the thriller and the detective story disappears: action and deduction are thoroughly mixed. Certainly it was Chandler who said: "When in doubt have a man come through the door with a gun in his hand"; but the reasons for the man's appearance would then be dissected logically. Such was the penetration of the American school that George Orwell was shocked and amazed to find that *No Orchids for Miss Blandish* (1939) was written by an Englishman, James Hadley Chase, "who had never been in the USA".

Even authors who preferred to stick to an English setting in the thirties and forties, such as Peter Cheyney and Leslie Charteris, adopted the tough style of the American "hard-boiled" school. Whether this was the cause of the demise of the English thriller à la Yates, Buchan and Sapper is questionable, but it is clear that their successors have inherited certain characteristics from across the Atlantic. First and most importantly, the mixture of action and deduction and the taste for explicit violence. Secondly, a dramatic reduction in snobbery and chauvinism: if James Bond is certainly a snob in some respects it is primarily a consumerist snobbery, not a class one, and his racism is extremely muted in comparison with his predecessors. Moreover he is no longer, like Yates' Berry Pleydell or Bulldog Drummond, a gentleman of independent means following the dictates of his conscience: he is a professional killer paid by the government. Thirdly, sexuality: at best a peripheral issue for the "clubland heroes" of the inter-war years, it became increasingly important in the hard-boiled school, central in Bond and even (in John Gardner's Boysie Oakes series) the hero's only skill. In the hard-boiled school sexuality's presence usually takes the form of a potential threat to the hero, since the woman he is attracted to may use her charms for other, treacherous purposes – *The Maltese Falcon* (1930) is the classic instance. In the Bond novels it is simultaneously pleasure and political therapy, as Bond converts lesbians, gangsters, Communists and frigid smugglers à gogo.

Ultimately the characteristics of the hero are relatively unimportant: that is to say, it is extremely important the he should have a set of characteristics that make him attractive to the reader, but beyond that it does not matter what they are. In the twenties and thirties in England the fashionable characteristics were breathless enthusiasm ("Great Scot! chaps, think of the bare possibility of having stumbled on something.") coupled with considerable arrogance. With Chandler's Philip Marlowe ironical distance claims pride of place ("On the smooth brown hair was a hat that had been taken from its mother too young"). Mickey Spillane's Mike Hammer breathes righteous hatred whereas Bond is cool and professional, but by the time we reach John le Carré's George Smiley a certain world-weariness has set in:

> ... all I know is that I have learned to interpret the whole of life in terms of conspiracy. That is the sword I have lived by, and as I look around me now I can see it is the sword I shall die by as well. These people terrify me but I am one of them. If they stab me in the back, then at least that is the judgement of my peers.

That is a long way from Bulldog Drummond, but across this variety of personalities runs a constant thread: courage, perseverance and intelligence – the qualities, in fact, demanded by the situations portrayed. This is a difficult matter, for the nature of these situations is by no means self-evident.

The emotion intended by the thriller is suspense; but there is no necessary connection between suspense and stories about criminal activity – disaster stories, for instance, are suspense stories but the disasters can as well be accidental as criminal in their origins. Neither is there any necessary connection between suspense and a story with a single charismatic hero – disaster stories commonly involve a group of people none of whom dominate the narrative and none of whom, perhaps, are particularly heroic. But thrillers are always about criminal activity, and focus around a single hero: it is this combination that is their defining feature.

But it is not crime in the legal sense, strictly speaking, that forms their subject matter. For instance, most real-life crime (excluding driving offences) consists of theft: but theft would rarely figure as the subject matter of a thriller, precisely because it is too ordinary. Only exotic crime – usually murder – can provide the necessary impact. And the necessary horror, for the crime that the hero confronts must also be disgusting, not just against the law: it is the excessive immorality of an action that makes it villainous, not its illegality. Usually, therefore, the action that starts the story of a thriller is a revolting act of violence against the person.

The nastiness of what the hero confronts both demands his intervention and justifies it. If there were no villains and villainy, Sherlock Holmes would have stuck to chemistry experiments and surrealist violin, and James Bond would presumably make a living as a professional golfer, gambler or gigolo. The hero always reacts to prior aggression, from a mysterious source: as a

Sean Connery as James Bond
*confronted by the evil Arno Goldfinger,
played by Gert Frobe in* Goldfinger
(1964).

result, from the beginning, we see things through his eyes. And this is essential, not only for moral reasons – so that we feel he is justified – but also in order to create our pleasure in the story: we want suspense, and we can only get suspense if we are 150 per cent on one side, and equally thoroughly against the others, for suspense consists of wholeheartedly wanting someone to succeed against extreme opposition.

The methods used by the hero may be every bit as nasty as those used by the villain: one of Mickey Spillane's heroes boasts of having tortured one of his enemies: "Goddam, I skinned a guy alive once and he screamed his state secrets with no trouble at all." This immorality has often been the source of concern among moralists. From the point of view of the thriller, of course, their concern misses the point: the hero is fighting evil men, and any means are justified that promise success. But that success must be achieved by the hero, for anyone who is dependent, in the final analysis, upon someone else is no hero – and the only way to show independence is to go it alone. That is why Doctor Watson is so stupid, and why James Bond's back-up team is regularly gunned down, burnt alive or dumped in a tank of barracuda.

Recently stories about criminal activity have shown a new feature: the hero is a criminal, the events narrated are his crime, and sometimes he even gets away with it. No longer are we on the hero's side because he is protecting the social order from evil – though sometimes the victims of his crimes are even more criminal than he is – but simply because he is engaged on a difficult "caper", and seems to have the ability to pull it off. The classic instance of this sympathy is probably Frederick Forsyth's *Day of the Jackal,* but there are many less famous versions. Morality no longer appears to play a part in our sympathies: skill and self-assertion are enough. Bulldog Drummond would turn in his grave.

Jerry Palmer is the author of Thrillers, Genesis and Structure of a Popular Genre. *He is Senior Lecturer in General Studies at the City of London Polytechnic.*

The Gothic

by Michele Slung

OSCAR WILDE remarked of Mrs Radcliffe that she "introduced the romantic novel, and consequently has much to answer for". Fashions change, but heroines go on, and Mrs Radcliffe's Emily St Aubert, whom we first see in *The Mysteries of Udolpho* rambling "among the scenes of nature" is not that removed from Anne who, 200 years later, in the latest novel of romantic suspense by Barbara Michaels, *Someone in the House* (1981), stands at her kitchen sink "mincing and chopping and braising and doing a lot of other things". Anne may be a modern woman – a self-confessed feminist, in fact – but it doesn't stop her from going off to spend her summer holiday at a menacing manor house complete with "strange subterranean chambers", "dank, stone-floored passageways", a disused chapel, and the mysterious portrait "of a medieval lady in long trailing robes".

The gothic romance – a phenomenon of popular culture for the last couple of centuries – is like a cake recipe that's been passed around a large circle of acquaintance. Some people add nuts, some raisins, others put in a few dates or take out a bit of sugar; no matter how you make it, to cognoscenti it's recognizably that same cake.

In the beginning there was Horace Walpole. He cooked up *The Castle of Otranto, a Gothic Story* (although the word "Gothic" does not appear on the title-page of the first edition), which he published in 1764 as by "William Marshall, Gent. from the original Italian of Onuphrio Muralto, Canon of the Church of St Nicholas at Otranto". A second printing brought the original 500 to a thousand copies, and Walpole by then was claiming such a popular book as his own.

The son of a prime minister, Walpole wasn't very amused by the politics of his day, preferring to dwell in his imagination in bygone halls. Eventually, he went to great efforts to turn his fantasies into reality and spent much of his life making his residence at Strawberry Hill, Twickenham, Surrey, into an elaborate but altogether sham Gothic castle. He soaked up the atmosphere there for almost fifteen years before delivering himself of *The Castle of Otranto* which had its origins, Xanadu-like, in a dream.

The Castle of Otranto *An illustration from an early edition of Horace Walpole's novel.*

Why Gothic? One might as well try to give an exact answer to why Art Nouveau resurfaced in the late sixties to give aesthetic shape to the counterculture. Someone is always reviving something in reaction to prevailing modes, from spare to ornate and back again. However, as E. F. Bleiler, editor of a 1966 collection of gothic novels, puts it, "Before Walpole (apart from Bishop Hurd's less important *Letters on Chivalry*) the word 'gothick' was almost always a synonym for rudeness, barbarousness, crudity, coarseness and lack of taste. After Walpole the word assumed two new major meanings: first, vigorous, bold, heroic and ancient, and second, quaint, charming, romantic but perhaps a little decadent in its association with Romanticism, but sentimental and interesting."

The plot of *The Castle of Otranto* is, despite scholars' claims for its continued readability, massively silly. *The Haunted Hat* might be a better name for it, since the action revolves around a gigantic helmet that falls plunk out of the sky, crushing beneath its weight a young prince. Then the homicidal helmet commences to wave its black plumes to indicate that it's still unappeased, while on the human front folks run back and forth, weeping, gnashing, brandishing, fleeing, hiding, denouncing, fainting, etc.

Now this may not sound exactly like what you expect to find between paperback covers, underneath illustrations of nubile females in filmy gowns running below battlements set against a clouded moon, but it was a start. Think of Walpole as the eccentric great-great-great uncle of the gothic novel of romantic suspense. And think of his Theodore and Isabella as the uppermost branches on a family tree which along the way includes Jane and Mr Rochester, Heathcliff and Catherine, the nameless narrator and Max de Winter of Daphne Du Maurier's *Rebecca*, and today has its offshoots catalogued in a newsletter published from Fairway, Kansas, entitled *Boy Meets Girl: A weekly review of romance authors, agents, publishers and fiction.*

Coincidentally, 1764, the year of *Otranto*, was the same as the birth of Ann Ward, later Mrs Ann Radcliffe, in London. She was to take what Walpole had started, in his desire "to blend the two kinds of romance, the ancient and the modern" (as he stated in his preface to the second edition) and give it what they call in the movie business "legs", or staying power. Though Clara Reeve's *The Old English Baron* (first called *The Champion of Virtue*) appeared in 1778 and was overtly modelled on *Otranto*, it was Mrs Radcliffe who, with *Udolpho* (1794) and *The Italian* (1797), claimed the gothic for her sex and thus for all time.

There, I've gone and said it: the gothic is women's fiction. Women read it, write it and, most importantly, identify with it. This, despite the hard evidence of Matthew Gregory Lewis' *The Monk* (1796), still thrillingly readable today; Charles Maturin's *Melmoth the Wanderer* (1820), an important development in the gothic progression; and all the other gentlemen – William Beckford, Charles Brockden Brown, William Godwin, Sir Walter Scott, Coleridge, Keats, Shelley, Byron, Poe, Hawthorne, Victor Hugo, George Du Maurier, Robert Browning, Dante Gabriel Rossetti, to name a few – who fertilized gothicism with their work. The exquisite horror tale, the more clanking ghost story, the early Victorian "bloods", the later swashbucklers: all of these can be considered fascinating gothic manifestations (romantic, exotic, thrilling in the most literal sense) but they will lead us along too circuitous a route to any discussion of what is currently designated "gothic fiction" in the modern market.

Jane Austen knew that gothics belonged to her sex and had great fun fleshing out this notion in *Northanger Abbey*, a sly, affectionate parody of the "horrid" novels of that era, in which Mrs Radcliffe's *Udolpho* is so

How to turn a gothic into an ordinary novel *and vice versa: a witty set of instructions produced by one C. J. Pitt in 1810.*

Where you find:	put:
A castle,	*an house*
A cavern,	*a bower*
A groan,	*a sigh*
A giant,	*a father*
A bloodstained dagger,	*a fan*
A knight,	*a gentleman without whiskers*
A lady who is the heroine,	*need not be changed, being versatile*
Assassins,	*telling glances*
A monk,	*an old steward*
Skeletons, skulls, &c	*compliments, sentiments, &c.*
A gliding ghost,	*a usurer, or an attorney*
A midnight murder,	*a marriage*

omnipresent as to be practically a character. The word "romance", as we know, has many meanings – among them, having to do with love, heightened imagination, and outright fabrication. And I'd like here to apply, with your indulgence, one of my favourite quotations – it's from Saki – for it is resonant in this context: "Romance at short notice was her speciality." Catherine Morland, the heroine of *Northanger Abbey*, is longing to give up her heart without too much reflection and, primed by the excesses of Mrs Radcliffe and others, she has the clichés of the genre at her fingertips.

Better still, to illustrate what Saki's daughter of the house in "The Open Window" later did as well, Austen's Eleanor Tilney, the hero's sister, reveals herself to be latently bloodthirsty, conjuring up real-life visions to match Catherine's fictive descriptions. But then, Austen has already told us that Miss Tilney likes the "little embellishments" of history and is "very well contented to take the false with the true". This is the lure of the safe frisson.

From Mrs Radcliffe to the Brontës is not a particularly complicated manoeuvre. The former eliminated the gross supernatural appurtenances that made Walpole's *Otranto* so grotesque (but which, in truth, give power to *The Monk* and *Melmoth*), but nonetheless felt compelled to set her books in the past. Emily St Aubert lives in the sixteenth century yet she has an eighteenth-century sensibility. Jane Eyre and Catherine Earnshaw are true gothic heroines but now the medieval trappings are gone, too. *Wuthering Heights* is probably best categorized as a "psychological gothic" but Emily Brontë knew what Ann Radcliffe had known before her: that wild scenery and wilder weather are a staple of the recipe. As for Charlotte Brontë, she made the "Reader, I married him" motif a standard ingredient as well.

In the space between *The Mysteries of Udolpho* and 1847, when the Brontë sisters took the English literary world by storm, Italianate romances enjoyed at least a couple of decades of vogue. Books with titles like *Rosaura di Viralva; or, The Homicide, The Italian Banditti, Italian Vengeance and English Forbearance, Sicilian Mysteries; Or, The Fortress Del Vechii, The Maid of Padua*, and *The Sicilian Boy* rolled off the presses. Others conveyed their message to the public with exclamation points, such as *Joan !!!, Astonishment !!!, The Three Monks !!!* and *The Reformist !!!*, while novels with names like *The Vampyre Bride, The Earl and the Maiden, Who Is The Bridegroom? or, Nuptial Discoveries*, and *The Nun's Picture* also signalled that gothic delights lurked inside.

Just past the middle of the nineteenth century, the "sensational novel", a close sister of the gothic, reached its apotheosis with M. E. Braddon's *Lady Audley's Secret* (1862), while at the same time Mrs Henry Wood issued her spectacularly successful sentimental melodrama, *East Lynne* (1861). These two divergent fictions of erring wives further fuelled the female appetite for reading matter that was more titillating than uplifting. They were like life in that they were set in a recognizably acceptable milieu but they were definitely fantasy – and thus like gothics – in that extreme events were allowed to occur and women could be active, even aggressive.

The rise of novels of mystery and detection is the next significant taste to be charted: more nuts and raisins. In the United States, in 1878, a lawyer's daughter, Anna Katharine Green, with *The Leavenworth Case,* added a substantial woman's touch to this budding genre, followed by such genteel plotters as Mary Roberts Rinehart and Carolyn Wells. The "Had-I-But Known" theme, to borrow an expression coined by Ogden Nash, though it had always been incipient, was the last to be informally added to the gothic concoction.

As I have implied, over the period of time in which the gothic romance became popular, women were rarely if ever in the same kind of danger outside of fiction as they were inside. Excessive childbearing, disease, and boredom were the greatest threats faced by women, and novels portraying *women in danger,* not surprisingly, became an antidote to the last-named. Brutish husbands and relations were not uncommon, but poisonous snakes in air-shafts stalking helpless heiresses were rare indeed (for what is "The Adventure of the Speckled Band" if not Sherlock Holmes investigating a gothic situation?). Just as the female sex could be more active in fiction, so could they be more menaced.

By the twentieth century, even as the formula was solidifying, women were moving out into the world, no longer just as governesses but in practically every profession. Oddly, however, the relatively passive Cinderella-type heroine, as in *Rebecca,* perhaps the premier gothic romance of our era, kept her hold on her audience. The Bluebeardish and Pandora's box aspects of the gothic romance have become increasingly pronounced while a great many best-selling romances (in paperback) are no longer "gothic" at all, slighting mysterious elements almost entirely in favour of the heroine's entanglements with seemingly unsuitable, initially indifferent men.

At the start of the 1980s, literary mitosis has created the "contemporary romance", which is now propagating itself at a rate far greater than the cell – the romantic/historical gothic-suspense novel – it originally split off from. Although the major modern writers of gothics, such as Daphne Du Maurier, Anya Seton, Victoria Holt, Phyllis Whitney, Susan Howatch, Barbara Michaels and Mary Stewart, still have devoted fans, other, lesser authors have been forced, like their heroines, to go underground..

To be fair, two of the most interesting gothics of the last ten years have been written by men. Although Henry Tilney in *Northanger Abbey* protests that "nearly as many" men as women read gothic romances (he himself claims to have finished "hundreds and hundreds"), the number of young males, or middle-aged or elderly ones, reading this genre has never really been a factor. After all, since I feel identification with the artificially endangered heroine to be crucial, who is there for them? In general, heroes like Mr Rochester and Heathcliff – the two basic models – are constructed to appeal to women, although there are, of course, men partial to Byronicism still. But whether they read gothics is another matter; it's enough for most to know the stereotype.

Thomas M. Disch's *Clara Reeve* (written under the nom de plume Leonie Hargrave) and Vincent Virga's *Gaywyck* are both tours de force; each is a meticulously recreated, affectionate homage to the eighteenth-century original. In *Clara Reeve* (1975), Disch, a poet and much acclaimed writer of speculative fiction under his own name, romps through the conventions while maintaining a scholar's eye on his detail. Every bit as much a lush production as *Clara Reeve* is *Gaywyck* (1980) which, with its mischievous titular allusion to Seton's *Dragonwyck,* lays claim to being the first homosexual gothic. That is to say, Virga has made the Cinderella/Pandora heroine a young man whose love affair with the lord-of-the-manor-who-has-a-secret-in-his-past is eventually consummated.

There have now also been gothic-type novels with disfigured and handicapped heroines, straight male "heroines" (with brooding lady love-objects withholding their favours for mysterious reasons), middle-aged heroines, and other well-intentioned efforts at pluralism. Like mystery and detective fiction, the gothic has become an equal-opportunity employer, but a recent American manifestation, a "No-Frills Book", guarantees for its Romance ("complete with everything") only that it has a "man, woman, large house, one walk, a kiss and an event near the sea".

That's a far cry from the nineteenth-century assessment by the literary historian Henry A. Beers of *The Monk* (1795) which he said

> used and abused the now familiar apparatus of Gothic romance. It had Spanish grandees, heroines of dazzling beauty, bravoes and forest banditti, foolish duennas and gabbling domestics, monks, nuns, inquisitors, magic mirrors, enchanted wands, midnight incantations, sorcerers, ghosts, demons; haunted chambers, wainscoted in dark oak; moonlit castles with ruined towers and ivied battlements, whose galleries rang with the shrieks and blasphemies of guilty spirits and from whose portals issued, when the castle clock tolled one, the spectre of a bleeding nun, with dagger and lamp in hand. There were poisonings, stabbings, and ministrations of sleeping potions; beauties who masqueraded as pages, and pages who masqueraded as wandering harpers; secret springs that gave admittance to winding stairs leading down into the charnel vaults of convents, where erring sisters were immured by cruel prioresses and fed on bread and water among the loathsome relics of the dead.

Other variables would, of course, include heirs, orphans, hermits, brides, beggars, outcasts, exiles, copses, corpses and curses, all ventilated by groaning winds.

Eventually, one's brain begins to clang shut like a drawbridge, refusing to admit any more caskets, portraits, mistaken identities, flickering candles, false closets, bloodstained documents, forged wills, mad first wives, and dour housekeepers who wear large bunches of keys at their waist. But it's been fun, hasn't it?

As I have been pointing out, the tradition is being carried on, whether in mainstream gothics (now called romantic suspense) or other sorts of mystery, romance and adventure tales. They all borrow bits from one another and adapt somewhat to current trends. It is impossible that Horace Walpole or Mrs Radcliffe, or even Oscar Wilde, could have foreseen a publishing climate in which coupons for free Harlequin romances would be given away in boxes of tampons in order to gain readership for pre-tested, interchangeable titles. But I think, despite this peculiar ploy, it's safe to assert that the gothic novel has not, after all, suffered a gothic fate.

Michele Slung is editor of Crime On Her Mind. *She contributes a column on books and authors to the* Washington Post.

The Espionage Novel

by John Gardner

"AND I WILL lead thee through the midst of Judea until thou come before Jerusalem; and I will set thy throne in the midst thereof; and thou shalt drive them as sheep that have no shepherd. . . ." So Judith, the first fictional spy – though fictional only if you do not believe the Biblical Apocrypha to be Holy Writ.

The Apocrypha consists, of course, of Old Testament books not written in the original Hebrew – discounted by the Jews, and removed from the Canon of the English Bible at the Reformation. In the Book of Judith we have an example of a very early glamour spy, who seduces Nebuchadnezzar's General, Holofernes, with promises to act as his informer and defeat her own people, the Israelites.

As a moral lesson the story is tried and true: never lose your head over a pretty woman; for Judith ends up by decapitating Holofernes, and saving the Israelites from slaughter.

Oddly, it is the Apocrypha which also contains one of the earliest detective stories – *The History of Susanna:* a tale of lust, a beautiful woman, blackmail, and the final rout of the blackmailers (dirty old men, all) at the hands of Daniel. This story is incidental to the spy genre, yet contains elements of the art of espionage: surveillance and interrogation.

Both the *Book of Judith* and *The History of Susanna* were added to the Apocrypha around the fifth century BC. Much muddied water was to pass under a lot of clandestine bridges before the next real piece of espionage fiction was to be written.

I do not, here, count the Chinese classic, *San Kuo – The Romance of the Three Kingdoms,* written at the end of the twelfth century, and crammed with incidental espionage detail. By the same token one cannot really call James Clavell or Frederick Forsyth authors of espionage fiction. Clavell uses KGB-SIS-CIA entanglements as a sub-plot to his masterly *Noble House,* but only as an ingenious aside; while Forsyth deals with espionage only as a background prop in *The Devil's Alternative* – though many would claim his villain/hero in *Day of the Jackal,* and his journalist, Peter Miller, of *The Odessa File,* as representatives of the two poles of espionage fiction: the professional (political killer in *Jackal*) and amateur (journalist seeking retribution and becoming deeply involved), as being true figures of spy fiction.

On the other hand, if one reduced a short history of espionage fiction only to those who have produced spy novels, it would make brief and boring reading.

Before World War I, the reading public were not treated to a great deal in the way of either literature, or pulp, based on the subject; though most authorities appear to agree that the first true spy novel appeared in 1821, J. Fenimore Cooper's aptly titled *The Spy.* As was the fashion of the time the novel is sub-titled, 'A Tale of the Neutral Ground', and it is set during the American War of Independence.

Harvey Birch, the central character, is the spy, and it is of passing interest to note that there is a very definite hint of the spy as anti-hero in Birch, a pedlar suspected of working for the British. In spite of saving a British Officer accused of spying, Birch appears to be a professional, working in the service of his country under a senior controller called Harper.

There is one incident in *The Spy* which marks the future path of many a real, and fictional, character. Towards the end of the war, the mysterious Mr Harper informs Birch that their partnership must end, and offers him money. Birch refuses the remuneration on the grounds that he will serve his country only for love, and not hard cash.

The echoes here, reach into reality. I once heard a senior member of the

Foreign Service say, of Kim Philby, "The thing I hated about him, was that he betrayed his country for love and belief in another ideal, and *not* for personal gain." I have never really understood this confusion in the real world of espionage, where, for some people, a man can be forgiven for being tempted by personal gain, but not for personal beliefs.

The spy, or "secret agent", did not begin really to come into his own, as a central character of fiction, however, until the end of the nineteenth century; and then in the appallingly-written works of William (Tufnell) Le Queux, a journalist, and probably more than that.

In 1890, Le Queux produced *Guilty Bonds*, after visiting Russia, where the book was banned, as was *A Secret Service* (1896). Both dealt with political conspiracy, but during the next couple of decades, Le Queux, for all his short-comings, set the pattern of the straightforward spy story – before the more literary devices elevated it to the title, "novel of espionage".

Le Queux's books all contain a garish hint of warning, first against the French, and then, by the end of the nineteenth century, the Germans, with titles like *England's Peril; The Invasion of 1910;* and *Spies of the Kaiser.*

In his clumsily-named *The Great War in England in 1897,* Le Queux introduces Count von Beilstein, an absurd villainous spy when set against even the most fantastic of today's creations: black-hearted, unscrupulous, and cunning to the point of diabolism.

The plight and invasion of England, by Franco-Russian forces, is sealed when von Beilstein "drops in" to visit young Engleheart at, would you believe?, the Foreign Office:

> *A quarter of an hour went by in silence, while Engleheart wrote on, calmly unconscious that there was a small rent in the newspaper the Count was reading, and through it he could plainly see each word of the treaty as it was transcribed from the secret code and written down in plain English!*

It is possible to reflect that Le Queux's characters were, in reality, written with tongue firmly in cheek. The names may give some clue – the spy/villain, Beilstein; the clean cut young hero, Engleheart. In fact, as in most of his spy fiction, the characters are subsidiary. The author is much more concerned with strategy, both military and naval; while his undoubted message was one of warning.

In *The Great War in England in 1897,* after a series of battles, reminiscent of Churchill's "We shall fight them on the beaches," speech of 1940, England triumphs, with the aid of the British Empire. Later, von Beilstein is arrested and executed on Horse Guards Parade, having, incidentally, doubled on his Russian masters to add to his infamy.

Le Queux had a low opinion of his own work, but certainly knew a good deal about politics and military matters. It is said that among his most ardent fans was A. J. Balfour, leader of the Conservative Party, who is reported to have said that Le Queux's works were worth several thousand votes to the Conservatives – presumably for constantly keeping up his main theme: the threats and dangers of foreign "infection and the hand of war".

If we are to believe his biographer, N. St. Barbe Sladen, Le Queux was a member of the Secret Service during – and prior to – World War I. Accepting this as a fact adds one more name to the many writers of spy fiction who have been an active part of what we now call the secret world. Compton Mackenzie, Somerset Maugham, A. E. W. Mason, Graham Greene, Dennis Wheatley, G. K. Chesterton, Ian Fleming, Sidney Horler, John Masterman, John Le Carré, John Buchan, Bernard Newman are all openly known to have served with, or been engaged in, Intelligence of one form or another. One suspects that short list to be but the visible tip of a much deeper hidden list of spy writers who may well range from important wheels in the machinery, to those who have done the odd job of clearing a letterbox, or acting as a one-time courier. Journalists and writers have exceptionally good cover, enabling them to move within that hidden labyrinth without causing undue suspicion. Though jittery security services can jump to wrong conclusions, a fact which I have personally experienced.

It is Erskine Childers, to whom goes the honour of writing the first espionage work of fiction to be regarded as literature: *The Riddle of the Sands,* a story of a pair of young Englishmen who accidentally come across German military and naval exercises in the Friesian Islands, taking place as a prelude to the invasion of Britain.

The Riddle of the Sands is still regarded by many as one of the best spy stories written (more than could ever be claimed for the relatively recent screenplay for the film version). However, the moral issues of espionage – like those in all early spy tales – are glossily and easily overcome. As Julian Symons so neatly sums it up in his book *Bloody Murder* (1972). "They (*the traitor to his own country; or the foreign national*) are viewed as spies pursuing evil ends, while We (*the English heroes*) are agents countering their wicked designs with good ones of our own. . . . the moral problem involved in spying was thus easily solved."

Childers, himself, became tragically involved in this double-standard dilemma. An Anglo-Irishman with a great sense of honour, he came to be regarded as a traitor by both the British and Irish governments during that confusion of political double- and treble-think which followed the founding of the Irish Free State. Arrested at his mother's house, refusing to give fight for fear that the women present might be injured, he declined to recognize the validity of a court-martial and was executed by firing squad on 24 November 1922.

Until the advent of Eric Ambler's books, most writers in this genre – good, bad, indifferent, and plain terrible – took a simplistic line with regard to the moral implications of spying: from Buchan, a good and practised writer, to 'Sapper', with his famous, unsophisticated, Bulldog Drummond yarns, the spy tale was mainly a case of the old Hollywood Western maxim that the good guys wore white hats while the bad favoured black. In the main, they are chauvinistic, in the true sense of that much misused word; in some cases even anti-Semitic; certainly anti-foreigner in most forms.

It could be said that, in spite of simplistic partisanship, Buchan's Hannay stories are classics in the history of espionography – in particular *The Thirty-Nine Steps* and *Greenmantle.* At the same time, one can be forgiven for imagining that 'Sapper' (Herman Cyril McNeile) invented that revolting phrase, "Wogs begin at Calais".

The story, or novel, of espionage has attracted our great men of letters as well as those who have specialized in that particular genre. So, many a literary lion has sniffed at the lure of the secret world and enjoyed the scent. Somerset Maugham found, in his own experiences within the Secret Service, ample material for his *Ashenden* stories, bringing a new reality to the world of espionage fiction – a cold wind of change, that was to be harnessed to the windmills of minds like Ambler and, later, John le Carré together with many others.

Earlier, Joseph Conrad had bitten at the clandestine hook with two books, each containing a character who falls within the range of spy fiction: Verloc, in *The Secret Agent*; and Razumov in *Under Western Eyes.* The true interest for the aficionado of the espionage novel, regarding these books, is that both

Verloc (*The Secret Agent* is based on a real incident in which a young man attempted to blow up Greenwich Observatory) and Razumov, are the first double agents to be painted as serious characters in fiction.

While on the subject of literary lions, a list of required reading for serious students of the spy novel has to include Rudyard Kipling's *Kim*, whose hero is Kimball O'Hara, orphaned son of an Irish colour-sergeant and the nurse-maid to a colonel's family, in the Punjab. Kim, as all who love that great book know, survives a rigorous apprenticeship for service as a government spy. It appears as an act of irony that Harold Adrian Russell Philby – born in the Punjab, burned brown by the sun, and speaking Hindi before English – should have been nicknamed Kim, after Kipling's character.

While thinking of literary lions who have been seduced into the world of espionage, one cannot forget that the background of Dickens' *A Tale of Two Cities* is one of espionage and counter-espionage; nor that, on at least three occasions, Conan Doyle's eternal Sherlock Holmes was engaged in espionage – in the part of a King's agent in *A Scandal in Bohemia;* in the adventure of the Bruce Partington plans; and again at the end of his career, in *His Last Bow.*

Here, writing with hindsight in 1917, Doyle sets the tale in the August of 1914, and recounts Holmes's nick-of-time capture of the German master spy, Von Bork. It has been noted that, of all the Holmes stories, *His Last Bow* is more concerned with the atmosphere of impending doom, just before the guns of August opened up, than the usual cold and analytical detection of the spy. Few can forget that last speech of Holmes – ". . . There's an East wind coming all the same, such a wind as never blew on England yet. It will be cold and bitter, Watson, and a good many of us may wither under its blast . . ."

The old world had already gone, and Conan Doyle, in 1917, recognized it more quickly than most.

As most scholars agree, the arrival of Eric Ambler on to the scene of spy fiction brought a new reality, together with political and moral ingredients, into the game.

It is, presumably, no accident that Ambler's work began during the depression of the 1930s, and so reflects a disenchantment, a subtle irony, and a greater sense of reality than any author of spy fiction to that date. He sounded the Last Post for the era of Richard Hannay, Bulldog Drummond, and the like. The spy, and the clandestine world, in literature came of age with Ambler, who has commented that this breakthrough ". . . was entirely Mr. Maugham's."

The depression during which Ambler began writing of the secret world, was not only one of economics. A blizzard of depressive disillusionment howled around thinking people, who recognized the serious novel of intrigue as an art form. It was as though they had suddenly awakened to the fact that the 1914-1918 war to end all wars had done nothing of the kind: that belligerence stalked the world in the wake of every ideology; and – most pertinent of all – that in the secret world there were no black and white hats: only shades of grey.

Ambler removed the glamour, presenting characters as they really are – not always heroic patriots, but people who did a dirty job and were tarnished by it. All this is found in his first, and far from best, novel *The Dark Frontier* (1936).

In all, Ambler wrote six books before World War II, *The Dark Frontier* being followed by *The Uncommon Danger, Epitaph For A Spy, Cause For Alarm, The Mask of Dimitrios,* and *Journey into Fear* (published in 1940). *The Mask of Dimitrios* is widely held to be his best book.

Nearly all of those early books deal with the theme of the hunted man, and all bear the professional hallmark of an author who takes exceptional care about detail. The European cities, against which the narratives are played out, live, breathe, and fill the nostrils from the page; while, for a man who claims never to have had any practical experience in the secret world, Ambler appears incredibly knowledgeable. He explains this by saying that he has to be very careful, because he knows so little. But adds, "Perhaps that isn't the same for everybody."

The "neutral" approach of the six earlier books could not survive in a post-war world. Yet the pundits are divided: some seeing Ambler's later work as straight thrillers more than spy stories; others claiming that, in spite of a natural datedness, their quality still stands up to comparison with anything written since. Certainly one would have thought that *The Intercom Conspiracy* (1970), presented as a dossier of tape transcripts and letters, *The Levanter* and *Dr. Frigo*, while arguably not all espionage novels in the purest sense, are brilliantly drawn and as good as, if not better than, eighty per cent of the more important novels in the spy genre.

So Eric Ambler, out of Somerset Maugham, had by the mid-1930s seriously questioned the role of the spy, or agent, as a constantly heroic figure. The so-called kitchen-sink theatre was not to arrive in drama until well into the 1950s, with Osborne's *Look Back In Anger*. The novel of espionage reached that point a good deal earlier – a fact which should be one of pride to all practitioners of the art.

Ambler's contemporary, and probably the best, if not greatest, British novelist of this century, Graham Greene, also holds a prime place in the development of the spy novel. Greene's cynical outlook, his search for the illuminating spark of good in every man, combined with what almost amounts to an obsession with the weaknesses of mankind, its follies and salvations, make the novels which can be listed as espionage fiction more than books of passing interest.

The first of his handful of books that can be classified within the genre, though espionage is but a prop and vehicle for something deeper, is *The Confidential Agent* (1939) written before, as far as one knows, Greene was personally embroiled in the work of MI6 (with, at one time, Kim Philby as his section officer). As in all Greene's books, including the so-called "entertainments", here he is far more concerned with character and motive, than a "spy story". The same is true of *The Third Man*, with its memorable picture of post-war Vienna as the city of spies; while there is a hard core of realistic corruption behind the, seemingly-gentle, satire on the Secret Service and its methods, in *Our Man in Havana* in which Wormold, the melancholy and failing vacuum cleaner salesman eking out a dull life in pre-Castro Cuba, is approached by the Secret Intelligence Service and supports the extravagances of his daughter by "inventing" a network of agents.

By far the best of Greene's novels in this field, however, is *The Quiet American* – a brutal and savage assault on the clandestine methods of modern superpowers.

Miles Copeland, former senior CIA officer, records that the oldest professional he knew, told him that if he was dropped on a desert island with just a few books, two of which had to be spy fiction, he would choose Graham Greene's *The Confidential Agent* and *Our Man in Havana*.

Within the confines of a chapter of this length, it is only possible to pinpoint the landmarks of history in the development of the spy story; yet an interesting, and more lengthy thesis, would be to trace this development next to the emotional needs of differing readerships.

What is now called the Novel of Espionage is regarded as at least a touch near to literature – first class prose, psychological reality in character, and a theme underlying a believable narrative. This kind of book will always, or nearly always (there is one extraordinary exception in recent years), triumph. Yet so will the kiss-kiss, bang-bang, blood and thunders, which rise, with seeming ease, to the top of best-seller lists (as if that really mattered).

The development of the spy story since World War II falls into two distinct halves, each of which has its own readership that, in turn, is cross-fertilized.

In the 1950s the reader longed for escape. The world was still war weary, and the man in the street, together with those of real consequence, were in need of adventure, combined with a sense of the wartime patriotism and, so-called, heroism, which appeared to have now passed into oblivion. The new/old enemy was Russia; and the Cold War made for anxiety.

The first major figure to appear, and appeal, was Ian Fleming; himself a former Naval Intelligence officer. His character, the incredible James Bond, serving under the crusty old Secret Service chief, M, and acting as "a blunt instrument" – a man with the Double-O prefix to his cipher: 007, Licensed to Kill.

There is little need to dwell on the phenomenon of James Bond. Between 1953 and 1964, when he died, Fleming produced twelve full-length James Bond novels, and two collections of Bond short stories.

The prose style, sex (tame by 1980s standards), possible brutality (tame by 1980s TV newsreels), and the criticism that Bond was a snob are all completely irrelevant.

Fleming was an immensely talented journalist, and he used those talents to create a super-spy; a hero who saved the world, again and again, from the KGB; from the outlandish Blofeld and his organization SPECTRE; from villains like Goldfinger, Sir Hugo Drax, Mr Big, and the like.

Bond had charm and elegance, enjoyed good living, and rarely failed to bed the lady of his choice (though examination of the books shows that *he* was usually the lady's choice).

Super-hero he may have been, yet he was all too fallible. He falls into traps, is captured, and sometimes – as in *From Russia With Love* – shows a remarkable lack of perception: the reader is aware, long before Bond, in the closing chapters, that danger is very near, and 007, the fast-thinking agent, genuinely appears to be exceptionally slow off the mark.

Nobody – Bond lover, or Bond loather – can deny the extraordinary appeal of Fleming's books to the reader: though some have tried to hive the success onto the vastly successful, though, for the most part, over-the-top, film versions.

As a personal note, I believe Bond is probably the only character in suspense fiction who will continue to live, be read, written about, and have a following for a very long time to come. His only rival for this kind of fictional longevity will be the great Sherlock Holmes.

The success of "series" novels, like the Bond books, automatically brings a backswing. It came first from Len Deighton, with his working-class, ex-NCO, nameless narrator (later to be named Harry Palmer in the films of his books; and played with cool insubordination by Michael Caine).

At first sight, Deighton's early books seem to be the complete antithesis of the Bond novels. They are certainly brilliant in their conception of character, and eye to detail. But, on deeper examination (I speak as an ardent and jealous admirer of Deighton), they contain a form of inverted snobbery which one likes to think is the author's intention.

Michael Caine as Harry Palmer *in* The Ipcress File *(1965).*

In the four major early novels, *The Ipcress File, Horse Under Water, Funeral in Berlin*, and *Billion-Dollar Brain*, we find the narrator as an habitué of Mario & Franco's Terrazza (One of the really "in" restaurants of "swinging sixties" London); a gourmet at home (Deighton is also a cook of some standing); and very knowledgeable about food and wine, just as he is with regard to locations, weapons, and military matters. He is a music lover (the works of Charles Ives receive special attention in one book), and knows his onions in that field also.

But the early Deighton spy novels are a delight; not on account of their plotting, but solely because of character and the standard of writing. Julian Symons writes of him as ". . . a kind of poetry of the spy novel", which, in those early books, is exactly what he is (Deighton's *An Expensive Place To Die*, not his best book by far, incidentally contains my own favourite opening line in all espionage fiction: "The birds flew around for nothing but the hell of it. It was that sort of day: a trailer for the coming summer.")

Rightly, and to his lasting credit, Len Deighton began to diversify after *Billion-Dollar Brain*, producing, among others, his *tour de force*, which has nothing to do with espionage – *Bomber*, a work that can be read again and again and is, undoubtedly, *the* classic novel of the air war against Germany during World War II.

His abiding interest is, obviously, military history, and, of late, Deighton has taken to producing works on that subject, *Fighter, Blitzkreig, The Battle of Britain*, of a very high standard. Happily, though, he has not entirely left the espionage field, and his last book at the time of writing, *XPD*, contains some of his best prose and observation.

While Bond stole the thunder, and Deighton built a valuable reputation, an unseen outsider was coming up on the rails.

In 1961, a year before Deighton published *The Ipcress File*, and the year Fleming produced *Thunderball*, a book titled *Call for the Dead* came out to a few reviews and only moderate success. The plot concerned a supposed suicide, by a senior civil servant, after a security vetting following an anonymous tip-off. The vetting was carried out by one George Smiley. The author of the book was David John Moore Cornwell, better known as John le Carré.

This first spy novel was followed, a year later, by an excellent detective story which had some links with the secret world, *A Murder of Quality*. Then, in 1963 le Carré published *The Spy Who Came in from the Cold*, a brilliant, dark, economically-written book which seemed, almost for the first time, to take us really to the heart of the true clandestine world. Leamas, a field officer almost burned out, is asked to take on one more assignment: to be set up as a tethered goat for an entrapment operation. A plot, which at first seems well-tried, is slowly revealed to be one of cross, double-cross, and – finally – intellectually a triple-cross of exceptional ingenuity.

Stated baldly, this appears to be run-of-the-mill stuff, but le Carré presents a special cynicism and deceit at the centre of all things secret. His forte lies in a particular talent for encapsulating characters caught up in the doom-laden duplicity of their trade, and time. In *The Spy Who Came in from the Cold* even the innocent cannot escape the long arm of bureaucratic fate. As John Snyder has written, le Carré's thesis ". . . sends real shivers down our moral spines."

The story goes that the book became an overnight triumph. This is more or less true, though I know the publishers, and Mr le Carré's then agent, sweated out a six week silence from the Press and public before, suddenly, recognition came, shooting the work, rightly, into the stratosphere.

In his next book, *The Looking Glass War*, much underrated by reviewers, and savaged by the movie industry, George Smiley makes a token appearance. He is not present at all in *A Small Town In Germany* (much loved by members of the Foreign Service), but comes into his own in the profound, if sometimes flawed, trilogy of *Tinker, Tailor, Soldier, Spy; The Honourable Schoolboy;* and *Smiley's People*.

Because of the subject matter of this undeniable achievement, le Carré has been forced to abandon his spare style, which still makes *The Spy Who Came in from the Cold* the great technical masterpiece of this writer. The trilogy, however, does a number of remarkable things, not least in the delineation of

The Spy Who Came in from the Cold *(1966) starred Richard Burton as Leamas.*

character – George Smiley in particular – clearly focusing on the dilemma of men and women working within the secret world, and creating that world, before our eyes, in a way never before managed by a British writer. It is the supreme act of suspending disbelief, and the reader really feels himself to be looking into the heart of the intelligence community, not to mention the hearts and souls of its members.

Undeniably, John le Carré is the supreme British writer of the Novel of Espionage, and, at the moment, remains so.

There are some who would like to attribute the "first cause" of le Carré's work as a reaction to the flamboyant success of the Bond-style novel, but that is a glib and easy simplification.

Donald McCormick, author of *Who's Who in Spy Fiction* (1977), has written that "One could almost picture le Carré and John Gardner carrying placards in a Chelsea demo, shouting 'Bond Out'!" I do not know about Mr le Carré, having never met him, but I would not have been there, holding a personal belief that there is room, within the readership of the spy genre, for many variations. It has been recorded elsewhere, that, for a time, I personally satirized "The Bond Genre" with the fatuous, clumsy Boysie Oakes who survived – to my surprise – eight books before I, rightly, left him for more serious matters.

While John le Carré remains the British guru of literary espionage fiction, there is no doubt in my mind that another author, the American ex-CIA officer, Charles McCarry, really leads the field in terms of the world league. This is a purely personal viewpoint, obviously not shared by the majority. Strangely, McCarry's books have never had the stratospheric success accorded to le Carré. The reasons for this are obscure, and one can only guess that the truth lies somewhere between bad publishing and McCarry's realistic eroticism, which removes the works from even intellectual "family reading".

McCarry's output is not large, *The Miernik Dossier* (the least impressive work), *The Tears of Autumn, The Secret Lovers* and – to date – *The Better Angels*.

The first three books have, at their heart, a CIA singleton (a roving case officer), Paul Christopher; and, like le Carré, the author deftly manages to carry his readers into the heart of the secret world. The same dilemmas are present, but amidst the sense of doom, there is a touch more humanity: a humanity which threatens to destroy the protagonists with the same ease as the political duplicity of our times. McCarry's sense of time and place is vivid and, for me, unbeatable; particularly in *The Secret Lovers,* a Cold War labyrinth which, one suspects, has its roots in reality.

It has only been possible, here, to invest the map of the spy genre's history with certain landmarks. One is all too conscious of having left out a mass of important figures whose varied contributions to the change, and development, of the espionage novel are of more than passing interest.

For instance, Ted Allbeury has added a new attention to detail; Evelyn Anthony skilfully shifts today's headlines into fictional suspense of a high order; Richard Condon has given us at least three major masterpieces, the best-known being *The Manchurian Candidate*; Kenneth Follett has filled a gap by dealing with industrial espionage in books like *The Shakeout* and *The Bear Raid*; Brian Freemantle, after numerous contributions, has scored highly with his character Charlie Muffin (humour is not dead in the espionage novel); Brian Garfield's *Hopscotch* deals excitingly with the problem of the dissatisfied agent, while his book, *The Paladin* caused considerable controversy, claiming, as it did, to be novelized truth, concerning Winston

Churchill's use of a boy spy in World War II; Geoffrey Household's *Rogue Male* must forever remain a classic; Nicholas Luard, Helen MacInnes and Anthony Price all deserve whole pages, as does the extraordinary 'Trevanian', a firm favourite with members of intelligence communities; not to forget Alan Williams, whose *Beria Papers* and *Gentleman Traitor* were both ahead of their time.

Where does the signpost lead us now? That most revered authority on detective, crime, suspense and spy fiction (not to mention criticism, poetry, and distinguished authorship in his own right), Julian Symons, wrote in 1972, "... it is difficult to see how the spy story can go much further at present, although perhaps it can be absorbed into a novel or be used as a basis for a new kind of documentary approach."

Well, even the most erudite can err, for Mr. Symons went on to suggest a moratorium should be called on espionage novels for the next ten years, which means that we would now be about to unleash the spies and spymasters of fiction after a decade's dearth. It is a good thing that publishers did not take the point seriously. If they had, we would have lost the whole of the *Tinker, Tailor* trilogy; *The Tears of Autumn; The Secret Lovers; The Better Angels; XPD;* and a number of other exceptional works.

Just as the old-fashioned detective story has adapted (and, for that matter, come back into vogue), so the permutations of the Novel of Espionage are endless; while the constantly-changing technology, methods and world conditions all provide a ripe soil in which it can grow. More, grow in varied and original ways.

The secret world still holds a fascination for readers, and, as the real intelligence world becomes more complex, so the novel will alter, perhaps even becoming part of the true literature of the future – for espionage has no frontiers, and is already part of a great time machine across which the experienced author can roam at will.

The Rules of the Espionage Novel

1   There are no rules, as such; except that, whether it is spy-adventure, spy-suspense, spy-realism or spy-literary, there must be a maze, a labyrinth, an unravelling, an equation of tension to be solved.

2   There are – as suggested above – a whole series of divisions and sub-divisions of the spy story, all of which can live together in harmony; all of which are attractive to a large readership. The main divisions are the old thud-and-blunder themes, brought up to date, as opposed to the more profound, even literary – wretched and pretentious word – novels of espionage.

Both can be divided several times over. There can be spy novels of the past, set firmly in the past; and novels of today (bearing in mind the vast changes in organization and technique); there can also be spy novels rooted in the present but tracing back to events of the past. Here, World War II is the favourite of the past, though Anthony Price managed it brilliantly with World War I in his award-winning piece of excellence, *Other Paths to Glory*. If World War II will not suffice, then there's the Cold War, the Korean War, Vietnam, or the political war which is waged around us – mainly unrecognized – in our own cities, towns and villages.

3   It should be remembered that the spy and the whore both vie for the

title of the oldest profession. The espionage novel, then, has the whole world, and all time – past, present and future – over which to travel.

4   The reader is, almost daily, becoming more sophisticated, and demands accuracy in detail. Friends of friends – espionage aficionados will know what I mean – can be useful, but unrewarding as they don't really say much. Far better to read the non-fictional books, and even then, read between the lines. It should also be remembered that there is another kind of spy fiction – that which is perpetrated by Intelligence and/or Security organizations. *The Penkovsky Papers* has long been suspect as a piece of CIA misdirection, though the case has yet to be proven. I would go as far as to say that, in reading the recently published memoirs of another self-confessed spy, one can almost detect the hand of his former masters.

So, beware, and read between the lines. On more mundane matters, check and double check from weapons to geography. It should be a moral to all that Eric Ambler himself once said, "It does seem rather odd that a man who was in Naval Intelligence, like Ian Fleming, should have got the Golden Horn mixed up with the Bosphorus (in *From Russia With Love*). It doesn't make one entirely confident about Naval Intelligence, does it?"

John Gardner is the author of a diversity of crime novels, among them a much-praised espionage series. He also writes the official successor stories to Ian Fleming's James Bond books.

HOW I WRITE MY BOOKS

STANLEY ELLIN
Under Financial Duress

"*HOW I WRITE MY BOOKS*".
There you have the precise wording the editor of this volume has provided me as inspiration and as instruction sheet. And I take it that when he says "*Write*" he means write in the physical sense, something to do with actually putting words on paper. This is good because it restricts my discussion here to twelve published novels, which means just enough discussion to enchant a reader short of paralysis.

If, on the other hand, this editor had also allowed me room for those works produced in the dim and vasty recesses of the mind, but where there is no connection between mind and hand, no words on paper to show, I would judge my production to be up there in the hundreds. I am always at my most prolific, most genius-struck, when I am away from pencil, paper, and typewriter. Then, countless nebulous ideas take form in the brain like brave new worlds being born. Vivid characters suddenly inhabit those worlds and undertake marvellously complex, though always logical, adventures. And all this in passages so fluent, so apt, so powerful that I can only be moved to wonderment by them.

Frankly, I never knew I had it in me.

And if I had any remaining doubt about it, it is easily put to rest by the glowing reviews which keep appearing – mental reviews, that is – even while the mental work on the dream narrative proceeds. Reviews of one's own work, say some authors, can never be too favourable, but watching those imaginary critiques parading before the mind's eye, well, though I can't really argue with their accuracy and sensitivity, I sometimes do find myself close to blushing at the overwhelming awe and admiration they convey.

So much for the good news.

The bad news is that there always seems to come a day when I must descend to reality and actually put some of those words on paper. And, in so doing, must recognize yet again that I was born with a faulty connection between mind and hand, something which suggests that I have been thinking those marvellous tales in Venusian, a language notoriously untranslatable into English. Willy-nilly, I must press forward with that translation, because – to descend into the grossly mundane – I put words on paper only under financial duress.

This does not mean that like Hogarth's pauperized poet I am reduced to rags and scraps before dragging myself to my labours, but there is inevitably a time during all that gaudy and profitless mental

-1-

"How I Write My Books."

There you have the precise wording ~~and instruction~~ the editor of
this ~~work~~ volume has provided ~~XXXXX~~ as inspiration ~~XX~~ and, instruction
sheet, ~~for the presentation of XXXXXXXXX~~ And I take it that when
he says 'Write' he means write in the physical sense, something to
do with actually putting words on paper. ~~XXXX XXX XX XXX XXXXXXX~~ This is
good ~~because~~ because it restricts/my discussion here to twelve
published novels, which means just enough ~~discussion~~ to enchant a
~~its~~ reader short of paralysis. this editor also
      If, on the other hand, ~~XX~~/allowed, room for those works pro-
duced in the dim and vasty recesses of the mind, but where there
is no connection between mind and hand, no words on paper to show, I would
judge my production to be up there in the hundreds. I am always at
my most prolific, most genius-struck, when I am away from ~~the tools~~
~~of the trade.~~ Nebulous ideas take form, like worlds being born. ~~Characters promptly~~
~~inhabit them. These characters XX/XXX~~ undertake ~~XXX~~ marvelously
complex, though always logical, adventures. they ~~express~~ themselves
And all this in passages ~~XX XXXXXX~~ so fluent, so apt, so powerful that I can
only be moved ~~by the wonder of~~ them.
      Frankly, I never knew I had it in me.
                              remaining
      And if I had any/doubt about it, it is easily put to rest
                 glowing
by the/reviews which keep appearing -- mental reviews, that is --
even before the mental work on ~~the opus is complete.~~ Reviews, say
                 never
some authors, can be too ~~good~~, but watching those imaginary critiques
~~file by in the mind like computer printouts~~, well, ~~while~~ I can't really
~~XXXXXXXXXX~~ their sensitivity
argue with ~~their~~ accuracy and/~~sensitivity of their XXXXXXX~~, I sometimes
do find myself close to blushing at the overwhelming awe and admiration
they convey.
      So much for the good news.
      The bad news is that there always ~~seems to~~ come/a ~~XXXX~~
~~XXXXXX~~ when I must descend to ~~XXXXXXXX~~ reality and actually put some of

writing of epics when the cash flow reverses direction. The realization of which direction it is now flowing in is the signal for me to approach my American book editor – longtime friend and co-signer – and to arrange with him a contract with fixed deadline for delivery of an acceptable novel. "Acceptable", aside from anything else, means visible words on paper. Then, with that deadline date posted large above my desk, I will sit down at the typewriter – I use both forefingers for rapid and inaccurate typing – roll in a sheet of clean paper, and remain there looking at it while I try to get a handle on my Venusian.

Eventually, I will write a page. Then I will study it with the horrified realization that, as all good things must, an otherwise promising literary career has just come to an abrupt end. However, there is that contract in the drawer and that deadline posted on the wall, and there is also my keen awareness that what I am trying to do is considerably easier on wind and limb than wielding pick and shovel at the bottom of a coal mine.

So I rewrite the page, striving to obtain some of that quality it had in mental Venusian, and this time it seems to go a little better. Sometimes, enough for me to risk a second page. And by way of this process, a third and fourth page and so on to *The End*. Which usually arrives about ten minutes before expiration of the deadline. Obviously, I am not going to be hanged for something or other if I miss that deadline, but the one sound work habit I have conditioned myself to is holding on to the idea that a deadline is sacred. If not for that, I'd be in the wrong business altogether.

Through this two-fingered exercise from *Page 1* to *The End* there are good days and bad days, frequent wild swings between the manic and the depressive. It has been some comfort to learn over the passing decades that I am not alone in alternating between emotional poles as I weave my magic spell, both fingers flying; I seem to have plenty of company in this. However, now and then I do encounter a colleague who, on a wing and a prayer, zooms through novel after novel – pretty good novels, mind you – without knowing even a qualm of nausea. Such specimens cannot seem to comprehend that at the daily grind one must suffer those qualms, ride those waves of manic-depression, and forever rest uneasy.

That is How I Write My Books.

P.D. JAMES
A Series of Scenes

IF WRITERS, LIKE THE REST OF HUMANITY, can be divided into larks and owls then I am and always have been a writing lark; my best time for working is in the early morning. There is no particular virtue in early rising, but there are a number of practical advantages. The city and the street haven't yet woken into noisy life, the telephone doesn't ring, the papers (always so seductive) haven't arrived and there is no temptation to switch on the television. When I was also a full-time bureaucrat I had no option but to get up early to write. Now I continue to do it for choice. I can use the evenings for revision, for planning or for research. But my creativity functions best before breakfast, stimulated by the essential early cup of tea.

My writing method has recently changed. I used to produce a first draft by hand and then dictate the hieroglyphics, which are my appalling handwriting, on tape before even I could no longer decipher them. The tape would then go to a professional typist and the first draft would be returned to me typed in double or treble spacing to facilitate the first revision. Now I use an electric typewriter, but I still prefer to scribble the first draft by hand. There is something satisfying about the contact of hand with pen and the physical production of words on paper. I am becoming more adept at creating directly on to the machine, but I am unlikely ever to dispense with my note book and when I am in the middle of a book I take it with me wherever I am.

I never begin at the beginning of a novel and work right through from the first chapter to the last. I visualize the book as a series of scenes rather as if I were shooting a film. These can be written in any order depending on how I am feeling at the time. Some mornings I am attracted to dialogue, perhaps to scenes where my detective is interviewing suspects and there is the cut and thrust of verbal confrontation. On others I draft descriptions of people, setting, scenery, weather, atmosphere, while sometimes I feel in the mood to tackle passages of violent action or horror. Even the weather can influence me in the scenes I choose to write at a particular time.

This jigsaw method of creation means, of course, that the whole book must be meticulously planned before any work begins. But this preliminary planning is always necessary when one is writing what I think of as the traditional British detective story. The genre is formalized, controlled and with its own conventions. There is always a mysterious death at the heart of the action; a closed circle of suspects (neither too confusing in number nor too few to provide a satisfying puzzle) each with his or her credible motive, opportunity and access to the means. The central character is the detective, either amateur or professional, whose job it is to solve the mystery not by luck or omniscient skill – although he is entitled to a measure of both – but by logical deduction from observed facts. And these facts must, of course, also be fairly available to the reader.

The attraction of the genre for the writer is to use this formal structure to produce, not a lifeless intellectual puzzle, but a book which has claims to be considered a novel. But the preliminary planning down to the last detail about the time of day, the weather, the setting and the crucial clues, must be carefully plotted. As with any novel, the characters and plot do develop and subtly change during the writing but all must be controlled within the basic structure. This means that much of the action is charted on paper hour by hour so that I can see where each of my suspects is at the crucial time of the victim's death.

But these are the mechanics of creation. What people usually ask is "How do you get your ideas?" And here the writer is as much at a loss as the questioner. Something sparks off the creative imagination; a character, a place, an original idea for the murder itself. With me it is often the setting; a desolate stretch of coast, an old and sinister house, an atmospheric part of London, a closed community such as a Nurses Home, a village, a forensic science laboratory. The central idea germinates over weeks, sometimes months and becomes clothed with the flesh of characters; literally the plot thickens. It is almost as if the whole book and the people already exist in some limbo outside myself and it is my business, by a long process of thought and effort, to get in touch with them and put them down on paper.

This is a lonely, disciplined and often frustrating process, and to the question "Do you enjoy writing?" I can only reply that I may not always be happy when writing but I would be miserable if I didn't write. And that is probably what it means to be an author.

A segment of the second draft of P. D. James' The Skull Beneath the Skin *(1982)*

DESMOND BAGLEY
Unprocessed Idea to Processed Word

WHEN I WAS ASKED TO WRITE AN ARTICLE with the above title for a book on crime and suspense I was mystified. My books are not specifically about crime although some people think they are, so I suppose I qualified under "suspense". Yet all novels must have suspense or they are nothing, Henry James to the contrary. And the title seemed to be another form of that perennial question guaranteed to drive any writer up the wall: "Where do you get your ideas?"

The act of writing may be divided into two parts – research and the physical act of putting down words. Some writers claim to do no research; that the words they put down come from some inner well of self-sufficiency. They are wrong; their research must be largely unconscious. The writer is, above all things, an observer; a watcher of people and places, especially people.

Other writers, myself included, put their research on an organized basis. An idea having occurred they deliberately seek to give that idea a backbone. Most of my own books begin with the question, "What if . . .?" The resolution of that question may lead to strange places and interesting people. And it can take time.

For instance, in going through old correspondence I came across a letter to my editor – I was going to write a story about an avalanche. The letter was written in 1963 and the book, *The Snow Tiger*, was published in 1975. What happened in the supervening 12 years? The short answer is that I did not know *anything* about avalanches. The search for information led me to the Antarctic, to the South Pole and to those interesting men, the snow and ice scientists. Other ideas have led across the Sahara and to Iceland and Greenland. Next year, China and Japan.

I take no notes. I have a retentive memory, a mind like flypaper to which facts stick. This disturbs people. I have interviewed specialists on technical subjects and they become worried. Only the other day, after an editorial session, my editor of 20 years' standing asked nervously, "Are you sure you can remember it all?" I can. But in my travels I take a plenitude of photographs.

Writers are terrible users of people. I have recommended the neophyte to cultivate socially a doctor, a lawyer and a policeman; those three professions cover 90 per cent of the human condition. And a writer reads, voluminously and perhaps indiscriminately, because he does not know where his next idea may come from. I don't know how many books I have in my own library but I have just added shelving for 2,500 more. It is a minor matter for pride that most library research is done in my own home. It saves valuable time.

I would say that 90 per cent of the information thus garnered does not appear in my books. As Hemingway said, "What you leave out of a book is more important than what you put into it". You may use but 10 per cent of the information painstakingly researched but you *must* know the other 90 per cent because this gives authority to the writing.

And so, having said "What if . . .?" – and research into this question leads to a bewildering variety of applications – one settles down to *write* the book. The act of putting words on paper can be done in different ways. Shakespeare would have used a quill pen, Trollope a steel pen, and Maugham a fountain pen. Robert Ruark used a typewriter which he called the "Iron Maiden". I use a word processor, hence the title of this piece.

There is nothing inherently wrong about using a word processor, or any other product of modern technology, except the difficulty of explaining to scientifically illiterate journalists and critics that the machine does not create or compose my books. Essentially it is a mechanized quill pen, no more and no less, which takes a lot of the hard work out of the job. If anyone thinks that writing a book is not physical hard labour then let him sit at a typewriter for ten or twelve consecutive hours.

I am sure that the reader is blinking at this point, saying plaintively, "But what about the plot?" Some writers like E. M. Forster have pushed the view that a novel should be a study of character in depth and that plot is unnecessary. To me this is like saying that a bicycle needs no wheels. That view is abhorrent because I am a storyteller and a story needs plot – a beginning, a middle and an end. The stories of Cinderella and Hamlet will be told when E. M. Forster and Virginia Woolf have been long forgotten.

But first comes *theme. Theme* is what a writer *has to say* – the particular point he is making. Theme is different than plot in this way: if we take the theme – "Jealousy is corrosive", a hundred plots can be written around it. Shakespeare chose to write *Othello* which, in my opinion, has an idiot plot. Shakespeare, however, was a genius, and genius can surmount anything.

So to plot. In discussions with fellow writers the general opinion is that my method would drive them mad. I write no synopsis. If I do my unconscious mind thinks I have written the novel and loses interest. I begin with the first chapter; a group of people in an interesting situation and environment. I have 300 blank sheets of paper to fill. I know roughly how I want the book to end, say, north-west. The characters and environment interact (I regard the place as another character in the book) and the plot grows organically like a tree. The book may end in the south-east but it has got there *naturally*, not constricted by a pre-planned synopsis, which strait-jacket could constrain a puppet to act out of character.

But are they puppets? The dying words of Balzac were, "Bian-chon! Summon Bianchon! He at any rate will save me!" Bianchon, an eminent physician, was a character created by Balzac in the *Comédie Humaine*. Who is the puppet?

And so the book is written, primarily because it interests me, and is sent to survive in a world where 40,000 titles are published annually in Britain alone. Fortunately my books also interest a lot of other people. I am a storyteller, a member of an old and honourable profession.

DOROTHY EDEN
Waiting Till They Talk

TIME WAS WHEN I WOULD find some unusual names, probably on old tombstones – Blandina, Hariot, Seraphine – and these would suggest to me a rather eccentric, rather flamboyant, very devious character. With luck a plot could be devised around her. She would spring, fully developed, into my view, and I would seize her triumphantly.

But that was long ago when I was young and romantic, and I adored characters of this kind. I still adore them but now I anchor them much more in reality. They must, however, talk to me. No book of mine ever comes alive until my characters talk of their own volition. Sometimes this doesn't happen until I am half way through. They lurk like ghostly images at the back of my mind, refusing to become flesh and blood. I am on the verge of discarding the whole project in misery when suddenly, in a scene, in a paragraph, even in a line of dialogue, the silence is broken and I listen and write and am willingly possessed.

How do I begin nowadays, with a great deal of experience behind me, but with a less fertile imagination and much less inspiration? The strange names no longer say things to me, so I have to somehow wrest the germ of an idea out of thin air, and slowly develop it into a plot. Then I make a list of suitable characters, with some notes about their appearance, their nature, their situation in life, and their motives, especially their motives. I name them carefully and sensibly, although I still find their names enormously important. Then I think of conflicts. A novelist thrives on conflicts and how people react to them, i.e. marriage, divorce, childbirth, loss, deception, accident, skulduggery, or sheer mystery. After all, a lot of things have to happen in 80,000 words, and the reader's interest must be held.

So, having assembled my characters, I then make a brief outline of the opening chapters. I don't get too far ahead as it is difficult to see clearly before my characters are pinned down on paper. But I always know the end. It is a signpost to work towards, and it would be impossible not to know my final destination. However, a lot of unplanned things can happen en route, and these spontaneous events are what gives a book its vitality.

The beginning is enormously difficult. Everyone is strange. Mostly I hate them all. I write by hand, as this was how I began, many years ago, on scraps of paper, during office work, during my lunch hour, in bed at night by candlelight when I lived on a remote New Zealand farm. The pen in my hand is familiar. Automatically my thoughts flow this way. But it is essential to be able to read back over previous pages, and this is not easy in my scrawl. So, after every twenty or thirty pages, I type my rough manuscript and have it ready for correction or re-writing. I re-write as I go along, and seldom do so after I have finished the book. I may re-write the beginning and the end several times, but mostly the rest has only minor alterations or some cutting.

My working time is usually in the mornings, with one or two coffee breaks. I frequently don't work any more in a day, unless I have reached a vital part where the story and the characters won't leave me alone. Then I sometimes work in the early hours of the morning, with a pot of tea beside me, and the magical quality of the quiet dark night around me. These occasions are fairly rare, and much to be savoured.

I finish a book with great regret. By then it has become my companion, my familiar. But I also finish with a sense of achievement and satisfaction. For a few days I take pleasure in my tidy desk. I get completed typescripts from my typist and read them carefully. Am I pleased or not? I wait eagerly to hear from my publishers. The book will be put into production. It will come out for Christmas, or next spring. I have earned a long rest, a holiday.

But then the void, the emptiness, begins. I am a creator. I must create. So slowly I gather my energies to start again. . . .

Dorothy Eden died while this book was in preparation.

A portion of an intermediate draft of Dorothy Eden's The Storrington Papers *(1979).*

Hannah

CHAPTER IV

Hannah's box had been carried upstairs while she was in the morning room being given instructions by her new mistress. Now she was shown to her room by an elderly servant whose name was Baxter.

She stared at Hannah a good deal. Her face was narrow and humourless, her small black eyes observant. She had a tight knot of grey hair wound tightly on the top of her head and wore an unadorned dark grey dress. She had thought Miss Knox would be older, she said.

"I'm twenty five," Hannah said, thinking that surely was old enough for anybody. "This is my third position." Because the woman was obviously waiting for this information to be enlarged on, she added, "I was with a family in Leicester, the Drews, for three years and then with the Woodcocks in London for two and a half years."

"And before that?" Baxter asked.

These were questions her employer should ask, and indeed had done so. But Baxter didn't look the sort of person with whom it

PATRICIA HIGHSMITH
Not-Thinking With the Dishes

I HAVE NO SET OF RULES for writing a book. I never think about who my readers may be. My book ideas begin with a situation of surprise or coincidence, some unusual circumstance, and around this, and forward and backward, I create a narrative with a beginning and an end. Or a novel can be inspired by a theme, as was *Edith's Diary*, a story in which the decline of a woman's life was more important than the euthanasic murder in it, and more important than any single incident.

I like to write three or four hours a day, taking a break frequently to do something such as finishing the last dishes in the sink, during which I am not-thinking about my work in progress. It is important that nobody else be in the house. Then my thoughts take a creative jump. Hard thought never did me very much good. I believe in letting one's mind alone. The only price I pay is having to rewrite, but not always a lot and mostly it is polishing, and having to cut a fair amount.

Under ideal conditions, I can write two thousand words a day, but conditions are ideal only half the time. In principle I work seven days a week, far from the truth, because something always happens to prevent work one or two days a week.

I wish I could adopt the method of a famous writer who said he writes the action parts first and fills in the gaps later. Unfortunately I am much more tedious and have to write all the in-between material as I go. Maybe this is inevitable because of the subjective attitude I generally take: I describe what is in the head of the protagonist,

psychopath or not, because what is in his or her head must explain as well as advance the story.

For settings, I have to have seen the places I am using, but so far I have gone to the places first, often by accident, and the story has come later. Sometimes I go back to a city a second time to get the details as right as I can.

How can a writer answer the question how does he write a book? A writer writes on enthusiasm, a rather embarrassing emotion to explain. Better just to write the book.

Right *A page from Patricia Highsmith's manuscript* The People Who Knock on the Door

-276-

he had the same blank but receptive expression that Arthur had seen
on his face in church, or when his father rambled on at the table,
either about the spiritual side of man. Irene, Arthur realized, was
talking about the physical side, about him, and Arthur struggled to
listen, not wanting to.

            "... young people have made a mistake-- they must realize
it, know it-- face it-- and say they're sorry. That way--"

            Lois shook her head and glanced at her mother. Lois
stood up. "If you'll excuse us now, we must be leaving soon. I'm
sure Richard can drive you both home."
            "You have been so kind-- both of you, all of you," said
        stood
Irene, standing up. "This is a household of goodness. Isn't it,
Louise?" She turned her red smile on her sister, who was just then
coming back.

            "What?" said Louise.

            Robbie fetched the coats. Thanks and good-byes, and
Richard went with the two out the kitchen door to his car.
                        Lois opened
            Oddly, Arthur his mother was opening the kitchen window
                        Arthur opened
a couple of inches, at the same time as he was opening a living room
window, as little as Arthur noticed. Just for a minute, Arthur thought,
        we'll open the windows
in spite of the cold, just to get those two out. And his mother felt
the same.

            Lois came into the living room. "The vulgarity!" she
said to both Joan and Arthur, and she could hardly smile except in
a twisted way. She put her hands over her face for an instant.

            "Dear Lois, we've got to think of it as funny-- the
                        Joan laughed. "Isn't that right,
way Arthur think sees them." Married Darkxxxxxx Arthur?"

            "When they're here, yes. Now that they're gone I feel
quite sober again-- almost normal!" He looked at Robbie, who was
        standing,
leaning against the armchair where is the fat Louise had sat.

            Robbie was not smiling, not if smiling. His brow was
as smooth as if he gazed out on Delmar Lake on a quiet day of fishing.
"They have to be managed," Robbie said, mainly to his grandmother.

GREGORY MCDONALD
On Getting Rid of An Idea

A T SCHOOL I HAD A TEACHER whose characteristic admonition was: "*Gentlemen, everyone else will tell you to develop a good memory. I tell you to develop a good forgettory. Every fact of any importance, including your own names, can be looked up in a book. Instead of cluttering up your mind with a trillion trivial facts, leave your mind unburdened and therefore open and free to deal creatively with what you are presently, freshly perceiving and assimilating*".

I took his advice to heart. I have never remembered a fact of any significance.

I would tell you that teacher's name if I were a less respectful, grateful, and obedient student and could remember it, or if I had time, at the moment, to look it up in a book.

Clearly this teacher was a major influence upon how I do my work.

When an Idea for a character or a story first enters this Author's head I do my best to forget it. No, I do not make notes. Such would flatter the idea unduly. Even making *a* note would be a kind of commitment, an admittance that the soft, inept, unformed *thing* is worth a jot. Although I know some fathers are so tempted, one just doesn't take a newborn at first sight and put him on the list for the national team.

I do my best to forget the Idea. And if I succeed in forgetting the Idea then I conclude it deserved to be forgotten. Simple as that. The Idea is not memorable and therefore not worth developing.

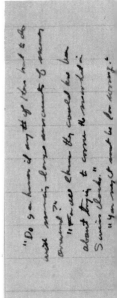

Right *A portion of Gregory Mcdonald's manuscript for one of his novels about his fantastic reporter hero, Fletch.*

You may ask what volume, what percentage of my ideas I therefore forget. The charming element of this technique is that I don't know. I can never remember.

If the Idea is memorable, all by itself, it will return, obviously. The next time it pops up it may even have a little more meat on its bones. Maybe it will have even washed and combed its hair. The wise Author looks at it, nods in recognition, then . . . does his best to forget it.

At that point the Idea may be truly forgotten. All well and good. If it doesn't have the strength to hang onto the conscious mind then it isn't worth conscious effort.

If the Idea is truly memorable it will continue to recur. And each time it pops up it brings with it more muscle, clothes, baggage from the unconscious.

. . . And each time a greater effort to suppress it is required.

Any good Idea flirts with the Author. It wills to come alive, to achieve its own kind of reality. It makes itself fuller, better and better, altogether more attractive. An Idea cannot enter reality without the Author. Asking the Author for an enormous amount of work bringing it into reality, the Idea must make itself very seductive indeed.

Then there comes the time when the Idea (a few, maybe, over a lifetime) can no longer be suppressed. It has become too strong, maybe strong enough to take over all of the Author's consciousness, so possess and obsess the Author that he has enough mind left to tie only one shoe string a day, brush either his uppers or his lowers but never all of his teeth.

It may not seem so, but the Author's job has not changed: now more than ever he has the need *to get rid of the idea*. Picking his teeth in public, tripping on his untied shoestring, forgetting the idea becomes a matter of life and death.

You might expect me to say at this point that the only way for the Author to get rid of the Idea is to write it.

Not yet. The Author should give the Idea one more chance to disappear. He tries a page or three, mostly looking for the point of view, the tone, the pacing, the decorum of a work. Then, again if he's wise, he throws it away. Finally he has expressed an openness to the Idea. If the idea is strong enough, irrepressible enough, witty enough to grab that opening and demand total possession of the Author's consciousness, then and only then must the poor Author, to restore his sanity, usually with a curse and a sigh, give himself in to the Idea.

Suppressing an Idea gives it its own power, its own energy, if it ever is to have such. If the Idea is suppressible, it deserves oblivion.

And if, at any point in the process of writing the work, the Author finds himself pushing too hard, or getting bored, he should quit. If he is pushing too hard, the reader will have to push equally hard. If he is bored, the reader will be bored. The Author should come back to the work only after the Idea has trimmed itself and developed new energies.

If, on the other hand, the Idea is so seductive, so powerful, it is the Author who is just barely hanging on, being pulled through the work, laughing with delight, it is reasonable for him to expect the Idea has created a Work others might enjoy.

An Author shouldn't work. An Idea should.

Then, of course, after the work is done, the Author has the toughest job of all, i.e., to forget it.

LIONEL DAVIDSON
Perspiration, A Constant Factor

ONE OF THE STRANGEST THINGS about writing books is that one forgets how to do it. I speak for myself, of course, but others are surely afflicted from time to time. Whether this forgetfulness is of that merciful kind covering things like childbirth or whether because a new book calls for a new method of narration, I've never known. What I do know is that for the first month or two of every book I am into stormy weather with numerous false tacks before "remembering" or discovering (or not as the case may be) how to carry on.

This is not altogether bad – something perhaps akin to the heavy schedules and the shadow boxing that prizefighters engage in before ducking under the ropes in earnest. It gets you up on your toes, legs in the right shape for all the footwork, round upon round upon round of it, that lies ahead. And it has other benefits. All kinds of developments, previously unthought of, seem to surface at this time. This is why I always keep these early pages (hundreds of them) and give them a going-over from time to time. It's nice to look over this early rubbish anyway, to marvel at the imbecility of it and to take heart that even the direst of the drivel seems to lick into some kind of shape.

All this calls for a lot of rewriting, of course, and accounts for what some critics have frowned on as the wilful obscurity of my openings. To me there is nothing obscure about my openings. They seem clear as day. What I forget (and this surely is true forgetfulness) is that others haven't that fine grasp on the stuff that I have, having gone so many rounds with it. And it also has benefits. Some people *like* obscurity and find huge depths of unintended profundity. But it cannot be good for trade.

Another puzzling thing is why books (mine) take so long to do. I can write a thousand words a day, often two or three. Allow, say, five days a week for writing and I ought to get 20,000 words a month. An 80,000 word book ought to take four months. Add a couple for getting started: six months. Why can't I write a book in six months? This is the record:

My first book *The Night of Wenceslas* took 120 writing days. But it took me three years! The second, *The Rose of Tibet*, a longer one (130,000 words cut down to 110,000), 390 writing days – and two years. Followed by *A Long Way to Shiloh* (in U.S. *The Menorah*

Men), 90,000 words and I don't know how many writing days, but eighteen months to the final bell. And so it goes, actually getting worse lately. My last book, a children's fantasy, 38,000 words, took two solid years and eleven complete rewrites. I haven't the faintest idea why. The whole thing is a total mystery, maddening to agents, publishers, conceivably even readers, but principally to me.

Ideas for books are another thing. Those I think about hard and long I never seem to do. The ones I do come about largely by accident. The second, for instance, surfaced abruptly during a winter walk in Kew Gardens. A thaw had started and I saw something pop suddenly out of a mound of melting snow. On closer inspection it proved to be an ear; a dog's, dead. For some reason this dead dog in the snow instantly transformed itself in my mind into a bear. I took a bus to the library for a book on bears. On the way in there was a display of books on Tibet – I don't know why, perhaps some fad of the librarian's. The library was thin on bear books but I took a couple of those on Tibet and was still reading them in bed that night. Next morning I woke up with practically the whole plot of a new book, and for the next two years, including research, sweated on *The Rose of Tibet*. Such, in my case, is the orderly process of inspiration, perspiration, realization. (The bear padded slowly into the book about three quarters of the way through.)

The perspiration, at any rate, is a constant factor. Because it never seems to me that I have enough plot, I research titanically to try and find more. This research always goes wild, the typewritten notes several times the length of the finished book. (The children's fantasy, for instance, generated 90,000 words of notes for 38,000 words of book.) Hardly any of it proves necessary – at least in its plot-providing function. In the very first flash I usually have far more plot than I can conceivably handle. The snag is, I don't know it; or rather, since it has happened every time, I *forget* it. I imagine this kind of thing happens most of the time with everybody, and in most departments, buying a house, a car, relationships, business, to name a few. It gives life its knockabout quality.

Of course, the research is not totally useless. All sorts of interesting things crop up which give a kind of authenticity to backgrounds: I become quite an expert in various recondite fields while writing a book, and instantly forget them as soon as I am finished. Perhaps this is why the experience of one book never seems to help much with the next.

The floundering about however does give the impression that something new and different is under way, which makes it quite fun, for the writer at least, and maybe some of it rubs off on the reader. This at any rate is the scientific process that puts the "how", speaking for myself alone in this helpful conspectus, into How I Write My Books.

LEN DEIGHTON
Even on Christmas Day

I HAVE NO FORMAL TRAINING and I have evolved a muddled sort of system by trial and error. Only after a decade or so did I find out there were books such as "How to Write a Novel" and I read them avidly. Usually such works are written by college professors in the USA and provide very good advice to anyone embarking on fiction writing. (John Braine's *Writing a Novel* published Eyre Methuen, London, and Coward McCann, New York, 1974 is in paperback from Methuen in Britain and from McGraw-Hill in the U.S.A.)

But the difficulty of saying anything about writing is that each writer has to find a way to winkle material out of his own brain. Furthermore each book has different problems that need to be tackled in a new way.

My own writing is characterized by an agonising reappraisal of everything I write so that I have to work seven days a week and usually do an hour or so even on Christmas Day, simply to keep all the problems fresh in my mind.

The most difficult lesson to learn is that thousands and thousands of words must go into the waste paper basket. To soften the blow I place scrapped chapters on a high shelf for a month before tossing them away.

Declarations of War was a book of short stories written over a period of a year during which my wife and I were living in hotels and temporary accommodation. We were looking for a house and in such conditions I could not have produced a long complete story but the travelling and talking provided material for the tales and *Declarations of War* turned out to be one of my favourite books.

The previous book *Bomber* was quite different. It took years of research and three trips to Germany – where much of the action takes place – as well as maps, charts, movies and recordings of interviews to get the material together. I had so many written notes – about half a million words – that I colour-coded the loose leaf notebook pages to help me find what I wanted. Colour can be a useful aid when taking notes; code always to the final use, not to the source. That is to say if a Luftwaffe pilot told me something that concerned the RAF flyers I

on the ground   Steeple Thaxted   220 FG   191 F.

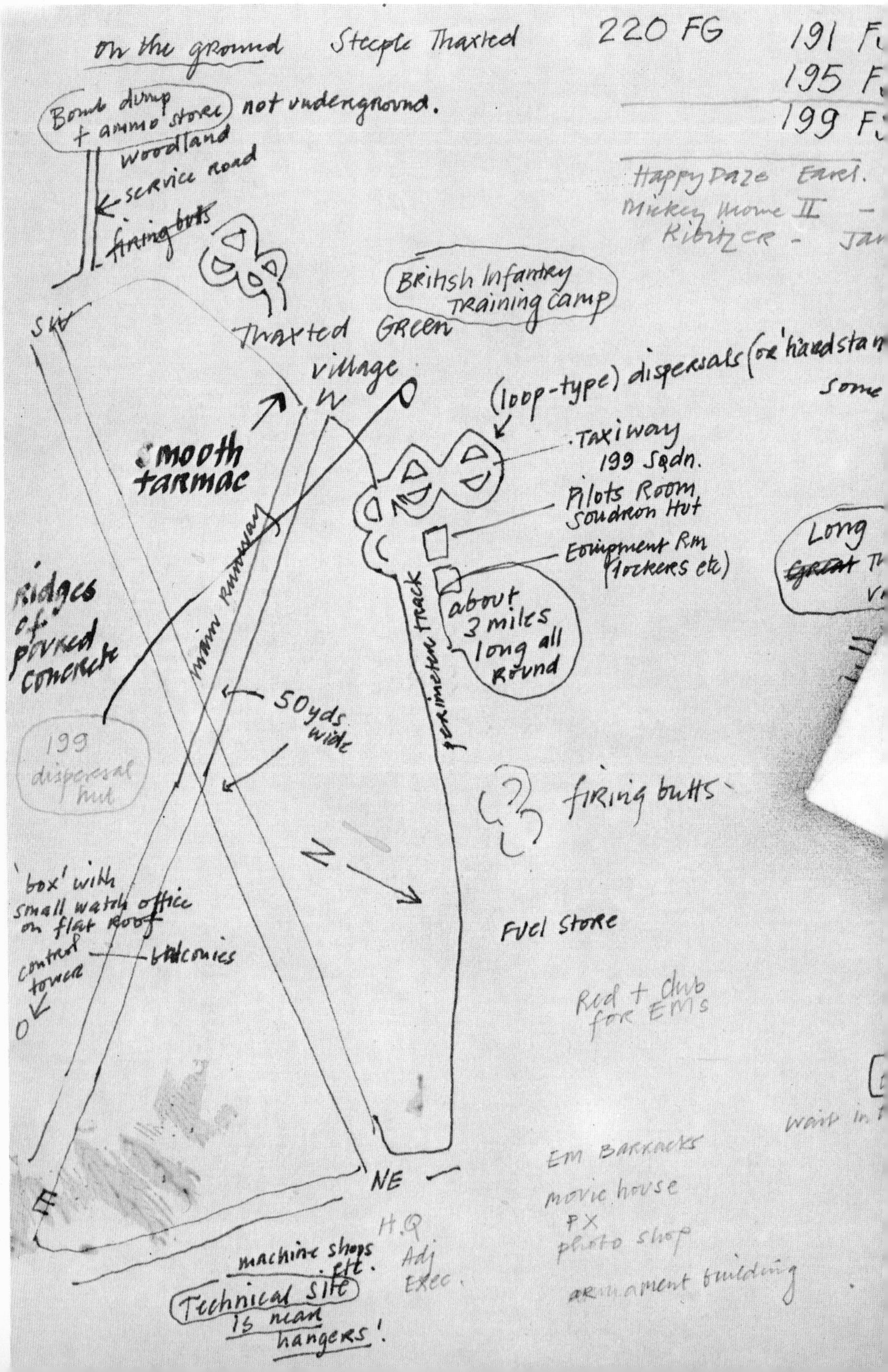

195 F.

199 F.

Bomb dump + ammo store   not underground.

woodland

service road

firing butts

Happy Daze Earl.

Mickey Mouse II –

Kibitzer – Jan

British Infantry
Training Camp

Thaxted Green
village
N

Sky

smooth
tarmac

(loop-type) dispersals (or 'hardstan

some

Taxiway
199 Sqdn.

Pilots Room
Squadron Hut

Equipment Rm
(lockers etc)

Long
Great Th
V

Ridges
of
poured
concrete

199
dispersal
hut

main runway

50 yds
wide

about
3 miles
long all
round

perimeter track

N

firing butts

'box' with
small watch office
on flat roof
control
tower   balconies

0

Fuel store

Red + Club
for EMs

NE

EM Barracks

movie house

PX

photo shop

armament building

H.Q
Adj
Exec.

machine shops
etc.

Technical site
is near
hangers!

wait in t

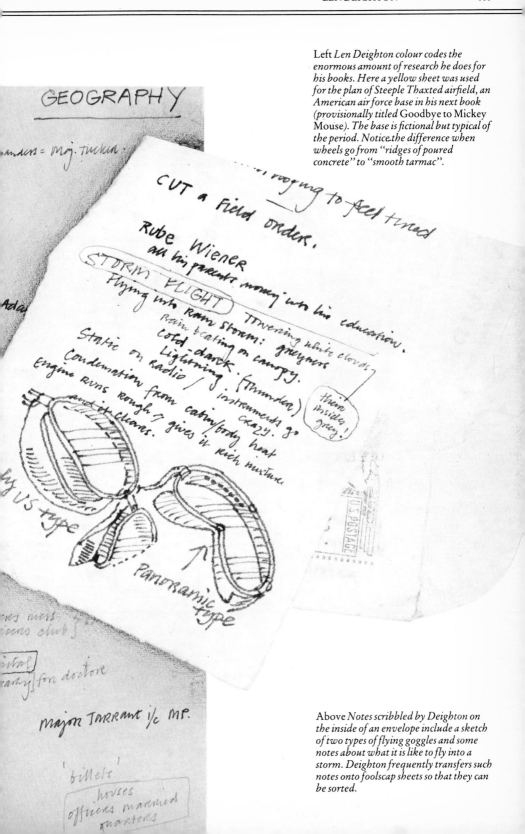

Left *Len Deighton colour codes the enormous amount of research he does for his books. Here a yellow sheet was used for the plan of Steeple Thaxted airfield, an American air force base in his next book (provisionally titled* Goodbye to Mickey Mouse*). The base is fictional but typical of the period. Notice the difference when wheels go from "ridges of poured concrete" to "smooth tarmac".*

Above *Notes scribbled by Deighton on the inside of an envelope include a sketch of two types of flying goggles and some notes about what it is like to fly into a storm. Deighton frequently transfers such notes onto foolscap sheets so that they can be sorted.*

would write it on blue sheets, if he told me something about the social life in Germany I would put it on white note pages, if he told me something that I wanted to know about the Luftwaffe it went on yellow pages. If this all sounds like an endless flurry of paper-work I should tell you that it must not be. A writer must keep his note-taking inconspicuous and he must have a plan of what information is needed and where it will be used.

By the time I finished *Bomber*, with a large number of characters – a high proportion of which were flyers and so physically and psychologically alike – and the dialogue confined to the words and mental attitudes of 1943 (a restriction which ensures that the more accurate you are the flatter and more cramped the result!), I was ready for *Close Up*.

For *Close Up* was not about lots of people, it was about just one person, an actor. Its dialogue was not that of wartime Britain but of contemporary show-biz. I'd spent a couple of years producing films and I wanted to use the knowledge I'd acquired. It was a safety valve; something I did instead of murdering certain movie people. Although writers are notoriously unreliable assessors of their own work, I believe that *Close Up* remains one of the best books I've ever written.

I'm often asked if I work directly on a typewriter. The answer is, yes if I have one to hand, otherwise I work on paper. Even in Latvia and Mexico I have never had much difficulty getting a school exercise book and a pencil. I write double-spaced to leave plenty of room for the inevitable revisions and I never write on both sides of the paper. I write on a right hand page, leaving the facing page blank for insertions and revisions. Then I leave the following double-page blank.

For me the first draft of a chapter is just a basis upon which to build. Once my secretary kept a note of my revisions and told me that one chapter was retyped 25 times. Now I have a word processor (an Olivetti TES 501 bought second hand from Richard Condon who had already written a couple of books on it) and my endless changes are done within the machine. This suits me very well but I know there are many writers who find any machine a barrier between them and the writing. The only implements needed to write a book are pencil and paper, everything else is luxury.

The question I'm asked most frequently is how long does it take to write a book. It's not easy to answer this because, although I spend at least a year "full time", I do, like most other writers, always have several other projects on the drawing board. Five or six years is by no means unusual from start to delivered manuscript. *Fighter* and *Blitzkrieg*, two non-fiction books about the war in 1940, required a great deal of travelling. Having been to the place where the German spearheads crossed the river Meuse, I later decided I would have to see them at the same season as the crossings took place and repeated the whole trip. I was able to combine some of the work for the two books, (the project began as a hobby and my original notes were not prepared for publication) and yet this all took eight or nine years from beginning to end. *Blitzkrieg* which dealt with the beginnings of the Nazi party and Hitler's control of the army was particularly demanding as I decided that I must go and sort out the material with people in Germany. I am most fortunate in having a wife who is a most gifted linguist; otherwise I would probably still be there.

I have heard that some writers are inspired by stories they read in the newspapers. While agreeing that each year fiction books contain more and more facts and newspapers more and more fiction, I have not found newspapers a source of stories. Books are about people and writers are best advised to go directly to a source. Neither is it true to say that stories are best based on facts; the greatest difficulty a writer faces is in reconciling reality with the needs of the story. When in doubt the requirements of the story must always prevail.

It's easy for writers to feel sorry for themselves. It is miserable to sit hammering away at that blank wall that we call "writer's block" but which we secretly know is incompetence. It is then that I wish I was flying a Phantom jet, working as a navy frogman, looking for alligators in the New York sewers, kicking my way into a narcotic dealer's apartment with the Los Angeles cops or even getting taken into custody by Russian soldiers in East Berlin. But in the course of my job I have done all those things and more. It's not such a bad job after all; except for sitting here at this damned typewriter.

ERIC AMBLER
Voyages – and Shipwrecks

For me, writing a book is a voyage of discovery. The metaphor, I know, is neither new nor particularly felicitous, but I can think of no better way of describing the process.

It begins, of course, with an idea. This may take many forms. The heart of it may be a character, either seen whole in real life or assembled from fragmentary observations made of different persons at different times in different places. The idea may have grown from some seed such as an unusual piece of information or anecdote. On occasion, though rarely, the idea has come from the experience of an unfamiliar danger like, say, a desert brushfire. More often it is the product of unusual conversations in strange surroundings.

Once, in Java, I was marooned by civil war in a small provincial town. The World Health Organisation had set up a pre-natal clinic there and I spent hours listening to what the Irish nursing sister in charge of the clinic had to say about her job and the people of the town. Ideas for stories do not often come wrapped in such an extraordinary cocoon of rare background information. Mostly they come unwrapped and often remain unnoticed for long periods, years sometimes. That is as it should be. Ideas should not be too raw when used.

The fun begins – and in the beginning stages it is all fun – when I start to work the thing out on paper. There will be many false starts and long pauses for reflection. The pauses may sometimes be devoted by the non-reflecting parts of my mind to the mechanical task of doing some piece of minor research that these early probings have shown to be necessary. Or I may do something unrelated to the work in hand. I may, for example, start to tidy up my workroom, a quinquennial task that can take weeks when I am forced to become serious about it.

Generally, the pauses can be measured in days. And all the time I am gradually discovering what the story I have embarked upon is about. However, I am not yet committed. I can still scrap the fifty or sixty pages of writing and rewriting that may have by then accumulated and turn to something else. I have no set plan for the book, only an idea and the loom of a possible story somewhere in the murk ahead.

This method of composing by discovery, of letting the material go its own way and then seeing what happens, is not unusual, though writers who always think their stories through completely and plan before they set pen to paper tend to dismiss it as an impossible way of working. I have been accused of being a secret planner and told that the very complexity of some of my plots proves that I must plan in advance. The only thing those complexities prove, I think, is that, if they work, I must rewrite carefully and often.

All the same, I do understand the planners' feelings. When working as a screenwriter I have always held that the "step-outline" – that is the breakdown of the film into a bleak series of numbered paragraphs describing the basic story content by sequences – is an essential first stage in the preparation of an effective screenplay. But for me

that is only to underline the differences between two writing disci-
plines. The planners could argue, I suppose, that all the *rewriting* I do
on a book proves their case and that my early drafts add up to a kind
of planning. I would say that they were quibbling.

Obviously, however one chooses to describe it, my way of working is slow. It can be wasteful too. I spoke casually of scrapping fifty
or sixty pages. That was to look on the brighter side. Not so long ago
I scrapped a book when the fourth attempt to make sense of it had
reached page 170. It had taken me almost a year to realize that none of
it was ever going to work and that the idea had been congenitally
defective. Odd as it may seem, the moment of decision was more
exhilarating than painful. I was relieved, no doubt, to find that I had
not been tempted to ignore the inner warnings and finish a book
knowing it to be substandard.

Once upon a time I used to write all the drafts by hand on ruled
foolscap paper. The final draft would be a fair copy of its predecessor,
fair enough that is for a copy-typist to read. Then osteo-arthritis
struck and I had to change my ways. One book I wrote mainly with
my left hand; but this was unsatisfactory because my left-hand
writing came out looking like old Siamese script, and by the time I
had reached the bottom of a page I had to rely upon memory to help
me decipher the paragraphs at the top. So I bought a dictating
machine. That was no use.

Finally, some months, much physiotherapy and a remission or two
later, I learned to type. I use an electric machine and the two-finger-
one-thumb method. The only thing I cannot do with it is compose a
first draft. The machine seems to inhibit thought. So, I still write first
drafts by hand. On a bad day the handwriting will become virtually

*A section from the first-draft manuscript
of Eric Ambler's* The Care of Time *(1981).*

Malpensa, the older and least fog-prone of
Milan's airports, is forty-five kilometers north of the
city along the autostrada to Como. Taxis, according
to the hotel doorman, were in short supply at that
time of day. Happily, though, he commanded the
allegiance of the driver of a Mercedes limousine.
To oblige the doorman, this good man was ready
to postpone his lunch in order to drive me wherever
I wanted to go.

The fare asked was exorbitant but I did not
argue. The Mercedes would be kinder to my developing

Eric Ambler

illegible; but, since I am now the only typist who is going to have to read it, legibility is of marginal importance.

I have been trying to think of some advantages of the voyage-of-discovery multiple-draft approach to the writing of thrillers. One is that you can clean up the worst litter of such things as faulty syntax, bad spelling and too many adverbs as you go. A more substantial advantage perhaps is the psychological one. Because you have not planned it all, you will not always know what is coming next. So, you will start work each day with hope in your heart and a sense of anticipation. That means that you will not easily be diverted from your true purpose by the outside world.

Have I any advice for would-be thriller writers? Yes, one piece.

Story ideas are fragile things. Never talk about them. Not, I hasten to add, because they may be stolen. Ideas that can be stolen and used by thieves are rarely worth having. No, it is simply that, in my experience, a story idea discussed, or even vaguely described, is an idea lost. Ideas should be written down but not spoken about. To explain or begin to describe a story aloud is to be trapped into developing it aloud. Once that act of communication has been performed the story is done for, it has gone. There is no point in trying to retrieve it. It has been told, so forget it. It will have forgotten you.

This may be a personal idiosyncracy. I have just realised that what I was describing there was the scar tissue of old wounds suffered at movie producers' story conferences. But let it stand. Some highly successful writers are quite capable of talking about a story, then writing it as a novel and then going on to write a screenplay based on the novel. I am not of that company. The only time I tried to write a screenplay based on a book of my own I failed because I became bored. The producer complained that I had ruined a good book. I had sense enough left to agree with him.

H. R. F. KEATING
Flying A Bit High

WHAT STARTS ME OFF writing a crime novel is, almost paradoxically, a philosophical idea. Flying a bit high? Well, like it or not, it is ideas of this sort – Can the world ever do without violence? How many lies should we tell? Ought you to try to be perfect or settle for getting something done? – that give my imaginative faculty the necessary fire.

Take the last of my three examples, something that in everyday life – say in sweeping leaves in the garden – has always bugged me. There came the day when I thought, yes, I can work this out in a book. I was at that time also a good deal worried by the purely commercial consideration of finding a crime book that would appeal not just to British publishers, as mine had done hitherto, but to American publishers who had found my work too British.

So the notion of setting a book outside England was in my head, and one day it combined with my more high-flying philosophical worry about perfectionism to give me the answer "India", a land which it would not be very unfair to see as a symbol of the imperfect (I was later to find it could equally have been a symbol of the perfect with the extraordinary feats of its mystics, its Taj Mahal, its discovery of the zero; but that's another story).

Very well. A murder mystery. To be set in India. With in the background well hidden, hidden even from the conscious minds of most readers, the theme of perfection and imperfection.

So, first, a murder had to be devised which was somehow not the perfect murder – the title for the book presented itself just like that – but an imperfect murder. What if the victim were not actually to die? Okay. And a somehow imperfect weapon? How about – my mind slowly hammered its way to a solution in jotted pencil notes – how about a classical weapon used somehow in the wrong way? A candlestick. Shades of Cluedo. But with its heavy base not used by the somewhat incompetent murderer (later named Dilip) to bash in the head of the victim (and what a piece of luck to discover that some Parsis have the family name of "Perfect"). Instead, Dilip, I thought, must use the top end of the candlestick – hence perhaps why Mr Perfect is not killed outright – and when the hunt for the weapon is first conducted the candlestick can be ruled out because it seems not to fit the wound in the old Parsi's skull.

So the murder outlined. The murderer dimly seen. The victim more clearly. Even the setting – a house in Bombay where a classical

A note, hastily scribbled by H. R. F.
Keating, when he hit on the idea of
murder committed with the wrong end of
a candlestick for The Perfect Murder.

candlestick might be found – beginning to show through.

Suspects needed now. Other people who could have had a reason for wanting an old Parsi out of the way. And each of them, of course, in some way to demonstrate one attitude or another to being perfect. Tugging away at the delicate threads these early notions left just dangling, bit by bit I began to see the bulk of the story to be called *The Perfect Murder*. I sketched it out muttering to my inner self all the while "The Reader, remember the Reader, tell him a story".

I tentatively assigned the various incidents I thought necessary to some twenty 3,000-word chapters. Too few happenings, as yet, it seemed, to have something meaty in each of the twenty awaiting spaces. A sub-plot then? Reflecting on the perfect, of course. How about the impossible? The classic locked-room mystery. So, painfully, there came into being another story, something that would doubly harass the already harassed Inspector Ghote as he investigated the murder.

Somebody important, "influential" as they say with awe in India, butting in all the time. A Minister. Yes. And what he wants investigating to be a locked-room puzzle, but a ridiculous one, irritatingly ridiculous to Ghote but such that he cannot possibly admit even to himself that it is ridiculous. Got it. The Minister finds a tiny sum, one rupee, missing from the desk in his guarded office. And the solution? Well, easy, he took the coin or the note himself for some curious reason.

So we're ready to go, pretty well. More about perfectionism, and how I feel about it when all's said and done, to be discovered in the process of writing, in asking myself what such-and-such a person would do, could do, in such-and-such a situation into which I have plunged him or her. All right. We're on the diving board. The cold water lies tranquilly below. The blank piece of paper. Think of the first sentence. *Type.*

WRITERS AND THEIR BOOKS:
A CONSUMER'S GUIDE

Writers and their books: A Consumers' Guide
H. R. F. Keating, Dorothy B. Hughes, Melvyn Barnes, Reginald Hill

I AM CONSCIOUS that in choosing the authors considered in the pages that follow I must have omitted some who should have been there. But my aim was to give a mention at least to the crime authors on both sides of the Atlantic who make their mark in the current scene, together with those names from the past that a regular reader might have heard of – and I have been unable to resist adding a few names more interesting perhaps for themselves than for their books.

To give some indication of the period of books mentioned we have included – everywhere I hope – the date of first publication, either in America or Britain.

The books listed after each author entry are recommended as an introduction to the author in question, and to provide a quick appraisal of each book we have awarded them stars, one to ten, for Characterization (**C**), Plot (**P**), Readability, or how quickly you turn the pages (**R**), and Tension, a measure of the suspense element (**T**).

H.R.F.K.

Dorothy B. Hughes is a distinguished American critic and historian of the mystery novel, with an Edgar Allan Poe award for her work. She has, too, written a number of acclaimed novels of suspense.

Melvyn Barnes is author of Best Detective Fiction: A Guide from Godwin to the Present, *advisor/ contributor to* Twentieth Century Crime and Mystery Writers, *and editor of the Remploy "Deerstalker" series of reprints of classic crime fiction. He is City Librarian to the City of Westminster, London.*

Reginald Hill is the author of many crime novels, including Who Guards the Prince *(1982), an international thriller.*

AIKEN, Joan (1942) British gothic and suspense novelist, daughter of the American poet, Conrad Aiken. From 1953 she wrote children's stories (*Guardian* award, 1969). In 1964 she began writing crime novels, which at their best shine with imagination, leaping quirkily from moment to moment in stories that are always gripping, often horrific, sometimes delightfully humorous.

The Ribs Of Death (1967)

C ★ ★ ★ ★ ★ ★ ★ ★	P ★ ★ ★ ★ ★
R ★ ★ ★ ★ ★ ★ ★ ★ ★ ★	T ★ ★ ★ ★ ★ ★ ★ ★ ★

Last Movement (1977)

C ★ ★ ★ ★ ★ ★ ★ ★	P ★ ★ ★ ★ ★ ★ ★ ★
R ★ ★ ★ ★ ★ ★ ★ ★ ★ ★	T ★ ★ ★ ★ ★ ★ ★

AIRD, Catherine (1930) British detective novelist. She writes the good old-fashioned whodunit, set in the English county of "Calleshire" with Inspector Sloan as hero, plentiful literary allusions, settings such as a flower show (with one, not altogether successful, foray into student life) and much contemporary detail.

The Religious Body (1966)

C ★ ★ ★ ★ ★	P ★ ★ ★ ★ ★
R ★ ★ ★ ★ ★ ★	T ★ ★ ★ ★

AIRTH, Rennie South African crime novelist and well-known foreign correspondent. Style and ingenuity mark out his rare books. He began in 1968 with a spoof kidnapping story *Snatch!*, and *Once A Spy* retains elements of that sort of humour in a more serious and wholly credible story of a retired agent forced back into the field.

Once A Spy (1981)

C ★ ★ ★ ★ ★ ★ ★	P ★ ★ ★ ★ ★ ★ ★ ★
R ★ ★ ★ ★ ★ ★	T ★ ★ ★ ★ ★ ★ ★ ★

C = Characterization   P = Plot   R = Readability   T = Tension

ALBRAND, Martha (1914) German/American suspense-espionage novelist. Known professionally by her writing name, she was born Heidi Huberta in Rostock, Germany, emigrating to the United States in 1937 at the rise of Hitler. She also used the pen-name Christine Lambert. Her work is distinguished by her personal knowledge of background material and by her understanding of pre- and Hitlerian Europe. She received Le Grand Prix de Littérature Policier for *Desperate Moment* (1951).

No Surrender (1942)

| C ★ ★ ★ ★ ★ ★ | P ★ ★ ★ ★ ★ ★ |
| R ★ ★ ★ ★ ★ ★ | T ★ ★ ★ ★ |

A Taste of Terror (1977)

| C ★ ★ ★ ★ ★ ★ | P ★ ★ ★ ★ ★ ★ |
| R ★ ★ ★ ★ ★ ★ ★ | T ★ ★ ★ ★ ★ |

ALEXANDER, Patrick British espionage novelist. An immensely successful first book, *Death of A Thin-skinned Animal*, followed by one less successful is his career in crime to date. But that first won in Britain the John Creasey first crime novel award, deservedly for its inside knowledge (Alexander was a foreign correspondent) and its humanity, let alone its excitement.

Death of A Thin-skinned Animal (1976)

| C ★ ★ ★ ★ ★ ★ ★ ★ | P ★ ★ ★ ★ ★ ★ ★ |
| R ★ ★ ★ ★ ★ ★ ★ | T ★ ★ ★ ★ ★ ★ ★ ★ ★ |

Show Me A Hero (1979)

| C ★ ★ ★ ★ ★ ★ ★ | P ★ ★ ★ ★ ★ ★ |
| R ★ ★ ★ ★ ★ ★ | T ★ ★ ★ ★ ★ ★ ★ |

ALLBEURY, Ted (1917) British espionage novelist and former Intelligence officer, who has said indeed, "Only someone who has done it knows what it is like to arrest a man, shoot a man . . ." And certainly the element of reality is very much present in his books, and is one of their particular attractions. But, with perhaps some exceptions in the earliest

volumes, he entirely subdues these factual elements to the purposes of fiction. He writes, in short, novels rather than fictionalized pamphlets on the art of spying. And it is because he writes novels and deals in truth that most of his books have a sad ending. But before that comes there is the exhilarating setting down of things truthfully, of details of spy tradecraft, of details of life in Moscow, Berlin, Washington, wherever, and above all of the movements of the human heart.

The Man with the President's Mind (1977)

| C ★ ★ ★ ★ ★ ★ ★ | P ★ ★ ★ ★ ★ ★ ★ ★ |
| R ★ ★ ★ ★ ★ ★ ★ ★ | T ★ ★ ★ ★ ★ ★ ★ |

The Twentieth Day of January (1980)

| C ★ ★ ★ ★ ★ ★ ★ | P ★ ★ ★ ★ ★ ★ ★ ★ |
| R ★ ★ ★ ★ ★ ★ ★ ★ | T ★ ★ ★ ★ ★ ★ ★ |

The Secret Whispers (1981)

| C ★ ★ ★ ★ ★ ★ | P ★ ★ ★ ★ ★ ★ ★ |
| R ★ ★ ★ ★ ★ ★ ★ | T ★ ★ ★ ★ ★ ★ ★ |

Ted Allbeury

C = Characterization   P = Plot

ALLINGHAM, Margery (1904-66) British detective novelist. Her first crime novel, written in her twenties, was full of the zing of youth and its happy-go-luckiness. And in the Golden Age of the detective story she was one of its most trusted practitioners, providing regular cases for the Scarlet Pimpernel-like Mr Campion (probably of royal descent). But by 1936 she could write, in *Flowers for the Judge*, a murder story that retained the dull incidents of investigation that other writers of the time were leaving out and yet, because of its author's superabundant energy, was still gripping. After the 1939-45 War Mr Campion changed a good deal, becoming a shrewd, compassionate observer rather than a foppish activist. The books of that time are among the best produced in the genre, individual, full of marvellous observation of London and the Essex marshes that were close to their author's home, darting with humour and fun, capable of the serious.

More Work for the Undertaker (1949)

C ★ ★ ★ ★ ★ ★ ★ ★	P ★ ★ ★ ★ ★ ★ ★ ★
R ★ ★ ★ ★ ★ ★ ★ ★	T ★ ★ ★ ★ ★ ★ ★ ★

The Tiger in the Smoke (1952)

C ★ ★ ★ ★ ★ ★ ★ ★	P ★ ★ ★ ★ ★ ★ ★ ★
R ★ ★ ★ ★ ★ ★ ★ ★	T ★ ★ ★ ★ ★ ★ ★ ★ ★ ★

The Beckoning Lady (1955)

C ★ ★ ★ ★ ★ ★ ★	P ★ ★ ★ ★ ★ ★ ★
R ★ ★ ★ ★ ★ ★ ★ ★	T ★ ★ ★ ★ ★ ★ ★ ★

AMBLER, Eric (1909) British espionage and adventure novelist. He initiated a new phase in the history of the spy story by choosing as hero, not an operative with right and the Establishment on his side, but a person caught up in the machinations of Giant Powers who was himself of the Left, a doubter and an innocent. After the 1939-45 War, in which he served in the Army film unit (he had before the war been a copywriter and to him we owe "Snap, crackle and pop"), his books took on a more varied hue, though always his mastery of narration and of construction made them marvellously readable. So much so indeed that he can, as in *The Schirmer Inheritance* (1953), make intensely gripping a story in which very little happens. Always, too, in the post-war books as in the pre-war he chooses interesting and exotic backgrounds and makes them come vividly to life, whether it is the Turkey of *The Mask of Dimitrios* and *The Light of Day* (1962) (filmed as *Topkapi*), or the Indonesia of the *Night-Comers* (1956) or the seedy Caribbean country of *Doctor Frigo* (1974), also a memorable characterization. The later books on the whole are marked by an interest in major problems confronting the world. *The Intercom Conspiracy* (1969) deals with the overkill effect

Margery
Allingham

R = Readability   T = Tension

Kingsley Amis

AMIS Kingsley (1922) British novelist, poet, critic. Amis's work as a university lecturer provided him with the background for his best selling first novel, *Lucky Jim* (1954). Essentially a satirist, he has occasionally ventured into crime fiction with a commendable lack of spoofery. *Colonel Sun* (1968) written under the pseudonym of Robert Markham, is a James Bond adventure with much of the authentic Fleming panache, and *The Riverside Villa Murders* (1973) is a 'Golden Age' detective story, with added sex for the modern palate.

Colonel Sun (1968)

C ★★★★★★★	P ★★★★★★★★
R ★★★★★★★★★	T ★★★★★★★

The Riverside Villa Murders (1973)

C ★★★★★★★	P ★★★★★★★★★
R ★★★★★★★★★	T ★★★★★

of too much spying and unceremoniously buries the hero of *The Mask of Dimitrios* in motorway concrete. *Send No More Roses* (1977) (*The Siege of the Villa Lipp* in U.S.) deals with the ungetatable criminal making millions through manipulating money and frontiers. *The Care of Time* (1981) deals with terrorism on an international plane. These are tougher books intellectually, but all the old skills are there, the sharp vividness, the ingenuity, the offbeat characterizations and, above all, the sheer storytelling. Both *Passage of Arms* and *The Levanter* of the postwar novels won the Crime Writers Association Gold Dagger awards in Britain and *A Kind of Anger* (1964) won a Mystery Writers Of America Edgar. Ambler is a Grand Master of the M.W.A. and of the Swedish Academy of Detection.

The Mask of Dimitrios (1939)

C ★★★★★★★★★	P ★★★★★★★★
R ★★★★★★★★★	T ★★★★★★★★

Passage of Arms (1959)

C ★★★★★★★★★	P ★★★★★★★★
R ★★★★★★★★★	T ★★★★★★★★★

The Levanter (1972)

C ★★★★★★★★★	P ★★★★★★★★★
R ★★★★★★★★★	T ★★★★★★★★★

ANDERSON, J. R. L. (1911-81) British espionage adventure writer, formerly a senior journalist. The sea features largely in the adventures of Colonel Peter Blair, retired and taken on as a secret agent. The stories, which Anderson began to write fairly late in life, are solid tales, generous with detail.

Death in A High Latitude (1981)

C ★★★★	P ★★★★★★★
R ★★★★★★★	T ★★★

ANDERSON, James British crime novelist. His books veer wildly from sub-genre to sub-genre, much as their plots are apt to veer wildly in the course of the telling. But they are written with great verve, and much may be forgiven for that.

The Abolition of Death (1974)

C ★★★★★★★	P ★★★★★★★
R ★★★★★★★★	T ★★★★★★★★

The Affair of the Blood-stained Egg Cosy (1975)

C ★★★★★★★	P ★★★★★★★★
R ★★★★★★★	T ★

C = Characterization   P = Plot

ANTHONY, Evelyn (1928) British romantic and suspense novelist, pen-name of Evelyn Ward Thomas. From well-researched historical novels, she turned to modern backgrounds of international espionage and political intrigue. Her subjects range from terrorism and kidnapping to the pursuit of war criminals; a strong love interest is often in conflict with politics or fanaticism.

The Tamarind Seed (1971)

C ★ ★ ★ ★	P ★ ★ ★ ★ ★ ★ ★
R ★ ★ ★ ★ ★ ★ ★	T ★ ★ ★ ★ ★ ★ ★

The Occupying Power (1973)
(Stranger at the Gates in U.S.)

C ★ ★ ★ ★ ★	P ★ ★ ★ ★ ★ ★
R ★ ★ ★ ★ ★ ★ ★	T ★ ★ ★ ★ ★ ★ ★

The Persian Ransom (1975)
(The Persian Price in U.S.)

C ★ ★ ★ ★ ★	P ★ ★ ★ ★ ★ ★ ★
R ★ ★ ★ ★ ★ ★ ★	T ★ ★ ★ ★ ★ ★ ★

Charlotte
Armstrong

ARCHER, Jeffrey (1940) British thriller writer and, as he records in *Who's Who,* "has-been politician" (he quit as an M.P. after a storm over financial dealings in 1974). His first book, *Not A Penny More, Not A Penny Less* (1975), echoes this affair, though its plot runs to wishful fantasy. Subsequent books have been bestsellers, stuffed with bestseller material (romance, inside knowledge), and certified by many reviewers as gripping from start to finish.

Shall We Tell the President? (1977)

C ★ ★ ★ ★	P ★ ★ ★ ★ ★ ★ ★
R ★ ★ ★ ★ ★ ★ ★	T ★ ★ ★ ★ ★ ★ ★

Kane and Abel (1979)

C ★ ★ ★ ★	P ★ ★ ★ ★ ★ ★ ★
R ★ ★ ★ ★ ★ ★ ★ ★	T ★ ★ ★ ★ ★ ★ ★

ARDIES, Tom (1931) American espionage novelist. His first three books, fast-moving tales of C.I.A. man Charlie Sparrow, are entertaining but with a certain lack of credibility. From *Kosygin is Coming* onwards, his books began to show greater skill in plot construction, complexity and characterization, some with touches of farce or debunking of the spy genre.

Kosygin is Coming (1974)

C ★ ★ ★ ★ ★ ★	P ★ ★ ★ ★ ★ ★ ★
R ★ ★ ★ ★ ★	T ★ ★ ★ ★ ★ ★

In a Lady's Service (1976)

C ★ ★ ★ ★ ★ ★	P ★ ★ ★ ★ ★ ★
R ★ ★ ★ ★ ★ ★	T ★ ★ ★ ★ ★

ARMSTRONG, Charlotte (1905-69) American mystery-suspense writer. She began as a successful Broadway playwright, turning to mystery novels in 1942 with *Lay On, MacDuff* and becoming an immediate star of the medium. She received the Mystery Writers of America award, the Edgar, in 1956 with *A Dram of Poison,* and was three times honoured with Edgar best short-story scrolls. Many of her books became successful motion

R = Readability T = Tension

pictures. Her final novels marked another successful and delightful transition, warm and witty inventions.

The Unsuspected (1946)

C ★ ★ ★ ★ ★	P ★ ★ ★ ★ ★ ★
R ★ ★ ★ ★ ★ ★ ★	T ★ ★ ★ ★ ★ ★

Mischief (1950)

C ★ ★ ★ ★ ★ ★	P ★ ★ ★ ★ ★ ★ ★
R ★ ★ ★ ★ ★ ★ ★	T ★ ★ ★ ★ ★ ★

Lemon in the Basket (1967)

C ★ ★ ★ ★ ★ ★	P ★ ★ ★ ★ ★ ★ ★
R ★ ★ ★ ★ ★ ★ ★ ★	T ★ ★ ★ ★ ★ ★

ASHE, Gordon (1908-73) Pseudonym of John Creasey (q.v.). Under the Ashe label, from 1939 onward, Creasey produced a long series of readable thrillers featuring Patrick Dawlish. Dawlish developed and matured with the times, from wartime espionage to post-war Scotland Yard investigations of international crime, culminating in leadership of "The Crime Haters".

The Crime Haters (1961)

C ★ ★	P ★ ★ ★ ★ ★
R ★ ★ ★ ★ ★ ★ ★ ★ ★	T ★ ★ ★ ★ ★ ★

A Plague of Demons (1976)

C ★ ★	P ★ ★ ★ ★ ★
R ★ ★ ★ ★ ★ ★ ★ ★ ★	T ★ ★ ★ ★ ★ ★

ASHFORD, Jeffrey (1926) Pseudonym of Roderic Jeffries (q.v.), which he employed for novels combining suspense with criminal psychology. This is not to say that they are of deep sociological import, however, being basically tales of unwitting victims enmeshed in matters criminal, with sanity normally restored by the use of solid police procedures.

The Double Run (1973)

C ★ ★ ★ ★ ★	P ★ ★ ★ ★ ★ ★ ★
R ★ ★ ★ ★ ★ ★ ★ ★	T ★ ★ ★

ASIMOV, Isaac (1920) Russian/American mystery and science writer. Born in the U.S.S.R., Asimov

Isaac Asimov

was brought to the United States when three years old, which gives America first claim on this unequalled science writer, whether writing pure science or science-fiction. A University professor since receiving his PhD from Columbia University, the number of books he has written is so enormous that he has said in a biographical sketch that he "long since decided to make it a rule to cease listing my books." Mystery writing is a sideline with Asimov. He writes mostly short stories in this field, and, as expected from a scientist mostly of the puzzle type. Also to be expected for those who know Asimov, his stories are heightened with good humour.

A Whiff of Death (1958)

C ★ ★ ★ ★ ★	P ★ ★ ★ ★ ★
R ★ ★ ★ ★ ★	T ★ ★ ★ ★ ★

More Tales of the Black Widowers (1976)

C ★ ★ ★ ★ ★	P ★ ★ ★ ★ ★ ★ ★
R ★ ★ ★ ★ ★	T ★ ★ ★ ★ ★

C = Characterization   P = Plot

ATLEE, Philip (1915) American espionage novelist, pen-name of James Atlee Phillips. After producing several creditable crime novels under his own name, he established a firm reputation with his spy stories featuring Joe Gall. From *The Green Wound* to *The Last Domino Contract*, Gall develops from all-action Bond figure to bitter and conscience-stricken maturity.

The Green Wound (1963)

C ★ ★ ★ ★	P ★ ★ ★ ★ ★
R ★ ★ ★ ★ ★ ★ ★ ★	T ★ ★ . ★ ★ ★ ★

The Trembling Earth Contract (1969)

C ★ ★ ★ ★	P ★ ★ ★ ★ ★
R ★ ★ ★ ★ ★ ★ ★ ★	T ★ ★ ★ ★ ★ ★ ★

The Last Domino Contract (1976)

C ★ ★ ★ ★ ★	P ★ ★ ★ ★ ★
R ★ ★ ★ ★ ★ ★ ★ ★	T ★ ★ ★ ★ ★ ★ ★

AUDEMARS, Pierre (1909) British author of French-set mysteries. Inspector Pinaud, Gallic, boastful, encounterer of beauties (frequently naked) is the hero of some 25 suspenseful adventures as typical of la belle France as Maurice Chevalier.

Audemars is his directly humorous "chronicler".

Gone to Her Death (1981)

C ★ ★ ★ ★ ★	P ★ ★ ★ ★ ★
R ★ ★ ★ ★ ★ ★ ★ ★	T ★ ★ ★ ★

AVALLONE, Michael, Jr (1924) American writer of considerable versatility, ranging from private eye and spy stories to science fiction and the supernatural, and involving many pseudonyms. Ed Noon, his best-known character, is personal investigator for the U.S. President. The Avallone hallmarks are effortless style and clipped dialogue, combined with racy action and larger-than-life characters.

The Tall Dolores (1953)

C ★ ★ ★	P ★ ★ ★ ★ ★
R ★ ★ ★ ★ ★ ★ ★	T ★ ★ ★ ★ ★ ★ ★

The February Doll Murders (1966)

C ★ ★ ★ ★	P ★ ★ ★ ★ ★ ★
R ★ ★ ★ ★ ★ ★ ★ ★	T ★ ★ ★ ★ ★ ★ ★

Shoot it Again, Sam (1972)
(The Moving Graveyard in U.K.)

C ★ ★ ★ ★	P ★ ★ ★ ★ ★ ★ ★
R ★ ★ ★ ★ ★ ★ ★ ★	T ★ ★ ★ ★ ★ ★ ★ ★

Marian Babson

BABSON, Marian American mystery writer, resident in Britain. She writes alternately suspense stories and mysteries-with-comedy, often with a particular London setting. At her best she hits off British types with insight and wit. At other times her plots strain credulity somewhat.

Murder, Murder, Little Star (1977)

C ★ ★ ★ ★ ★ ★	P ★ ★ ★ ★ ★ ★
R ★ ★ ★ ★ ★ ★ ★	T ★ ★ ★ ★ ★ ★ ★

Dangerous to Know (1980)

C ★ ★ ★ ★ ★ ★	P ★ ★ ★ ★ ★ ★ ★
R ★ ★ ★ ★ ★ ★	T ★ ★ ★ ★ ★ ★ ★

R = Readability   T = Tension

BAGBY, George (1906) American mystery writer. Bagby, best known pseudonym of the prolific Aaron Marc Stein (q.v.), narrates as the amanuensis of Inspector Schmidt of the New York police. The first Bagby story was *Bachelor's Wife* (1932); the first with Inspector Schmidt was *Bird Walking Weather* (1939). The stories are upbeat, the New York background as real as being there, and for about fifty years Bagby has never aged, always a pleasure to read.

Here Comes the Corpse (1941)

C ★★★★	P ★★★★★
R ★★★★	T ★★★★

Scared to Death (1952)

C ★★★★★	P ★★★★★
R ★★★★	T ★★★★

Another Day, Another Death (1968)

C ★★★★★	P ★★★★★
R ★★★★★	T ★★★★

H. C. Bailey

BAGLEY, Desmond (1923) British thriller/adventure novelist, born in South Africa. He has brought to a high pitch the art of creating excitement, excitement of a genuine sort arising from the predicaments of people in whom one can believe, as much as from the nature of the predicaments themselves. He derives a good deal of his creative force from the choice of exotic settings, carefully visited in advance. These have ranged from Iceland (*Running*

Blind, 1970) to the Sahara (*Flyaway*), from northernmost Scotland (*The Enemy*) to southern New Zealand (*The Snow Tiger*). But he never allows his research, however massive, eventually to get in the way of his story, although what facts he does let on to the pages greatly enhance the authenticity and interest of those stories.

The Snow Tiger (1974)

C ★★★★★★★	P ★★★★★★
R ★★★★★★★	T ★★★★★★★★

The Enemy (1977)

C ★★★★★★★	P ★★★★★★★
R ★★★★★★★★	T ★★★★★★★★

Flyaway (1979)

C ★★★★★★	P ★★★★★★
R ★★★★★★★★★	T ★★★★★★★★

BAILEY, H. C. (1878-1961) British detective-story writer. One of the Golden Age brigade who deserves to live on, he invented the sanctimonious solicitor Joshua Clunk and the genial, humane, whimsical scientific adviser, Dr Reggie Fortune. The books are almost always intricate puzzles strictly of the fair-play school, and are now becoming increasingly interesting as well as social history.

The Sullen Sky Mystery (1935)

C ★★★★★	P ★★★★★★
R ★★★★★★	T ★★★★

Black Land, White Land (1937)

C ★★★★★★	P ★★★★★★★
R ★★★★★★	T ★★★

BALCHIN, Nigel (1908-70) British novelist and scientist, who in at least one of his novels moved clearly into the suspense field. This was *Mine Own Executioner*, a psychological thriller, still worth reading more than thirty years after its publication.

Mine Own Executioner (1945)

C ★★★★★★	P ★★★★★
R ★★★★★★	T ★★★★★★★

BALL, John (1911) American mystery writer. Born in Schenectady, New York, Ball worked on newspapers and published technical books before he wrote his first mystery, *In The Heat of the Night* (1964). It was an immediate sensation. Ball distilled the essence of the Deep South in his story of a Northern black police officer working with a Mississippi sheriff to solve a small town Southern murder. The book received the Edgar for Best First Novel in 1965, a Crime Writers award in Britain in 1967, and five Academy of Motion Picture awards also in 1967. Ball has written numerous, well-received police stories since, but none with the perfect story-telling of his first.

In The Heat of the Night (1964)

C ★ ★ ★ ★ ★ ★ ★	P ★ ★ ★ ★ ★ ★ ★
R ★ ★ ★ ★ ★ ★ ★ ★	T ★ ★ ★ ★ ★ ★ ★ ★

Five Pieces of Jade (1971)

C ★ ★ ★ ★	P ★ ★ ★ ★ ★
R ★ ★ ★ ★ ★ ★	T ★ ★ ★ ★ ★ ★

BALLARD, Willis Todhunter (1903) American hardboiled detective and western novelist, also using numerous pseudonyms. His most popular character, Bill Lennox, appeared regularly in the legendary *Black Mask* magazine before his full-length debut. Hollywood or Las Vegas backdrops, money and immorality, corruption and tough wisecracking dialogue are all fused most effectively.

Say Yes to Murder (1942)

C ★ ★ ★ ★ ★	P ★ ★ ★ ★ ★
R ★ ★ ★ ★ ★ ★ ★	T ★ ★ ★ ★ ★ ★

Murder Las Vegas Style (1967)

C ★ ★ ★ ★ ★	P ★ ★ ★ ★ ★
R ★ ★ ★ ★ ★ ★ ★	T ★ ★ ★ ★ ★

BALINGER, Bill S. (1912) American mystery writer. Prolific in all of his fields, long and short mysteries, westerns, motion picture, radio and television dramas, Ballinger published his first mystery novel, *The Body in the Bed,* in 1948. More than 10 million copies of his books have been sold in the United States alone. His books are characterized as semi-tough but intelligent. In 1965 he diverted to write a series of spy novels against unusual foreign backgrounds such as Angkor, the Java Sea, Bangkok. He received the Edgar award in 1960 for a television suspense drama.

The Longest Second (1957)

C ★ ★ ★ ★ ★	P ★ ★ ★ ★ ★ ★
R ★ ★ ★ ★ ★ ★	T ★ ★ ★ ★ ★

BANKIER, William (1928) Canadian crime short-story writer, resident in Britain and freelance writer since a holiday trip there. If that was taking a risk, the stories he writes are generally about people doing that too, acting out of long-pent desperation. Many of his stories are concerned with sports. His 1980 story *The Choirboy* was nominated for a Mystery Writers of America Edgar. There is no collected edition.

BARDIN, John Franklin (1916) American mystery story writer and legal editor. He wrote three books in the 1940s, much admired by the cognoscenti but soon totally ignored until in 1976 Julian Symons (q.v.) found their author, who had completely lost touch with his publishers, and brought out the books again as an omnibus Penguin paperback. The novels are intensely romantic explorations of the human mind under stress, curious and compelling.

The Deadly Percheron (1946)

C ★ ★ ★ ★ ★ ★ ★ ★	P ★ ★ ★ ★ ★ ★
R ★ ★ ★ ★ ★ ★ ★ ★ ★	T ★ ★ ★ ★ ★ ★ ★ ★ ★

The Last of Philip Banter (1947)

C ★ ★ ★ ★ ★ ★ ★	P ★ ★ ★ ★ ★ ★
R ★ ★ ★ ★ ★ ★ ★ ★ ★	T ★ ★ ★ ★ ★ ★ ★

Devil Take the Blue-Tail Fly (1948)

C ★ ★ ★ ★ ★ ★ ★	P ★ ★ ★ ★ ★ ★ ★
R ★ ★ ★ ★ ★ ★ ★ ★	T ★ ★ ★ ★ ★ ★ ★ ★

R = Readability   T = Tension

BARNARD, Robert (1940) British mystery novelist. Professor of English at the University of Tromso, Norway, Barnard writes outwardly conventional whodunits, mostly set in England, that flail with little mercy the pretensions and prejudices of the British middle class (and up) in settings usually of more than average interest. But the pretensions and prejudices are such that they are easily transferable to the pretensions and prejudices of other societies in other parts of the world, a quality which, as Barnard himself has pointed out in his study of Agatha Christie (*A Talent to Deceive*, 1980), makes the books widely acceptable.

Death in A Cold Climate (1979)

C ★ ★ ★ ★ ★ ★	P ★ ★ ★ ★ ★ ★ ★
R ★ ★ ★ ★ ★ ★ ★	T ★ ★ ★ ★ ★ ★

Mother's Boys (1980)

C ★ ★ ★ ★ ★ ★ ★	P ★ ★ ★ ★ ★ ★
R ★ ★ ★ ★ ★ ★ ★	T ★ ★ ★ ★ ★ ★

Sheer Torture (1981)

C ★ ★ ★ ★ ★ ★ ★ ★	P ★ ★ ★ ★ ★ ★ ★ ★
R ★ ★ ★ ★ ★ ★ ★ ★	T ★ ★ ★ ★ ★

BARNETT, James (1920) British thriller novelist. After a successful police career ending as a CID Commander, Barnett took to the typewriter and over five books achieved a very high standard. *The Firing Squad,* brought off the difficult feat of being both exciting as a thriller and penetrating as a novel.

The Head of the Force (1978)

C ★ ★ ★	P ★ ★ ★ ★ ★ ★ ★
R ★ ★ ★ ★ ★	T ★ ★ ★ ★ ★

The Firing Squad (1981)

C ★ ★ ★ ★ ★ ★ ★	P ★ ★ ★ ★ ★ ★ ★
R ★ ★ ★ ★ ★ ★ ★ ★	T ★ ★ ★ ★ ★ ★ ★ ★

BAXT, George (1923) American mystery writer. Baxt was in the forefront of the writers of the sixties with their emphasis on black humour. More importantly, he was possibly the first writer in mystery to handle the homosexual scene with verisimilitude. His first mysteries evoked such adjectives as "grotesque . . . nasty". Evidently by 1967 he was found more amusing than "revolting", as his third book, *A Parade of Cockeyed Creatures* or *Did Someone Murder Our Wandering Boy?*, received an Edgar scroll that year. Baxt is also a motion picture and television writer.

A Queer Kind of Death (1966)

C ★ ★ ★ ★ ★	P ★ ★ ★ ★ ★ ★
R ★ ★ ★ ★ ★	T ★ ★ ★

Swing Low, Sweet Harriet (1967)

C ★ ★ ★ ★ ★	P ★ ★ ★ ★ ★ ★
R ★ ★ ★ ★ ★	T ★ ★ ★ ★

A Parade of Cockeyed Creatures (1967)

C ★ ★ ★ ★ ★ ★	P ★ ★ ★ ★ ★ ★
R ★ ★ ★ ★ ★ ★	T ★ ★ ★ ★ ★

Robert Barnard

BEEDING, Francis British detective and espionage novelist, collaborative pen-name of John Leslie Palmer (1885-1944) and Hilary St. George Saunders (1898-1951). Their many entertaining spy thrillers feature Colonel Alastair Granby, but their smaller number of detective novels deserve to be more enduringly recognized as competent, suspenseful, and well characterized examples of the classic tradition.

The House of Dr Edwardes (1927)

C ★ ★ ★ ★ ★ ★	P ★ ★ ★ ★ ★ ★ ★
R ★ ★ ★ ★ ★ ★ ★	T ★ ★ ★ ★

The Norwich Victims (1935)

C ★ ★ ★ ★ ★ ★	P ★ ★ ★ ★ ★ ★
R ★ ★ ★ ★ ★ ★ ★	T ★ ★ ★ ★

BEHN, Noel (1928) American espionage novelist, whose small output belies his significance. Not for Behn the jollification of the spy escapade nor the excessive patriotism of some other writers; instead he makes the point that ruthlessness and treachery are by no means the prerogative of the other side.

The Kremlin Letter (1966)

C ★ ★ ★ ★ ★ ★ ★ ★	P ★ ★ ★ ★ ★ ★ ★ ★
R ★ ★ ★ ★ ★ ★ ★	T ★ ★ ★ ★ ★ ★ ★

The Shadowboxer (1969)

C ★ ★ ★ ★ ★ ★ ★ ★	P ★ ★ ★ ★ ★ ★ ★
R ★ ★ ★ ★ ★ ★ ★	T ★ ★ ★ ★ ★ ★ ★

BELL, Josephine (1897) British detective novelist. Over 45 years and nearly as many crime books Josephine Bell has entertained her public, often with medical settings (she is a doctor). The later books, certainly, add to often clever puzzles a bracing edge of social criticism. She is also a novelist, particularly in the historical field.

A Flat Tyre in Fulham (1963)

C ★ ★ ★ ★ ★ ★ ★ ★	P ★ ★ ★ ★
R ★ ★ ★ ★ ★ ★ ★ ★	T ★ ★

Wolf! Wolf! (1979)

C ★ ★ ★ ★ ★ ★ ★ ★	P ★ ★ ★ ★ ★ ★
R ★ ★ ★ ★ ★ ★ ★	T ★ ★ ★ ★ ★

BELLAIRS, George (1902) British detective novelist. Thomas Littlejohn of Scotland Yard features throughout a long series of competent novels in the English detective tradition, laced with humour and eccentricity. Bellairs' clever alibis and neat puzzles amply compensate for his deficiencies in credible characterization.

Death of a Busybody (1942)

C ★ ★ ★ ★ ★	P ★ ★ ★ ★ ★ ★
R ★ ★ ★ ★ ★ ★ ★	T ★ ★

Pomeroy, Deceased (1971)

C ★ ★ ★ ★	P ★ ★ ★ ★ ★ ★ ★
R ★ ★ ★ ★ ★ ★ ★	T ★ ★

BENNETT, Dorothea (1924) British crime novelist, wife of Terence Young, film producer (among others of James Bond stories). She writes little, but she writes with wit and style and a confidence that gives her books a touch of distinction.

The Maynard Hayes Affair (1981)

C ★ ★ ★ ★ ★ ★ ★ ★	P ★ ★ ★ ★ ★ ★
R ★ ★ ★ ★ ★ ★ ★ ★	T ★ ★ ★ ★ ★

BENNETT, Margot (1912) British crime novelist. She wrote only six crime books but they assure her a high place for their variedness, their wit, their ingenuity, the reality of their people. Indeed, the idea for *The Man Who Didn't Fly* (four set out by plane from England to Ireland but only three are found when it crashes) is a classic of originality.

The Widow of Bath (1952)

C ★ ★ ★ ★ ★ ★ ★ ★ ★	P ★ ★ ★ ★ ★ ★ ★ ★
R ★ ★ ★ ★ ★ ★ ★ ★	T ★ ★ ★

The Man Who Didn't Fly (1956)

C ★ ★ ★ ★ ★ ★ ★ ★ ★ ★	P ★ ★ ★ ★ ★ ★ ★ ★ ★ ★
R ★ ★ ★ ★ ★ ★ ★ ★	T ★ ★ ★ ★

Someone from the Past (1958)

C ★ ★ ★ ★ ★ ★ ★ ★ ★ ★	P ★ ★ ★ ★ ★ ★ ★ ★
R ★ ★ ★ ★ ★ ★ ★ ★	T ★ ★ ★

BENTLEY, E. C. (1875-1956) British detective novelist. Inventor of

R = Readability T = Tension

that oddest of verse forms, the cleri-hew, Bentley wrote three whodunits of which two make the classics list. *Trent's Last Case* was intended to be a light-hearted rebuke to the rule-bound Golden Age detective story: it ended as a classic of the sub-genre.

Trent's Last Case (1913)

C ★ ★ ★ ★ ★ ★ ★ ★	P ★ ★ ★ ★ ★ ★
R ★ ★ ★ ★ ★ ★ ★ ★ ★	T ★ ★ ★ ★

Trent's Own Case (1936)

C ★ ★ ★ ★ ★ ★ ★	P ★ ★ ★ ★ ★
R ★ ★ ★ ★ ★ ★ ★ ★	T ★ ★ ★

BENTLEY, Nicholas (1907-78) British humorous crime writer. Son of E. C. Bentley (q.v.), he was pri-marily an illustrator (he drew a charming caricature of Agatha Christie). His six crime books are more notable for their wit and high spirits than for plot or tension.

Inside Information (1974)

C ★ ★ ★ ★ ★	P ★ ★ ★
R ★ ★ ★ ★ ★ ★ ★	T ★

BENTON, Kenneth (1909) British espionage novelist. A retired diplo-mat, Benton brought his knowledge of foreign countries to chronicling the adventures of Peter Craig, special adviser on policing. Some of the later books (*A Single Monstrous Act*, 1976) contain hammered-home warnings on the dangers of subver-sion, on which Benton is an expert.

Craig and the Midas Touch (1975)

C ★ ★ ★ ★ ★	P ★ ★ ★ ★ ★ ★ ★
R ★ ★ ★ ★ ★ ★ ★ ★	T ★ ★ ★ ★ ★ ★ ★

BERCKMAN, Evelyn (1900-78) American crime novelist, long resi-dent in England. Her output has varied greatly in approach, from de-tective story to gothic the thriller, but her standard of writing was al-ways decidedly high. Indeed, the difficulty of labelling her as a writer (she was also an authority on the history of the British Navy) has re-sulted in her excellent work being frequently much under-estimated.

A Simple Case of Ill-Will (1964)

C ★ ★ ★ ★ ★ ★ ★ ★	P ★ ★ ★ ★ ★ ★ ★
R ★ ★ ★ ★ ★ ★ ★ ★	T ★ ★ ★ ★ ★ ★

The Heir of Starvelings (1967)

C ★ ★ ★ ★ ★ ★ ★ ★	P ★ ★ ★ ★ ★ ★ ★
R ★ ★ ★ ★ ★ ★ ★ ★	T ★ ★ ★ ★ ★ ★ ★ ★ ★ ★

The Victorian Album (1973)

C ★ ★ ★ ★ ★ ★ ★ ★	P ★ ★ ★ ★ ★ ★ ★
R ★ ★ ★ ★ ★ ★ ★ ★	T ★ ★ ★ ★ ★ ★ ★ ★

BERGMAN, Andrew American private-detective novelist. His Jack Le Vine novels, set in the 1940s, have a great period atmosphere and the added flavour of such characters as Dewey, the younger Nixon and Humphrey Bogart. His fascination with politics and movie history leads to effective portrayals of corruption and the threat to Hollywood of McCarthyism.

The Big Kiss-Off of 1944 (1974)

C ★ ★ ★ ★ ★ ★	P ★ ★ ★ ★ ★ ★ ★
R ★ ★ ★ ★ ★ ★ ★	T ★ ★ ★ ★ ★ ★ ★

Hollywood and Le Vine (1975)

C ★ ★ ★ ★ ★ ★	P ★ ★ ★ ★ ★ ★ ★
R ★ ★ ★ ★ ★ ★ ★	T ★ ★ ★ ★ ★ ★ ★

BERKELEY, Anthony (1893-1971) British detective novelist. His real name was Anthony Cox and he also wrote as Francis Iles (q.v.). The Berkeley books are conventional, and very clever, detective stories, with a bright, rather whimsical sleuth, Roger Sheringham, journal-ist. He is charmingly debunked in the multi-solutioned *The Poisoned Chocolates Case*.

The Poisoned Chocolates Case (1929)

C ★ ★ ★ ★ ★ ★	P ★ ★ ★ ★ ★ ★ ★ ★ ★ ★
R ★ ★ ★ ★ ★ ★ ★ ★	T ★ ★

Trail and Error (1937)

C ★ ★ ★ ★ ★ ★ ★	P ★ ★ ★ ★ ★ ★ ★ ★
R ★ ★ ★ ★ ★ ★ ★ ★	T ★ ★

BIGGERS, Earl Derr (1884-1933) American mystery writer. Biggers is one of the major names in American

John Bingham

mystery of the early twentieth-century. A Boston newspaperman, his first mystery novel, *Seven Keys to Baldpate,* became the sensationally successful George M. Cohan play, Cohan producing and starring in it. In 1925, Biggers created Charlie Chan, deliberately choosing to show a Chinese gentleman, not a "sinister and wicked" villain, but an "amiable" character on the side of law and order. All six Chan novels were serialized in the prestigious *Saturday Evening Post,* and made a classic statement in mystery fiction and also in motion pictures. Biggers' work remains good reading and Baldpate appears regularly in repertory.

BINGHAM, John (1908) British crime novelist. Otherwise Lord Clanmorris, retired Intelligence officer, sometimes said to be the physical model for John Le Carré's (q.v.) George Smiley. Interested more in the psychology leading to murder than in who done it, Bingham was something of an innovator in Britain with novels in which the police did not always behave as impeccable "bobbies" (*My Name Is Michael Sibley*). He has also written in the espionage field and he is in particular a dab hand with the intriguing situation, if sometimes straining credulity.

Seven Keys to Baldpate (1913)

C ★ ★ ★ ★ ★	P ★ ★ ★ ★ ★ ★
R ★ ★ ★ ★ ★ ★ ★ ★	T ★ ★ ★ ★ ★ ★ ★ ★

The House without A Key (1952)

C ★ ★ ★ ★ ★ ★ ★	P ★ ★ ★ ★ ★ ★
R ★ ★ ★ ★ ★ ★ ★ ★	T ★ ★ ★ ★ ★ ★

The Keeper of the Keys (1932)

C ★ ★ ★ ★ ★ ★ ★	P ★ ★ ★ ★ ★ ★
R ★ ★ ★ ★ ★ ★ ★ ★	T ★ ★ ★ ★ ★ ★

My Name Is Michael Sibley (1952)

C ★ ★ ★ ★ ★ ★ ★ ★	P ★ ★ ★ ★ ★ ★ ★ ★
R ★ ★ ★ ★ ★ ★ ★ ★	T ★ ★ ★ ★ ★ ★ ★

A Fragment of Fear (1966)

C ★ ★ ★ ★ ★ ★ ★	P ★ ★ ★ ★ ★ ★
R ★ ★ ★ ★ ★ ★ ★ ★	T ★ ★ ★ ★ ★ ★ ★ ★

God's Defector (1976)
(*Ministry of Death* in U.S.)

C ★ ★ ★ ★ ★	P ★ ★ ★ ★ ★ ★ ★
R ★ ★ ★ ★ ★ ★ ★ ★	T ★ ★ ★ ★ ★

BLACK, Gavin (1913) Scottish thriller writer, real name Oswald Wynd, under which he has also written crime novels. Born in Tokyo, he writes chiefly about the Far East (occasionally about Scotland) with as his frequent hero, Paul Harris, Singapore owner of a small shipping company. The books are notable for the likeliness of the adventures that happen in them, the authenticity of their settings and their reticent masculinity.

Suddenly, in Singapore (1961)

| C ★ ★ ★ ★ ★ ★ | P ★ ★ ★ ★ ★ ★ |
| R ★ ★ ★ ★ ★ ★ ★ | T ★ ★ ★ ★ ★ ★ ★ |

Night Run from Java (1979)

| C ★ ★ ★ ★ ★ ★ ★ | P ★ ★ ★ ★ ★ ★ |
| R ★ ★ ★ ★ ★ ★ ★ | T ★ ★ ★ ★ ★ ★ |

BLACK, Lionel (1910-80) British detective novelist. Well-known under his real name, Dudley Barker, for varied works of fiction and non-fiction (including a biography of G. K. Chesterton (q.v.) (1973)) he wrote between 1960 and 1980 fifteen or so detective stories, many featuring an inquisitive crime reporter, Kate Theobald. He is particularly notable for his settings in various parts of England.

Death Has Green Fingers (1971)

| C ★ ★ ★ ★ ★ ★ | P ★ ★ ★ ★ ★ |
| R ★ ★ ★ ★ ★ ★ ★ | T ★ ★ ★ ★ ★ |

BLACKBURN, John (1923) British supernatural suspense writer. A gift for the almost outrageously macabre combined with a talent for making the events he writes about seem plausible, and even ordinary, marks him out. Sometimes the element of the occult takes the books out of the strict crime category.

Bury Him Darkly (1969)

| C ★ ★ ★ ★ ★ ★ | P ★ ★ ★ ★ ★ |
| R ★ ★ ★ ★ ★ ★ ★ | T ★ ★ ★ ★ ★ ★ ★ |

BLACKSTOCK, Charity British psychological crime novelist and mainstream novelist. More interested, it seems, in emotion than murder, she is a chronicler of hatred, passion and, occasionally, the intrigue of espionage.

I Met Murder on the Way (1977) *(The Shirt Front* in U.S.)

| C ★ ★ ★ ★ ★ ★ | P ★ ★ ★ ★ ★ |
| R ★ ★ ★ ★ ★ ★ ★ | T ★ ★ ★ ★ ★ ★ |

Nicholas Blake

BLAKE, Nicholas (1904-72) British detective novelist under this pen-name, otherwise Cecil Day-Lewis, Poet Laureate. He began in 1935, golden heyday of the detective story, with a book in the full tradition but which yet had in it a touch of salt deriving from radical beliefs, seen in such minute things as a quotation from T. S. Eliot, fearful modern poet of those days, and in a hero, Nigel Strangeways then quite closely based on the poet W. H. Auden and a man really imbued with literature rather than a mere mouthpiece for an author's stock of literary allusions. The earlier books are marked by a fun-filled zest that still comes over clearly. There was perhaps some falling away in zest in later books as well as a perhaps wise backing off from Auden as Strangeways' prototype. But there were always liable to be interesting ideas, as for instance the notion of a poet suddenly finding access to a period of past experience because of the murder he eventually confesses to (*Head of A Traveller*, 1949), a valuable commentary on the poetic process. The last book, *The Private Wound*, however, is not in any way below the highest achievement, at once a poignant love story, pitted with truth, and a murder puzzle fairly clued and providing all that can be looked for in the genre on which Blake was a perceptive commentator, notably in his introduction to Howard Haycraft's *Murder for Pleasure* (1941).

The Beast Must Die (1938)

| C ★ ★ ★ ★ ★ ★ ★ ★ | P ★ ★ ★ ★ ★ ★ ★ ★ ★ |
| R ★ ★ ★ ★ ★ ★ ★ ★ ★ ★ | T ★ ★ ★ ★ ★ ★ ★ ★ |

The Case of the Abominable Snowman (1941)
(*The Corpse in the Snowman* in U.S.)

| C ★ ★ ★ ★ ★ ★ ★ | P ★ ★ ★ ★ ★ ★ ★ ★ |
| R ★ ★ ★ ★ ★ ★ ★ | T ★ ★ ★ ★ ★ ★ |

The Private Wound (1968)

| C ★ ★ ★ ★ ★ ★ ★ ★ ★ ★ | P ★ ★ ★ ★ ★ ★ ★ ★ |
| R ★ ★ ★ ★ ★ ★ ★ ★ ★ ★ | T ★ ★ ★ ★ ★ ★ ★ ★ |

BLEECK, Oliver see THOMAS, Ross

BLOCH, Robert (1917) American mystery writer. Born in Chicago, Bloch is one of the most prolific and entertaining of today's writers. He has extensive honours in science fiction, is an active screen and television writer, and has published more than 500 short stories and novelettes. Although his novels should be classified more as horror

stories than mysteries, his tongue in cheek treatment sets them far above the ludicrousness of usual horror material. Bloch was presented with a special scroll by the Mystery Writers of America in 1961.

Psycho (1959)

| C ★ ★ ★ ★ ★ ★ | P ★ ★ ★ ★ ★ ★ ★ ★ |
| R ★ ★ ★ ★ ★ ★ ★ ★ | T ★ ★ ★ ★ ★ ★ ★ ★ ★ |

Yours Truly, Jack the Ripper (1962)

| C ★ ★ ★ ★ ★ ★ | P ★ ★ ★ ★ ★ ★ ★ |
| R ★ ★ ★ ★ ★ ★ ★ ★ | T ★ ★ ★ ★ ★ ★ ★ ★ |

BLOCHMAN, Lawrence G. (1900-75) American mystery writer. California born and educated, Blochman had a newspaper career before becoming a full-time, freelance writer in 1928. Not only did he become a prolific writer of short stories, novels and screenplays, but as he was bi-lingual, he was in constant demand as a French translator, translating among others some of Simenon's Maigret stories. His later career included work for the U.S. Office of War Information, for the Commission on Government Security, for the U.S. Information Agency and for the Department of State. His best-known fictional character was the forensic expert Dr Daniel Webster Coffee of India. In 1950 he received an Edgar for his collection of stories, *Diagnosis: Homicide*.

Rather Cool for Mayhem (1951)

| C ★ ★ ★ ★ ★ | P ★ ★ ★ ★ ★ ★ ★ |
| R ★ ★ ★ ★ ★ | T ★ ★ ★ ★ ★ |

Recipe for Homicide (1952)

| C ★ ★ ★ ★ ★ | P ★ ★ ★ ★ ★ ★ ★ |
| R ★ ★ ★ ★ ★ ★ | T ★ ★ ★ ★ ★ |

BLOCK, Lawrence (1938) American mystery writer. There are two sides to Lawrence Block's writings, one serious, one comic. On the serious side is a book such as *Ariel*, the story of an evil child, which was a Book of the Month Club selection, no small honour. On the comic side is one of the most delectable char-

R = Readability   T = Tension

acters of the day, Bernie Rhodenbarr, the inimitable, unexpected burglar. Other series characters invented by Block are Evan Tanner and Matthew Scudder.

The Burglar Who Liked to Quote Kipling (1979)

C ★ ★ ★ ★ ★ ★	P ★ ★ ★ ★ ★ ★
R ★ ★ ★ ★ ★ ★	T ★ ★ ★ ★

Ariel (1980)

C ★ ★ ★ ★ ★ ★	P ★ ★ ★ ★ ★ ★
R ★ ★ ★ ★ ★ ★	T ★ ★ ★ ★ ★ ★

BOGGIS, David (1946) British spy writer and journalist, who has also written suspense stories as Gary Vaughan. The two Boggis books so far feature an ex-Australian Air Force freelance agent, David Bellamy, and are remarkable for technological expertise, made reasonably understandable. Otherwise adventure packs the pages.

A Time to Betray (1981)

C ★ ★ ★ ★ ★ ★	P ★ ★ ★ ★ ★ ★ ★
R ★ ★ ★ ★ ★ ★ ★	T ★ ★ ★ ★ ★ ★

BOLAND, John (1913-76) British thriller writer and playwright. Pretty prolific, Boland scored chiefly with *The League of Gentlemen,* a story of jobless ex-officers of the 1939-45 War banding together for a monster bank robbery. The participants featured in several later books. Boland is notable mainly for his unremitting inventiveness of plot, something that enabled him to write hundreds of short stories and several plays.

The League of Gentlemen (1958)

C ★ ★ ★	P ★ ★ ★ ★ ★ ★ ★ ★
R ★ ★ ★ ★ ★ ★ ★ ★	T ★ ★ ★ ★ ★

BONETT, John and Emery (both, 1906) Primarily British cinema writer-producers, John and Emery Bonett are adept mystery writers. Their stories are sophisticated, light and bright in their touch, with enough bite to keep the reader on his toes. Since their move to the Costa Brava some years back, they seem too busy with sun and sea to write mysteries. Their real names are John and Felicity Coulson.

This Side Murder (1967)
(*Murder on the Costa Brava* in U.S.)

C ★ ★ ★ ★ ★ ★	P ★ ★ ★ ★ ★ ★
R ★ ★ ★ ★ ★ ★	T ★ ★ ★ ★ ★ ★

BOUCHER, Anthony (1911-68) American mystery writer and critic. Anthony Boucher took over so completely from William A(nthony) P(arker) White that the true name seems the pseudonym. Before he became the noted mystery critic of the *New York Times,* he was mystery reviewer for the *San Francisco Chronicle.* He was also writing then his delightful mystery novels, both as Boucher and as H. H. Holmes. He had total recall memory for books and music, and for years produced an operatic radio programme in Berkeley, his home city. He turned from mystery to writing science-fiction and with a bookman friend, Jesse McComas, edited a top-ranking science-fiction magazine. His critiques had literary style, but also simplicity of style which made them collector's items. He always intended to write more books but once he was launched at the *New York Times* there was never enough time. The few Boucher and Holmes books extant are as delightful on re-reading as they were the first time around. He won a great many Edgars for criticism.

The Case of the Seven of Calvary (1937)

C ★ ★ ★ ★ ★ ★	P ★ ★ ★ ★ ★ ★
R ★ ★ ★ ★ ★ ★ ★	T ★ ★ ★ ★ ★

The Case of the Baker Street Irregulars (1940)

C ★ ★ ★ ★ ★ ★	P ★ ★ ★ ★ ★ ★
R ★ ★ ★ ★ ★ ★ ★	T ★ ★ ★ ★ ★

Nine Times Nine (Holmes) (1940)

C ★ ★ ★ ★ ★	P ★ ★ ★ ★ ★
R ★ ★ ★ ★ ★ ★ ★	T ★ ★ ★ ★ ★

C = Characterization   P = Plot

BOX, Edgar (1925) Gore Vidal, outstanding American novelist, wrote three highly amusing mysteries under the pseudonym of Edgar Box. The pseudonym was kept secret for many years, although Vidal did leak it to a few persons in the literary world. As Box, Vidal was a forerunner of the explicit sex scenes of today's mysteries. He however, satirized such scenes rather than permeating his pages with sophomoric hang-ups. His mysteries have been reprinted recently both in paperback editions and in an omnibus collection, with Edgar Box revealed as Gore Vidal.

Death in the Fifth Position (1952)

C ★★★★★★★	P ★★★★★★
R ★★★★★★★★	T ★★★★★

Death before Bedtime (1953)

C ★★★★★★★	P ★★★★★★
R ★★★★★★★★	T ★★★★★

Death Likes It Hot (1954)

C ★★★★★★★	P ★★★★★
R ★★★★★★★★	T ★★★★★

BRAHMS Caryl (1901) Pseudonym of Doris Caroline Abrahams. British novelist and playwright. Caryl Brahms in collaboration with S. J. Simon wrote (among a whole host of other novels) four crime fictions featuring Inspector Adam Quill. Distinguished by the characteristic Brahms/Simon free-wheeling wit, these novels belong strictly with the rest of the *oeuvre* in the world of comic rather than detective fiction.

A Bullet in the Ballet (1937)

C ★★★★★★★	P ★★★★★★
R ★★★★★★★	T ★★★★

BRAMAH, Ernest (1868-1942) British short story writer. One of the crime writers of the early days who has survived (just, perhaps) into a sort of classic status. He invented the blind detective, Max Carrados. At their best the Carrados stories use the hero's disability in a strikingly positive way to solve riddles or escape from fraught situations which only a blind person could. Bramah also wrote the Chinese pastiche stories about Kai Lung.

Best Max Carrados Detective Stories (1972)

C ★★★★★★★	P ★★★★★★★★
R ★★★★★★★★	T ★★★★★★★

BRAND, Christianna (1909) British detective novelist. (Also writes as China Thompson; Mary Anne Ashe; Mary Roland; Annabel Jones). After an Eastern childhood, Christianna Brand had many jobs, including governess, shop-assistant, model, secretary, before her first book appeared in 1941. A light humorous touch, a shrewd eye and a considerable talent for puzzling are the qualities which give her books their characteristic flavour.

Green for Danger (1944)

C ★★★★★★★★	P ★★★★★★★★★
R ★★★★★★★	T ★★★★★★★

Cat and Mouse (1950)

C ★★★★★★★	P ★★★★★★★★
R ★★★★★★★★	T ★★★★★★★★

Christianna Brand

R = Readability   T = Tension

BREAN, Herbert (1907-73) American mystery writer. Brean, a noted newsman and magazine editor (United Press International, *Life*), and lecturer on mystery writing, (Columbia University and New York University), was an author of special quality in mystery. Two of his books received Edgar nominations for Best of Year. He wrote numerous non-fiction books and edited the *Life Treasury of American Folklore,* a subject he had used to fine advantage in his mystery books.

Wilders Walk Away (1948)

C ★ ★ ★ ★ ★	P ★ ★ ★ ★ ★ ★
R ★ ★ ★ ★ ★ ★	T ★ ★ ★ ★ ★ ★

The Clock Strikes Thirteen (1952)

C ★ ★ ★ ★ ★	P ★ ★ ★ ★ ★ ★ ★
R ★ ★ ★ ★ ★ ★ ★	T ★ ★ ★ ★ ★ ★ ★

The Traces of Brillhart (1960)

C ★ ★ ★ ★ ★	P ★ ★ ★ ★ ★ ★ ★
R ★ ★ ★ ★ ★ ★ ★	T ★ ★ ★ ★ ★ ★

BRETT, Simon (1945) British detective novelist. A playwright and former radio and television producer, Brett has as his hero the seedy but sympathetic actor, Charles Paris, and each book depicts, often with tart criticism, a different facet of British showbusiness. Their murder plots are plainly less interesting to the author.

The Dead Side of the Mike (1980)

C ★ ★ ★ ★ ★ ★	P ★ ★ ★ ★
R ★ ★ ★ ★ ★ ★ ★	T ★ ★ ★

Murder Unprompted (1982)

C ★ ★ ★ ★ ★ ★	P ★ ★ ★ ★
R ★ ★ ★ ★ ★ ★ ★	T ★ ★ ★ ★

BRIDGE, Ann (1889-1974) British espionage novelist, pen-name of Lady Mary Dolling O'Malley. The resourceful Julia Probyn, an amateur in the field of espionage, is the protagonist in eight novels which are exciting, sometimes wryly amusing, enjoyable as travelogues, but devoid of the obligatory brutality of so many other spy writers.

The Lighthearted Quest (1956)

C ★ ★ ★ ★ ★	P ★ ★ ★ ★ ★ ★
R ★ ★ ★ ★ ★ ★ ★	T ★ ★ ★ ★ ★ ★

Emergency in the Pyrenees (1965)

C ★ ★ ★ ★ ★	P ★ ★ ★ ★ ★
R ★ ★ ★ ★ ★ ★	T ★ ★ ★ ★ ★ ★

BRIERLEY, David (1936) British espionage novelist. The two books he wrote up to 1981 showed a mind of considerable intelligence, sharp observation of contemporary mores in Europe and Britain and something of the early Le Carré (q.v.) mould.

Big Bear, Little Bear (1981)

C ★ ★ ★ ★ ★ ★	P ★ ★ ★ ★ ★ ★
R ★ ★ ★ ★ ★	T ★ ★ ★ ★ ★ ★

Ann Bridge

BROCK, Lynn (1877-1943) Irish detective novelist. Although often ranked with the Crofts (q.v.) school of meticulous plotting, he could be (as in *The Kink*) sexually explicit for his time. Colonel Gore's investigations contained more action than those of his contemporaries, as he pursued ingenious criminals against well-drawn settings.

The Deductions of Colonel Gore (1924)

C ★ ★ ★ ★	P ★ ★ ★ ★ ★
R ★ ★ ★ ★ ★ ★	T ★ ★

Colonel Gore's Third Case: The Kink (1927)

C ★ ★ ★ ★ ★	P ★ ★ ★ ★ ★ ★ ★
R ★ ★ ★ ★ ★ ★ ★	T ★ ★ ★

The Stoat (1940)

C ★ ★ ★ ★	P ★ ★ ★ ★ ★ ★
R ★ ★ ★ ★ ★ ★ ★	T ★ ★

BROWN, Carter (1923) British hardboiled private eye novelist, pen-name of Alan Geoffrey Yates, who has spent his writing career in Australia but has set innumerable "pulp" novels against the glamour, sex and corruption of Los Angeles, San Francisco and Hollywood. His men are men, and his women are willing.

The Lover (1958)

C ★ ★	P ★ ★ ★ ★
R ★ ★ ★ ★ ★ ★ ★ ★	T ★ ★ ★ ★ ★ ★

The Bump and Grind Murders (1964)

C ★ ★	P ★ ★ ★ ★
R ★ ★ ★ ★ ★ ★ ★ ★	T ★ ★ ★ ★ ★ ★ ★

BROWN, Frederic (1906-72) American mystery writer. Brown was one of the leading writers to come out of the pulps in the thirties and forties to become noted in mystery short story and novel as well as a leader in science fiction and fantasy. *A Key to Frederic Brown's Wonderland*, an introduction to his work was published in 1981, complete with bibliography. A critic

called him "one of the most original and complex writers", and Mickey Spillane (q.v.) is quoted as naming him "his favourite writer of all time." His first novel, *The Fabulous Clipjoint* took Edgar honours for Best First Novel of its year.

The Fabulous Clipjoint (1949)

C ★ ★ ★ ★ ★ ★	P ★ ★ ★ ★ ★ ★ ★
R ★ ★ ★ ★ ★ ★ ★	T ★ ★ ★ ★ ★ ★ ★ ★

The Screaming Mimi (1950)

C ★ ★ ★ ★ ★ ★	P ★ ★ ★ ★ ★ ★
R ★ ★ ★ ★ ★ ★	T ★ ★ ★ ★ ★ ★ ★

The Five Day Nightmare (1963)

C ★ ★ ★ ★ ★ ★	P ★ ★ ★ ★ ★ ★ ★
R ★ ★ ★ ★ ★ ★	T ★ ★ ★ ★ ★ ★ ★

BRUCE, Leo (1903-79) British detective novelist, pen-name of Rupert Croft-Cooke, novelist and autobiographer over many volumes. A consistently excellent purveyor of the classic detective puzzle, whether featuring Sergeant Beef in humorous and often satirical vein or the more conventional schoolmaster-detective Carolus Deene; literate, ingenious, and often displaying a devastating sleight of hand.

Case for Three Detectives (1936)

C ★ ★ ★ ★ ★ ★ ★ ★	P ★ ★ ★ ★ ★ ★ ★ ★
R ★ ★ ★ ★ ★ ★ ★ ★	T ★ ★ ★

A Bone and a Hank of Hair (1961)

C ★ ★ ★ ★ ★ ★ ★ ★	P ★ ★ ★ ★ ★ ★ ★
R ★ ★ ★ ★ ★ ★ ★ ★	T ★ ★ ★

BUCHAN, John (1875-1940) Scottish adventure novelist and, as a primary career, statesman, eventually Lord Tweedsmuir, Governor-General of Canada. "Buchanesque" has become a standard reviewer's adjective to describe the adventure story that is unhesitating, real owing to the decent depth of its characters, totally plausible and finally having about it some hint of powerful forces affecting a society. Writing during and after World War I, naturally the theme of the glory of the British imperial idea lies firmly behind his work. That idea is no longer popu-

R = Readability   T = Tension

lar, but it was so at a period now so distant that any offensiveness it may have had has long since been dissipated. The same can be said of his portrayals of "gentlemen" imbued with loyalties and notions no longer universally upheld. The books have become historical novels, but the stories they tell are so well done that they defy time. In his autobiography *Memory Hold-the-Door* (1940) Buchan writes interestingly of his art. He says he always told his stories to himself, or rather found them being "told to him", before he set pen to paper, putting his people into difficult situations and waiting to see how they behaved. He liked people with "the knack of just squeezing out of unpleasant places" and found excitement best generated by giving them hurried journeys, races against time.

John Buchan

The Thirty-nine Steps (1915)

C ★ ★ ★ ★ ★ ★ ★	P ★ ★ ★ ★ ★ ★ ★ ★
R ★ ★ ★ ★ ★ ★ ★ ★ ★	T ★ ★ ★ ★ ★ ★ ★ ★

Greenmantle (1916)

C ★ ★ ★ ★ ★ ★ ★	P ★ ★ ★ ★ ★ ★ ★
R ★ ★ ★ ★ ★ ★ ★ ★ ★	T ★ ★ ★ ★ ★ ★ ★

Huntingtower (1922)

C ★ ★ ★ ★ ★ ★ ★	P ★ ★ ★ ★ ★ ★ ★
R ★ ★ ★ ★ ★ ★ ★ ★ ★	T ★ ★ ★ ★ ★ ★

BUCKLEY, William F., Jr (1925) American mystery writer. New York born William Buckley, controversial personality in print and on television, educated as a boy in England, was graduated with honours from Yale University in 1950. It was at Yale that he first came to notoriety with his writings, ultra-conservative at a time of ultra-liberalism. Buckley is an esteemed intellectual and the controversies he delights in are leavened by his humour. He came recently into mystery with two books in espionage style.

Saving the Queen (1976)

C ★ ★ ★ ★ ★	P ★ ★ ★ ★ ★
R ★ ★ ★ ★ ★ ★	T ★ ★ ★ ★

William Buckley

BURKE, John (1922) British thriller writer, who writes also as Jonathan Burke. Suspense is the key feature of his work rather than the puzzle element, but he displays great versatility. Among his prolific output, his forays into psychology and the macabre are of note, including the cases of psychic investigator Dr Caspian.

Echo of Barbara (1959)

C ★★★★★★	P ★★★★★★★★
R ★★★★★★★★★	T ★★★★★★★★

The Devil's Footsteps (1976)

C ★★★★★	P ★★★★★★★
R ★★★★★★★	T ★★★★★★★

BURLEY, W. J. (1914) British detective novelist. His books generally feature Superintendent Wycliffe, a West Country detective with something of the introspective outlook and immersive technique of a Maigret. The result is crime novels of unusual thoughtfulness.

Wycliffe and the Pea-green Boat (1975)

C ★★★★★★★	P ★★★★★★★
R ★★★★★★	T ★★★★

Wycliffe's Wild-goose Chase (1982)

C ★★★★★★★	P ★★★★★★★
R ★★★★★★	T ★★★★

BURNETT, W. R. (1899) American novelist. W. R. Burnett is one of the most important American fiction writers of the twentieth century. He is not a mystery writer and has never been one. He was primarily a writer of westerns until in 1929, he created *Little Caesar*, the first important piece of fiction about the power of the underworld. Burnett became labeled as a "tough" writer and miscalled on occasion a mystery writer. His awards are too many to list. They include: the prestigious O. Henry Memorial award for short story in 1930, Writers' Guild best screenplay 1963, Academy Award nominations for several of his screenplays. In 1980 the Mystery Writers of America honoured him with a Grand Masters Edgar.

Little Caesar (1929)

C ★★★★★★	P ★★★★★★★
R ★★★★★★★	T ★★★★★★★

High Sierra (1940)

C ★★★★★★	P ★★★★★★
R ★★★★★★★	T ★★★★★★

The Asphalt Jungle (1949)

C ★★★★★★	P ★★★★★★
R ★★★★★★★	T ★★★★★★★

BURNS, Rex (1935) American mystery writer. Burns is San Diego, California born. He received degrees from Stanford University and the University of Minnesota, taught English in Missouri, and since 1968 has been a professor of English at the University of Colorado in Denver. Anyone not knowing his background would believe him to be native to Denver, he has made this location so much his own. His particular interest is in the native-born Spanish-Americans and their varying position in the community. Burns took the Best First Novel Edgar from the Mystery Writers of America for *The Alvarez Journal*.

The Alvarez Journal (1975)

C ★★★★★★★	P ★★★★★★
R ★★★★★★	T ★★★★★

Speak for the Dead (1978)

C ★★★★★★★	P ★★★★★★
R ★★★★★★★	T ★★★★★

BURTON, Miles (1884-1965) British detective story writer. He was also John Rhode (q.v.), the somewhat better known writer in much the same vein of classic-type detective stories (a total of 63 between 1930 and 1960). For long he contrived to keep the secret of his two identities, which continued even after his death. The Burton books feature Desmond Merrion, amateur sleuth, and stolid, sometimes wide-eyed Inspector Arnold.

R = Readability   T = Tension

Gwendoline Butler

BUTLER, Gwendoline (1922) British detective novelist, who began writing in 1956. A good many of her odd, intuitive, compelling books featured a rootless, self-educated London policeman named Coffin. *Coffin for Pandora* (*Olivia* in U.S.) won the Silver Dagger of the Crime Writers Association in Britain in 1973. Under the Butler name she has also written Victorian crime romances, and she is, too, Jennie Melville (q.v.)

Coffin for Pandora (1973)

C ★ ★ ★ ★ ★ ★ ★	P ★ ★ ★ ★ ★
R ★ ★ ★ ★ ★ ★ ★	T ★ ★ ★ ★ ★

A Coffin for the Canary (1974)

C ★ ★ ★ ★ ★ ★ ★	P ★ ★ ★ ★ ★
R ★ ★ ★ ★ ★ ★ ★	T ★ ★ ★ ★ ★ ★

The Brides of Friedberg (1977)

C ★ ★ ★ ★ ★ ★	P ★ ★ ★ ★ ★
R ★ ★ ★ ★ ★ ★ ★	T ★ ★ ★ ★ ★ ★

Death in the Tunnel (1936)
(*Dark in the Tunnel* in U.S.)

C ★ ★ ★	P ★ ★ ★ ★ ★ ★ ★
R ★ ★ ★ ★ ★ ★ ★	T ★ ★

BUSBY, Roger (1941) British police procedural novelist. A journalist and later a police public relations officer, Busby's books are among the best informed and most effective police procedurals of the British school. They are also by no means lacking in the human touch.

Pattern of Violence (1973)

C ★ ★ ★ ★ ★ ★ ★	P ★ ★ ★ ★ ★
R ★ ★ ★ ★ ★ ★ ★	T ★ ★ ★ ★ ★ ★ ★

Garvey's Code (1978)

C ★ ★ ★ ★ ★ ★	P ★ ★ ★ ★ ★
R ★ ★ ★ ★ ★ ★ ★	T ★ ★ ★ ★ ★ ★

BUSH, Christopher (1885-1973) British detective novelist. Throughout some eighty books, except when writing as Michael Home, he never forsook his genial detective Ludovic Travers. Competent, at times erudite, and a neat purveyor of the seemingly unbreakable alibi, Bush was one of the hardy perennials of the thoroughly English school.

The Case of the Burnt Bohemian (1953)

C ★ ★ ★ ★ ★	P ★ ★ ★ ★ ★ ★ ★
R ★ ★ ★ ★ ★ ★ ★	T ★ ★

CAIN, James M. (1892-1977) American novelist. Cain was a bigger than life man, as hot-headed and tough-minded as any of his characters. He was a fighter for what he believed to be right, and a man to have on your side in a fight. He wasn't a tough guy. His father was a college president, and after Cain took his Bachelor's and Master's degrees, he was for several years a professor at St. John's College in his home town of Annapolis, Maryland. He became a top newspaperman on the Baltimore papers, and later on the great *New York World*. He gravitated to Hollywood where he was to become an important screenwriter. His first book, *The Postman Always Rings Twice*, was written when he was 42 years old. It was an instant classic, and is still a major sales item after almost fifty years in print. It was written in the lean dialogue and terse narrative style of the late twenties and early thirties, often attributed to Hemingway, but actually the style of the pulp magazines of that day. Although Cain was never in the mystery writer category, because of his crime novels, notably *Postman* and *Double Indemnity*, he was honoured by The Mystery Writers of America with a Grand Master Edgar in 1969.

The Postman Always Rings Twice (1934)

C ★ ★ ★ ★ ★ ★	P ★ ★ ★ ★ ★ ★
R ★ ★ ★ ★ ★ ★	T ★ ★ ★ ★ ★ ★

Serenade (1937)

C ★ ★ ★ ★ ★ ★	P ★ ★ ★ ★ ★
R ★ ★ ★ ★ ★ ★	T ★ ★ ★ ★ ★ ★

Double Indemnity (1943)

C ★ ★ ★ ★ ★ ★ ★	P ★ ★ ★ ★ ★ ★ ★
R ★ ★ ★ ★ ★ ★ ★	T ★ ★ ★ ★ ★ ★ ★

CANDY, Edward (1925) British novelist, not all detection, pen-name of Barbara Alison Neville. Her medical qualifications and experience serve her well in presenting authentic backgrounds and sympathetic characterization. Elegant, clever and literate, her detective novels have been few in number but very highly regarded in the field.

Which Doctor (1953)

C ★ ★ ★ ★ ★ ★ ★	P ★ ★ ★ ★ ★ ★ ★
R ★ ★ ★ ★ ★ ★	T ★ ★ ★

Bones of Contention (1954)

C ★ ★ ★ ★ ★ ★ ★	P ★ ★ ★ ★ ★ ★
R ★ ★ ★ ★ ★ ★	T ★ ★ ★

Words for Murder, Perhaps (1971)

C ★ ★ ★ ★ ★ ★ ★	P ★ ★ ★ ★ ★ ★
R ★ ★ ★ ★ ★	T ★ ★

CANNAN, Joanna (1898-1961) British novelist, not all detection. Her tales of unexceptional Inspectors Northeast and Price are not strictly in the mould of the classical English mystery, but are interesting for their exposure of smouldering emotions under the mask of domesticity; more than adequate in her plotting and characterization, she can also spring a surprise.

Death at The Dog (1940)

C ★ ★ ★ ★ ★ ★	P ★ ★ ★ ★ ★ ★
R ★ ★ ★ ★ ★ ★ ★	T ★ ★

Murder Included (1950)
(*Poisonous Relations* in U.S.)

C ★ ★ ★ ★ ★ ★	P ★ ★ ★ ★ ★ ★ ★
R ★ ★ ★ ★ ★ ★ ★	T ★ ★

Victor Canning

CANNING, Victor (1911) English novelist who in his later works turned mostly to espionage and adventure, writing some 40 such books between 1947 and 1980. The best of his espionage novels are marked out by a strong feeling for the life of the countryside, whether in England or elsewhere, an awareness of man's links with the unsleeping universe of instinct. It is this that gives the strain of romantic love which frequently appears in the books its truth, power and compellingness. His people are almost always totally convincing even when they become involved in situations of high melodrama, again a not infrequent occurrence. Wisdom is not perhaps the quality one

R = Readability   T = Tension

would expect to find in crime novels, nor might it be thought an asset; yet Canning has it, and in the best of his suspense stories it gives an added depth which makes for a tension that is the more powerful for being real.

The Rainbird Pattern (1972)

C ★ ★ ★ ★ ★ ★ ★	P ★ ★ ★ ★ ★ ★ ★ ★ ★ ★
R ★ ★ ★ ★ ★ ★ ★ ★	T ★ ★ ★ ★ ★ ★ ★ ★ ★

The Mask of Memory (1974)

C ★ ★ ★ ★ ★ ★ ★	P ★ ★ ★ ★ ★ ★ ★
R ★ ★ ★ ★ ★ ★ ★ ★ ★	T ★ ★ ★ ★ ★ ★ ★ ★

Birdcage (1978)

C ★ ★ ★ ★ ★ ★ ★ ★	P ★ ★ ★ ★ ★ ★ ★
R ★ ★ ★ ★ ★ ★ ★ ★ ★ ★	T ★ ★ ★ ★ ★ ★ ★ ★ ★

CARMICHAEL, Harry (1908-79) British detective novelist. Between 1952 and 1978 he wrote 41 novels, mostly featuring Quinn, an obnoxious, flippant journalist, and Piper, an insurance assessor, working in tandem. The books are in the Golden Age style, notably accurate in detail, their puzzles to be solved by ratiocination. He was also Hartley Howard (q.v.)

False Evidence (1976)

C ★ ★ ★ ★	P ★ ★ ★ ★ ★ ★ ★
R ★ ★ ★ ★ ★ ★ ★	T ★ ★ ★ ★

CARNAC, Carol (1894-1958) British detective novelist. She wrote between 1936 and 1958, a stalwart of the Golden Age. The better books under thei pseudonym (she is also E. C. R. Lorac q.v.) feature Inspector Rivers and the lively Inspector Laing. The puzzle is the thing.

Impact of the Evidence (1954)

C ★ ★ ★ ★ ★	P ★ ★ ★ ★ ★ ★ ★
R ★ ★ ★ ★ ★	T ★

CARR, A. H. Z. (1902-1971) American writer whose works include many short mystery stories and one significant detective novel, *Finding Maubee*. This novel, with voodoo murder against a skilfully presented Caribbean background, is a most memorable vehicle for one of the few black fictional detectives and interest is heightened by contrasts of ethnic cultures.

Finding Maubee (1970)
(*The Calypso Murders* in U.K.)

C ★ ★ ★ ★ ★ ★ ★	P ★ ★ ★ ★ ★ ★ ★ ★
R ★ ★ ★ ★ ★ ★	T ★ ★ ★ ★

CARR, Glyn (1908) British detective novelist, pen-name of Showell Styles, novelist. He specializes in murder with a mountaineering or rock-climbing background, always featuring pompous actor-manager Sir Abercrombie Lewker, and this provides some unusual murder methods and a very closed circle of suspects. Clever plotting and characterization predominate, together with topographical skill.

Murder of an Owl (1956)

C ★ ★ ★ ★ ★ ★	P ★ ★ ★ ★ ★ ★ ★
R ★ ★ ★ ★ ★ ★ ★ ★	T ★ ★ ★ ★

CARR, John Dickson (1906-77) American detective novelist resident in England for many years, also using the pseudonym Carter Dickson (q.v.) and specializing in "locked room" mysteries and other seemingly impossible crimes, often with apparently supernatural elements but always with satisfyingly logical solutions. Carr is incomparable in this sub-genre, his ingenious variations giving every appearance of being inexhaustible; basically his skill is in misdirection, and many of his explanations are so simple as to be easily overlooked by even the most vigilant reader. His early novels feature a colourful Parisian *juge,* Bencolin, but his most memorable character is Dr. Gideon Fell; a Chestertonian figure, Fell thunders through a long series of novels with a consistently high standard of plot construction down to the last dovetail, and liberal dashes of humour. From 1950, Carr occasionally rang the changes on his enthralling crimes and his penchant for the macabre by using historical settings to good effect.

The Three Coffins (1935)
(*The Hollow Man* in U.K.)

C ★ ★ ★ ★ ★ ★	P ★ ★ ★ ★ ★ ★ ★ ★ ★
R ★ ★ ★ ★ ★ ★ ★ ★ ★	T ★ ★ ★ ★ ★

The Burning Court (1937)

C ★ ★ ★ ★ ★ ★	P ★ ★ ★ ★ ★ ★ ★ ★ ★
R ★ ★ ★ ★ ★ ★ ★ ★ ★	T ★ ★ ★

The Devil in Velvet (1951)

C ★ ★ ★ ★ ★	P ★ ★ ★ ★ ★ ★ ★ ★
R ★ ★ ★ ★ ★ ★ ★ ★	T ★ ★ ★ ★

CARVIC, Heron British detective novelist and, primarily, actor. He wrote five novels about Miss Seeton, part Victorian spinster, part fey lady. The setting is the English village, and the dialogue, as is to be expected from an actor, is a pleasure to read. The tone is brisk and somewhat facetious.

Miss Seeton Draws the Line (1969)

C ★ ★ ★ ★ ★ ★	P ★ ★ ★ ★ ★
R ★ ★ ★ ★ ★ ★ ★	T ★

CASPARY, Vera (1904) American novelist and playwright. Vera Caspary has written more for theatre and screen, and more non-mystery novels than mystery, but because of the classic *Laura*, she is always deemed a mystery author. Without any clutter of adjectives or picture words, Caspary has the gift of creating a character from within, exposing the inherent sadness beneath a polished surface. *Laura* was a critical and commercial success not only in book form but also on stage and screen.

Laura (1942)

C ★ ★ ★ ★ ★ ★ ★	P ★ ★ ★ ★ ★ ★ ★
R ★ ★ ★ ★ ★ ★ ★ ★ ★	T ★ ★ ★ ★ ★ ★ ★

Bedelia (1944)

C ★ ★ ★ ★ ★ ★ ★	P ★ ★ ★ ★ ★ ★ ★
R ★ ★ ★ ★ ★ ★ ★ ★	T ★ ★ ★ ★ ★ ★ ★

Evvie (1960)

C ★ ★ ★ ★ ★ ★ ★	P ★ ★ ★ ★ ★ ★ ★
R ★ ★ ★ ★ ★ ★ ★ ★	T ★ ★ ★ ★ ★ ★ ★

CECIL, Henry (1902-76) British humorous crime writer. A County Court judge (Henry Leon), he wrote successful plays, lightly learned law works and crime stories that featured aspects of the law, some veering towards the pure puzzle tale, mostly frankly amusing though often with something quite serious to say underneath. The style is notably easy and wit-sprinkled.

Brothers in Law (1955)

C ★ ★ ★ ★ ★ ★ ★	P ★ ★ ★ ★ ★ ★ ★ ★
R ★ ★ ★ ★ ★ ★ ★ ★	T ★

Alibi for A Judge (1960)

C ★ ★ ★ ★ ★ ★ ★ ★	P ★ ★ ★ ★ ★ ★ ★ ★
R ★ ★ ★ ★ ★ ★ ★ ★ ★	T ★ ★ ★

The Asking Price (1966)

C ★ ★ ★ ★ ★ ★ ★ ★	P ★ ★ ★ ★ ★ ★ ★
R ★ ★ ★ ★ ★ ★ ★ ★	T ★ ★

CHANCE, John Newton (1911) British writer of thrillers and (as John Lymington) science fiction, who also produced (as J. Drummond) many Sexton Blake novelettes of the forties and fifties. His prolific thriller output has been patchy in quality, with his early titles generally displaying a more craftsmanlike attention to plotting and characterization than his later ones.

The Eye in Darkness (1946)

C ★ ★ ★ ★ ★	P ★ ★ ★ ★ ★ ★
R ★ ★ ★ ★ ★ ★ ★ ★ ★	T ★ ★ ★ ★ ★

CHANDLER, Raymond (1888-1959) American detective novelist. Born in Chicago, he was educated in Britain, at Dulwich College, and in the 1914-18 War fought with the Gordon Highlanders and was twice decorated. Afterwards he became a successful oil executive in Los Angeles until the Depression when, jobless and needing money, he began to write for the pulp magazines and produced his first novel, *The Big Sleep*, in 1939. He soon attained tremendous popularity, retained to this day, chiefly from the persona of

R = Readability   T = Tension

his private-eye hero, Philip Marlowe, tough, laconically wise-cracking, fearlessly judging, a man of honour, never rich despite the cases he gets to the bottom of usually among clients who are both very wealthy and not a little corrupt. All the seven novels that brought Chandler to the heights of the genre and many of his short stories are set in California, chiefly in the Los Angeles of the thirties and forties, a city which he depicts in its seaminess but also in its beauty with love and a sharp eye and a tremendous evocativeness. The books have received enormous and discerning praise. W. H. Auden, the poet, called them "works of art" rather than crime novels, but their achievement is that they are both. Yet it may be said against them that they are sometimes over-lush in the language, that Chandler was too conscious of being a writer, even a phrase maker, to do for this sort of story, which he with Dashiell Hammett (q.v.) dragged from the formless body of sensation literature, what could at the very best be done with it. There is, too, an occasional hint of the send-up in his writing, as if he did not altogether trust the sub-genre he had helped discover and had memorably defined in a famous essay "The Simple Art of Murder" (1944). Yet the books are likely to live as long as crime is written of and readers want to read about it.

Raymond Chandler

Leslie Charteris

The Big Sleep (1939)

C ★ ★ ★ ★ ★ ★ ★ ★   P ★ ★ ★ ★ ★ ★ ★
R ★ ★ ★ ★ ★ ★ ★ ★ ★   T ★ ★ ★ ★ ★ ★ ★ ★

The High Window (1942)

C ★ ★ ★ ★ ★ ★ ★ ★   P ★ ★ ★ ★ ★ ★ ★ ★
R ★ ★ ★ ★ ★ ★ ★ ★ ★   T ★ ★ ★ ★ ★ ★ ★ ★

The Little Sister (1949)

C ★ ★ ★ ★ ★ ★ ★ ★   P ★ ★ ★ ★ ★ ★ ★ ★
R ★ ★ ★ ★ ★ ★ ★ ★ ★   T ★ ★ ★ ★ ★ ★ ★ ★

CHARTERIS, Leslie (1907) Naturalized American mystery writer. Born Leslie Charles Bowyer Yin of a Chinese father and English mother, Charteris's reputation rests almost entirely on his 'Saint' books. These feature Simon Templar, a smooth, hedonistic, likeable Robin Hood character, and their bright and breezy style and slightly sketched backgrounds have preserved them from dating as quickly as some others in this vein.

The Saint in New York (1935)

C ★ ★ ★ ★ ★   P ★ ★ ★ ★ ★ ★ ★
R ★ ★ ★ ★ ★ ★ ★ ★   T ★ ★ ★ ★ ★ ★ ★

The Saint Goes West (1942)

C ★ ★ ★ ★ ★   P ★ ★ ★ ★ ★ ★
R ★ ★ ★ ★ ★ ★ ★   T ★ ★ ★ ★ ★ ★ ★ ★

G. K. Chesterton

CHASE, James Hadley (1906) British crime novelist. Born in London, a Children's Encyclopaedia salesman in his teens, Chase utilized more adult reference books to project pictures of the American crime scene which even Americans enjoy. Violence and sex plus an insistent narrative technique are the key.

No Orchids For Miss Blandish (1939) (*The Villain and the Virgin* in U.S.)

C ★ ★ ★ ★ ★	P ★ ★ ★ ★ ★ ★ ★ ★
R ★ ★ ★ ★ ★ ★ ★ ★	T ★ ★ ★ ★ ★ ★ ★ ★

CHASTAIN, Thomas American police procedural novelist and journalist. He writes chiefly police stories starring Inspector Max Kauffman, of New York's Sixteenth Precinct, who to the usual attributes of a successful senior detective adds large personal wealth. The cases he gets involved in have a similar dimension of the super – a plot to black out all New York, a plot to take over a whole precinct house.

High Voltage (1980)

C ★ ★ ★ ★ ★	P ★ ★ ★ ★ ★ ★ ★
R ★ ★ ★ ★ ★ ★ ★	T ★ ★ ★ ★ ★ ★ ★ ★

The Diamond Exchange (1981)

C ★ ★ ★ ★ ★	P ★ ★ ★ ★ ★ ★
R ★ ★ ★ ★ ★ ★ ★	T ★ ★ ★ ★ ★ ★ ★

CHESTERTON, G. K. (1874-1936) English novelist, poet, essayist, literary critic, polemicist, biographer and first President of the Detection Club. His fame in the crime field rests on his stories of Father Brown, the inoffensive little priest with the gift of solving the most impenetrable puzzles. But his novel *The Man Who Was Thursday*, while from its serious intent (carried out with immense brio) it must be ranked as a pure novel is also a fine story of anarchists at work. Indeed, there is also a considerable measure of moral intent in the engaging Father Brown tales. Chesterton saw paradox as a mainspring of existence, and almost all the stories are paradoxes ingeniously made to reveal the reality of mysterious events. "A splash of blood that grew vivid as it cried for vengeance" is at last seen to be just the red light cast by stained glass; a man wears a purple wig, so that no one will look at his deformed, giveaway ear; a black man makes himself inconspicuous by posing as a blacked-up minstrel. But the stories work, most of them, as pure crime puzzles, some dazzlingly.

The Man Who Was Thursday (1908)

C ★ ★ ★ ★ ★	P ★ ★ ★ ★ ★ ★ ★
R ★ ★ ★ ★ ★ ★ ★ ★	T ★ ★ ★ ★ ★ ★ ★

The Innocence of Father Brown (1911)

C ★ ★ ★ ★ ★ ★ ★	P ★ ★ ★ ★ ★ ★ ★ ★ ★
R ★ ★ ★ ★ ★ ★ ★ ★ ★	T ★ ★ ★ ★ ★ ★ ★

The Wisdom of Father Brown (1929)

C ★ ★ ★ ★ ★ ★ ★	P ★ ★ ★ ★ ★ ★ ★ ★
R ★ ★ ★ ★ ★ ★ ★ ★ ★	T ★ ★ ★ ★ ★ ★ ★

CHEYNEY, Peter (1896-1951) British mystery writer. Songwriter, bookmaker, politician, journalist, Cheyney was almost as prolific in his careers as he was in his writing. Best known for his Lemmy Caution books which brought the feel of the American hard nosed private-eye novel to a London setting, he was accused of being sadistic, spurious

R = Readability   T = Tension

and fascist in his writing. His books were certainly tough and excitingly different from most contemporaneous British crime writing.

This Man is Dangerous (1936)

C ★ ★ ★ ★ ★	P ★ ★ ★ ★ ★
R ★ ★ ★ ★ ★ ★ ★	T ★ ★ ★ ★ ★ ★

CHILDERS, Erskine (1870-1922) British novelist and Irish patriot. He wrote only one work of fiction, *The Riddle of the Sands*, but it is a sober classic, a tale of yachting and spying written to warn Britain of the German menace in 1903 and still grippingly readable long after its message is meaningless. After the 1914-18 War Childers settled in Dublin, became heavily involved in politics, joined the Irish Republican Army and was caught and shot.

The Riddle of the Sands (1903)

C ★ ★ ★ ★ ★ ★ ★	P ★ ★ ★ ★ ★ ★ ★ ★ ★
R ★ ★ ★ ★ ★ ★ ★ ★ ★	T ★ ★ ★ ★ ★ ★ ★

CHRISTIE, Agatha (1890-1976) British detective story and thriller writer. Created a Dame Commander of the Order of the British Empire, 1971. She was a towering figure in crime literature. First, as the author more than any other who consolidated the classic mystery novel in many books that were this alone, five or six of which set a standard that bettered anything written earlier and are unlikely ever to be excelled. Secondly, she towers simply because she sold more books than any other writer in any field, barring only the Bible and Shakespeare. To some extent she owed this to the bandwagon effect. For people the world over her name became a shorthand symbol for "the mystery story". But her work was good enough to stand up to this. She wrote splendidly simply, in simple, good English with plenty of accurately rendered dialogue, however marvellously complicated her plots were. She told a good story and resisted regularly any temptation to digress or embroider. She knew just what she wanted to do and just what she could do, and she did just that and no more. Yet her first book, the excellent *The Mysterious Affair at Styles* (1920) was rejected by six publishers before gaining a modest success, and even the controversial *The Murder of Roger Ackroyd* (1926) which came out shortly before she disappeared for nine days and was the centre of a sensational press jamboree sold by later standards a modest enough initial count. Yet gradually, interspersing thrillers, which she found easy to do though she did not do them with any of the brilliance of her mysteries, with the classical whodunits that constitute her chief claim

to enduring fame, her sales rose and rose until at last they became simply too numerous to tally.

Agatha
Christie

The Murder of Roger Ackroyd (1920)

C ★ ★ ★ ★ ★ ★ ★	P ★ ★ ★ ★ ★ ★ ★ ★ ★
R ★ ★ ★ ★ ★ ★ ★ ★ ★	T ★ ★ ★ ★ ★ ★ ★

Ten Little Niggers (1939)
(*And Then There Were None* in U.S.)

C ★ ★ ★ ★ ★	P ★ ★ ★ ★ ★ ★ ★ ★ ★
R ★ ★ ★ ★ ★ ★ ★ ★	T ★ ★ ★ ★ ★ ★ ★ ★

Sleeping Murder (1976)

C ★ ★ ★ ★ ★	P ★ ★ ★ ★ ★ ★ ★ ★
R ★ ★ ★ ★ ★ ★ ★	T ★ ★ ★ ★ ★

C = Characterization   P = Plot

CLARK, Douglas (1919) British detective novelist and pharmaceutical advertising executive. His mysteries generally have some medical point embedded in them. His detectives are Chief Superintendent Masters "who's reckoned to be the Great-I-Am" of Scotland Yard, and Chief Inspector Green, between whom there is a quiet running war laced with mutual respect. The books are notable for their solid detail. Douglas Clark has also written as Peter Hosier and James Ditton.

The Longest Pleasure (1981)

| C ★ ★ ★ ★ ★ | P ★ ★ ★ ★ ★ ★ ★ |
| R ★ ★ ★ ★ ★ ★ | T ★ ★ ★ |

CLARK, Eric (1937) British espionage novelist. A highly experienced foreign correspondent he has brought his expert knowledge to bear on spy stories notable for the accuracy of their backgrounds and the daring of their ideas.

Send in the Lions (1981)

| C ★ ★ ★ ★ | P ★ ★ ★ ★ ★ ★ |
| R ★ ★ ★ ★ ★ ★ ★ | T ★ ★ ★ ★ ★ ★ ★ |

CLARK, Mary Higgins (1931) American mystery writer. One of the new bright stars of American mystery, whose novels of ordinary persons in situations of terror made her an instant best-seller. She writes straight line prose, allowing the strength of the story to make its impact without gew-gaws.

Where Are the Children (1975)

| C ★ ★ ★ ★ | P ★ ★ ★ ★ ★ ★ |
| R ★ ★ ★ ★ ★ ★ | T ★ ★ ★ ★ ★ |

A Stranger Is Watching (1978)

| C ★ ★ ★ ★ | P ★ ★ ★ ★ ★ |
| R ★ ★ ★ ★ ★ | T ★ ★ ★ ★ ★ |

The Cradle Will Fall (1980)

| C ★ ★ ★ ★ | P ★ ★ ★ ★ ★ |
| R ★ ★ ★ ★ ★ | T ★ ★ ★ ★ ★ |

CLARKE, Anna (1919) British detective novelist. One-time secretary to Victor Gollancz, the noted British crime publisher, she began writing comparatively late in life. She claims never to know where her novels will end. They vary a good deal in their success, but at their height they achieve the total immersion of the best fiction.

My Search for Ruth (1975)

| C ★ ★ ★ ★ ★ ★ | P ★ ★ ★ ★ ★ |
| R ★ ★ ★ ★ ★ ★ ★ | T ★ ★ ★ ★ ★ ★ |

The Lady in Black (1977)

| C ★ ★ ★ ★ ★ | P ★ ★ ★ ★ ★ ★ ★ |
| R ★ ★ ★ ★ ★ ★ ★ | T ★ ★ ★ ★ |

CLEARY, Jon (1917) Australian novelist, who has written many thrillers of distinction. His writing and characterization are always of a high standard; his subjects and backgrounds range throughout the world with versatility and descriptive skill. Whether creating suspense or romantic interest, he displays the artistry of the first-class storyteller.

The High Commissioner (1966)

| C ★ ★ ★ ★ ★ | P ★ ★ ★ ★ ★ ★ |
| R ★ ★ ★ ★ ★ ★ | T ★ ★ ★ ★ ★ ★ |

Mask of the Andes (1971)
(The Liberators in U.S.)

| C ★ ★ ★ ★ ★ ★ | P ★ ★ ★ ★ ★ ★ |
| R ★ ★ ★ ★ ★ ★ | T ★ ★ ★ ★ ★ ★ ★ |

Peter's Pence (1974)

| C ★ ★ ★ ★ ★ ★ | P ★ ★ ★ ★ ★ ★ ★ |
| R ★ ★ ★ ★ ★ ★ | T ★ ★ ★ ★ ★ ★ ★ |

CLEEVE, Brian (1921) Irish novelist of suspense and espionage, who paints the Irish scene with skill and understanding including characters from throughout the social strata. They are not merely stage furniture, but vital components of his often brutal tales of intrigue and counterplot.

Death of a Painted Lady (1962)

| C ★ ★ ★ ★ ★ | P ★ ★ ★ ★ ★ |
| R ★ ★ ★ ★ ★ ★ ★ | T ★ ★ ★ ★ |

Vote X for Treason (1964)

| C ★ ★ ★ ★ | P ★ ★ ★ ★ ★ |
| R ★ ★ ★ ★ ★ ★ ★ | T ★ ★ ★ ★ ★ |

R = Readability   T = Tension

CLIFFORD, Francis (1917-1975) English spy and suspense novelist. a wartime soldier who underwent a 1,000-mile journey through Japanese-occupied Burma (*Desperate Journey,* 1979) and was later an officer in the Special Operations Executive, he began writing in order to discover the meaning for him of his war experiences. Yet he never put himself before his potential readers and his novels are remarkable for their high level of tension, produced by a combination of people with whom one deeply sympathizes and situations carefully calculated to put them under most strain. To this he added a remarkable ability to conjure up scenes that an unknown reader will see and remember. The remembering comes from the sure authority with which he wrote, an authority all the more sure for being modest. He said once of his writing "I use a very large rubber and a very small pencil." With them he produced some very good books.

Francis Clifford

The Naked Runner (1966)

C ★ ★ ★ ★ ★ ★ ★ ★	P ★ ★ ★ ★ ★ ★ ★
R ★ ★ ★ ★ ★ ★ ★ ★	T ★ ★ ★ ★ ★ ★ ★ ★ ★

Amigo, Amigo (1973)

C ★ ★ ★ ★ ★ ★ ★ ★	P ★ ★ ★ ★ ★ ★ ★
R ★ ★ ★ ★ ★ ★ ★ ★ ★	T ★ ★ ★ ★ ★ ★ ★ ★ ★

Drummer in the Dark (1976)

C ★ ★ ★ ★ ★ ★ ★ ★	P ★ ★ ★ ★ ★ ★ ★ ★
R ★ ★ ★ ★ ★ ★ ★ ★ ★	T ★ ★ ★ ★ ★ ★ ★ ★ ★

CLINTON-BADDELEY, V. C. (1900-70) British detective novelist, sometime actor and editor for Encyclopedia Britannica. Late in life he produced five books featuring an elderly don sleuth, Dr Davie, fairplay books if ever there were, marked out by some delightful, if unashamedly digressive, dialogue.

To Study A Long Silence (1972)

C ★ ★ ★ ★ ★ ★	P ★ ★ ★ ★
R ★ ★ ★ ★ ★ ★ ★	T ★

COBB, Belton (1892-1971) British detective novelist. He produced over fifty carefully plotted stories, mostly featuring Inspector Cheviot Burmann. They are unremarkable pieces of escapism, although his patient detective work (with poison a speciality) is sometimes relieved by racier action than is displayed by many of his contemporaries in the classic English tradition.

Poisoner's Base (1957)

C ★ ★ ★ ★	P ★ ★ ★ ★ ★ ★
R ★ ★ ★ ★ ★ ★ ★ ★	T ★ ★

COBURN, Andrew (1932) American suspense novelist, reporter and editor. He wrote his first book, *The Trespassers* (1974), latish in life and by 1981, when he produced *Off Duty*, had reached a high level. This is a sombre, leanly told tale of a battle in Boston between a good cop and a bad one with an authentic tang of evil in its pages.

Off Duty (1981)

C ★ ★ ★ ★ ★ ★ ★ ★	P ★ ★ ★ ★ ★ ★ ★
R ★ ★ ★ ★ ★ ★ ★ ★ ★	T ★ ★ ★ ★ ★ ★ ★ ★

COLE, G. D. H. (1889-1959) and **Margaret** (1893-1980) British detective story writers. He was a highly influential left-wing economist and biographer, victim of diabetes, which made him his wife, Margaret, said "write faster and faster, larger and more complicated books." The detective stories they collaborated on, 30 in all, are complicated too, typical thirties products, "competent but no more," in Dame Margaret Cole's own words in her life of her husband.

Counterpoint Murder (1940)

| C ★ ★ ★ ★ | P ★ ★ ★ ★ ★ ★ ★ |
| R ★ ★ ★ ★ ★ | T ★ |

CODY, Lisa British Crime suspense writer. She won with her first book, *Dupe*, the John Creasey award for the best first crime novel published in Britain. The book featured a girl private-eye, delightfully life-like even to forgetting to put important questions, and was marked by its up-to-the-minute setting in the lower reaches of the London film world.

Dupe (1980)

| C ★ ★ ★ ★ ★ ★ ★ | P ★ ★ ★ ★ ★ |
| R ★ ★ ★ ★ ★ ★ ★ | T ★ ★ ★ ★ ★ ★ |

COLES, Manning British espionage novelist, collaborative pen-name of Cyril Coles (1899-1965) and Adelaide Manning (1891-1959). Most of their novels feature Tommy Hambledon of British Intelligence. The earlier titles appeared when the reading public was hungry for tales of derring-do against the Nazi menace; well plotted and authentic, they established a reputation for Manning Coles which post-war titles failed to justify.

Drink to Yesterday (1940)

| C ★ ★ ★ ★ ★ | P ★ ★ ★ ★ ★ ★ ★ |
| R ★ ★ ★ ★ ★ ★ ★ | T ★ ★ ★ ★ ★ ★ ★ |

Pray Silence (1940)
(A Toast to Tomorrow in U.S.)

| C ★ ★ ★ ★ ★ | P ★ ★ ★ ★ ★ ★ ★ |
| R ★ ★ ★ ★ ★ ★ ★ | T ★ ★ ★ ★ ★ ★ |

COLLIER, John (1901-81) British fantasy novelist (*His Monkey Wife*), short-story writer and Hollywood scriptwriter. Some of Collier's much-praised, somewhat whimsical horror stories edge into the crime category and indeed he was awarded the Mystery Writers of America short-story Edgar in 1951. Most are to be found in a big collection, *Fancies and Goodnights*, an abridged version of which, *Demons and Darkness*, was published in Britain as a paperback.

Fancies and Goodnights (1951)

| C ★ ★ ★ ★ ★ ★ ★ | P ★ ★ ★ ★ ★ ★ ★ ★ |
| R ★ ★ ★ ★ ★ ★ ★ | T ★ ★ ★ ★ ★ ★ ★ ★ |

COLLINS, Michael (1924) American mystery writer. Michael Collins is the best known of Dennis Lynds' pseudonyms, others being John Crowe and William Arden. Collins was a popular short story crime writer before starting his hard-boiled series featuring the one-armed private eye, Dan Fortune. Fortune under a different name and different character was previously Slot-Machine Kelly of a series of short stories. The first Fortune novel *Act of Fear* (1966) was awarded the Edgar for Best First Novel.

Night of the Toads (1970)

| C ★ ★ ★ ★ ★ | P ★ ★ ★ ★ ★ |
| R ★ ★ ★ ★ ★ ★ | T ★ ★ ★ ★ ★ |

The Nightrunners (1978)

| C ★ ★ ★ ★ ★ | P ★ ★ ★ ★ ★ |
| R ★ ★ ★ ★ ★ ★ | T ★ ★ ★ ★ ★ |

COLLINS, Wilkie (1824-89) English novelist who produced the book which T. S. Eliot called "the first, the longest and the best" English detective novel, *The Moonstone*, and a thriller novel of equal power and delight, *The Woman in White*. Collins was a marvellous writer. His mainstream novels, some of which like *Armadale* (1866) and *No Name* (1862) are not far off being crime stories, are well worth reading if they can be found. He could create on occasion characters every bit as remarkable as those of his close

R = Readability T = Tension

Wilkie Collins

friend, Dickens. He wrote with splendid easiness. His humour is proof against time. He could handle the tenderest feelings. His plots are as well worked out as Eliot suggested. Even his melodrama, for which today's taste is different, is very well done and takes little real swallowing. He once said his formula for success was "Make 'em laugh, make 'em weep, make 'em wait." He does all three superbly.

The Woman in White (1860)

C ★★★★★★★★★	P ★★★★★★★★★
R ★★★★★★★★★★	T ★★★★★★★★★

The Moonstone (1868)

C ★★★★★★★★★	P ★★★★★★★★★★
R ★★★★★★★★★★	T ★★★★★★★★

CONDON, Richard (1915)

American novelist. New York born, Irish domiciled, Richard Condon's early career was in the American film and theatre industry. As a novelist, he has latterly tended to a convoluted self-indulgence. Elements of crime fiction appear in several of his books, but *The Manchurian Candidate* is certainly his best and most sustained piece of crime writing.

The Manchurian Candidate (1959)

C ★★★★★★★★★	P ★★★★★★★★★
R ★★★★★★★★	T ★★★★★★★★★★

CONNINGTON, J. J. (1880-1947)

British detective novelist. Connington's stories mostly feature Chief Constable Driffield and Squire Wendover, and are in the Crofts (q.v.) mould of unsensational and meticulous detection, with ingenious murder methods and alibis.

The Eye in the Museum (1929)

C ★★★★	P ★★★★★★★
R ★★★★★★★	T ★★★

CONRAD, Joseph (1857-1924)

English novelist of Polish origin whose work includes at least two great novels that are at the same time espionage stories, using his experience as a young man in Poland of the Russian world of agents and double-crossing, and his knowledge of why men became revolutionaries. He writes with tremendous power, the fruit of long and deep thought and a fierce determination not to set down anything other than what he exactly means.

The Secret Agent (1907)

C ★★★★★★★★★★	P ★★★★★★★★★★
R ★★★★★★★★	T ★★★★★★★★★

Under Western Eyes (1911)

C ★★★★★★★★★★	P ★★★★★★★★★★
R ★★★★★★★★	T ★★★★★★★★

Richard Condon

C = Characterization   P = Plot

COPPER, Basil (1924) British detective novelist and writer of macabre short stories, who has also edited and continued the Solar Pons stories of August Derleth (q.v.). His many hard-boiled novels, featuring Los Angeles private eye Mike Faraday, have a degree of authenticity achieved by few British writers in this predominantly American field.

The Dark Mirror (1966)

C ★★★★★	P ★★★★★
R ★★★★★★★★★	T ★★★★★

No Letters from the Grave (1971)

C ★★★★★★	P ★★★★★★★
R ★★★★★★★★★	T ★★★★★

The Further Adventures of Solar Pons (1979)

C ★★★★★	P ★★★★★★
R ★★★★★★★★	T ★

CORY, Desmond (1928) British crime writer, of varied output, and university lecturer. He began, at age 23, writing enjoyable spy novels with a hero called Johnny Fedora, but felt that Ian Fleming (q.v.) spoilt the game in making it mass popular. The books after about 1970 are very different, often relying heavily on psychological expertise, sometimes dazzlingly clever play with the rules of crime writing and indeed of all fiction.

High Requiem (1956)

C ★★★★★★	P ★★★★★★★★
R ★★★★★★★	T ★★★★★

The Circe Complex (1975)

C ★★★★★★★★	P ★★★★★★★★★★
R ★★★★★★	T ★★★★

Bennett (1977)

C ★★★★★★★★	P ★★★★★★★★
R ★★★★★★★★	T ★★★★

COSGRAVE, Patrick (1941) British espionage novelist, crime reviewer, sometime crime publisher and sometime political editor of *The Spectator* and speech-writer for and biographer of Mrs Margaret Thatcher. Son of a former Irish prime minister, in a busy life he has produced a handful of spy stories in the old Dornford Yates (q.v.) tradition, good reads not immune from forthright right-wing philosophy.

The Three Colonels

C ★★★★★★★	P ★★★★★★★★
R ★★★★★★★★	T ★★★★★★

COULTER, Stephen (1914) British writer of thrillers and espionage novels, also using the pseudonym James Mayo (q.v.). He displays a versatility of subject matter and background, with well-paced action in many parts of the world. Whether he is dealing with corruption, hazardous adventure at sea or political intrigue, he combines narrative skill with competent characterization.

Offshore! (1965)

C ★★★★★★	P ★★★★★★★★
R ★★★★★★★★	T ★★★★★★★★

An Account to Render (1970)

C ★★★★★★★★	P ★★★★★★★
R ★★★★★★★★	T ★★★★★★

COURTIER, S. H. (1904-74) Australian detective novelist. One tends to think of Arthur Upfield (q.v.) as the personification of the Australian detective story and Courtier, later on the scene, is unjustly neglected. His works show a good narrative style, ingenious plots, and integral settings which are powerfully atmospheric.

Now Seek My Bones (1957)

C ★★★★	P ★★★★★★★
R ★★★★★★★★★	T ★★★★

Death in Dream Time (1959)

C ★★★★	P ★★★★★★★★
R ★★★★★★★★★	T ★★★★

Murder's Burning (1967)

C ★★★★	P ★★★★★★★
R ★★★★★★★★★	T ★★★★★★

COXE, George Harmon (1901) American mystery writer. Since 1932, more than fifty books ago,

R = Readability   T = Tension

John Creasey

George Harmon Coxe has been writing his classic Boston police novels featuring Kent Murdock, a news photographer thus legitimately on the scene of the crime. Kent Murdock has also appeared in many films and television dramas. Coxe was a newspaperman for some ten years before becoming a full time fiction writer, beginning as most of his peers in the pulps. He writes with the skill of a newsman in uncluttered prose. In 1964 he was honoured by Mystery Writers of America with a Grand Masters Edgar.

Murder with Pictures (1935)

C ★ ★ ★ ★ ★	P ★ ★ ★ ★ ★
R ★ ★ ★ ★ ★	T ★ ★ ★ ★ ★

The Glass Triangle (1940)

C ★ ★ ★ ★ ★ ★	P ★ ★ ★ ★ ★ ★
R ★ ★ ★ ★ ★ ★	T ★ ★ ★ ★ ★ ★

Woman with a Gun (1972)

C ★ ★ ★ ★ ★ ★	P ★ ★ ★ ★ ★ ★
R ★ ★ ★ ★ ★ ★	T ★ ★ ★ ★ ★

CRANE, Frances (1891-1981) American mystery writer. Frances Crane was a well-known short-story writer before turning to the novel, publishing more than 100 stories in such fashionable magazines as the *New Yorker* and *Harper's Bazaar*. The Abbotts, Pat and Jean, are the bright young detecting team she featured in more than twenty-five of her mystery novels. A world traveller, verisimilitude of city backgrounds was no small part of the popularity of Mrs Crane's novels. She used colour titles for the Abbott cases, beginning with *The Turquoise Shop*, set in Taos, New Mexico. In her later years, Mrs Crane made her home in New Mexico, both in Taos and Santa Fe.

The Turquoise Shop (1941)

C ★ ★ ★ ★ ★ ★	P ★ ★ ★ ★ ★
R ★ ★ ★ ★ ★ ★	T ★ ★ ★ ★ ★ ★

Thirteen White Tulips (1953)

C ★ ★ ★ ★ ★ ★	P ★ ★ ★ ★ ★
R ★ ★ ★ ★ ★ ★	T ★ ★ ★ ★

CREASEY, John (1908-73) British mystery writer. Also wrote as Gordon Ashe (q.v.); M. E. Cooke; Margaret Cooke; Henry St John Cooper; Norman Deane; Elise Fecamps; Robert Caine Frazer; Patrick Gill; Michael Halliday; Charles Hogarth; Brian Hope; Colin Hughes; Kyle Hunt; Peter Manton; J. J. Marric (q.v.); Richard Martin; Rodney Mattheson; Anthony Morton; Ken Ranger; William K. Reilly; Tex Riley; Jeremy York. Creasey had a variety of jobs and over 700 rejection slips before his first book was accepted in 1932, after which he seemed determined to match his rejections with published books. Under his own name and his numerous pseudonyms, he certainly got past 600. They run the whole gamut of crime writing from police procedurals via private-eyes to light comedy thrillers. He was a skilful plotter but naturally such an output required a heavy leaning upon the labour-saving device of established series

C = Characterization   P = Plot

characters, such as The Toff, The Baron, Inspector West and, perhaps best known of all, Commander Gideon in the books written as J. J. Marric (q.v.).

Inspector West Alone (1950)

C ★★★★★	P ★★★★★★★
R ★★★★★★★	T ★★★★★★

Danger for the Baron
(Anthony Morton) (1953)

C ★★★★★	P ★★★★★★★★
R ★★★★★★★	T ★★★★★★

CRISPIN, Edmund (1921-78) British detective novelist, crime critic and under his own name, Bruce Montgomery, composer. The first of his nine donnish detective stories, *The Case of the Gilded Fly* (1944), was written while he was still an Oxford undergraduate. Seven

while yet capable of pausing in the midst of a case and "making up titles for Crispin". You have to be bright to get the most out of this author who used to the full the resources of a well-stocked mind, had a great gift for the magnificently inappropriate metaphor as well as the sharp literary dig and a wild sense of the bizarre. But for the bright the rewards are munificent.

The Moving Toyshop (1946)

C ★★★★★★★★	P ★★★★★★★★★★★
R ★★★★★★★★	T ★★★★★★

Love Lies Bleeding (1948)

C ★★★★★★★★	P ★★★★★★★★★
R ★★★★★★★★	T ★★★★★★

The Glimpses of the Moon (1977)

C ★★★★★★★★	P ★★★★★★★★
R ★★★★★★★★★	T ★★★★★★

Edmund
Crispin

Freeman Willis
Crofts (right)

others followed in the years up to 1951, all marked with the intellectual fizz of the first and by a sense of sheer fun. The ninth book did not come until 1977, though there were occasional short stories, some splendidly ingenious, others gigglingly hilarious. His running hero was Professor Gervase Fen, engagingly always delighting in his sleuthery

CROFTS, Freeman Wills (1879-1957) British detective story writer. He was the master of timetables and alibis, beginning in 1924 with the immensely successful *The Cask*, a shipping story, and carrying on at something like a book a year till 1952. His sleuth is painstaking, stopping-for-meals Inspector French, whose very ploddingness

R = Readability   T = Tension

now has a strong period charm, combined as it is with meticulous detail of 1930s middle-class life in Britain.

The Cask (1924)

C ★★★★★	P ★★★★★★★★★★
R ★★★★★★	T ★★

Death of A Train (1946)

C ★★★★★	P ★★★★★★★★★★
R ★★★★★★	T ★★★

CROSS, Amanda (1926) American mystery writer. The pseudonymous Amanda Cross is an English professor at Columbia University. Her mysteries are involved entertainingly with such writers as James Joyce, T. S. Eliot, and yes, Will Shakespeare. An academic background is usually featured.

The James Joyce Murder (1967)

C ★★★★★	P ★★★★★★
R ★★★★★	T ★★★★★

Poetic Justice (1970)

C ★★★★★	P ★★★★★★
R ★★★★★★	T ★★★★★

The Theban Mysteries (1972)

C ★★★★★★	P ★★★★★★
R ★★★★★★	T ★★★★★

CULLINGFORD, Guy (1907) British detective novelist, pseudonym of Constance Lindsay Taylor. In twenty years from 1948 she (or he) produced ten books only. Then silence fell, except for a few short stories and a handful of excellent television plays. In very English settings she told curious and ingenious tales of classical murder with a difference, as for instance *Post Mortem* in which the sleuth is the ghost of the victim.

If Wishes Were Hearses (1952)

C ★★★★★★★★	P ★★★★★★
R ★★★★★★★★	T ★★

Post Mortem (1953)

C ★★★★★★★★	P ★★★★★★★★
R ★★★★★★★★	T ★★★

CUMBERLAND, Marten (1892-1972) British detective story writer and journalist, finally resident in Ireland. He created Commissaire Saturnin Dax who featured in most of his prolific output after 1940, though his earliest crime story was in 1926. Dax's detection involves highly intricate plots and plenty of very French locales. Cumberland also wrote as Kevin O'Hara (q.v.).

No Sentiment in Murder (1966)

C ★★★★★	P ★★★★★★★★
R ★★★★★★	T ★★★★

CUNNINGHAM, E. V. (1914) American mystery writer (pseudonym of Howard Fast). Howard Fast takes a breather from his serious fiction and non-fiction, a lengthy list, with the light non-preaching mysteries of E. V. Cunningham. Each is titled with a girl's name, and all are good entertainment and set in New York.

Margie (1966)

C ★★★★★★★	P ★★★★★★
R ★★★★★★★	T ★★★★★

CURTISS, Ursula R. (1923) American mystery writer. Ursula Curtiss is one of the writing daughters of Helen Reilly, until her death one of the front-ranked mystery writers of the mid-twentieth century. Mrs Curtiss is one of the best practitioners of the domestic mystery, stories which arise from unusual happenings to everyday people in everyday life. Her first book was the prize-winning *Voice Out Of Darkness* (1948).

The Noonday Devil (1951)

C ★★★★★★	P ★★★★★★
R ★★★★★★★	T ★★★★★★★

The Deadly Climate (1954)

C ★★★★★★	P ★★★★★
R ★★★★★★★	T ★★★★★★★

Hours to Kill (1961)

C ★★★★★★	P ★★★★★★
R ★★★★★★★	T ★★★★★★★★

D'AGNEAU, Marcel English humorous crime writer, whose real name is the jealously guarded one of a major British writer who lives chiefly in Monte Carlo. As a sideline he has dashed off two spoofs, *Eeny Meeny Miny Mole* (1979) which sent up the Le Carré (q.v.) and Deighton (q.v.) world of treble-crossing, and *The Curse of the Nibelung* "The last case of Lord Holmes of Baker Street." Both hit a high level of zaniness.

The Curse of the Nibelung (1981)

C ★ ★ ★ ★	P ★ ★ ★ ★
R ★ ★ ★ ★ ★ ★ ★	T ★

DAHL, Roald (1916) British horror crime short-story writer, novelist and children's writer. His stories, over which he takes enormous care, combine clockwork precision of plot with a unique gift for the outré, such as the murder committed with the frozen leg of lamb which is then eaten to dispose definitively of the weapon. They have been well called "tales of the unexpected".

Some Like You (1953)

C ★ ★ ★ ★ ★ ★	P ★ ★ ★ ★ ★ ★ ★ ★
R ★ ★ ★ ★ ★ ★ ★ ★	T ★ ★ ★ ★ ★ ★ ★

Kiss, Kiss (Stories, 1960)

C ★ ★ ★ ★ ★ ★	P ★ ★ ★ ★ ★ ★ ★ ★ ★
R ★ ★ ★ ★ ★ ★ ★ ★	T ★ ★ ★ ★ ★ ★ ★ ★

Switch Bitch (Stories, 1974)

C ★ ★ ★ ★ ★ ★	P ★ ★ ★ ★ ★ ★ ★ ★ ★
R ★ ★ ★ ★ ★ ★ ★ ★	T ★ ★ ★ ★ ★ ★ ★

DALY, Carroll John (1889-1958) American crime novelist and theatre-owner. Between 1927 and 1951 he wrote 27 crime novels, many featuring Race Williams, gunman trading on his reputation as a killer, as well as numerous short stories for the pulp magazines. His *Black Mask* tale "The False Burton Combs" is often cited as the first "hardboiled" crime story, but Daly seems little to have understood the innovation he was responsible for and indeed frequently mixed realism and rank melodrama.

The Snarl of the Beast (1927)

C ★ ★ ★ ★ ★	P ★ ★ ★ ★ ★ ★ ★
R ★ ★ ★ ★ ★ ★ ★ ★	T ★ ★ ★ ★ ★ ★ ★ ★

DALY, Elizabeth (1878-1967) American mystery suspense novelist. The Daly books were a cut above the norm because of their literary quality and because of her fine hand in weaving the eerie into the story line. They featured an amateur detective, Henry Gamadge, a New York bibliophile, whose research into old books added to the background. Miss Daly received an Edgar from Mystery Writers of America in 1960 for the body of her work.

Murder in Volume 2 (1941)

C ★ ★ ★ ★ ★ ★	P ★ ★ ★ ★ ★ ★ ★
R ★ ★ ★ ★ ★ ★ ★ ★	T ★ ★ ★ ★ ★ ★ ★

Book of the Lion (1948)

C ★ ★ ★ ★ ★ ★	P ★ ★ ★ ★ ★ ★ ★
R ★ ★ ★ ★ ★ ★ ★ ★	T ★ ★ ★ ★ ★ ★ ★

Roald Dahl

R = Readability T = Tension

DANIEL, Glyn (1914) British archaeologist and television popularizer and occasional detective novelist. *The Cambridge Murders,* which he wrote under the pen-name Dilwyn Rees, was acclaimed as a brilliant debut, a fine example of the donnish puzzle. Under his own name he subsequently enhanced his reputation for ingenuity and clever character observation.

The Cambridge Murders (1945)

C ★★★★★★★	P ★★★★★★★★
R ★★★★★★★★	T ★★★

Welcome Death (1954)

C ★★★★★★★★	P ★★★★★★★
R ★★★★★★★★	T ★★★

DAVEY, Jocelyn (1908) British espionage writer, in real life Chaim Raphael, civil servant and historian of Judaism. He has produced only five books, but they rate high. Their hero is an Oxford philosopher, Ambrose Usher, a not unerudite figure and a smart hand with a cocktail. The books are somewhat farfetched, but highly entertaining.

A Treasury Alarm (1976)

C ★★★★★★★	P ★★★★★★★
R ★★★★★	T ★

DAVIDSON, Lionel (1922) English suspense novelist, for a long period resident in Israel. He has produced a wide variety of novels in the different crime sub-genres as well as novels that fall, just, outside the crime boundaries. All of them are marked by an extraordinary vividness, so much so that reading his pure adventure story *The Rose of Tibet* (1962), a land he never went near, you find yourself wondering seriously whether all its events did not actually take place. This, backed in almost all the later books by a deeply serious sense of purpose, makes images and characters from his writing lodge themselves in the mind. They stay there often enough, too, as images of hope. From the darkest moments of recent history he pulls out this vision. But any solemnity is never allowed to dampen sheer entertainment. His books are ceaselessly gripping, and funny often to laugh-aloud point.

The Night of Wenceslas (1960)

C ★★★★★★★★	P ★★★★★★★★
R ★★★★★★★★★	T ★★★★★★★★★

A Long Way to Shiloh (1966)
(The Menorah Men in U.S.)

C ★★★★★★★★	P ★★★★★★★★★
R ★★★★★★★★★★	T ★★★★★★★★★★

Making Good Again (1968)

C ★★★★★★★★★	P ★★★★★★★★★
R ★★★★★★★★★★	T ★★★★★★★★★★

DAVIS, Dorothy Salisbury (1916) American mystery-suspense novelist. One of the finest of American suspense authors, Mrs. Davis' work is distinguished both for creativity and for skill. The main body of the work centres on serious studies of character against environment. Only recently has she taken on the diversion of the New York street scene played for comedy not tension, and this is as rewarding as her serious novels. Mrs Davis has received many Edgar scrolls both for novel and for short story.

The Judas Cat (1949)

C ★★★★★★★	P ★★★★★★★
R ★★★★★★★★	T ★★★★★★

A Gentle Murderer (1951)

C ★★★★★★★	P ★★★★★★★
R ★★★★★★★★	T ★★★★★★★

A Death in the Life (1976)

C ★★★★★★★	P ★★★★★★
R ★★★★★★★★	T ★★★★★★

DEIGHTON, Len (1929) British espionage novelist, mainstream novelist, short-story writer, cookery writer and air-war historian. From his first book, *The Ipcress File* (1962), he became a major influence on the course of espionage fiction, steering it from the glossiness of the

C = Characterization   P = Plot

James Bond fashion into a marked reality. Partly this is done through a humorous distrust of Establishment figures embodied in the working class origins of his unnamed hero (called Harry Palmer in the films). Partly it is done by a certain emphasis on the everyday business of spying, the expenses claims, the procedures over fire-arms issue. Partly it is done by his extraordinarily keen interest in the mechanics, based on research of unusual pertinacity. After a period of some years (1967-74) in which he let espionage writing lie fallow he brought to the art a wide-ranging authority that has made his subsequent books classic examples. They are cram-full of virtues: writing of great sensitivity, strongly told stories, character drawing that ranges confidently through countries and classes, the presentation of hard-to-learn facts, sharp and flawlessly accurate dialogue, well worked-out plots, a marvellous vividness and an overall intelligence that seems to spark out from every line. A must for all who enjoy espionage fiction.

Spy Story (1974)

C ★★★★★★★★	P ★★★★★★★★
R ★★★★★★★★★	T ★★★★★★★

SS-GB (1978)

C ★★★★★★★★	P ★★★★★★★
R ★★★★★★★★	T ★★★★★★★★

XPD (1981)

C ★★★★★★★	P ★★★★★★★★★
R ★★★★★★★★★	T ★★★★★★★★

DE LARRABEITI, Michael (1936) British suspense writer and highly unusual children's writer. His single crime book, *The Bunce*, was a strong contender for the 1980 Gold Dagger award in Britain. "Bunce" is bribe-money and one strand of the book is concerned with that and the wide-reaching effects it might have. But there is much else. De Larrabeiti thinks long and writes short, a fine recipe.

The Bunce (1980)

C ★★★★★★★	P ★★★★★★★★
R ★★★★★★★★★	T ★★★★★★★

DE LA TORRE, Lilian (1902) American mystery writer. She stands alone in her mystery career, bringing to life Dr Sam Johnson as an amateur detective, and using her knowledge of eighteenth-century life to make the background as real as the present. All of Lilian de la Torre's books and short stories are based on real persons and events, researched to scholarly perfection and then made lively by her own skill. She has won many awards and is as highly regarded in academic and theatrical circles as in mystery.

Elizabeth Is Missing (1945)

C ★★★★★★★	P ★★★★★★★
R ★★★★★★★	T ★★★★★★

Dr. Sam: Johnson, Detector (stories, 1946)

C ★★★★★★★	P ★★★★★★★
R ★★★★★★★	T ★★★★

The Heir of Douglas (1952)

C ★★★★★★★	P ★★★★★★★
R ★★★★★★★	T ★★★★★★

DELVING, Michael (1914-78) American mystery writer, novelist and under his real name, Jay Williams, children's writer, latterly resident in England. His sleuths were two antique dealers, Dave Cannon and Bob Edison (a Cherokee) and his seven crime stories draw on his knowledge of antiques.

Die Like A Man (1970)

C ★★★★★★	P ★★★★★★★
R ★★★★★★★	T ★★

DENT, Lester (1904-79) American pulp story writer and novelist who between 1933 and 1979 wrote just short of 200 novels about Doc Savage, hardboiled investigator, under the name Kenneth Robeson. Under his own name he wrote only a handful of books in which he tried,

R = Readability   T = Tension

without complete success, to break out of the enforced mediocrity of pulp writing at its most commercial.

The Red Spider (1979)

C★★	P★★★★★
R★★★★★★	T★★★★★

DERLETH, August (1909-71) American writer in many fields of fiction, including detection and the macabre. The prolific and imaginative Derleth carved a niche for himself in the mystery genre with his several volumes of Holmes pastiches featuring Solar Pons, and to a lesser extent with his novels of Judge Ephraim Peck.

The Man on All Fours (1934)

C★★★★★	P★★★★★★★
R★★★★★★★★★	T★★★

No Future for Luana (1945)

C★★★★★	P★★★★★
R★★★★★★★★★	T★★

The Chronicles of Solar Pons stories, 1973)

C★★★★★	P★★★★★★
R★★★★★★★★★	T★

DEVINE, D. M. (1920-80) British detective novelist (who latterly wrote as Dominic Devine) and university administrator. His books mixed thoughtful, if occasionally ponderous, characterization with the traditional puzzle element, often in a Scottish setting. They showed the classical detective story is alive and well and living in the 1980s.

My Brother's Keeper (1961)

C★★★★★★★	P★★★★★★★★
R★★★★★★★	T★★★★★★

This Is Your Death (1981)

C★★★★★★★	P★★★★★★★★
R★★★★★★★	T★★★★

DEXTER, Colin (1930) British detective novelist and university administrator. His novels are set in Oxford and feature the introverted, intelligent Inspector Morse. A crossword puzzle composer, Dexter's plots are marvels of complication, that of *Service for All the Dead* winning him in Britain the Crime Writers Association Silver Dagger for 1979.

Service for All the Dead (1979)

C★★★★★★★★	P★★★★★★★★★
R★★★★★★	T★★

The Dead of Jericho (1981)

C★★★★★★★★	P★★★★★★★★
R★★★★★★★★	T★★★★

DICKENS, Charles (1812-70) English novelist, and in his last, unfinished book, *The Mystery of Edwin Drood,* crime novelist. Crime, had played a large part in earlier novels, notably in *Bleak House* (1853) but that is a novel using criminal actions as part only of its story. In *Drood* Dickens embraced the crime novel proper in a story whose whole action and *raison d'être* was the mystery of the death of young Edwin Drood. The book was written at the height of his powers, despite the strain he was putting on himself with his reading tours that contributed to his comparatively early death. Even as the mere stump of what it might have been (and it is more than that) the book is enormously rewarding to read. Many attempts have been made to complete it, perhaps the most successful is by Leon Garfield (1981).

The Mystery of Edwin Drood (1870)

C★★★★★★★★★★	P UNFINISHED
R★★★★★★★★★★	T★★★★★★★★

DICKINSON, Peter (1927) British crime novelist and children's writer, formerly assistant editor of *Punch.* Dickinson is, in a crude generalization, a typical British eccentric. His books have the oddest of backgrounds, a New Guinea tribe living in London attics, an oil-sheik's palace where a chimpanzee is learning grammar, a home for children whose illness makes them psychic

Peter Dickinson

Little wonder he gained the Crime Writers Association Gold Dagger in two successive years, 1968 and 1969.

The Glass-sided Ants' Nest (1968) (*Skin-deep* as U.K. hardback)

C ★ ★ ★ ★ ★ ★ ★	P ★ ★ ★ ★ ★ ★ ★
R ★ ★ ★ ★ ★ ★ ★ ★	T ★ ★ ★ ★ ★ ★

The Poison Oracle (1974)

C ★ ★ ★ ★ ★ ★ ★ ★	P ★ ★ ★ ★ ★ ★ ★
R ★ ★ ★ ★ ★ ★ ★ ★	T ★ ★ ★ ★ ★ ★ ★ ★

One Foot in the Grave (1979)

C ★ ★ ★ ★ ★ ★ ★	P ★ ★ ★ ★ ★ ★ ★ ★
R ★ ★ ★ ★ ★ ★ ★ ★	T ★ ★ ★ ★ ★ ★ ★ ★

DICKSON, Carter (1906-77) Pseudonym of John Dickson Carr (q.v.). Most of his novels feature Sir Henry Merrivale, a blustery and colourful character with a twinkling eye and a habit of knowingly describing himself as "the Old Man". The books are similar to Carr's Dr Fell series, with seemingly inexplicable murders and ample comedy.

The Plague Court Murders (1934)

C ★ ★ ★ ★ ★	P ★ ★ ★ ★ ★ ★ ★
R ★ ★ ★ ★ ★ ★ ★ ★	T ★ ★ ★

The Red Widow Murders (1935)

C ★ ★ ★ ★ ★	P ★ ★ ★ ★ ★ ★ ★
R ★ ★ ★ ★ ★ ★ ★ ★	T ★ ★ ★

The Judas Window (1938)

C ★ ★ ★ ★ ★	P ★ ★ ★ ★ ★ ★ ★ ★
R ★ ★ ★ ★ ★ ★ ★ ★	T ★ ★ ★

DISNEY, Doris Miles (1907-76) American mystery writer. A prolific writer of mysteries set mostly in New England and the suburban East, Mrs Disney's apprenticeship was in publicity work for social agencies. Two of her books became films, *Stella* and *Fugitive Lady*. Her first mystery was *A Compound for Death* (1943) and for more than 25 years Mrs Disney published another of her popular books annually.

Night of Clear Choice (1967)

C ★ ★ ★ ★ ★ ★	P ★ ★ ★ ★ ★ ★
R ★ ★ ★ ★ ★ ★ ★	T ★ ★ ★ ★ ★

sensitives. And there is, another sign of the eccentric, a deliberate smallness in each of these enclosed worlds. But, increasingly as he wrote, these limited settings rode on themes of more and more power, man's destruction of his living base, man's disregard of his instinctual mainsprings, the danger of ignoring immediate life in favour of distant dreams. Yet all is done within the confines of the classical detective story. There are proper clues (and devilishly cunningly they are sown, as examining the clue of the roly-poly pudding in *One Foot in the Grave* will show); there is the closed circle of suspects; there is a detective (in most books the reticent, very British Superintendent Pibble – significant name); there is on occasion a final confrontation before all the witnesses. Dickinson, too, is a marvellously vivid writer. His characters, often a little larger than life, stand out with splendid clearness. He can in a single phrase make a setting spring to life. And there is behind it all a charge, a power that makes some of his scenes stick in the mind for many a year after reading.

R = Readability   T = Tension

DODGE, David (1910) American mystery-suspense writer. One of the exceptional suspense novelists of the forties and fifties, David Dodge may have deserted the mystery because of the equally exceptional success of his global travel books. His Poor Man's and Rich Man's guides to travel have been best sellers for many years. His first mystery was *Death and Taxes* (1941) and his first travel book the classic *How Green Was My Father* (1947). Dodge had literary style as well as being a fine story teller.

The Long Escape (1948)

C ★ ★ ★ ★ ★	P ★ ★ ★ ★ ★ ★
R ★ ★ ★ ★ ★ ★ ★	T ★ ★ ★ ★ ★ ★

Plunder of the Sun (1949)

C ★ ★ ★ ★ ★	P ★ ★ ★ ★ ★
R ★ ★ ★ ★ ★ ★ ★	T ★ ★ ★ ★ ★

To Catch A Thief (1952)

C ★ ★ ★ ★ ★	P ★ ★ ★ ★ ★ ★
R ★ ★ ★ ★ ★ ★ ★	T ★ ★ ★ ★ ★ ★

DOMINIC, R. B. see LATHEN, Emma

DOYLE, Sir Arthur Conan (1859-1930) British novelist, historian, campaigner for spiritualism and creator of Sherlock Holmes. When in *A Study in Scarlet* (1888) he created his great detective (in early notes called Sherrinford Holmes), although he was paid only £25 for full rights in the tale, he nevertheless altered literary history. When, with the short Holmes stories published in the *Strand* magazine from July 1891 onwards, his tremendous success began he established a form which almost at once brought imitators and followers of all sorts. The detective story was singled out as being something different from other stories, different even from melodrama or sensation stories. This was due, perhaps, to two other factors than Doyle's marvellous natural skill as a storyteller. First, his scientific detective appealed to a huge new public that knew something of scientific method and felt that here was something that appealed to all that was newest and most interesting in their lives. Second, by hitting on the idea of a running hero, a man who would appear in story after story, Doyle established a public so faithful that when, after not so many years, he tried to kill off Holmes in the concluding story of *The Memoirs of Sherlock Holmes* (1894) there were processions of black armbanded mourners seen in the Strand. But none of this should be allowed to detract from Doyle's skill as a writer, underpraised surely by critics who distrust the popularity the Holmes stories achieved. Holmes himself is a towering piece of character creation, so real that it is no wonder real appeals were made for his help, contradictory as only a real human being can be, of heroic stature nevertheless, and reflecting in countless ways small and large the very spirit of his times. And the people he encounters are brought to life with marvellous swiftness in stories that very seldom move away in the least from their straight course. The descriptions,

Sir Arthur
Conan Doyle

especially of London, are splendidly evocative while being rigidly economical. The dialogue is excellent, ringing true and conveying much in little. Above all, Doyle was a teller of tales, those pieces of imaginative fiction that somehow go to the depths in us however outwardly simple and easy they may seem.

The Adventures of Sherlock Holmes
(Stories, 1892)

C ★★★★★★★★★★	P ★★★★★★★★★★
R ★★★★★★★★★★	T ★★★★★★★★

The Memoirs of Sherlock Holmes
(Stories, 1894)

C ★★★★★★★★★★	P ★★★★★★★★★★
R ★★★★★★★★★★	T ★★★★★★★★

The Hound of the Baskervilles
(1902)

C ★★★★★★★★★	P ★★★★★★★★
R ★★★★★★★★★	T ★★★★★★★★

DRISCOLL, Peter (1942) British thriller writer, born and educated in South Africa. Place is the driving force in his well-told stories of high adventure, generally place chosen for its political tensions, whether that is South Africa, Northern Ireland or the China Seas. His heroes, in the Buchan (q.v.) tradition, tend to become caught up in their tense situations willy-nilly.

The Wilby Conspiracy (1973)

C ★★★★★★	P ★★★★★★★
R ★★★★★★★★★	T ★★★★★★★★

Pangolin (1979)

C ★★★★★★	P ★★★★★★★
R ★★★★★★★★★	T ★★★★★★★★★

DRUMMOND, Charles (1922-77) British police mystery writer, who also wrote as Edmund McGirr and Kenneth Giles. A versatile performer, under his Drummond pseudonym he produced five memorable stories between 1967 and 1973 featuring Sergeant Reed, of Scotland Yard, a drink-fixated odd-man-out suspected of disciplinary offences, who solves tricky mysteries with brilliance and unorthodoxy.

A Death at the Bar (1972)

C ★★★★★★★	P ★★★★★★★★
R ★★★★★★★	T ★★★

DRUMMOND, Ivor (1929) British spy-adventure novelist, and under his real name, Roger Longrigg, novelist. His pacy stories featuring Lady Jennifer Norrington, deb and tough with it, Count Sandro de Ganzarello, maxi-masculine Italian bear, and Colly Tucker III, American millionaire Pimpernel figure, are in the James Bond tradition, and at their best are not far behind Fleming.

The Man with the Tiny Head (1970)

C ★★★★★★	P ★★★★★★★★
R ★★★★★★★★	T ★★★★★★★★★

The Necklace of Skulls (1977)

C ★★★★★★	P ★★★★★★★★
R ★★★★★★★★	T ★★★★★★★★★

DRUMMOND, June (1923) South African suspense writer. Her novels, set in different parts of the world though they are, all have an oddness of flavour about them, something extra besides the mystery to be solved, sometimes produced by a deliberate total vagueness of background. Frequently they feature powerful women, ambivalently hovering between good and evil.

Slowly the Poison (1975)

C ★★★★★	P ★★★★★★★
R ★★★★★★★★	T ★★★★★★★

DUKE, Madeleine British novelist, crime novelist, doctor of medicine. Born in Switzerland, she had a remarkable and adventurous war (1939-45). Among the many books she writes are mysteries with an attractive medical background.

Death of A Dandie Dinmont (1978)

C ★★★★★★★	P ★★★★★★★
R ★★★★★★★	T ★★★★

DU MAURIER, Daphne (1907)

R = Readability   T = Tension

Daphne du Maurier

British romantic novelist. Grand-daughter of George du Maurier (author of *Trilby*) and daughter of Sir Gerald du Maurier, the actor, she has maintained the family tradition of high drama in her writing. A fine plotter with a love of the gothic, she has frequently been drawn to the mystery-suspense field where she specializes in surprise endings, either ironic or bizarre.

Rebecca (1938)

| C ★ ★ ★ ★ ★ ★ ★ | P ★ ★ ★ ★ ★ ★ ★ ★ |
| R ★ ★ ★ ★ ★ ★ ★ ★ | T ★ ★ ★ ★ ★ ★ ★ ★ |

My Cousin Rachel (1951)

| C ★ ★ ★ ★ ★ ★ ★ ★ | P ★ ★ ★ ★ ★ ★ ★ ★ |
| R ★ ★ ★ ★ ★ ★ ★ ★ | T ★ ★ ★ ★ ★ ★ ★ ★ ★ ★ |

The Scapegoat (1957)

| C ★ ★ ★ ★ ★ ★ ★ ★ | P ★ ★ ★ ★ ★ ★ ★ ★ ★ |
| R ★ ★ ★ ★ ★ ★ ★ ★ | T ★ ★ ★ ★ ★ ★ ★ |

DUNCAN, W. Murdoch (1909-76)

British writer of over two hundred detective novels and thrillers, also using several pseudonyms. As Duncan and as John Cassells, his detection is competent and his plots entertaining; his private eye stories as Neill Graham and Lovat Marshall are racy; while his thrillers as Peter Malloch can be toughly realistic.

The Hooded Man (1960)

| C ★ ★ ★ ★ | P ★ ★ ★ ★ ★ ★ |
| R ★ ★ ★ ★ ★ ★ ★ ★ ★ | T ★ ★ ★ ★ ★ |

Meet the Dreamer (1963)

| C ★ ★ ★ ★ | P ★ ★ ★ ★ ★ |
| R ★ ★ ★ ★ ★ ★ ★ ★ ★ | T ★ ★ ★ ★ |

DUNNETT, Dorothy (1923)

Scottish humorous crime writer, published as Dorothy Halliday in Britain, and historical novelist. She produced a handful of lightweight, engaging suspense stories featuring a portrait painter, Johnson Johnson, and in each book his dolly of the moment, a girl who got a large share of the preposterous but very readable action.

Dolly and the Nanny Bird (1976)

| C ★ ★ ★ ★ ★ | P ★ ★ ★ ★ ★ ★ |
| R ★ ★ ★ ★ ★ ★ ★ ★ | T ★ ★ ★ ★ ★ ★ |

DURBRIDGE, Francis (1912)

British suspense writer. First a radio and television serial constructor (the books are chiefly novelizations), he has a tremendous and deserved reputation both in Britain and in Europe for the cliff-hanging surprises he has been so adept at producing, in clipped, Surrey stockbroker-style dialogue, from his earliest Paul Temple radio serial before World War II to television serials in the 1980s.

A Man Called Harry Brent (1970)

| C ★ ★ ★ ★ ★ | P ★ ★ ★ ★ ★ ★ ★ ★ |
| R ★ ★ ★ ★ ★ ★ ★ | T ★ ★ ★ ★ ★ ★ ★ ★ ★ |

E

EBERHART, Mignon G. (1899)

American mystery writer. Eberhart has been one of the most important of American mystery novelists from the publication of her first book, *The Patient In Room 18* (1929), through the more than fifty books and collections and numerous motion pictures which have followed. The first serious contender to Mary Roberts Rinehart, she herself has never been successfully challenged over the years. She received the Grand Masters Edgar from Mystery Writers of America in 1970.

While the Patient Slept (1930)

C ★★★★★★★	P ★★★★★★★
R ★★★★★★★	T ★★★★★

Five Passengers from Lisbon (1946)

C ★★★★★★★	P ★★★★★★
R ★★★★★★★	T ★★★★★

Message from Hong Kong (1969)

C ★★★★★★★	P ★★★★★★★★
R ★★★★★★★	T ★★★★★★★

EBERSOHN, Wessel (1940) South African suspense writer and novelist. He has used the crime novel to indict the excesses of apartheid and the security police in his country, but he by no means neglects the mystery, excitement and tension of the genre he uses. His hero is an unorthodox, highly sympathetic Jewish psychiatrist.

Divide the Night (1981)

C ★★★★★★★★	P ★★★★★★★
R ★★★★★★★★	T ★★★★★★★

EDEN, Dorothy (1912-82) New Zealand gothic and historical novelist, long resident in Britain. Her gothic novels have their share of the standard ingredients, the heroine with the romantic name, the dangers she gets herself into, the love she finds in the end, the exotic setting that it all takes place in. But the books are written with a good deal more distinction than the great majority of the genre. The characters bear a closer relation to life than to pasteboard. And, above all, each book has a splendid story, carrying the reader unerringly forward from one point of tension to the next with a limpid directness that is much harder to achieve than its clarity and simplicity would indicate.

Bride by Candlelight (1954)

C ★★★★★★★	P ★★★★★★★
R ★★★★★★★★★	T ★★★★★★★★

Waiting for Willa (1970)

C ★★★★★★★★	P ★★★★★★★★
R ★★★★★★★★★★	T ★★★★★★★★★

Afternoon Walk (1971)

C ★★★★★★★★	P ★★★★★★★★
R ★★★★★★★★★★	T ★★★★★★★★★★

EGAN, Leslie see LININGTON, Elizabeth

Clive Egleton

EGLETON, Clive (1927) British thriller writer. A former senior army officer, with Intelligence work in his record, he always wanted to write but succeeded only with his eleventh effort. His books are tough and uncompromising, with plenty of action, plenty of blood spilt and often audacious plots.

Backfire (1979)

C ★★★★★	P ★★★★★★★★
R ★★★★★★★★	T ★★★★★★★★

ELLIN, Stanley (1916) American suspense novelist and crime short-story writer. In each field he has a very high reputation. As a short-story writer his debut (after many tries), "The Specialty of the House"

R = Readability   T = Tension

(1954), has been so much anthologized ever since that it has acquired, properly, the status of a classic. Seven Ellin stories won contests sponsored by *Ellery Queen's Mystery Magazine*, two ("The House Party" and "The Blessington Method") won Edgars from the Mystery Writers of America (as did the novel *The Eighth Circle*). Enormously varied in plot and setting, his stories are perhaps linked first by their hammered-out clarity of style and, second, by a fascinatingly bizarre view of the world and its people (and one flea). The novels, too, are extraordinarily different one from the other. Ellin has said that the crime field offers opportunities for an infinite diversity of theme and treatment, which he likes to take advantage of. So we have in *The Eighth Circle* a long, serious (only what a story) study of the modern American private investigator. In *Mirror, Mirror on the Wall* we have an investigation conducted entirely within the sexuality of its protagonist, a remarkable *tour de force* and a pioneering development, hardly followed up in the decade after it by any writer. In *The Stronghold* we have a study (tense as a bowstring) of the clash between two views on violence, the Quaker way and the murderous.

The Eighth Circle (1958)

| C ★ ★ ★ ★ ★ ★ ★ ★ | P ★ ★ ★ ★ ★ ★ ★ |
| R ★ ★ ★ ★ ★ ★ ★ ★ | T ★ ★ ★ ★ ★ ★ ★ ★ |

Mirror, Mirror on the Wall (1972)

| C ★ ★ ★ ★ ★ ★ ★ ★ ★ | P ★ ★ ★ ★ ★ ★ ★ ★ ★ |
| R ★ ★ ★ ★ ★ ★ ★ ★ ★ | T ★ ★ ★ ★ ★ ★ ★ ★ ★ |

The Specialty of the House (Complete Stories) (1979)

| C ★ ★ ★ ★ ★ ★ ★ ★ | P ★ ★ ★ ★ ★ ★ ★ ★ ★ |
| R ★ ★ ★ ★ ★ ★ ★ ★ ★ | T ★ ★ ★ ★ ★ ★ ★ ★ |

ERDMAN, Paul E. (1932) American suspense novelist. An economist and banker, Paul Erdman did not begin fiction writing until he was incarcerated in a Swiss prison where he, like the protagonist of his first book, was the "fall guy" in a money man escapade. As of now he has written four books, each one of star quality. The first three are also highly rated motion pictures.

The Billion Dollar Sure Thing (1972) (*The Billion Dollar Killing* in U.K.)

| C ★ ★ ★ ★ ★ | P ★ ★ ★ ★ ★ ★ ★ ★ ★ |
| R ★ ★ ★ ★ ★ ★ ★ | T ★ ★ ★ ★ ★ ★ ★ ★ |

The Silver Bears (1974)

| C ★ ★ ★ ★ ★ | P ★ ★ ★ ★ ★ ★ ★ ★ ★ |
| R ★ ★ ★ ★ ★ ★ ★ ★ | T ★ ★ ★ ★ ★ ★ ★ ★ |

The Crash of '79 (1976)

| C ★ ★ ★ ★ ★ ★ | P ★ ★ ★ ★ ★ ★ ★ ★ ★ |
| R ★ ★ ★ ★ ★ ★ ★ ★ | T ★ ★ ★ ★ ★ ★ ★ |

EUSTIS, Helen (1916) American mystery novelist. Helen Eustis published her first novel, *The Horizontal Man* in 1946. It was a brilliant *tour de force*, a psychological story set in the verisimilitude of a girl's college. It was awarded the Edgar for Best First Mystery of its year. This unusual and beautifully written book was not only the beginning but was to be almost the end of her writing career. Her only other mystery, *The Fool Killer,* based on a fearful folk legend, appeared almost twenty years later. There have been no books from her since.

The Horizontal Man (1946)

| C ★ ★ ★ ★ ★ ★ ★ ★ | P ★ ★ ★ ★ ★ ★ ★ ★ |
| R ★ ★ ★ ★ ★ ★ ★ ★ | T ★ ★ ★ ★ ★ ★ ★ ★ |

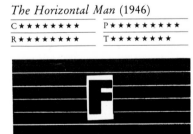

FAIR, A. A. see GARDNER, Erle Stanley

FAIRLIE, Gerard (1899) British thriller writer who produced some exciting tales of international crime and espionage, including series characters Victor Caryll and Johnny

William
Faulkner

FAULKNER, William (1897-1962) American novelist. Nobel prize-winner William Faulker, one of the greatest names in American literature, was always bemused by the criminal mind. It surfaces in most of his writings, colouring his novels of Yoknapatawpha County, and certainly is an integral part of the Snopes volumes. *Sanctuary,* his first "popular" novel, belongs in the library of crime as does its sequel, *Requiem for A Nun.* But it is for *Intruder in the Dust* that he will be remembered in mystery annals, certainly one of the finest mysteries ever written.

Sanctuary (1931)

C ★★★★★★★★★	P ★★★★★★★★
R ★★★★★★★★★	T ★★★★★★★★

Intruder in the Dust (1948)

C ★★★★★★★★★	P ★★★★★★★★★★
R ★★★★★★★★★	T ★★★★★★★★★★

Requiem for A Nun (1951)

C ★★★★★★★★★	P ★★★★★★★★★★
R ★★★★★★★★★★	T ★★★★★★★★★★

FEARING, Kenneth (1902-61) American poet and novelist with a small but significant output in the field of crime fiction. His perception of urban society, his fine characterization and his Faulkneresque technique combine to make him much more than a purveyor of enthralling stories of suspense.

Dagger of the Mind (1941)

C ★★★★★★★★	P ★★★★★★★
R ★★★★★★★	T ★★★★★

The Big Clock (1946)

C ★★★★★★★★★	P ★★★★★★★★★
R ★★★★★★★	T ★★★★★★

The Crozart Story (1960)

C ★★★★★★★	P ★★★★★★
R ★★★★★★	T ★★★

FENISONG, Ruth American gothic mystery writer. Ruth Fenisong's American publishers, Crime Club, used their "Damsel In Distress" colophon as the clue to her

---

Macall, but whose principal claim to fame is that he continued – and in some respects improved upon – the Bulldog Drummond stories initiated by Sapper (q.v.).

They Found Each Other (1946)

C ★★★★	P ★★★★★★
R ★★★★★★★★	T ★★★★★★

Bulldog Drummond Stands Fast (1947)

C ★★★	P ★★★★★
R ★★★★★★★★★	T ★★★★★★★

FARRER, Katharine (1911) British detective novelist. Her disappointingly small output is a refreshing mixture of intellectual problem, action, well drawn settings and good characterization. Inspector Ringwood, who brings erudition to some unusual puzzles, is sadly neglected by historians of the classic English detective novel; he belongs in the front rank.

The Missing Link (1952)

C ★★★★★★★★	P ★★★★★★★
R ★★★★★★★	T ★★★

The Cretan Counterfeit (1954)

C ★★★★★★★★	P ★★★★★★★★
R ★★★★★★★	T ★★★

R = Readability   T = Tension

stories. She had, however, more bite than the usual in Damsel stories, and was for many years one of the more prolific writers in the genre.

But Not Forgotten (1960)

C ★ ★ ★ ★ ★	P ★ ★ ★ ★ ★ ★
R ★ ★ ★ ★ ★	T ★ ★ ★ ★ ★

FENWICK, Elizabeth American mystery suspense writer. Each of Elizabeth Fenwick's suspense novels has as its seed the strange sort of terror that emerges from a quiet setting and from characters who, to say the least, are a little strange, not quite normal. She received an Edgar scroll in 1963 for her book *The Make-Believe Man.*

The Make-Believe Man (1962)

C ★ ★ ★ ★ ★ ★	P ★ ★ ★ ★ ★ ★ ★
R ★ ★ ★ ★ ★ ★	T ★ ★ ★ ★ ★ ★

Goodbye Aunt Elva (1968)

C ★ ★ ★ ★ ★ ★	P ★ ★ ★ ★ ★ ★ ★
R ★ ★ ★ ★ ★ ★	T ★ ★ ★ ★ ★ ★ ★

FERRARS, Elizabeth (1907) British detective novelist, published in the U.S. as E.X. Ferrars. With 50 books behind her, starting in 1940, she is one of the stalwarts of the traditional British-style crime novel. But she keeps her backgrounds and characters well up to date, frequently choosing as a theme some contemporary dilemma. Her books always give the reader something to think about, as well as a good puzzle to unravel. Her people are notably real. They eat; they choose clothes.

Enough To Kill A Horse (1955)

C ★ ★ ★ ★ ★ ★	P ★ ★ ★ ★ ★ ★
R ★ ★ ★ ★ ★ ★ ★	T ★ ★ ★

Witness Before the Fact (1979)

C ★ ★ ★ ★ ★ ★ ★	P ★ ★ ★ ★ ★
R ★ ★ ★ ★ ★ ★ ★	T ★ ★ ★ ★

Experiment with Death (1981)

C ★ ★ ★ ★ ★ ★	P ★ ★ ★ ★ ★ ★
R ★ ★ ★ ★ ★ ★ ★ ★	T ★ ★ ★ ★

FISH, Robert L. (1912-81) American mystery writer. A consulting engineer in demand around the world, Fish was equally as proficient as a writer. His entrance into fiction writing was through short story, in particular through his pastiche character Schlock Homes, published by Ellery Queen's Mystery Magazine. His best known character in books was Captain Jose Da Silva of Brazil, a country in which Fish lived for ten years. *Bullitt,* one of the most successful crime motion pictures in recent years was based on Fish's book, *Mute Witness.* Fish was so prolific as a fiction writer that he also used two pseudonyms, Robert L. Pike, almost as successful as Fish, and A. C. Lamprey for sideline writing. He received Edgars both for Best First Novel and for Short Story.

The Quarry (1964)

C ★ ★ ★ ★ ★	P ★ ★ ★ ★ ★ ★
R ★ ★ ★ ★ ★ ★	T ★ ★ ★ ★ ★

The Incredible Schlock Homes (1966)

C ★ ★ ★ ★	P ★ ★ ★ ★ ★ ★ ★
R ★ ★ ★ ★ ★ ★	T ★ ★ ★

The Bridge That Went Nowhere (1968)

C ★ ★ ★ ★ ★	P ★ ★ ★ ★ ★ ★
R ★ ★ ★ ★ ★ ★	T ★ ★ ★ ★ ★

FISHER, David E. (1932) American detective novelist, novelist, scientist, sometime gopher in the Philadelphia garment district and howdy-doody man in the Connecticut tobacco fields. If ever a writer deserves to be remembered for one book, though he has written more, it is Fisher, and the book is *The Man You Sleep With,* a dazzlingly told affair with a new-twist alibi that should be kept out of the hands of potential murderers plus characterization fit for a first-class novel.

The Man You Sleep With (1981)

C ★ ★ ★ ★ ★ ★ ★ ★	P ★ ★ ★ ★ ★ ★ ★ ★
R ★ ★ ★ ★ ★ ★ ★	T ★ ★ ★ ★ ★ ★ ★

FITT, Mary (1897-1959) British detective novelist, lecturer in Classical Greek and, under her own name of

C = Characterization   P = Plot

Ian
Fleming

Kathleen Freeman, novelist. She was a crime writer in the Dorothy L. Sayers (q.v.) tradition, providing meaty mystery in good English, laced with easy learning, from *Murder Mars the Tour* in 1926 until *There Are More Ways of Killing*, published in 1960. Stolidly efficient Inspector Mallett features in most of her books.

Death and the Pleasant Voices (1946)

C ★ ★ ★ ★ ★ ★ ★	P ★ ★ ★ ★ ★ ★
R ★ ★ ★ ★ ★ ★ ★	T ★ ★

FITZGERALD, Nigel (1906) Irish detective novelist whose home country has provided highly effective backgrounds for many of his intricate, exciting and witty mysteries. Deft characterization, some ingenious murder methods, and an accomplished atmospheric touch are key features of his work, which is in the classic tradition.

This Won't Hurt You (1959)

C ★ ★ ★ ★ ★ ★	P ★ ★ ★ ★ ★ ★ ★
R ★ ★ ★ ★ ★ ★	T ★ ★ ★

Affairs of Death (1967)

C ★ ★ ★ ★ ★ ★	P ★ ★ ★ ★ ★ ★
R ★ ★ ★ ★ ★ ★ ★	T ★ ★ ★

FLEMING, Ian (1908-64) British spy novelist, former personal assistant to the Director of Naval Intelligence and newspaper executive. Fleming created James Bond. And it is not many writers who bring to life a myth. But Bond, after a pretty shaky start, revived the whole subgenre of the spy novel. When he caught on he caught on but good, especially when towards the end of Fleming's life the movies started to come out and the cult became as down-market popular in America as it had been up-market popular chiefly in Britain, though President Kennedy was a notorious Bond fan. Imitators and parodists arose as clusteringly as they had done for Conan Doyle's Sherlock Holmes. Among the best of them was Kingsley Amis (q.v.), writing as Robert Markham, and the most recent and perhaps most successful reviver of the Bond image has been John Gardner (q.v.). What accounted for Bond's sweeping success? Principally perhaps that he came at the right time, just. The Cold War was at its chilliest and Bond showed that it could be won (at least in miniature) and that it could be fun. In Britain at that time fun was hard to find in the dull, rationed days of post-war austerity, and this certainly contributed to the first wave of success. Bond, too, with his insistence on the good things of life, meticulously catalogued with brand-names, and his easy trips to exotic locales appealed to the nascent materialism of those years, and with his promiscuous and reasonably detailed love-life he appealed to the earliest manifestations of the permissive society. But if there was that much of the forward-looking in him, there was also something of the backward-looking. Bond was, it could be said, the last of the gentlemen, the last of those figures nurtured in Victorian Britain that set an example to the world (an example shown at its finest, if flawed, in Sherlock

R = Readability   T = Tension

Holmes). Finally, whether consciously or not, Fleming wrote stories, of "penny-dreadful improbability" one commentator said, which deep down were the great tales of old, the tales which appeal to the most buried parts of the psyche, the story of Midas (*Goldfinger*), the story of the demi-god who had to be killed (*Dr No*, 1958), the story of the dragon slayer (*Moonraker*, 1955).

Casino Royale (1953)

C ★ ★ ★ ★ ★	P ★ ★ ★ ★ ★ ★ ★ ★
R ★ ★ ★ ★ ★ ★ ★ ★	T ★ ★ ★ ★ ★ ★ ★ ★

From Russia With Love (1957)

C ★ ★ ★ ★ ★	P ★ ★ ★ ★ ★ ★ ★ ★
R ★ ★ ★ ★ ★ ★ ★ ★	T ★ ★ ★ ★ ★ ★ ★ ★

Goldfinger (1959)

C ★ ★ ★ ★ ★	P ★ ★ ★ ★ ★ ★ ★
R ★ ★ ★ ★ ★ ★ ★ ★	T ★ ★ ★ ★ ★ ★ ★

FLEMING, Joan (1908-80) British detective novelist. Twice winner of the Crime Writers Association Gold Dagger in Britain (1962 and 1970), she was nevertheless a most erratic writer, switching from one type of crime story to another, often hitting, sometimes missing, flirting with a Turkish sleuth (Nuri Iskirlak), with Victorian crime, with the gothic.

When I Grow Rich (1962)

C ★ ★ ★ ★ ★ ★ ★	P ★ ★ ★ ★ ★ ★ ★ ★
R ★ ★ ★ ★ ★ ★ ★ ★	T ★ ★ ★ ★ ★ ★

Young Man, I Think You're Dying (1970)

C ★ ★ ★ ★ ★ ★	P ★ ★ ★ ★ ★ ★ ★
R ★ ★ ★ ★ ★ ★ ★ ★	T ★ ★ ★ ★ ★ ★ ★

FLETCHER, J. S. (1863-1935) British detective novelist, novelist, poet, writer on religion, writer about Yorkshire. Incredibly prolific, at the height of his fame in the twenties and thirties he rivalled Edgar Wallace (q.v.) and his *The Middle Temple Murder* was hailed by no less a person than President Woodrow Wilson. Between 1889 and 1937 he published no fewer than 93 novels of detection alongside all his other work. Yet his two best books, at least, deserve to be dragged from limbo.

The Middle Temple Murder (1919)

C ★ ★ ★	P ★ ★ ★ ★ ★ ★ ★
R ★ ★ ★ ★ ★ ★ ★	T ★ ★ ★ ★ ★

The Charing Cross Murder (1923)

C ★ ★ ★	P ★ ★ ★ ★ ★ ★ ★
R ★ ★ ★ ★ ★ ★ ★ ★	T ★ ★ ★ ★ ★

FLETCHER, Lucille (1912) American mystery writer. Primarily a radio and television suspense writer, Lucille Fletcher (with Allen Ullman) wrote the *tour de force, Sorry, Wrong Number,* for which she is best remembered, in 1949. She has published only a few books since then, two of which, *Blindfold* and *And Presumed Dead* have been filmed. In 1959 a special award, the Raven, was given by Mystery Writers of America to Miss Fletcher for her radio play, the earliest form of *Sorry, Wrong Number.*

Sorry, Wrong Number (1949)

C ★ ★ ★ ★ ★	P ★ ★ ★ ★ ★ ★ ★
R ★ ★ ★ ★ ★ ★	T ★ ★ ★ ★ ★ ★ ★

FOLEY, Rae (?-1978) American mystery writer. Born in North Dakota, Rae Foley lived for many years in New York and later in nearby suburban Connecticut. Her books are "women type", romantic, well plotted, involving ordinary people. She wrote more than 40 mysteries and also wrote books for young people. Her interest in current history and world politics led her to several collaborative books on these subjects.

The Brownstone House (1974)

C ★ ★ ★ ★ ★	P ★ ★ ★ ★ ★
R ★ ★ ★ ★ ★	T ★ ★ ★ ★

FOLLETT, Ken (1949) British thriller writer. He has risen to a decently high position, perhaps more, in the thriller ranks by virtue of books that are satisfyingly big, smooth to read, arrow-direct in the telling, peaked with action as a mountain range and that assimilate massive research like a boa constrictor.

Storm Island (1978)

C ★ ★ ★ ★ ★ ★	P ★ ★ ★ ★ ★ ★ ★ ★
R ★ ★ ★ ★ ★ ★ ★ ★ ★	T ★ ★ ★ ★ ★ ★ ★ ★ ★

The Key to Rebecca (1980)

C ★ ★ ★ ★ ★ ★ ★	P ★ ★ ★ ★ ★ ★ ★ ★
R ★ ★ ★ ★ ★ ★ ★ ★ ★	T ★ ★ ★ ★ ★ ★ ★ ★ ★

FORBES, Stanton (1923) American mystery writer. Whether she writes as Stanton Forbes or Tobias Wells or Forbes Rydell (with Helen Rydell) or is editing the *Wellesley* (Mass.) *Townsman*, Mrs Forbes is a creative writer. As Stanton Forbes she is the author of *Grieve for the Past*, one of the most sensitive and understanding pictures of an adolescent girl in a small midwestern town. For this classic study Mrs Forbes received Edgar Scroll honours in 1963.

Grieve for the Past (1962)

C ★ ★ ★ ★ ★ ★ ★	P ★ ★ ★ ★ ★ ★
R ★ ★ ★ ★ ★ ★ ★	T ★ ★ ★ ★ ★ ★

If Laurel Shot Hardy the World Would End (1970)

C ★ ★ ★ ★ ★ ★ ★	P ★ ★ ★ ★ ★ ★
R ★ ★ ★ ★ ★ ★ ★	T ★ ★ ★ ★ ★

How To Kill A Man (As Tobias Wells) (1972)

C ★ ★ ★ ★ ★ ★ ★	P ★ ★ ★ ★ ★ ★
R ★ ★ ★ ★ ★ ★ ★	T ★ ★ ★ ★ ★ ★

FORD, Leslie (1898) American mystery writer. Mrs Zenith Jones Brown wrote first under the pseudonym David Frome; she was resident in England and the books featured Mr Pinkerton of Wales and Inspector Bull of Scotland Yard. She adopted the Leslie Ford pseudonym for her Washington, D.C. stories of the trio Grace Lathem, (a widow), Colonel Primrose and Sergeant Buck, whose popularity was immediate. All of her stories have been

delightfully perceptive, most were serialized in the *Saturday Evening Post* to a wide audience.

Ill Met By Moonlight (1937)

C ★ ★ ★ ★ ★ ★ ★	P ★ ★ ★ ★ ★ ★ ★
R ★ ★ ★ ★ ★ ★ ★ ★	T ★ ★ ★ ★ ★ ★

Trial by Ambush (1962)

C ★ ★ ★ ★ ★ ★ ★	P ★ ★ ★ ★ ★ ★ ★
R ★ ★ ★ ★ ★ ★ ★ ★	T ★ ★ ★ ★ ★ ★

FORESTER, C. S. (1899-1966) British historical novelist who wrote two interesting crime novels. *Payment Deferred*, which was in fact his first book, is a strong example of the inverted detective story in which we know the murderer from the beginning, a device first used by R. Austin Freeman (q.v.) and classically later by Francis Iles (q.v.). *Plain Murder*, Forester's other crime novel, is similar though not so powerful.

Payment Deferred (1926)

C ★ ★ ★ ★ ★ ★ ★ ★	P ★ ★ ★ ★ ★ ★ ★ ★ ★ ★ ★
R ★ ★ ★ ★ ★ ★ ★ ★	T ★ ★ ★ ★ ★ ★

C. S. Forester

R = Readability   T = Tension

Frederick Forsyth

The Day of the Jackal (1971)	
C ★ ★ ★ ★ ★	P ★ ★ ★ ★ ★ ★ ★ ★
R ★ ★ ★ ★ ★ ★ ★ ★	T ★ ★ ★ ★ ★ ★ ★ ★

The Odessa File (1972)	
C ★ ★ ★ ★ ★	P ★ ★ ★ ★ ★ ★ ★
R ★ ★ ★ ★ ★ ★ ★	T ★ ★ ★ ★ ★ ★ ★

The Devil's Alternative (1979)	
C ★ ★ ★ ★ ★	P ★ ★ ★ ★ ★ ★ ★ ★
R ★ ★ ★ ★ ★ ★ ★	T ★ ★ ★ ★ ★ ★ ★

FORSYTH, Frederick (1938) British thriller writer. Journalists, in particular foreign correspondents, who turn aside from reportage to use their special knowledge and special talents in the service of fiction are a not uncommon species, but by far the most successful of them has been Frederick Forsyth. With *The Day of the Jackal* (1971) he set himself on top of the pile and each of his three subsequent novels has confirmed his position as the best of the current "documentary" thriller writers. Authenticity is to Forsyth what imagination is to many other writers. It is the quality by which he involves his readers totally in his narratives, which themselves are firmly grounded in political and historical factualities. *The Devil's Alternative,* his detailed account of the hi-jacking of a supertanker, demonstrates that convincing familiarity with both modern political crime and modern super-technology (either of which may destroy us), gives even his dullest passages the compulsion of "the real". His fictional characters benefit from this too. What they lack in depth and subtlety, they compensate for by existing in this "authentic" world where they rub shoulders with "real" people and react to "real" events.

FRANCIS, Dick (1920) British suspense novelist, formerly National Hunt Champion jockey. Modestly he took to crime writing because his sitting-room badly needed a new carpet. That first book, *Dead Cert* (1962), achieved immediate success, both commercial and artistic. Since then, each October, there has been a new Francis thriller, mostly with a racing setting though often with another background interlaced with that. There have been some that have been less good than others, but the latter titles have reached extraordinary heights. Yet the stories

Dick Francis

seem simple. Francis simply says what he has to say, but because what he intends to say is a good deal more than just surface skimming he produces finally books that are tensely exciting thrillers and at the same time compassionate comment on some aspect of life. To write simply and truthfully about simple truths is a high achievement in any field of fiction. Francis does both. His books are very well plotted. They are clearly told. The timing (remember that Turf career that brought him once within an ace of winning the Grand National, bar the last-minute collapse of his mount) is brilliant. They are gripping as anything being written because of the simple humanity that underlies them. These virtues are attested by two Edgars from the Mystery Writers of America (for *Enquiry*, 1969, and *Reflex*, 1980) and a Gold Dagger of the Crime Writers Association for *Whip Hand* in 1979.

Whip Hand (1979)

| C ★ ★ ★ ★ ★ ★ ★ ★ | P ★ ★ ★ ★ ★ ★ ★ ★ |
| R ★ ★ ★ ★ ★ ★ ★ ★ ★ ★ | T ★ ★ ★ ★ ★ ★ ★ ★ ★ ★ |

Reflex (1980)

| C ★ ★ ★ ★ ★ ★ ★ ★ | P ★ ★ ★ ★ ★ ★ ★ ★ ★ |
| R ★ ★ ★ ★ ★ ★ ★ ★ ★ ★ | T ★ ★ ★ ★ ★ ★ ★ ★ ★ ★ |

Twice Shy (1981)

| C ★ ★ ★ ★ ★ ★ ★ ★ | P ★ ★ ★ ★ ★ ★ ★ ★ |
| R ★ ★ ★ ★ ★ ★ ★ ★ ★ ★ | T ★ ★ ★ ★ ★ ★ ★ ★ ★ ★ |

FRASER, Antonia (1932) British detective novelist and, primarily, historian and biographer. Lady Antonia writes a series of attractive novels featuring Jemima Shore, a television investigator apt to become involved in crime, a figure very feminine and very much of her moment.

A Splash of Red (1981)

| C ★ ★ ★ ★ ★ ★ ★ | P ★ ★ ★ ★ ★ ★ ★ |
| R ★ ★ ★ ★ ★ ★ ★ ★ | T ★ ★ ★ ★ ★ ★ ★ |

FREELING, Nicolas (1927) British crime novelist, resident in Strasbourg. He both created and killed off Inspector Van der Valk, Dutch detective, whose main task was to carry his creator's messages about the state of the world, man's humanity and man's inhumanity, an investigator who mingled the understanding with the sceptical. The patently intelligent probing that constitutes a Freeling novel, a simultaneous investigation of a crime and a facet of society somewhat in the manner of Simenon (q.v.), brought him much critical acclaim, the second award of the Crime Writers Association in Britain in 1963 for *Gun Before Butter (A Question of Loyalty* in U.S.), the Grand Prix du Roman Policier and an Edgar from the Mystery Writers of America in 1966 for *King of the Rainy Country*. Yet there has always been something wilful about his writing, witness the killing of Van der Valk in mid-book (*A Long Silence*, 1972, *Auprès de Ma Blonde* in U.S.). His stories are apt to wander; his prose is erratic; his opinions are often eccentric and at times intrusive; his titles are odd. In recent books he has taken as running heroes either a French detective, Henri Castang, or Van der Valk's widow, Arlette, who works in Strasbourg, most European of cities.

Antonia Fraser

R = Readability   T = Tension

Criminal Conversation (1965)

C ★★★★★★★	P ★★★★★★★
R ★★★★★★	T ★★★★★★

Gadget (1977)

C ★★★★★★	P ★★★★★★★
R ★★★★★★★	T ★★★★★★★★

The Night Lords (1978)

C ★★★★★	P ★★★★★★
R ★★★★★★	T ★★★★★

FREEMAN, R. Austin (1862-1943) British detective story writer. He is numbered among the classics on two counts. First for the creation of Dr Thorndyke, the scientific investigator. And a real scientist he was, actually using the facts of science, clearly explained, to track down murderers. Secondly, Freeman was one of the inventors, if not the inventor, of the inverted detective story, in which we know who the murderer is and the interest is in the way he is at last pinned down. Freeman himself said his ideal reader would be "a clergyman of studious and scholarly habit" more interested in the explanation than in the puzzle. But unideal readers can still take pleasure in his drily humorous, solidly scientific stories.

The Red Thumb Mark (1911)

C ★★★★★	P ★★★★★★★★
R ★★★★★★★	T ★★

The Cat's Eye (1923)

C ★★★★★	P ★★★★★★★★★
R ★★★★★★★	T ★★★

FREEMANTLE, Brian (1936) British espionage writer. A former foreign correspondent who worked in more than 40 countries, Freemantle created Charlie Muffin, an agent in the tradition of Deighton's anti-snob figure, almost always very much on the wrong side of the British spy establishment, an organization shown as working often more for its own presitge than out of patriotism. The other people in his books are swiftly well-drawn characters.

Charlie Muffin (1977)
(*Charlie M.* in U.S.)

C ★★★★★★	P ★★★★★★★★
R ★★★★★★★	T ★★★★★

Celia
Fremlin

FREMLIN, Celia (1914) British suspense writer. She achieves a very high standard in books that range fairly widely, being awarded the Mystery Writers of America Edgar in 1960 for *Uncle Paul*. Her novels seldom have policemen or detectives in them and often they have no murder, only a feeling, cleverly and strongly conveyed, of ever-escalating threat. She combines this with a sharp eye for hypocrisy and a fine touch with the details of domestic life. "You can," one of her publishers once said, "feel the hanging wet nappies (diapers) brushing your face." Her prose is fastidiously excellent.

Uncle Paul (1959)

C ★★★★★★★	P ★★★★★★★
R ★★★★★★★	T ★★★★★★★

The Spider-Orchid (1977)

C ★★★★★★★	P ★★★★★★★★
R ★★★★★★★	T ★★★★★★★

With No Crying (1980)

C ★★★★★★★★	P ★★★★★★★
R ★★★★★★★★	T ★★★★★★

FULLER, Roy (1912) British poet, lawyer, novelist and author of three crime stories, of which the most distinguished is *The Second Curtain.* This is the story of the Power Industries Corporation, a huge criminal organisation, and one rather ineffectual novelist's struggle against it.

The Second Curtain (1953)

C ★ ★ ★ ★ ★ ★ ★ ★	P ★ ★ ★ ★ ★ ★
R ★ ★ ★ ★ ★ ★ ★	T ★ ★ ★ ★ ★ ★

FUTRELLE, Jacques (1875-1912) American author of crime short stories and journalist. Futrelle invented as sleuth The Thinking Machine, otherwise Professor S. F. X. Van Dusen, solver of impossible riddles. His story "The Problem of Cell 13" (1905), a locked-room challenge, is one of the classics of crime. He perished in the sinking of *The Titanic,* after pushing his wife into a lifeboat and so saving her.

Best Thinking Machine Detective Stories (1973)

C ★ ★ ★ ★ ★	P ★ ★ ★ ★ ★ ★ ★ ★ ★
R ★ ★ ★ ★ ★ ★	T ★ ★ ★ ★ ★ ★

GABORIAU, Emile (1833-73) French sensation novelist. He was a precursor of the detective story and, daringly when the police were much distrusted, made his detective a young policeman, Lecoq (though on occasion the detection goes to an old pawnbroker, Père Tabaret, called "Tir-au-clair"). Much that was later used and used in British detection, and American, first saw the light in his pages.

The Mystery of Orcival (1884)

C ★ ★ ★ ★	P ★ ★ ★ ★ ★ ★ ★
R ★ ★ ★ ★ ★ ★	T ★ ★ ★ ★

The Lerouge Case (1885)

C ★ ★ ★ ★	P ★ ★ ★ ★ ★ ★ ★
R ★ ★ ★ ★ ★ ★	T ★ ★ ★ ★

GADNEY, Reg (1941) British espionage novelist and art historian. He wrote six novels between 1972 and 1977, since when academic duties at the Royal College of Art seem to have silenced him. But the six were each well worth having, swiftly told in sharp, packed prose, they gave us portraits of the underside of Europe, surrealist at times.

Drawn Blanc (1970)

C ★ ★ ★ ★ ★ ★ ★	P ★ ★ ★ ★ ★ ★ ★ ★
R ★ ★ ★ ★ ★ ★ ★	T ★ ★ ★ ★ ★ ★ ★ ★

GAINHAM, Sarah (1922) British novelist, pen-name of Sarah Rachel Ames, whose earlier works were in the espionage field. Extensive travel in Europe since the war, and her work as a journalist, have endowed her with the sense of political atmosphere and upheaval which are so evident in her disturbingly authentic stories of intrigue and revolution.

Time Right Deadly (1956)

C ★ ★ ★ ★ ★	P ★ ★ ★ ★ ★ ★ ★
R ★ ★ ★ ★ ★ ★	T ★ ★ ★ ★ ★ ★

The Mythmaker (1957)
(*Appointment in Vienna* in U.S.)

C ★ ★ ★ ★ ★	P ★ ★ ★ ★ ★ ★ ★ ★
R ★ ★ ★ ★ ★	T ★ ★ ★ ★ ★ ★ ★

The Silent Hostage (1960)

C ★ ★ ★ ★ ★ ★	P ★ ★ ★ ★ ★ ★ ★
R ★ ★ ★ ★ ★	T ★ ★ ★ ★ ★ ★

GARDNER, Erle Stanley (1889-1970) American mystery author. Gardner was the most published American author of his time, sharing the world record with the queen herself, Agatha Christie. A lawyer for twenty years before deciding to become a writer, Gardner learned by writing short stories for the pulps, and when he turned to full length mystery devised the lawyer character Perry Mason, an immediate star. Mason was known throughout the world not only from the Gardner books but from his television appearances. Gardner wrote under numerous pen names, A. A. Fair be-

R = Readability   T = Tension

ing best known. Although not a stylist, Gardner was a perfectionist in his writing, both in his books, his articles, his short stories, and his travel series of Baja California, which peninsula he pioneered. His great contribution to mystery was in taking the detective story away from the eccentric sleuthing amateur, such as Philo Vance and other variations of Sherlock Holmes, and establishing in his stead through Perry Mason, a hard-working, normal intelligent man who solved cases to defend his clients. The titles of the Gardner works cover two and a half book pages. He was honoured with a Grand Master Edgar by Mystery Writers of America in 1961.

Erle Stanley Gardner

The Case of the Velvet Claws (1933)

C ★ ★ ★ ★ ★ ★	P ★ ★ ★ ★ ★ ★ ★
R ★ ★ ★ ★ ★ ★	T ★ ★ ★ ★ ★ ★

The Case of the Howling Dog (1934)

C ★ ★ ★ ★ ★ ★	P ★ ★ ★ ★ ★ ★ ★
R ★ ★ ★ ★ ★ ★	T ★ ★ ★ ★ ★ ★

The Case of the Caretakers Cat (1935)

C ★ ★ ★ ★ ★ ★	P ★ ★ ★ ★ ★ ★ ★
R ★ ★ ★ ★ ★ ★	T ★ ★ ★ ★ ★ ★

GARDNER, John (1926) British suspense writer and novelist. He is remarkable for the width and success of his work in the field. He began in 1964 at the height of the Bond era in spy fiction with a highly amusing series starring Boysie Oakes, cowardly, lascivious and made an 007-type agent in error. In 1969 he wrote a police procedural novel with strong religious undertones in the Graham Greene mode, *A Complete State of Death*, with as hero a C.I.D. man, Derek Torry, who was to feature in one other similar book. Another five years on, in 1974, he launched out again with *The Return of Moriarty*, with as anti-hero Sherlock Holmes' opponent of old, backed by a great deal of good historical research. This again had a sequel. Then in 1976 with *To Run A*

Little Faster he turned to the suspense novel proper in the style of, say, Francis Clifford (q.v.) and continued somewhat in this vein with the compulsively readable *The Werewolf Trace*, which mingled espionage with a touch of the occult. He was to stay in the espionage sub-genre, it seemed, with his well-conceived group of agents and spymasters comparable to those of Le Carré (q.v.), notably the massive,

John Gardner

C = Characterization   P = Plot

intellectual Big Herbie Kruger. But there was to be another change of direction when in 1981 Gardner was entrusted with the task of reviving James Bond, a feat he brought off with admirable judgment in *Licence Renewed* and its sequel, *For Special Services* (1982).

The Liquidator (1964)

C ★ ★ ★ ★ ★ ★	P ★ ★ ★ ★ ★ ★ ★
R ★ ★ ★ ★ ★ ★ ★ ★	T ★ ★ ★ ★ ★ ★ ★

The Werewolf Trace (1977)

C ★ ★ ★ ★ ★ ★ ★ ★	P ★ ★ ★ ★ ★ ★ ★
R ★ ★ ★ ★ ★ ★ ★ ★	T ★ ★ ★ ★ ★ ★ ★

Licence Renewed (1981)

C ★ ★ ★ ★ ★ ★ ★	P ★ ★ ★ ★ ★ ★ ★ ★
R ★ ★ ★ ★ ★ ★ ★ ★ ★	T ★ ★ ★ ★ ★ ★ ★

GARFIELD, Brian (1939) American mystery writer. A prolific writer of Westerns under his own name and under many pseudonyms, Brian Garfield moved into the mystery field to an immediate and equal success. He writes the hard-boiled

novel and many of his stories have been filmed. In 1975, Garfield received the Edgar for Best Novel with *Hopscotch*. *Recoil*, one of his latest, was an alternate Book of the Month selection.

Hopscotch (1974)

C ★ ★ ★ ★ ★	P ★ ★ ★ ★ ★ ★ ★ ★
R ★ ★ ★ ★ ★ ★ ★	T ★ ★ ★ ★ ★ ★ ★ ★

Recoil (1977)

C ★ ★ ★ ★ ★	P ★ ★ ★ ★ ★ ★ ★
R ★ ★ ★ ★ ★ ★ ★	T ★ ★ ★ ★ ★ ★ ★

GARNER, William (1932) British thriller novelist who worked for 20 years in industrial public relations before achieving a long-held ambition to be a full-time novelist and "forsake red-carpet life". His books generally have an accurate scientific background and they do not lack an underlying seriousness (which makes the tension more tense). He says: "I think a lot *all* the time. I never switch off."

The Us or Them War (1969)

C ★ ★ ★ ★ ★ ★	P ★ ★ ★ ★ ★ ★ ★
R ★ ★ ★ ★ ★ ★ ★ ★	T ★ ★ ★ ★ ★ ★ ★

The Möbuys trip (1979)

C ★ ★ ★ ★ ★ ★ ★	P ★ ★ ★ ★ ★ ★ ★ ★
R ★ ★ ★ ★ ★ ★ ★ ★	T ★ ★ ★ ★ ★ ★ ★ ★

GARVE, Andrew (1908) British suspense writer, pseudonym for Paul Winterton, a distinguished journalist. From 1950 on, when he ceased writing books on Soviet affairs, he produced a steady stream of crime novels of varying sorts and varied settings, but all written with a craftsman's skill. With him you can always be sure of a good, clearly told story and generally of plenty of by-the-way information.

The Sea Monks (1963)

C ★ ★ ★ ★ ★ ★	P ★ ★ ★ ★ ★ ★
R ★ ★ ★ ★ ★ ★ ★ ★	T ★ ★ ★ ★ ★ ★ ★

Counterstroke (1978)

C ★ ★ ★ ★ ★ ★ ★	P ★ ★ ★ ★ ★ ★
R ★ ★ ★ ★ ★ ★ ★ ★	T ★ ★ ★ ★ ★ ★

William
Garner

R = Readability   T = Tension

GASH, Jonathan (1935) British mystery writer, and as Dr John Grant head of a bacteriology unit at the University of London. As a medical student he worked in various London street markets for pocket money and began to learn about antiques. His running hero is one Lovejoy, an antiques dealer not above going to the edge of the legal and a bit beyond, a person impressively knowledgeable as well as being a great goer-to-bed with assorted ladies. The books are written from his viewpoint, with immense gusto.

Spend Game (1980)

C ★ ★ ★ ★ ★ ★ ★	P ★ ★ ★ ★ ★ ★ ★
R ★ ★ ★ ★ ★ ★ ★ ★	T ★ ★ ★ ★ ★

The Vatican Rip (1981)

C ★ ★ ★ ★ ★ ★ ★	P ★ ★ ★ ★ ★ ★ ★ ★
R ★ ★ ★ ★ ★ ★ ★ ★ ★	T ★ ★ ★ ★ ★ ★

GAULT, William Campbell (1910) American mystery writer. Gault has had an award winning double career, both in mystery and for his juvenile novels. He wrote 300 short stories before turning to mystery, winning Best First Edgar in 1952 for *Don't Cry For Me*. His chief interest is sports and best known of his private eyes is a former player for the Los Angeles Rams, a professional football team. His juvenile books are also sports oriented, and for this body of work he received awards from the Boys' Club of America in 1957.

Michael Gilbert

Day of the Ram (1956)

C ★ ★ ★ ★ ★ ★ ★	P ★ ★ ★ ★ ★ ★ ★
R ★ ★ ★ ★ ★ ★ ★	T ★ ★ ★ ★ ★ ★

Dead Hero (1963)

C ★ ★ ★ ★ ★ ★ ★	P ★ ★ ★ ★ ★ ★
R ★ ★ ★ ★ ★ ★ ★	T ★ ★ ★ ★ ★ ★

GIELGUD, Val (1900) British playwright and detective novelist, whose experience in drama and at the B.B.C. has provided a number of his mysteries with much technical authenticity. A competent purveyor of the old-fashioned mystery and also those which move with the times, his London backgrounds are particularly good.

Prinvest – London (1963)

C ★ ★ ★ ★ ★	P ★ ★ ★ ★ ★ ★
R ★ ★ ★ ★ ★ ★ ★ ★	T ★ ★ ★

A Necessary End (1969)

C ★ ★ ★ ★ ★ ★	P ★ ★ ★ ★ ★ ★ ★
R ★ ★ ★ ★ ★ ★ ★ ★	T ★ ★ ★

GILBERT, Anthony (1899-1973) British detective novelist, pseudonym for Lucy Malleson. Between 1925 and 1974 she published 69 crime novels, a few as J. Kilmeny Keith or Anne Meredith. From 1937 onwards she mostly chronicled with tearaway enjoyment the cases of the highly engaging shyster lawyer Arthur Crook (in his earlier days less likeable), "the criminal's hope, the judge's despair."

The Visitor (1967)

C ★ ★ ★ ★ ★ ★ ★ ★	P ★ ★ ★ ★ ★ ★
R ★ ★ ★ ★ ★ ★ ★	T ★ ★ ★ ★ ★ ★

Death Wears A Mask (1970)

C ★ ★ ★ ★ ★ ★ ★ ★	P ★ ★ ★ ★ ★ ★ ★
R ★ ★ ★ ★ ★ ★ ★ ★	T ★ ★ ★ ★ ★

GILBERT, Michael (1912) British crime novelist and lawyer. Over half a century (his first book *Close Quarters* was written in 1930, though not published until 1947 after a wartime interval) Michael Gilbert has written a large number of books in a number of different criminous sub-genres. All are mark-ed by good straightforward story-telling and an ambition simply to entertain whether in the police pro-cedural (Petrella is his British detec-tive), the thriller, the murder puzzle or in espionage stories. They rank him high.

Smallbone Deceased (1950)

C ★ ★ ★ ★ ★ ★ ★	P ★ ★ ★ ★ ★ ★ ★
R ★ ★ ★ ★ ★ ★ ★ ★	T ★ ★ ★ ★ ★

Flash Point (1974)

C ★ ★ ★ ★ ★ ★ ★	P ★ ★ ★ ★ ★ ★ ★
R ★ ★ ★ ★ ★ ★ ★ ★	T ★ ★ ★ ★ ★ ★

GILL, B. M. (1921) British mystery writer and novelist. With only two ventures into crime fiction she made her mark. She writes about localized British settings, a boarding school, a hospital, with sympathy and an accuracy that has led some critics to compare her with P. D. James (q.v.)

Victims (1981)

C ★ ★ ★ ★ ★ ★ ★	P ★ ★ ★ ★ ★
R ★ ★ ★ ★ ★ ★	T ★ ★ ★ ★ ★

GILMAN, Dorothy (1923) American suspense novelist. She turned from writing juvenile fiction to create the most unlikely C.I.A. agent imaginable, the charming and elderly widow Mrs Pollifax, who faces many a grim situation with resourcefulness and humour, and gives us unashamed escapism.

A Nun in the Closet (1975)
(A Nun in the Cupboard in U.K.)

C ★ ★ ★ ★ ★	P ★ ★ ★ ★ ★ ★ ★
R ★ ★ ★ ★ ★ ★ ★ ★	T ★ ★ ★ ★ ★

GLEN WINSLOW, Pauline Brit-ish-born suspense novelist, resident in New York. Because her first, mainstream novel, *The Strawberry Marten* (*Gallows Child* in U.S.) was based on Ruth Ellis, the last woman to hang in Britain, she found herself fixed in the mystery category, in which she produced books with a curious power to them, somewhat in the Margery Allingham (q.v.) mould.

She has also written faction works with a crime or espionage flavour, such as *The Windsor Plot*.

Coppergold (1978)

C ★ ★ ★ ★ ★ ★ ★ ★	P ★ ★ ★ ★ ★ ★ ★
R ★ ★ ★ ★ ★ ★ ★	T ★ ★ ★ ★ ★

The Windsor Plot (1981)

C ★ ★ ★ ★ ★ ★	P ★ ★ ★ ★ ★ ★
R ★ ★ ★ ★ ★ ★ ★ ★	T ★ ★

GODEY, John (1912) American mystery writer, who published numerous short stories before turn-ing to novels. His first full length novels featured Jack Albany, an un-successful actor. With *The Taking of Pelham One Two Three*, about the high-jacking of a New York sub-way, he gained a Book of the Month choice, a best seller and a best motion picture. From a literary standpoint, *The Snake* was an even greater success, a new classic in mystery fiction, honoured by an Edgar scroll in 1979.

A Thrill a Minute with Jack Albany (1967)

C ★ ★ ★ ★ ★	P ★ ★ ★ ★ ★ ★ ★
R ★ ★ ★ ★ ★ ★	T ★ ★ ★ ★ ★ ★ ★

The Taking of Pelham One Two Three (1973)

C ★ ★ ★ ★ ★	P ★ ★ ★ ★ ★ ★ ★
R ★ ★ ★ ★ ★ ★ ★ ★	T ★ ★ ★ ★ ★ ★ ★ ★

The Snake (1978)

C ★ ★ ★ ★ ★	P ★ ★ ★ ★ ★ ★ ★
R ★ ★ ★ ★ ★ ★ ★ ★ ★	T ★ ★ ★ ★ ★ ★ ★ ★ ★

GOLDSTEIN, Arthur D. (1937) American mystery writer. Brook-lyn-born Arthur Goldstein worked in public relations and as an editor for news releases of the American Stock Exchange and Securities markets before writing a book. His first mystery, *A Person Shouldn't Die Like That*, was published in 1971 and took honours from the Mystery Writers of America the fol-lowing year as one of the best first novels of its year. Goldstein writes of the Jewish community on the East

R = Readability   T = Tension

Side of New York, of the old men who sit together in the park, remembering old times. He has the perfect ear for dialogue, the eye for detail, and a heart attuned to this community within a community.

A Person Shouldn't Die Like That (1971)

C ★★★★★★★	P ★★★★★★
R ★★★★★★★★	T ★★★★★★★

Nobody Was Sorry He Got Killed (1976)

C ★★★★★★★	P ★★★★★★
R ★★★★★★★★	T ★★★★★★

THE GORDONS (Gordon, Gordon) (1912), **(Gordon, Mildred)** (1912-1979) American mystery writers. Both the Gordons were Arizona journalists and he was also in publicity for motion picture companies before they began their mystery career. Mildred wrote her first mystery, a solo, *The Little Man Who Wasn't There,* when her husband was serving as an FBI special agent in World War II. Their collaboration began after the war, and it meshed so perfectly that no one could distinguish where one writer took over from another. Their first book was *The FBI Story* (1950). After more than a decade of straight mysteries they diversified into comedy mystery with *Undercover Cat,* an imaginative feline detective who brought a new career to the Gordons. They received Edgar recognition for both *The Talking Bug* and for *Undercover Cat.* Many of their books were made into successful motion pictures.

Campaign Train (1952)

C ★★★★★★	P ★★★★★★★
R ★★★★★★	T ★★★★★

The Talking Bug (1955)

C ★★★★★★	P ★★★★★★★★
R ★★★★★★★	T ★★★★★★

Undercover Cat (1963)

C ★★★★★★	P ★★★★★★★★
R ★★★★★★★	T ★★★★★★

GORES, Joe (1931) American mystery writer. Joe Gores was a prolific short story writer, more than 100 published before his first novel, *Time of Predators* appeared. It launched a new star of the hard-boiled school, taking Best First Novel Edgar in 1969. The same year he also took top Edgar for Best Short Story for "Goodbye, Pops". A regular writer for the Kojak television series, he received a third Edgar in 1975 for his episode, "No Immunity for Murder". In spite of his listing his background as a hod carrier, a carnival worker and a private eye, he holds a Bachelor's degree from Notre Dame University and a Master's degree from Stanford University. And he makes a point, in biographical material, that "Gores" rhymes with "Roars".

A Time of Predators (1968)

C ★★★★★	P ★★★★★
R ★★★★★★	T ★★★★★

Dead Skip (1972)

C ★★★★★	P ★★★★★
R ★★★★★★	T ★★★★★

Final Notice (1973)

C ★★★★★	P ★★★★★★
R ★★★★★★★	T ★★★★★

GOSLING, Paula American suspense writer, resident in England. She has a marked gift for the creation of tension, and as well in *Zero Trap* has successfully invaded the male territory of Alistair MacLean (q.v.) and Desmond Bagley (q.v.).

A Running Duck (1978)

C ★★★★★★★	P ★★★★★★★
R ★★★★★★★★★	T ★★★★★★★★

Zero Trap (1979)

C ★★★★★	P ★★★★★★★
R ★★★★★★★★★	T ★★★★★★★★★

GRAEME, Bruce (1900) British writer of thrillers and detective stories. His most enduring series features gentlemen-burglars Blackshirt and Son, and (under the pseudonym

David Graeme) their Seventeenth-century forefather Monsieur Blackshirt. Lesser known today, but with neat detection in the classic mould, are his novels of Superintendent Stevens and Inspector Allain, and bookseller-sleuth Theodore I. Terhune.

Blackshirt (stories, 1925)

C ★ ★ ★ ★	P ★ ★ ★ ★ ★
R ★ ★ ★ ★ ★ ★ ★ ★ ★	T ★ ★

The Quiet Ones (1970)

C ★ ★ ★ ★ ★	P ★ ★ ★ ★ ★
R ★ ★ ★ ★ ★ ★ ★ ★ ★	T ★ ★ ★

Winston
Graham

GRAHAM, Winston (1909) British novelist of considerable range, whose Poldark family saga unfortunately overshadows his many excellent crime novels. From near-traditional detective stories, through espionage and psychological suspense, his standard is consistently high; he likes to explore motivation, with an implicated protagonist rather than a neutral investigator,

and hence is much more than just a top rate storyteller.

The Little Walls (1955)

C ★ ★ ★ ★ ★ ★ ★	P ★ ★ ★ ★ ★ ★ ★
R ★ ★ ★ ★ ★ ★ ★ ★ ★	T ★ ★ ★ ★

Marnie (1961)

C ★ ★ ★ ★ ★ ★ ★	P ★ ★ ★ ★ ★ ★
R ★ ★ ★ ★ ★ ★ ★ ★	T ★ ★ ★

The Walking Stick (1967)

C ★ ★ ★ ★ ★ ★ ★	P ★ ★ ★ ★ ★ ★ ★
R ★ ★ ★ ★ ★ ★ ★ ★	T ★ ★ ★

GRAY, Dulcie (1920) British suspense writer, actress and film star. Her crime stories, initially detective tales, later psychological studies, are marked by their excellent dialogue, keen interest in human beings and zestful telling, occasionally over-detailed and sometimes wildly inaccurate in matters other than the theatrical.

For Richer, For Richer (1970)

C ★ ★ ★ ★ ★ ★ ★	P ★ ★ ★ ★
R ★ ★ ★ ★ ★ ★ ★ ★	T ★ ★ ★ ★

GRAYSON, Richard (1922) British historical mystery writer. He sets his stories in Paris, round about the turn of the century and has a considerable gift for evoking the atmosphere of zestful decadence, even if detail is sometimes piled on to excess. His first book, *The Murders at Impasse Louvain*, won the popularly-voted Current Crime cup in Britain.

The Murders at Impasse Louvain (1978)

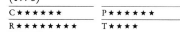

C ★ ★ ★ ★ ★ ★	P ★ ★ ★ ★ ★ ★
R ★ ★ ★ ★ ★ ★ ★ ★	T ★ ★ ★ ★

GREEN, Anna Katherine (1846-1935) American mystery writer. Anna Katherine Green is generally considered to be the first woman in America to write a detective story. She was indeed the first woman to use a working detective in her books, Ebenezer Gryce. Daughter of a noted New York lawyer, Green was

R = Readability   T = Tension

immensely popular in her fifty years of writing. Her first mystery, *The Leavenworth Case*, is considered an American mystery classic.

The Leavenworth Case (1878)

C ★★★★★	P ★★★★★★
R ★★★★★★★	T ★★★★★

The Step on the Stair (1923)

C ★★★★★	P ★★★★★★
R ★★★★★★★	T ★★★★★

GREENE, Graham (1904) British novelist, former secret agent and, in the books he once labelled as "entertainments", crime novelist. Indeed, his novel of 1978, *The Human Factor*, differs so little from the classic contemporary espionage novel that it is hard not to claim it as an example, and a marvellously tense one, of the genre. *Brighton Rock* (1938), too, which Greene swiftly shifted out of its original "entertainment" category, was begun avowedly as a detective thriller, though, suspenseful as it is, it hardly ended up as one. Even the entertainments are redolent of that particular view of existence that has been called the atmosphere of "Greeneland", the unique mixture of the seedy and the extraordinarily funny and the sad, the whole running in a story, swift-flowing and easy, told in quiet prose that carries a high charge in every syllable.

A Gun for Sale (1936)
(This Gun for Hire in US)

C ★★★★★★★★	P ★★★★★★★★★
R ★★★★★★★★★	T ★★★★★★★★★

The Third Man (1950)

C ★★★★★★★★	P ★★★★★★★★★
R ★★★★★★★★★	T ★★★★★★★★★

Our Man in Havana (1958)

C ★★★★★★★★★★	P ★★★★★★★★★
R ★★★★★★★★★★	T ★★★★★★★★★

GREENLEAF, Stephen American mystery writer. A newcomer to the private-eye story, he hit with his first novel, *Grave Error*, the full classical style while contriving to delve deep into psychology in the Ross Macdonald (q.v.) manner.

Grave Error (1981)

C ★★★★★★★	P ★★★★★★★
R ★★★★★★★★	T ★★★★★★★

GRIBBLE, Leonard (1908) British writer of detective fiction and true crime stories, with prolific output under at least six names. His principal character, Slade of Scotland Yard, is solid and dependable; well plotted and economical in style, normally with typically English settings, Slade's exploits entertainingly convey the message that crime does not pay.

They Kidnapped Stanley Matthews (1950)

C ★★★	P ★★★★★★★
R ★★★★★★★★	T ★★★

GRIERSON, Edward (1914-75) British crime novelist, whose examination of human relationships and questioning of legal conventions are more important than the crime content. Powerful characterization and a mastery of dialogue predominate. He wrote only four crime novels, but his contribution to the field was considerable in terms of originality and quality.

Reputation for a Song (1952)

C ★★★★★★★★★	P ★★★★★★★
R ★★★★★★	T ★★★★

The Second Man (1956)

C ★★★★★★★★★	P ★★★★★★★★
R ★★★★★★	T ★★★

The Massingham Affair (1962)

C ★★★★★★★	P ★★★★★★★★
R ★★★★★★	T ★★★

GRUBER, Frank (1904-69) American mystery writer. Frank Gruber was an indefatigable writer with many pseudonyms, equally at home in westerns and in mystery. As a sideline he wrote more than fifty motion picture scripts and more than 200 television scripts. He taught himself to write while working on trade journals in the midwest. His inimitable characters were Oliver Quade, the "Human Encyclopedia", and Charles Boston, a comic team in the Laurel and Hardy tradition. Gruber's Johnny Fletcher and Simon Lash stories were highly popular for many years, part of the semi-tough tradition of the forties.

The Etruscan Bull (1969)

C ★ ★ ★ ★ ★ ★	P ★ ★ ★ ★ ★ ★ ★
R ★ ★ ★ ★ ★ ★ ★	T ★ ★ ★ ★ ★

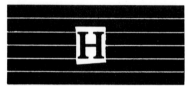

HADDAD, C. A. American mystery writer. Haddad is so well hidden behind his/her pseudonym that the anonymity has not yet been breached. He is however one of the most exciting and amusing new names in American mystery. His scene is Israel and his lead character a Jew from Morocco who in spite of being a self-declared coward becomes a member of the Israeli security service. The scene is so real that it seems Haddad must be a born and bred Israeli citizen. Over and above the hilarious misfortunes of Judah, there is Jewish wisdom.

The Moroccan (1975)

C ★ ★ ★ ★ ★ ★	P ★ ★ ★ ★ ★ ★ ★
R ★ ★ ★ ★ ★ ★ ★	T ★ ★ ★ ★ ★ ★

Operation Apricot (1978)

C ★ ★ ★ ★ ★ ★	P ★ ★ ★ ★ ★ ★
R ★ ★ ★ ★ ★ ★ ★	T ★ ★ ★ ★ ★ ★

William
Haggard

HAGGARD, William (1907) British espionage novelist, former Controller of Enemy Property for the British government. From 1958, at about the rate of one a year, he has produced a series of action novels of international politics, marked out by an idiosyncratic view of all human activity, by a trick of placing many of his narratives in the highest citadels of government (where they look down on mere passing Prime Ministers) and by the frequent presence of Colonel Russell of the Security Executive, latterly retired, a gentleman of the old school and a sardonic realist in outlook. Even Haggard's style of writing is stamped with the impress of a personality tartly at odds with the bland acceptances of contemporary society.

The Conspirators (1967)

C ★ ★ ★ ★ ★ ★ ★	P ★ ★ ★ ★ ★ ★ ★
R ★ ★ ★ ★ ★ ★	T ★ ★ ★ ★ ★ ★

The Doubtful Disciple (1969)

C ★ ★ ★ ★ ★ ★ ★	P ★ ★ ★ ★ ★ ★ ★
R ★ ★ ★ ★ ★ ★ ★	T ★ ★ ★ ★ ★ ★

The Protectors (1972)

C ★ ★ ★ ★ ★ ★ ★	P ★ ★ ★ ★ ★ ★
R ★ ★ ★ ★ ★ ★ ★	T ★ ★ ★ ★ ★ ★ ★

R = Readability   T = Tension

HALL, Adam (1920) British spy adventure writer, real name Elleston Trevor (q.v.). The Adam Hall books, with one exception, feature Quiller, a British Intelligence trouble-shooter, working for an organization yet more mysterious and unacknowledged than MI5 or DI6. They are written in a hectic, even bullying, style making few concessions to the reader and packed with authentic-sounding spy jargon, car expertise and fight analysis.

The Striker Portfolio (1969)

C ★ ★ ★ ★ ★	P ★ ★ ★ ★ ★ ★ ★ ★
R ★ ★ ★ ★ ★ ★ ★ ★	T ★ ★ ★ ★ ★ ★ ★ ★ ★

The Pekin Target (1981)

C ★ ★ ★ ★ ★	P ★ ★ ★ ★ ★ ★ ★ ★
R ★ ★ ★ ★ ★ ★ ★ ★	T ★ ★ ★ ★ ★ ★ ★ ★ ★

HALLAHAN, William American mystery writer. Hallahan was Edgar winner for Best Novel in 1977 with *Catch Me, Kill Me*, characterized by New York critics as "a thriller" and a "masterpiece of bamboozlement". One of the new mystery writers, Hallahan mixes suspense with unusual plot developments.

Catch Me, Kill Me (1976)

C ★ ★ ★ ★ ★ ★	P ★ ★ ★ ★ ★ ★ ★ ★
R ★ ★ ★ ★ ★ ★ ★	T ★ ★ ★ ★ ★ ★ ★

Keeper of the Children (1978)

C ★ ★ ★ ★ ★ ★	P ★ ★ ★ ★ ★ ★ ★
R ★ ★ ★ ★ ★ ★ ★	T ★ ★ ★ ★ ★ ★ ★

HALLIDAY, Brett (1904-77) American mystery writer, pseudonym of Davis Dresser. Dresser had any number of pseudonyms but the principal one was Brett Halliday. Halliday authored Michael Shayne, a semi-hardboiled Florida private eye who appeared in countless books and for many years had a magazine bearing his name. Dresser was a prolific writer of westerns as well as mysteries; many of both were filmed, included two well remembered crime classics, *Before I Wake* (1949) and *A Lonely Way To Die* (1950).

Dividend on Death (1939)

C ★ ★ ★ ★	P ★ ★ ★ ★ ★ ★
R ★ ★ ★ ★ ★ ★	T ★ ★ ★ ★ ★

Murder In Haste (1961)

C ★ ★ ★ ★ ★	P ★ ★ ★ ★ ★ ★
R ★ ★ ★ ★ ★ ★	T ★ ★ ★ ★ ★

HALLIDAY, Dorothy see DUNNETT, Dorothy

HAMILTON, Donald (1916) American mystery writer. Swedish-born Donald Hamilton has lived in the United States since he was a small boy. He served as a chemist in the Naval Reserve during World War II, and on leaving the service in 1946 he turned to writing, both in the western and the mystery fields. His first mystery, *Date With Darkness,* was published the following year. He wrote fine espionage novels for a number of years but not until his creation of Matt Helm did he become a world wide best seller. The Helm series appears as original paperbacks and is distinguished in that field by the fact that Hamilton's writing has literary quality as well as rousing action. Matt Helm's *The Terrorizers* received an Edgar Scroll for Best Paperback original in 1977. Matt Helm was also featured in a motion picture series.

The Ambushers (1963)

C ★ ★ ★ ★ ★ ★ ★	P ★ ★ ★ ★ ★ ★ ★
R ★ ★ ★ ★ ★ ★ ★ ★	T ★ ★ ★ ★ ★ ★ ★

The Terminators (1975)

C ★ ★ ★ ★ ★ ★ ★	P ★ ★ ★ ★ ★ ★ ★
R ★ ★ ★ ★ ★ ★ ★ ★	T ★ ★ ★ ★ ★ ★ ★

HAMILTON, Patrick (1904-62) British novelist and playwright. Patrick Hamilton, in his young days an actor and stage-manager, is perhaps most easily identified as the writer of two plays later made into successful films – *Rope* (1929) and *Gas Light* (1933). His crime novels consist of a claustrophobic study of schizophrenia, *Hangover Square* (1939), and the first three books of

C = Characterization   P = Plot

an unfinished quartet featuring a villain called Gorse.

Hangover Square (1939)

C ★ ★ ★ ★ ★ ★ ★ ★	P ★ ★ ★ ★ ★ ★
R ★ ★ ★ ★ ★ ★ ★	T ★ ★ ★ ★ ★ ★ ★

HAMMETT, Dashiell (1894-1961) American private-eye novelist, former Pinkerton's agent. In 1922, fearing that he had not long to live because of a lung disease he had contracted while in the Army Ambulance corps in World War I, he quit Pinkerton's and began to write, advertising copy for a jewel store so as to live and pieces for *Black Mask* magazine and *Smart Set*. His writing developed rapidly and by 1927 he was contributing long stories to *Black Mask* which, revised, became his first novels, *Red Harvest* and *The Dain Curse* (both 1929). Thereafter books came out in quick succession, but by 1934 his career as a creative writer was over, though he long nourished ambitions to do more.

Dashiell
Hammett

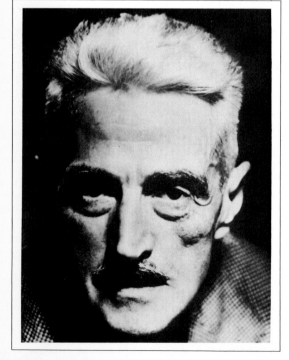

But he had done enough. He is the toughest and the greatest of the once-called ''hardboiled'' crime novelists, America's prime contribution to the art. He is, too, a novelist proper of stature, a seer of things hitherto unseen. But however much his novels and some of his short stories are literature they were first published because they were, simply, gripping reading. Nor has time dulled their edge. Sometimes, indeed, it gives us an odd bonus of sociological fact, such as the ultra-tough detective scrambling out of bed and into a union suit, combination top and bottom underwear. Hammett's achievement, however, stems from more than just being tough, or even just telling the truth about murder and detective work. He had a vision. He saw life as a precarious existence we each fabricate in pathetic defiance of the ever-looming sudden. It is this view that gives his work consistency and gives him his unique tone of voice, simultaneously fiercely pacy and quietly distanced. He never has to strive for a violent effect; only very occasionally does he become a trace literary.

The Novels of Dashiell Hammett (1966)

C ★ ★ ★ ★ ★ ★ ★ ★ ★	P ★ ★ ★ ★ ★ ★ ★ ★
R ★ ★ ★ ★ ★ ★ ★ ★ ★	T ★ ★ ★ ★ ★ ★ ★ ★ ★

The Big Knockover (stories, 1966)

C ★ ★ ★ ★ ★ ★ ★ ★	P ★ ★ ★ ★ ★ ★ ★
R ★ ★ ★ ★ ★ ★ ★ ★	T ★ ★ ★ ★ ★ ★ ★ ★

The Continental Op (stories, 1974)

C ★ ★ ★ ★ ★ ★ ★	P ★ ★ ★ ★ ★ ★ ★
R ★ ★ ★ ★ ★ ★ ★ ★	T ★ ★ ★ ★ ★ ★ ★ ★

HAMMOND, Gerald (1926) British suspense writer and humorist. His books have as hero Keith Calder, a Scottish gunsmith and poacher, and are firmly set in the Borders country, evoked in accurate detail. Calder is an outsize personality, though very credible, a life-lover and for all his illegalities plainly on the side of the good.

R = Readability   T = Tension

The Reward Game (1980)

C ★★★★★★★	P ★★★★★★★
R ★★★★★★★	T ★★★★★★

Fair Game (1982)

C ★★★★★★★	P ★★★★★★★
R ★★★★★★★★	T ★★★★★★★

HANSEN, Joseph (1923) American private-eye novelist, who has also written novels as Rose Brock and James Colton. The most obvious thing about Hansen's books is that his private eye is a homosexual and his investigations often lead him into the half-world of the gays. But, far more important, is that Hansen writes excellent private-eye novels (his Dave Brandstetter is a shrewd, tough-minded insurance investigator), at once exactly in the classical mould and able to say as much about life in general as many a hailed straight novelist. The books were arguably the best novels in this sub-genre written in the seventies.

Fadeout (1970)

C ★★★★★★★	P ★★★★★★
R ★★★★★★★★	T ★★★★★★★

The Man Everybody Was Afraid Of (1978)

C ★★★★★★★	P ★★★★★★
R ★★★★★★★★	T ★★★★★★

Skinflick (1979)

C ★★★★★★★★	P ★★★★★★★★
R ★★★★★★★★	T ★★★★★★★

HARCOURT, Palma British espionage writer, formerly employed in British Intelligence where she met her husband. With him she has travelled widely, and her books are set in places she knows and often in the diplomatic world, accurately chronicled if romantically seen. The richer appurtenances of life abound, but there is excitement too as well as easy, lucid writing.

Tomorrow's Treason (1980)

C ★★★★★	P ★★★★★★
R ★★★★★★★★	T ★★★★★★

Joseph Hansen

HARE, Cyril (1900-58) British detective-story writer and County Court judge. He wrote nine excellent mystery puzzles, mostly featuring Inspector Mallett of Scotland Yard and Francis Pettigrew, an aging and not very successful barrister. Hare was also a particularly skilled writer of crime short stories.

Tragedy at Law (1942)

C ★★★★★★★★	P ★★★★★★★
R ★★★★★★	T ★★

When the Wind blows (1949)
(*The Wind Blows Death* in U.S.)

C ★★★★★★★	P ★★★★★★★
R ★★★★★★★	T ★★

Best Detective Stories of Cyril Hare (1959)

C ★★★★★★	P ★★★★★★★★
R ★★★★★★★	T ★★

HARLING, Robert (1910) British suspense writer, magazine editor and design consultant. He wrote six novels all set in the world of journalism, which he knew well. They are of a quality to have retained their places on library shelves over the years though the last appeared in 1974 and the first in 1951. Betrayal and irony run like dark, but humanizing, threads through most of what he wrote.

The Paper Palace (1951)

C ★ ★ ★ ★ ★ ★ ★		P ★ ★ ★ ★ ★ ★ ★ ★	
R ★ ★ ★ ★ ★ ★ ★		T ★ ★ ★ ★ ★ ★	

The Enormous Shadow (1955)

C ★ ★ ★ ★ ★ ★ ★ ★		P ★ ★ ★ ★ ★ ★	
R ★ ★ ★ ★ ★ ★ ★		T ★ ★ ★ ★ ★ ★ ★ ★	

HARRIS, Rosemary (1923) British suspense novelist, novelist and children's writer. She has written only five crime novels, but they have such a strongly individual flavour that they give her a respectable place on the ladder. Written from the point-of-view of a young female narrator, with no lack of love interest, as such they head for many pitfalls but by and large scrape past.

A Wicked Pack of Cards (1969)

C ★ ★ ★ ★ ★ ★ ★		P ★ ★ ★ ★ ★	
R ★ ★ ★ ★ ★ ★ ★ ★		T ★ ★ ★ ★ ★ ★	

HARVESTER, Simon (1910-75) British espionage novelist, and, as Henry Gibbs, novelist. Real name Henry St John Clair Rumbold-Gibbs. He wrote 44 thrillers between 1942 and his death (plus nineteen books under the Henry Gibbs name). Smoothness and ease of reading characterize them all. His most popular hero was Dorian Silk (each of his titles contains the word "Road"), expert equally with exotic ladies, flying bullets and double-crossings. An unswerving anti-Communist philosophy underlies the tales.

Siberian Road (1976)

C ★ ★ ★ ★ ★		P ★ ★ ★ ★ ★ ★	
R ★ ★ ★ ★ ★ ★ ★ ★		T ★ ★ ★ ★ ★ ★ ★	

HASTINGS, Macdonald (1909) British journalist and writer on country sports, whose mystery novels feature insurance investigator Montague Cork. The books are not elaborate in plot or detection, but are good on country atmosphere and lore, with Hastings' knowledge of shooting and fishing and some nice character sketches making for a pleasant read.

Cork in the Doghouse (1957)

C ★ ★ ★ ★ ★ ★		P ★ ★ ★ ★ ★	
R ★ ★ ★ ★ ★ ★ ★ ★		T ★	

HAWKEY, Raymond (1930) British suspense novelist and designer. He was responsible for the covers of all the Len Deighton British hardback editions up to *SS-GB,* the first of which contributed in no small measure to the success of *The Ipcress File.* He began to write himself, in collaboration with Roger Bingham, in 1975 with *Wild Card* and later branched out on his own. Massive research to support a well worked-out if fantastic plot is his hallmark.

Side-effect (1979)

C ★ ★ ★ ★ ★ ★		P ★ ★ ★ ★ ★ ★ ★ ★ ★	
R ★ ★ ★ ★ ★ ★ ★ ★		T ★ ★ ★ ★ ★ ★ ★ ★	

HAYES, Joseph (1918) American playwright and mystery novelist. Primarily a playwright, Hayes first novel, *The Desperate Hours* gave him immediate success in mystery. It was accepted before publication as a Literary Guild selection and became a hit Broadway production and motion picture. Hayes received the Tony award in theatre as author of the play and a mystery Edgar for best screenplay of the film version.

The Desperate Hours (1954)

C ★ ★ ★ ★ ★		P ★ ★ ★ ★ ★ ★ ★	
R ★ ★ ★ ★ ★ ★ ★		T ★ ★ ★ ★ ★ ★ ★	

The Long Dark Night (1974)

C ★ ★ ★ ★ ★		P ★ ★ ★ ★ ★ ★ ★	
R ★ ★ ★ ★ ★ ★		T ★ ★ ★ ★ ★ ★ ★	

HEAD, Matthew (1907) American mystery writer. Real name John E. Canady, painter, historian and, since 1959, art critic of the *New York Times.* As Matthew Head, he be-

R = Readability T = Tension

came one of the classic American mystery writers. In 1943 in a three-week period he wrote his first, *The Smell of Money*, using a pseudonym because he was afraid the book would not be a success and he wanted to save his own name for the books on art he planned to write. Although it was not unil 1959 that he published his first book on art, he is today the leading American writer in that field. His mysteries set in Africa, the first to present twentieth-century Africa with verisimilitude, are bright with humour and subtly satiric. Although he has written no mysteries for a number of years, his books continue to be reprinted.

The Devil in the Bush (1945)

C ★★★★★★★	P ★★★★★★★
R ★★★★★★★★	T ★★★★★★

The Cabinda Affair (1949)

C ★★★★★★★	P ★★★★★★★★
R ★★★★★★★★	T ★★★★★★★

The Congo Venus (1950)

C ★★★★★★★	P ★★★★★★
R ★★★★★★★★	T ★★★★★

HEALD, Tim (1944) British mystery farce writer. A journalist-of-all-work, he uses the various backgrounds he acquires to add an extra dimension to his skim-along mysteries featuring Simon Bognor, more or less inept Board of Trade investigator. The books are light and the easiest of reading.

Masterstroke (1982)

C ★★★★★	P ★★★★★
R ★★★★★★★★	T ★★★★★

HEARD, H. F. (1889-1971) British detective novelist and (as Gerald Heard) author of many sociological and religious works. His detective Mr Mycroft appeared in three novels and two short stories with (as his name implies) Holmesian overtones. The first novel, *A Taste for Honey,* is regarded as a minor classic of the genre.

A Taste for Honey (1941)

C ★★★★★★★	P ★★★★★★★★
R ★★★★★★★	T ★★

HEBDEN, Mark (1916) British police novelist, using French settings, and also John Harris, adventure novelist. The Hebden books, begun in 1971 and in a regular stream since, feature Inspector Pel in their more recent appearances. Pel is a Burgundian, senior in the force, henpecked by his landlady, apt to feel under the weather. But he always gets his man, and the atmosphere is French as Gauloise smoke.

Pel Under Pressure (1981)

C ★★★★★★	P ★★★★★★★
R ★★★★★★★★	T ★★★★★★

HENDERSON, Laurence (1928) British police procedural writer. He has not produced a great deal of work, but what there is is of a high standard. He has the gift of making what seems to be a straightforward account of an investigation grip through the sheer economy and accuracy of the writing.

Major Enquiry (1976)

C ★★★★★★★	P ★★★★★★★
R ★★★★★★★★	T ★★★★★★★★

HENISSART, Paul (1923) British spy novelist. He writes intense stories of agents and assassinations. Indeed, *Margin of Error* forecast in advance the killing of President Sadat as well as being a portrait of the super-terrorist, with sex.

Margin of Error (1980)

C ★★★★★★★	P ★★★★★★★★★
R ★★★★★★★★	T ★★★★★★★

HERRON, Shaun (1912) Canadian espionage writer and novelist, born and educated in Ulster. He has moved from early spy tales that were almost pure entertainment, through crime novels of considerable power on to mainstream novels that still have in them a considerable admixture of excitement and entertainment. A hatred of large, anonymous organizations of all sorts informs much of his work and gives it its charge.

Through the Dark and Hairy Wood (1972)

C ★ ★ ★ ★ ★ ★ ★	P ★ ★ ★ ★ ★
R ★ ★ ★ ★ ★ ★ ★ ★	T ★ ★ ★ ★ ★ ★ ★ ★

HEYER, Georgette (1902-74) British detective novelist and, above all, Regency romance writer. Her detective stories, though outshone by her historical novels, were in the Golden Age tradition and popular. Country houses figure largely and the puzzle is all, but the style is light and agreeable and many of the characters deftly comic.

Death in the Stocks (1935)

C ★ ★ ★ ★ ★ ★	P ★ ★ ★ ★ ★ ★ ★
R ★ ★ ★ ★ ★ ★ ★ ★	T ★ ★

HIGGINS, George V. (1939) American crime novelist and former assistant U.S. district attorney. He shot to the top rank with his first book, *The Friends of Eddie Coyle*, a story set in the lower reaches of the Boston underworld, sordid, naturally, but ringing deadly true and marked above all by its plentiful dialogue, coarse and everyday, yet resonating with much more than its simple outward appearance. His extraordinary ear for the words people actually use, for the hesitations and back-tracks in the way they actually use them, stood him in good stead over several similar books in the years immediately following 1972. This rediscovery of actual speech is a necessary process of literature, necessarily repeated at intervals, although each time the words that get on to paper are not exactly the words used on the street. They can never be. If they were they would read appallingly dully. But they are each time a better stylized approximation. Dashiell Hammett (q.v.) contributed to this process in the twenties and thirties. Higgins did it again in the seventies. But, as if to demonstrate this was not his only talent, in 1980 he produced a more conventional crime novel, *Kennedy for the Defense* (separated from the underworld stories by two mainstream novels). In this we are in the upper-echelon world of Boston lawyers and a lot of the dialogue overheard is different. But equally well caught.

George V. Higgins

The Friends of Eddie Coyle (1972)

C ★ ★ ★ ★ ★ ★ ★	P ★ ★ ★ ★ ★ ★
R ★ ★ ★ ★ ★ ★ ★ ★	T ★ ★ ★ ★ ★ ★ ★ ★

Cogan's Trade (1974)

C ★ ★ ★ ★ ★ ★ ★	P ★ ★ ★ ★ ★
R ★ ★ ★ ★ ★ ★ ★ ★	T ★ ★ ★ ★ ★ ★ ★

Kennedy for the Defense (1980)

C ★ ★ ★ ★ ★ ★ ★	P ★ ★ ★ ★ ★ ★
R ★ ★ ★ ★ ★ ★ ★	T ★ ★ ★ ★ ★ ★

HIGGINS, Jack (1929) British thriller writer, pseudonym of Harry Patterson (q.v.). After half a dozen books under the Higgins pseudonym, the breakthrough was made into the international best-seller lists

R = Readability   T = Tension

Jack Higgins

with *The Eagle Has Landed* (1975), where his talents for pacy narrative, convoluted plotting and exciting action were at last applied to a story with that extra dimension of memorability.

The Eagle Has Landed (1975)

C ★★★★★★	P ★★★★★★★★
R ★★★★★★★★	T ★★★★★★★★★

HIGHSMITH, Patricia (1921) American suspense novelist, long resident in Europe. She is a figure of considerable importance in the history of crime writing, though more appreciated always in Europe than in the United States. The claim rests on two factors. First, she is one of the writers of the second half of the twentieth century who most consistently edged the crime genre in the direction of the mainstream novel (while always keeping it in the crime, entertainment-first field). Second, with her Tom Ripley, hero of four books, she confirmed the possibility of a protagonist who is amoral yet still a figure with whom to identify and in more than a merely "Evil be thou my good" fashion. Her books are notable for the theme of guilt that runs through them, sometimes, as in the Ripley titles, taking the form of

an extra-ordinary absence of guilt. She has also almost always, though increasingly as time passed, used the method of taking situations to an extreme, often going to the very edge of credibility. It gives her writing an extraordinary power. From the first, too, she has shown a highly characteristic style, colloquial, laconic, matter-of-fact. She gives her readers brief statements about her people that by their very lack of flourishes, their businesslike terseness claim absolute belief. She creates a world. It is one that Graham Greene characterized as claustrophobic and irrational, one "we enter each time with a sense of personal danger." It is a world supremely of intuition, a method that seems to lie at the heart of her writing more obviously perhaps than in any other novelist in the crime field. It makes her books, frankly, repellent to some readers, but to others one of the greatest pleasures the field affords.

The Talented Mr Ripley (1955)

C ★★★★★★★★	P ★★★★★★
R ★★★★★★★★	T ★★★★★★★★

This Sweet Sickness (1960)

C ★★★★★★★★	P ★★★★★★★
R ★★★★★★★★★	T ★★★★★★★★★★

The Boy Who Followed Ripley (1980)

C ★★★★★★★★	P ★★★★★★
R ★★★★★★★★★	T ★★★★★★★★★

HILL, Peter (1939) British thriller writer and television scriptwriter. He has contributed to many of the most prestigious crime series on British television, *Z-Cars, The Sweeney* etc, and has written half-a-dozen fast-paced thrillers with sex spicily sandwiched in. His characters live and his backgrounds can be notably original.

The Washermen (1979)

C ★★★★★★★	P ★★★★★★
R ★★★★★★★★	T ★★★★★★★

C = Characterization   P = Plot

Reginald Hill

HILL, Reginald (1936) British detective novelist, and formerly Lecturer in English (see also Patrick Ruell). He is perhaps the most interesting of his generation of British crime writers, literate, amusing (often downright funny), skilful in using the detective genre, writing about real people with roots in a past and capable of going deep. Perhaps his most notable score has been the creation of a detective duo that is admirably useful for his particular branch of the art. The combination of fat, coarse Superintendent Dalziel, a pragmatic realist, with Sergeant (later Detective Inspector) Pascoe, sociology graduate, acute, sensitive, up-to-date, gives him a wide spread. Neither is Watson to the other's Holmes, but on occasion each will learn from his counterpart. Hill's other notable contribution to the crime novel lies in his handling of absolutely contemporary material, in the style of speech of his characters, in their life styles and in the sort of crime he chooses for them to be involved in (i.e. in *A Pinch of Snuff*, which has nothing to do with snuff-taking from elegant little boxes, he tackles not simply sex but that peculiar combination of sex with violence, the so-called 'snuff' blue movies, which is a mark of our times).

A Fairly Dangerous thing (1972)

C ★ ★ ★ ★ ★ ★ ★	P ★ ★ ★ ★ ★ ★ ★
R ★ ★ ★ ★ ★ ★ ★ ★	T ★ ★ ★ ★ ★ ★

Ruling Passion (1973)

C ★ ★ ★ ★ ★ ★ ★	P ★ ★ ★ ★ ★ ★ ★
R ★ ★ ★ ★ ★ ★ ★ ★	T ★ ★ ★ ★ ★ ★

A Pinch of Snuff (1978)

C ★ ★ ★ ★ ★ ★ ★ ★	P ★ ★ ★ ★ ★ ★ ★
R ★ ★ ★ ★ ★ ★ ★ ★	T ★ ★ ★ ★ ★ ★ ★

HILLERMAN, Tony (1925) American mystery writer. Hillerman, newspaperman, later journalism professor, had served his apprenticeship for more than twenty years before his first novel, *The Blessing Way* was published in 1969. His immediate success as a mystery writer is unparalleled. He has received Edgar recognition for each of his novels and the Edgar award for Best Novel in 1974. Hillerman spent his early years with Indians in Oklahoma, and has, since his move to New Mexico, been their associate as a newsman and a university professor. He stands alone in writing of Southwest Indians as they are, not as they appear to outsiders.

The Fly on the Wall (1971)

C ★ ★ ★ ★ ★ ★	P ★ ★ ★ ★ ★ ★
R ★ ★ ★ ★ ★ ★ ★	T ★ ★ ★ ★ ★ ★

Dance Hall of the Dead (1973)

C ★ ★ ★ ★ ★ ★	P ★ ★ ★ ★ ★
R ★ ★ ★ ★ ★ ★ ★	T ★ ★ ★ ★ ★

People of Darkness (1981)

C ★ ★ ★ ★ ★ ★	P ★ ★ ★ ★ ★ ★
R ★ ★ ★ ★ ★ ★ ★	T ★ ★ ★ ★ ★ ★

HILTON, James (1900-54) British novelist. Best-selling author (*Lost Horizon, Random Harvest, Goodbye Mr Chips*) Hilton wrote just one detective story, or detective fantasia as he called it. It is set in a British public school when such institutions

R = Readability   T = Tension

were at the height of their self-confidence, and is well worth keeping alive.

Murder at School (1931)
(Was it Murder? in U.S.)

C ★ ★ ★ ★ ★ ★	P ★ ★ ★ ★ ★ ★ ★
R ★ ★ ★ ★ ★ ★ ★	T ★

HILTON, John Buxton (1921) British detective novelist. He began writing only when on the verge of retirement as an Inspector of Schools (like Matthew Arnold before him) and produces curious books, sometimes excellent, at others off-beam. There is frequently a strong element of social history in them and folklore is also a notable element. Three of them, among the best, were set between 1877 and 1911. The others good and less so, feature Superintendent Kenworthy, the introspective.

No Birds Sang (1975)

C ★ ★ ★ ★ ★ ★ ★	P ★ ★ ★ ★ ★ ★ ★
R ★ ★ ★ ★ ★ ★	T ★ ★ ★ ★ ★ ★ ★

Playground of Death (1981)

C ★ ★ ★ ★ ★ ★ ★	P ★ ★ ★ ★ ★ ★ ★ ★
R ★ ★ ★ ★ ★ ★ ★	T ★ ★ ★

HIMES, Chester (1909) American mystery writer and novelist. He began writing only when almost fifty and, though American to the core, his books were published first in French in Paris, where he had gone to live after finishing a seven-year term in the Ohio State Penitentiary. There, having read Hammett (q.v.), he conceived the notion that "to tell it like it is" would produce a parallel result. Whether the wierd events that happen in New York's black districts to his two black detectives, Coffin Ed Johnson and Grave Digger Jones, are "like it is" or not, the books certainly rate very high. He wields that pure revealing magnifying-glass on life, showing it to us clearly for what it is, a weapon not given to every fiction writer by any means. He is extra-

ordinarily funny: his vision is fundamentally tragic.

The Real Cool Killers (1959)

C ★ ★ ★ ★ ★ ★	P ★ ★ ★ ★ ★ ★ ★
R ★ ★ ★ ★ ★ ★ ★	T ★ ★ ★ ★ ★

Cotton Comes to Harlem (1965)

C ★ ★ ★ ★ ★ ★ ★	P ★ ★ ★ ★ ★ ★ ★
R ★ ★ ★ ★ ★ ★ ★	T ★ ★ ★ ★ ★ ★

Blind Man with A Pistol (1969)

C ★ ★ ★ ★ ★ ★ ★ ★	P ★ ★ ★ ★ ★ ★ ★
R ★ ★ ★ ★ ★ ★ ★	T ★ ★ ★ ★ ★ ★ ★

HOCH, Edward D. (1930) American mystery writer. Primarily a short story writer, Hoch has more than 400 on his published record, with a regular series appearing in *Ellery Queen's Mystery Magazine*. A number of his stories have appeared as television dramas. Hoch has also edited numerous short story collections.

The Frankenstein Factory (1975)

C ★ ★ ★ ★	P ★ ★ ★ ★ ★ ★
R ★ ★ ★ ★ ★	T ★ ★ ★ ★ ★

HOCKING, Anne (1895) British detective novelist who changed course from suspense stories to the

Chester
Himes

classical detective format, normally featuring personable and literate William Austen of Scotland Yard. Austen is much travelled; the series has him popping up in murder cases all over the world, and quietly competent they are too.

Night's Candles (1941)

C ★ ★ ★ ★ ★ ★	P ★ ★ ★ ★ ★ ★ ★
R ★ ★ ★ ★ ★ ★ ★	T ★ ★ ★

Prussian Blue (1947)
(*The Finishing Touch* in U.S.)

C ★ ★ ★ ★ ★	P ★ ★ ★ ★ ★ ★
R ★ ★ ★ ★ ★ ★	T ★ ★

HOLME, Timothy (1928) British police procedural writer, journalist and former actor. On holiday in Italy he married his Italian teacher and has lived there ever since. His books are firmly set in Italy and feature a Neapolitan detective, Inspector Peroni, charmingly boastful, amorous and individual. His adventures are full of humour, and of Italian facts.

A Funeral of Gondolas (1981)

C ★ ★ ★ ★ ★ ★ ★	P ★ ★ ★ ★ ★ ★ ★
R ★ ★ ★ ★ ★ ★ ★	T ★ ★ ★ ★ ★ ★

HOLT, Victoria (1906) British gothic and romantic novelist. She is enormously successful, knowing well just what readers she is writing for (she has said that it is "nicer" to be read than to be reviewed) and aiming to do no more, but no less, than provide pure entertainment. This over many books, some written as Elbur Ford, Kathleen Kellow, Ellalice Tate and (her own name) Eleanor Hibbert, she has done.

The Shivering Sands (1969)

C ★ ★ ★ ★ ★ ★	P ★ ★ ★ ★ ★ ★
R ★ ★ ★ ★ ★ ★ ★	T ★ ★ ★ ★ ★ ★ ★

HOLTON, Leonard (1915) Irish mystery writer and novelist, eventually resident in America. From 1959 on he has written a series of mysteries almost always set in seamy east Los Angeles and featuring a Catholic priest, Father Bredder. But as Leonard Whibberley he is a prolific novelist, best known for *The Mouse That Roared* (1955), and he has also written non-fiction on a wide variety of subjects under this name. The Bredder novels expertly avoid the traps set both by having an amateur (and therefore unlikely, not to say unreal) detective and those set by having a religious figure as hero (preaching).

The Saint Maker (1959)

C ★ ★ ★ ★ ★	P ★ ★ ★ ★ ★ ★
R ★ ★ ★ ★ ★ ★ ★	T ★ ★ ★ ★ ★

Flowers by Request (1964)

C ★ ★ ★ ★ ★ ★	P ★ ★ ★ ★ ★ ★ ★
R ★ ★ ★ ★ ★ ★ ★	T ★ ★ ★ ★ ★ ★

HONE, Joseph (1938) British espionage novelist. He began writing spy fiction with *The Private Sector* (1971), the first of a trilogy with as hero one Marlow, an English teacher in Cairo originally (as was his creator), who gets caught up in international espionage and its ruthlessness. Hone uses espionage fiction (which he produces only at rare intervals) to explore the springs of human personality, something which it is markedly fitted for, and writes with a splendid gift for dramatic dialogue.

The Sixth Directorate (1975)

C ★ ★ ★ ★ ★ ★ ★ ★	P ★ ★ ★ ★ ★ ★
R ★ ★ ★ ★ ★ ★	T ★ ★ ★ ★ ★ ★ ★

HORLER, Sydney (1888-1954) British mystery writer. A Fleet Street journalist, Horler resigned to write fiction full time, and his prolific output covers a wide range of genres from the espionage thriller to the society 'cracksman' story. His plots are fast-moving, his backgrounds upper class, his characters wooden and his viewpoint Boys' Own-patriotic.

Tiger Standish (1932)

C ★ ★ ★ ★	P ★ ★ ★ ★ ★ ★
R ★ ★ ★ ★ ★ ★	T ★ ★ ★ ★ ★ ★

R = Readability   T = Tension

HORNUNG, E. W. (1866-1921) British crime short-story writer and novelist, creator of A. J. Raffles, gentleman burglar, one of the inextinguishable characters of crime fiction and one of the few given the accolade of imitation (see Perowne, Barry). Hornung was Conan Doyle's (q.v.) brother-in-law, and Raffles was to some extent designed as a contrast to Sherlock Holmes (Doyle frowned). As a character Raffles is indeed fit to hold a candle to the great man.

The Amateur Cracksman (1899)

C ★★★★★★★★	P ★★★★★★★★
R ★★★★★★★★★	T ★★★★★★★★

The Black Mask (1901)

C ★★★★★★★★	P ★★★★★★★
R ★★★★★★★★★	T ★★★★★★★★

A Thief in the Night (1905)

C ★★★★★★★★	P ★★★★★★★
R ★★★★★★★★★	T ★★★★★★★★

HOUSEHOLD, Geoffrey (1900) British suspense adventure writer. One superb book, his second, *Rogue Male*, the wonderfully tense story of a man who tried to assassinate Hitler and is pursued relentlessly for it in just pre-war England, has always tended to overshadow Household's other work. But these are considerable books, individual, even awkward, imbued with the life of the countryside often, strange.

Rogue Male (1939)

C ★★★★★★★★	P ★★★★★★★★★★
R ★★★★★★★★★★	T ★★★★★★★★★★

Summon the Bright Water (1981)

C ★★★★★★★	P ★★★★★★★
R ★★★★★★★★	T ★★★★★★★★

HOWARD, Clark American mystery novelist, author of true crime books and crime short-story writer. His 1980 short story, Horn Man, won the Edgar of the Mystery Writers of America. His father was a well-known bootlegger in Tennessee in the 1930s, and from an early age he lived in foster homes (and frequently ran away). But the Marine Corps gave him self-confidence and he enrolled at university for journalism and writing courses. *The Arm*, his first novel, was the story of a professional crap-shooter.

The Arm (1967)

C ★★★★★★★	P ★★★★★★★★
R ★★★★★★★★	T ★★★★★★★★

HOWARD, Hartley (1908-1979) British private-eye novelist. While writing his English-set books as Harry Carmichael (q.v.), he also produced a series, chiefly featuring one Glenn Bowman, of hardboiled classic-type American stories. There are 44 of them, written between 1951 and 1979.

The Sealed Envelope (1979)

C ★★★★	P ★★★★★★★
R ★★★★★★★	T ★★★★★

Geoffrey Household

HUBBARD, P. M. (1910-80) British suspense novelist. A writer who quietly elevated the suspense story into something unique, memorable, different, compelling. His stories usually feature a man alone. Very often there is a countryside setting, beautifully and accurately rendered.

Or a sea setting, done as well. There is, too, almost always, a quality of something approaching fantasy (for all that, detail is always of the earth, simple and unexaggerated). Sex, too, powerful though understated, runs like a dark thread through many of the tales. And violence, half welcomed, half deplored, plays its strong part.

The Causeway (1976)

| C ★ ★ ★ ★ ★ ★ ★ | P ★ ★ ★ ★ ★ ★ |
| R ★ ★ ★ ★ ★ ★ ★ ★ | T ★ ★ ★ ★ ★ ★ ★ |

The Quiet River (1978)

| C ★ ★ ★ ★ ★ ★ ★ ★ | P ★ ★ ★ ★ ★ ★ |
| R ★ ★ ★ ★ ★ ★ ★ ★ ★ | T ★ ★ ★ ★ ★ ★ ★ ★ |

Kill Claudio (1979)

| C ★ ★ ★ ★ ★ ★ ★ | P ★ ★ ★ ★ ★ ★ ★ |
| R ★ ★ ★ ★ ★ ★ ★ | T ★ ★ ★ ★ ★ ★ ★ |

HUGHES, Dorothy B. (1904) American suspense novelist, mystery fiction critic and biographer (of Erle Stanley Gardner (q.v.)). Between 1940 and 1952 she wrote thirteen suspense novels, with one more added in 1964, that have given her a high place in the mystery hierarchy (she is a Grand Master of the Mystery Writers of America and of the Swedish Academy of Detection). Her work is marked by its combination of unrelenting suspense with penetrating comment on society.

Dorothy B. Hughes

Her typical situation is to take a civilized person, usually a woman, and to plunge them into a tangle of evil in which they find in themselves hidden strengths. Through it she says a great deal about the human condition.

The So Blue Marble (1940)

| C ★ ★ ★ ★ ★ ★ ★ ★ | P ★ ★ ★ ★ ★ ★ ★ |
| R ★ ★ ★ ★ ★ ★ ★ ★ | T ★ ★ ★ ★ ★ ★ ★ ★ |

Ride the Pink Horse (1946)

| C ★ ★ ★ ★ ★ ★ ★ | P ★ ★ ★ ★ ★ ★ ★ ★ |
| R ★ ★ ★ ★ ★ ★ ★ ★ | T ★ ★ ★ ★ ★ ★ ★ ★ |

The Expendable Man (1964)

| C ★ ★ ★ ★ ★ ★ ★ ★ | P ★ ★ ★ ★ ★ ★ ★ |
| R ★ ★ ★ ★ ★ ★ ★ ★ | T ★ ★ ★ ★ ★ ★ ★ ★ |

HULL, Richard (1896-1973) British detective-story writer. He scored so well with his first book, *The Murder of My Aunt* (not to be confused with C. H. B. Kitchin (q.v.) *Death of My Aunt*) that his others, fourteen in all, have tended to get put in the shade. But that first ranks high. An inverted whodunit, it recounts the attempts of a not very pleasing young man to kill his even less pleasing old aunt. It was hailed on publication in America by Christopher Morley as a "brilliant savage comedy".

The Murder of My Aunt (1934)

| C ★ ★ ★ ★ ★ ★ ★ ★ | P ★ ★ ★ ★ ★ ★ ★ ★ |
| R ★ ★ ★ ★ ★ ★ | T ★ ★ ★ ★ ★ ★ |

HUME, Fergus (1859-1932) British sensational novelist, mainly crime and mystery. Although he could descend to crude melodrama, his best work in the detective field was clearly influenced by Gaboriau (q.v.) and Wilkie Collins (q.v.). Hume enthusiasts complain that, of some 140 novels, critics only ever mention one; there seems little reason to break with tradition.

The Mystery of a Hansom Cab (1886)

| C ★ ★ ★ ★ | P ★ ★ ★ ★ ★ ★ ★ ★ |
| R ★ ★ ★ ★ ★ | T ★ ★ |

R = Readability   T = Tension

HUNTER, Alan (1922) British detective novelist, creator of Inspector (later Chief Superintendent) Gently, and poet. Most of his books incorporate the word "gently" in the title. As a detective he is somewhat of an English Maigret, but very much a model Scotland Yard man. The books are apt to conceal various literary allusions, to Proust, to Walter Scott, to Shakespeare, and are sometimes somewhat experimental. They vary in locale from Norfolk (frequent) to Scotland and France.

Gently Instrumental (1977)

C	P
★★★★★★★★	★★★★★★★
R ★★★★★★★	T ★★★★★★

Fields of Heather (1981)

C	P
★★★★★★★	★★★★★★★★★
R ★★★★★★★	T ★★★★★

HURD, Douglas (1930) British politician and occasional spy/adventure novelist, a former member of the British Foreign Service. In collaboration with Andrew Osmond (q.v.) he wrote a number of political spy thrillers, marked as might be expected by a high degree of awareness of the implications of then current policies. They are notably sophisticated and intelligent. Out of office in 1975, he wrote similar books without his collaborator.

Douglas Hurd

Scotch on the Rocks (1971)

C	P
★★★★★★	★★★★★★★★
R ★★★★★★★★	T ★★★★★★★

HYLAND, Stanley (1914) British detective novelist, former House of Commons research librarian and television producer. He has written only three crime novels, but they have been much praised. In *Who Goes Hang?*, his first, he used his knowledge of Parliament to write a Dorothy Sayers (q.v.) style whodunit, witty and knowledgeable. In *Green Grow the Tresses-O* (1965) he delivered some good rapier thrusts at M.I.5. In *Top Bloody Secret* (1969) both M.I.5 and Parliament get the sharp edge of his wit.

Who Goes Hang? (1958)

C	P
★★★★★★★★	★★★★★★★★★
R ★★★★★★★★	T ★★★★★★★

IAMS, Jack (1910) American mystery novelist. His aim was to give mystery readers an enjoyable, fun-spattered time, and in the majority of his eight books this is precisely what he did. His first was a little different, set in Brazzaville, West Africa, and based on his wartime experience for the Office of War Information. More typical is *Death Draws A Line*, set in a strip-cartoon factory.

Death Draws A Line (1949)

C	P
★★★★★★★	★★★★★★★
R ★★★★★★★★★	T ★★★

ILES, Francis (1893-1971) English crime novelist, who also wrote as Anthony Berkeley (q.v.). As Iles he was for some years an influential reviewer, but it was as an author of just three books that his importance lay. In two of them he revolutionized the

C = Characterization   P = Plot

traditional English detective story. The opening sentence of *Malice Aforethought* is: "It was not until several weeks after he had decided to murder his wife that Dr Bickleigh took any active steps in the matter." The perennial question Who dun it? was answered before it had been asked. He was not the first to write what has become known as the inverted story (in an introduction to the Berkeley book *The Second Shot* he acknowledges R. Austin Freeman (q.v.)), but he established this new sub-genre. *Before the Fact,* his other revolutionary book, which followed, deserves its place in crime fiction history for two reasons. First, because it took the murder victim's point of view, an advance on taking the murderer's. Second, because it shifted the whole genre's interest in the direction of character rather than plot, people rather than mere puzzle. In his preface to *The Second Shot* Iles hazarded that soon "the question will not be 'Who killed the old man in the bath-room?' but 'What on earth induced X of all people to kill the old man in the bath-room?'." His own writing helped to make his prophecy come true. The books, too, have nowadays the extra virtue of presenting a sharply observed picture of British society of their day. But they do more. Iles was a good writer. He puts, in these books, an individual and coherent view of life in a lively and attractive manner. It is often a savage view. Of the middle-class attitude to his heroine in *Before the Fact* he wrote "Kleptomania could always be excused; intelligence never." It is sometimes more gently pinpricking as in his lightly disguised portrait of Dorothy Sayers (q.v.) in the same book where the heroine wishes this person could be "fitted with a volume control like the wireless." A final innovation in the Iles books lies in his treatment of sex. He snapped the existing taboo on that subject like a dry stick. No other writer till then had dared say of

their heroine that she was "a stingy bitch in bed". And he was able, too, to do that rare thing in novels, and until then unheard of in crime novels, make a person change and develop. A considerable innovator and a fascinating writer.

Malice Aforethought (1931)

| C ★ ★ ★ ★ ★ ★ ★ ★ | P ★ ★ ★ ★ ★ ★ ★ ★ |
| R ★ ★ ★ ★ ★ ★ ★ ★ | T ★ ★ ★ ★ ★ ★ ★ ★ |

Before the Fact (1932)

| C ★ ★ ★ ★ ★ ★ ★ ★ | P ★ ★ ★ ★ ★ ★ ★ ★ |
| R ★ ★ ★ ★ ★ ★ ★ ★ | T ★ ★ ★ ★ ★ ★ ★ ★ |

Hammond Innes

INNES, Hammond (1913) British suspense novelist, probably incomparable among living writers in his power to depict man against the elements in the four corners of the world. Crime does not always play a part, but adventure and conflict on land or at sea are his key elements. He travels widely, and writes from personal experience of the terrain.

The Lonely Skier (1947)
(Fire in the Snow in U.S.)

| C ★ ★ ★ ★ ★ ★ | P ★ ★ ★ ★ ★ ★ ★ |
| R ★ ★ ★ ★ ★ ★ ★ | T ★ ★ ★ ★ ★ ★ ★ |

Campbell's Kingdom (1952)

| C ★ ★ ★ ★ ★ ★ | P ★ ★ ★ ★ ★ ★ ★ |
| R ★ ★ ★ ★ ★ ★ ★ ★ | T ★ ★ ★ ★ ★ ★ |

The Mary Deare (1956)

| C ★ ★ ★ ★ ★ ★ | P ★ ★ ★ ★ ★ ★ ★ |
| R ★ ★ ★ ★ ★ ★ ★ | T ★ ★ ★ ★ ★ ★ ★ |

R = Readability   T = Tension

INNES, Michael (1906) English detective-story writer, mainstream novelist, Reader in English Literature at Oxford, visiting professor at American universities. It was in 1936 that we read (many of us as yet unborn) Innes's splendid debut, *Death at the President's Lodging* (pusillanimously re-titled in America *Seven Suspects*) and since then he has given us more than 50 volumes of detection to enrich our wayward hours by their intellectual chamois-leaping and stylistic coral-building. Not quite all of the fifty were pure detective stories. There are a handful of excellent spy pursuit tales such as *The Journeying Boy*. But in the majority of them we follow with delight and bewilderment first Inspector Appleby, eventually Sir John Appleby, Commissioner of the Metropolitan Police, retired, as he gravely trumps every literary ace and with calm ingenuity solves every complex case. As the years go by a soupçon of the perfunctory perhaps creeps in, but even these later books can still surprise us. Innes is the donniest of the donnish school of detective story writing, always a joke ahead of every reader.

Hamlet, Revenge! (1937)

C ★ ★ ★ ★ ★ ★ ★	P ★ ★ ★ ★ ★ ★ ★ ★
R ★ ★ ★ ★ ★ ★ ★ ★	T ★ ★ ★ ★ ★ ★ ★

The Journeying Boy (1949)

C ★ ★ ★ ★ ★ ★ ★	P ★ ★ ★ ★ ★ ★ ★ ★
R ★ ★ ★ ★ ★ ★ ★ ★	T ★ ★ ★ ★ ★ ★ ★ ★

The New Sonia Wayward (1960)

C ★ ★ ★ ★ ★ ★	P ★ ★ ★ ★ ★ ★ ★
R ★ ★ ★ ★ ★ ★ ★ ★	T ★ ★ ★ ★ ★ ★ ★

IRISH, William see WOOLRICH, Cornell

ISRAEL, Peter (1933) American suspense novelist and publisher. His books are set in France (where he was adviser formerly to a French publishing house) and his hero is one B. F. Cage, balanced on the line between the law and illegality and a

Michael Innes

very smart guy. The books are both violent and cheerful, a fine combination.

The Stiff Upper Lip (1978)

C ★ ★ ★ ★ ★ ★ ★	P ★ ★ ★ ★ ★ ★ ★
R ★ ★ ★ ★ ★ ★ ★	T ★ ★ ★ ★ ★ ★ ★

J

JACKSON, Shirley (1919-65) American suspense novelist. She wrote six novels and a number of short stories that have a unique flavour. She dealt in the mysteries of the mind under stress, but wrote with a formality and preciseness in strong counterpart to the terrors she described. Witchcraft and the mythological play a strong part in her powerful stories, which nevertheless avoid overt violence.

Hangsaman (1951)

C ★ ★ ★ ★ ★ ★ ★	P ★ ★ ★ ★ ★ ★ ★
R ★ ★ ★ ★ ★ ★ ★	T ★ ★ ★ ★ ★ ★ ★ ★

We Have Always Lived in the Castle (1962)

C ★ ★ ★ ★ ★ ★ ★	P ★ ★ ★ ★ ★ ★ ★
R ★ ★ ★ ★ ★ ★ ★ ★	T ★ ★ ★ ★ ★ ★ ★

C = Characterization   P = Plot

JACQUEMARD, Yves and **SÉNÉCAL, Jean Michel** (both 1943) French playwrights and crime novelists. Friends at school, they came together again in 1963 to write the first of a long series of plays. Admiration of Agatha Christie inspired *The Eleventh Little Nigger* which owes much to her, both in its theatrical setting and its complex puzzle plot.

The Eleventh Little Nigger (1977)

C ★★★★★★	P ★★★★★★★★★
R ★★★★★★★	T ★★★★★★

JAMES, P. D. (1920) British detective novelist. She seemed to alight fully-fledged on the crime tree with her first book *Cover Her Face* (1962), a straight mystery distinguished by the depth of its characterization and the pleasure of its detective, Inspector Adam Dalgleish, poet. In later books, though there were clues neatly tucked away, masquerading as pure description or disguised with an ambiguity worthy of Agatha Christie (q.v.), keeping close to life brought such things as endings that were not happy (*A Mind to Murder*, 1963). The tone was a commonsensical decisiveness of judgment, a feminine characteristic different indeed from any male authoritarianism. There was, too, excellent descriptive writing and sometimes a touch of a deeper elemental feeling, a hint of hidden powers. All flowered in her later books, in *The Black Tower* with its multi-layered discussion of that banned subject (especially in murder books) death, and in *Innocent Blood,* perhaps more a novel than a crime novel: a peak of the art nevertheless.

An Unsuitable Job for A Woman (1972)

C ★★★★★★★★	P ★★★★★★★
R ★★★★★★★★	T ★★★★★★★★

The Black Tower (1975)

C ★★★★★★★★★	P ★★★★★★★★
R ★★★★★★★★★	T ★★★★★★★★★★

Innocent Blood (1980)

C ★★★★★★★★★	P ★★★★★★★★
R ★★★★★★★★★	T ★★★★★★★★

JAPRISOT, Sebastien (1931) Pseudonym of Jean-Baptiste Rossi, French novelist. Japrisot's fast-moving, ingenious and carefully structured crime novels have won awards both in his native land and abroad. Many have become successful films. One, *Goodbye Friend* was published as it was conceived, in scenario form.

Goodbye Friend (1969)

C ★★★★★★★★	P ★★★★★★★★★★
R ★★★★★★★★★★	T ★★★★★★★

JEFFRIES, Roderic (1926) British detective novelist, who began with thoroughly competent mysteries with ingenious legal twists, then turned to puzzles in Mallorca featuring Enrique Alvarez. A prolific writer, his pseudonyms include Peter Alding and Jeffrey Ashford (q.v.), and he has continued the Blackshirt stories of Bruce Graeme (his father, q.v.) as Roderic Graeme.

Evidence of the Accused (1961)

C ★★★★★★	P ★★★★★★★★★
R ★★★★★★★★★	T ★★★

Mistakenly in Mallorca (1974)

C ★★★★★★★	P ★★★★★★★
R ★★★★★★★★	T ★★

JEPSON, Selwyn (1899) British thriller writer, best known for his series in which the lovely Eve Gill gets into all manner of dangerous situations. The first of these, *Man Running,* became a creditable Hitchcock film as *Stage Fright.* Jepson's non-series novels are equally readable, and provide more scope for ingenuity and the unpredictable.

Keep Murder Quiet (1940)

C ★★★★★	P ★★★★★★★
R ★★★★★★★★	T ★★

R = Readability   T = Tension

Man Running (1948)
(*Outrun the Constable* in U.S.)

C ★ ★ ★ ★ ★	P ★ ★ ★ ★ ★ ★
R ★ ★ ★ ★ ★ ★ ★ ★	T ★ ★ ★

JESSE, F. Tennyson (1889-1958) British journalist, novelist and playwright. Her principal contribution to crime fiction was *A Pin to See the Peepshow*, a powerful novel based upon the Thompson and Bywaters murder case; romantic, harrowing, an indictment of 1920s hypocrisy and the horror of capital punishment. Her short stories of the extra-sensory Solange Fontaine are unjustly neglected today.

The Solange Stories (1931)

C ★ ★ ★ ★ ★	P ★ ★ ★ ★ ★ ★
R ★ ★ ★ ★ ★ ★ ★ ★	T ★ ★

A Pin to See the Peepshow (1934)

C ★ ★ ★ ★ ★ ★ ★ ★	P ★ ★ ★ ★ ★ ★ ★ ★
R ★ ★ ★ ★ ★ ★	T ★ ★ ★ ★

JOBSON, Hamilton (1914) British police procedural writer. Thirty years a policeman, with nine commendations for special arrests, Jobson writes solid stories of policework, notable for their lack of contrived situations, if somewhat slow in the telling. His running hero was Inspector Anders, the same rank as he himself attained.

Smile and Be A Villain (1969)

C ★ ★ ★ ★ ★ ★ ★ ★	P ★ ★ ★ ★ ★ ★
R ★ ★ ★ ★ ★ ★ ★	T ★ ★ ★ ★ ★

JORDAN, David Pseudonymous British financial thriller novelist. The world of international merchant banks is a closed one to most people, but Jordan opens it up, in a way that is easily understood and with occasions of genuine excitement thrown in. He writes splendidly crisply; he is awesomely clever; he can be funny.

Double Red (1981)

C ★ ★ ★ ★ ★ ★ ★	P ★ ★ ★ ★ ★ ★ ★ ★
R ★ ★ ★ ★ ★ ★ ★ ★	T ★ ★ ★ ★ ★ ★ ★ ★

KALLEN, Louise American detective story writer. Louise Kallen was one of the brightest off-camera stars of early day television. She was for many years a head writer of the Sid Caesar *Show of Shows*. Her recent mystery series about Maggie Rome and C. B. Greenfield, newspaper reporter and editor, could be a hit series of the amateur detective form. Kallen has wit, good humour, and an eye and ear which distill life on the back roads of Westchester County.

The Tanglewood Murder (1980)

C ★ ★ ★ ★ ★ ★ ★	P ★ ★ ★ ★ ★ ★ ★
R ★ ★ ★ ★ ★ ★ ★ ★	T ★ ★ ★ ★ ★

KAMINSKY, Stuart M. (1934) American suspense writer and professor of radio, television and film. A compulsive writer, his books vary in subject and setting, though more than one has featured Toby Peters, a Hollywood private eye of the forties, investigating in the world of the stars. His most successful work, however, is perhaps *Rostnikov's Corpse*, set in Russia and featuring the persevering Inspector Porfiry Rostnikov, battling Moscow's cold, the hovering K.G.B. and Soviet bureaucracy equally.

Murder on the Yellow Brick Road (1977)

C ★ ★ ★ ★ ★ ★ ★	P ★ ★ ★ ★ ★ ★ ★ ★
R ★ ★ ★ ★ ★ ★ ★ ★ ★	T ★ ★ ★ ★ ★ ★ ★

Rostnikov's Corpse (1981)

C ★ ★ ★ ★ ★ ★ ★ ★	P ★ ★ ★ ★ ★ ★ ★
R ★ ★ ★ ★ ★ ★ ★ ★	T ★ ★ ★ ★ ★ ★ ★

KEATING, H. R. F. (1926) British novelist. H. R. F. Keating began his writing career as a journalist and may seem to have consummated it with his Inspector Ghote books which for a decade and a half have been providing their readers with a powerful evocation of modern India as well as with teasing puzzles and one of the most amiable and humane of modern detectives. But fans who can recall the subtle pleasures of the pre-Ghote books, and who have enjoyed his three "straight" novels would not be surprised to find this writer seeking new directions in the eighties.

A Rush on the Ultimate (1961)

C ★ ★ ★ ★ ★ ★ ★ ★	P ★ ★ ★ ★ ★ ★ ★ ★
R ★ ★ ★ ★ ★ ★ ★ ★	T ★ ★ ★ ★ ★ ★ ★

Inspector Ghote Trusts The Heart (1972)

C ★ ★ ★ ★ ★ ★ ★ ★	P ★ ★ ★ ★ ★ ★ ★ ★
R ★ ★ ★ ★ ★ ★ ★ ★	T ★ ★ ★ ★ ★ ★ ★

A Remarkable Case of Burglary (1975)

C ★ ★ ★ ★ ★ ★ ★	P ★ ★ ★ ★ ★ ★ ★ ★
R ★ ★ ★ ★ ★ ★ ★ ★	T ★ ★ ★ ★ ★ ★ ★ ★

KELLY, Mary (1927) British suspense novelist. She began with a series of detective novels set in contemporary industrial locales (papermaking, pottery manufacture), but abandoning this she produced books designed entirely to sweep the reader into a different, more gripping, more alive world. In this she succeeds admirably, chiefly by virtue of fine writing, of description carried out with a never-blinking eye and by bringing to us characters who are always real people seen in depth. She is, alas, apt to give less attention to plot, but the handful of books she has written give her a high place in contemporary crime writing.

Write on Both Sides of the Paper (1969)

C ★ ★ ★ ★ ★ ★ ★ ★	P ★ ★ ★ ★ ★ ★
R ★ ★ ★ ★ ★ ★ ★ ★	T ★ ★ ★ ★ ★ ★ ★ ★

The Twenty-fifth Hour (1971)

C ★ ★ ★ ★ ★ ★ ★ ★	P ★ ★ ★ ★ ★
R ★ ★ ★ ★ ★ ★ ★ ★	T ★ ★ ★ ★ ★ ★ ★ ★ ★

KEMELMAN, Harry (1908) American mystery novelist. He began in 1964 producing a series of which the first title was *Friday the Rabbi Slept Late*. The other days of the week have subsequently been gone through. In many ways the Edgar-awarded first book was the best. In it Kemelman succeeded in his implicit promise to use Talmudic reasoning to solve crimes where the less sophisticated logic of the police had failed. But the books have another purpose, itself twofold. First Kemelman wished to explain Jewish religion by his stories of Rabbi Small of Barnard's Crossing. Second he set out to portray, which he does very well, the everyday tensions and complications of the conduct of a Jewish temple in Middle America. The later books sometimes diverged from these aims. Kemelman is also the author of a series of brilliantly clever short crime stories, *The Nine Mile Walk*.

Friday the Rabbi Slept Late (1964)

C ★ ★ ★ ★ ★ ★ ★ ★	P ★ ★ ★ ★ ★ ★ ★ ★
R ★ ★ ★ ★ ★ ★ ★ ★	T ★ ★ ★ ★ ★ ★ ★

The Nine Mile Walk (1967)

C ★ ★ ★ ★ ★	P ★ ★ ★ ★ ★ ★ ★ ★ ★
R ★ ★ ★ ★ ★ ★ ★	T ★ ★ ★ ★ ★

KENNEDY, Adam American novelist whose slick, versatile performances include suspense stories that have won from Harold Robbins the accolade "I couldn't put it down." He writes with swift efficiency, using plentiful dialogue and can achieve an impression of thundering power. He has also used the pen-name John Redgate.

Debt of Honour (1981)

C ★ ★ ★ ★ ★	P ★ ★ ★ ★ ★ ★ ★ ★
R ★ ★ ★ ★ ★ ★ ★ ★	T ★ ★ ★ ★ ★ ★ ★

KENRICK, Tony (1935) British thriller writer, born and educated in Australia but much travelled since. He specializes in big (really big) caper stories, but liberally lards them with comedy. Novels about hi-jacking, extortion and large-scale rob-

R = Readability   T = Tension

bery ought to be suspenseful; Kenrick's are just that, but with hilarity.

A Tough One to Lose (1972)

C ★ ★ ★ ★ ★	P ★ ★ ★ ★ ★ ★ ★
R ★ ★ ★ ★ ★ ★	T ★ ★ ★ ★ ★ ★

Two for the Price of One (1974)

C ★ ★ ★ ★ ★	P ★ ★ ★ ★ ★ ★
R ★ ★ ★ ★ ★ ★	T ★ ★ ★ ★ ★ ★

KENYON, Michael (1931) British crime novelist. He began with a deserved bestseller, *May You Die in Ireland,* a spy novel humorously seen, followed it with less successful books in a similar jokey vein, but gradually allowed seriousness occasionally to creep in achieving a high degree of literary success. Though not Irish, he sets many of his books there, to excellent comic effect. He has a fine touch of wicked wit.

May You Die in Ireland (1965)

C ★ ★ ★ ★ ★ ★	P ★ ★ ★ ★ ★ ★
R ★ ★ ★ ★ ★ ★	T ★ ★ ★ ★ ★ ★

The Rapist (1977)
(Daniel Forbes in U.S.)

C ★ ★ ★ ★ ★ ★	P ★ ★ ★ ★ ★ ★ ★
R ★ ★ ★ ★ ★ ★	T ★ ★ ★ ★ ★ ★ ★

Zigzag (1981)

C ★ ★ ★ ★ ★ ★	P ★ ★ ★ ★ ★ ★ ★
R ★ ★ ★ ★ ★	T ★ ★ ★ ★ ★ ★

KERSH, Gerald (1911-68) Naturalized American novelist. Baker, bouncer, cook, wrestler, journalist and wartime Army Film Unit scriptwriter, Kersh's life was as strange and varied as his writing. His imaginative powers and his taste for the grotesque and the bizarre are displayed to best advantage in his short stories.

Nightshade and Damnation
(Stories, 1968)

C ★ ★ ★ ★ ★ ★	P ★ ★ ★ ★ ★ ★ ★
R ★ ★ ★ ★ ★ ★ ★	T ★ ★ ★ ★ ★ ★ ★

KIENZLE, William X. (1928) American mystery writer. A Roman Catholic priest for more than a quarter of a century, Kienzle, after leaving the religious life in the seventies, turned to mystery writing at the suggestion of his agent. *The Rosary Murders* was published in 1979 to immediate success, a selection of the Mystery Guild, the Literary Guild and the Detective Book Club. The protagonist is Father Koesler, a young priest working in a large city, Detroit. Kienzle's mysteries are amusing, exciting, and informative about church personnel and day by day work.

The Rosary Murders (1979)

C ★ ★ ★ ★ ★ ★	P ★ ★ ★ ★ ★ ★
R ★ ★ ★ ★ ★	T ★ ★ ★ ★ ★

Death Wears A Red Hat (1980)

C ★ ★ ★ ★ ★ ★	P ★ ★ ★ ★ ★
R ★ ★ ★ ★ ★	T ★ ★ ★ ★

KING, C. Daly (1895-1963) American detective novelist, lecturer in and writer on psychology. A very uneven writer, at his best he constructed a dazzling plot. His short story 'The Episode of the Nail and the Requiem' in *The Curious Mr Tarrant* has been hailed as "one of the most ingenious locked-room puzzles ever". His most successful novel was *Obelists Fly High* (an "obelist", King's own word, being a person of little importance but much suspiciousness).

The Curious Mr Tarrant (Stories, 1935)

C ★ ★ ★ ★	P ★ ★ ★ ★ ★ ★ ★ ★ ★
R ★ ★ ★ ★ ★	T ★ ★

Obelists Fly High (1935)

C ★ ★ ★ ★	P ★ ★ ★ ★ ★ ★ ★ ★
R ★ ★ ★ ★ ★ ★	T ★ ★ ★ ★ ★

KIRST, H. H. (1914) German novelist and crime novelist. Bestknown for his Gunner Asch satires on German army life, Kirst also wrote three linked satirical crime novels set in Munich and attacking in no uncertain terms the materialism and corruption of Germany in the

C = Characterization   P = Plot

1970s. They have been well translated.

A Time for Truth (1974)

C ★★★★★★★	P ★★★★★★★★
R ★★★★★★★★	T ★★★★★★

A Time for Payment (1976)

C ★★★★★★★	P ★★★★★★★★
R ★★★★★★★★	T ★★★★★★★

KITCHIN, C. H. B. (1895-1967) British detective novelist, lawyer and Stock Exchange member. He wrote four detective novels (and nine straight novels), of which *Death of My Aunt* has been enshrined in the crime Valhalla. As might be expected of a pure novelist, his chief strength is in characterization, but this goes far to carry his books.

Death of My Aunt (1929)

C ★★★★★★★★★	P ★★★★★★
R ★★★★★★★★	T ★★★★★★

Death of My Uncle (1939)

C ★★★★★★★★★	P ★★★★★★
R ★★★★★★★★	T ★★★★

KNOX, Bill (1928) Scottish crime novelist and former crime reporter, also writing as Michael Kirk, Robert MacLeod and Noah Webster. He is solidly prolific. There are more than fifteen police procedural stories set in Glasgow and featuring Detective Chief Inspector Thane, a tough but human character. There are nearly as many stories about a Scottish Fishery Protection officer, Webb Garrick. These all reek of local colour. Moving away from Scotland somewhat (as MacLeod in the U.K., and as Webster in the U.S.), he has half-a-dozen stories about a slightly less believable "Queen's Remembrancer", Jonathan Gaunt, operating from Edinburgh to various foreign locations. He always tells a good story.

Live Bait (1979)

C ★★★★★★★	P ★★★★★★★★
R ★★★★★★★★	T ★★★★★★★

KNOX, Ronald (1888-1957) British detective story writer and humorous critic of the genre, better known as a theologian (he was a Monsignor of the Roman Catholic Church and produced a new English version of the Bible). He wrote five detective stories. Curiously, in view of his exceptional intelligence, wit and interest in the genre, they are of the most moderate standard. However, his Decalogue of Detection (forbidding mysterious Chinese, confining secret passages to one per book, insisting that the criminal be introduced early) did encapsulate with nice wit the rules that guided the art in its Golden Age. He was also the first of the Sherlockian scholars, exposing for instance Doyle's error over the clue of the bicycle wheels in 'The Priory School' (read it and pit your wits).

KYLE, Duncan (1930) British suspense novelist and former journalist. He began writing, in 1970, comparatively late in life but *A Cage of Ice* was successful and since then he has produced more or less a book a year. He likes using unusual locations, and visiting them, even taking a long log-raft trip in British Columbia. But the locations are not all, nor the adventures. His people are real, often somewhat offbeat and interesting.

In Deep (1976)

C ★★★★★★★	P ★★★★★★★★
R ★★★★★★★★★	T ★★★★★★★★★

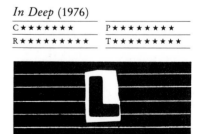

LAMBERT, Derek British thriller writer. He likes to write novels with more than a touch of topical controversy about them in the faction mode, though he embodies his re-

R = Readability T = Tension

searches always in a swiftly told story. *I Said the Spy*, for instance is about the little-reported Bilderburg Conference while *Trance* is concerned with the use of hypnotism by the American police.

Trance (1981)

C ★ ★ ★ ★ ★	P ★ ★ ★ ★ ★ ★ ★
R ★ ★ ★ ★ ★ ★ ★ ★	T ★ ★ ★ ★ ★ ★ ★

LANGLEY, Bob (1936) British espionage novelist and television presenter. He is a skilful builder of books with plenty of action, efficiently constructed characters and plots that have the necessary magnitude. His handling of his material can be judged by his success, as an Englishman, in setting most of *Autumn Tiger* in an American prison camp for Germans in 1945.

Autumn Tiger (1981)

C ★ ★ ★ ★ ★	P ★ ★ ★ ★ ★ ★ ★ ★
R ★ ★ ★ ★ ★ ★ ★	T ★ ★ ★ ★ ★ ★ ★

LATHEN, Emma Pseudonym of mystery-writing team Mary Latsis and Martha Hennissart. The writing team of Emma Lathen which debuted in 1961 with *Banking On Murder* is the only genuine five-star mystery writer to appear in the late twentieth century. Lathen is inimitable, witty, intelligent, honest, and just an all-round terrific writer. The key man and crime solver of the Lathen books is John Putnam

James Leasor

Thatcher, New York banker. He and his story reflect the modes and manners of today's Manhattan and the surrounding suburbs. Under the pseudonym R. B. Dominic, the Lathen collaborators have also introduced a Congressman who is gaining recognition among mystery readers. All the Lathen books are best, the three below just a sampling.

A Place for Murder (1963)

C ★ ★ ★ ★ ★ ★ ★ ★	P ★ ★ ★ ★ ★ ★ ★ ★
R ★ ★ ★ ★ ★ ★ ★ ★	T ★ ★ ★ ★ ★ ★ ★

Murder to Go (1969)

C ★ ★ ★ ★ ★ ★ ★ ★	P ★ ★ ★ ★ ★ ★ ★ ★
R ★ ★ ★ ★ ★ ★ ★ ★	T ★ ★ ★ ★ ★ ★ ★

Double, Double, Oil and Trouble (1978)

C ★ ★ ★ ★ ★ ★ ★ ★	P ★ ★ ★ ★ ★ ★ ★
R ★ ★ ★ ★ ★ ★ ★ ★	T ★ ★ ★ ★ ★ ★

LATIMER, Jonathan (1906) American crime novelist and screenwriter. Latimer's crime novels are a fast-moving, wise-cracking and often blackly comic variety of the American hard-nosed private-eye school. His alcoholic detective, Bill Crane, is unusual in that drink makes him drunk.

The Lady in the Morgue (1936)

C ★ ★ ★ ★ ★ ★	P ★ ★ ★ ★ ★ ★ ★
R ★ ★ ★ ★ ★ ★ ★ ★	T ★ ★ ★ ★ ★ ★ ★

LEASOR, James (1923) British thriller writer and historical novelist. He chronicles the adventures of Dr Jason Love, devotee of the vintage American Cord car, as is his creator. Love, a simple Somerset doctor, contrives or happens to get sent here and there in the world on dangerous missions. The locales, visited by Leasor, are invariably well and accurately described and the adventures are in the tradition of Buchan (q.v.), with sex by Bond.

Host of Extras (1973)

C ★ ★ ★ ★ ★	P ★ ★ ★ ★ ★ ★
R ★ ★ ★ ★ ★ ★ ★ ★	T ★ ★ ★ ★ ★ ★ ★ ★

C = Characterization   P = Plot

LEATHER, Edwin (1919) British espionage novelist. After a notable career in business and public life as a Member of Parliament and ultimately Governor and Commander-in-Chief, Bermuda, he turned to writing spy stories with as hero an impeccable British ex-Intelligence officer, settled in Vienna as a dealer in superb antiques. The books are awash with the artefacts and graces of the rich life. Fine wine is drunk, fine paintings stolen and dashingly retrieved.

The Duveen Letter (1980)

C ★★★★★★	P ★★★★★★★
R ★★★★★★★	T ★★★★★★★

LE CARRE, John (1931) British espionage novelist. Although beginning in quite a minor key with the pleasant detective story *Call for the Dead* (1961) which incidentally featured his later towering hero, George Smiley, he was eventually to write espionage novels that brought this literary sub-genre of age. but it was with his third book, *The Spy Who Came In from the Cold*, that in 1963 he (together with Len Deighton (q.v.) who was simultaneously finding a new way) moved the spy story from the slick, if enjoyable, nonsense of the James Bond books into a world of reality, of meanness, betrayal and bureaucracy. But, excellent though his subsequent espionage novels often were, they were to an extent limited. They were in essence single point-of-view books, following a single agent or tracing out a single adventure. It was in 1977 with *The Honourable Schoolboy* that it became apparent that Le Carré was producing something on a whole new scale, the massive George Smiley trilogy, later to include *Smiley's People* and putting into its place the earlier *Tinker, Tailor, Soldier, Spy*. In these three books he used the spy story to do more than simply spin an exciting tale, more even than merely to illuminate a particular facet of the human mind. He used the form to penetrate a whole world in a way that can be compared to the great novels of the nineteenth century. He sought to show the spy ethos, and all the complications that gives rise to seeping through whole societies. He produced espionage novels that had both sweep and vision. He asked on a massive scale a question that goes to the heart of Western democracy today: the dilemma that crouches at the heart of espionage and snakes out its tentacles everywhere, how is it possible to defend humanity in inhuman ways? It is a tremendous achievement.

The Spy Who Came in from the Cold (1963)

C ★★★★★★★★★	P ★★★★★★★
R ★★★★★★★★★	T ★★★★★★★★★★

Tinker, Tailor, Soldier, Spy (1974)

C ★★★★★★★★★	P ★★★★★★★★★
R ★★★★★★★★	T ★★★★★★★★

Smiley's People (1980)

C ★★★★★★★★★	P ★★★★★★★★
R ★★★★★★★★★	T ★★★★★★★★

John
Le Carré

R = Readability   T = Tension

LEMARCHAND, Elizabeth (1906) English detective novelist. A headmistress who retired early because of illness, she began then to write old-fashioned detective stories with often a map, a timetable and a cast list of characters. "Genteel" is the word, but it should not be thought of as disparaging, nor should "old-fashioned".

Change for the Worse (1980)

C ★ ★ ★ ★ ★ ★ ★	P ★ ★ ★ ★ ★ ★ ★
R ★ ★ ★ ★ ★ ★ ★	T ★ ★

LEOPOLD, Christopher Penname of two British collaborators as novelists and in the thriller field. Theirs is a classy product, with books set in chic locales such as the South of France and in periods, such as the 1930s, when the world was chicer too. A pleasant wit extends over all, in incidental touches, to the thriller genre being half-parodied. Learning is lightly worn.

The Night Fishers of Antibes (1981)

C ★ ★ ★ ★ ★ ★ ★ ★	P ★ ★ ★ ★ ★ ★ ★ ★
R ★ ★ ★ ★ ★ ★	T ★ ★ ★ ★ ★ ★

LE QUEUX, William, (1864-1927) British mystery and espionage writer. A journalist and sometime Secret Service agent, le Queux has some claim to be the first writer of spy fiction. His novels which depended more upon contemporary sensationalism than literary merit have not withstood the test of time.

The Mystery of a Motor Car (1906)

C ★ ★ ★ ★	P ★ ★ ★ ★ ★ ★
R ★ ★ ★ ★ ★ ★	T ★ ★ ★ ★ ★ ★ ★ ★

LEROUX, Gaston (1868-1972) French crime novelist. Leroux's varied and eventful career which included working as a journalist and as a lawyer and involved him in wide-ranging travel is reflected in the variety of his thirty-plus crime novels which are all narratively compelling if not altogether narratively convincing.

The Mystery of the Yellow Room (1908)

C ★ ★ ★ ★ ★ ★	P ★ ★ ★ ★ ★ ★ ★ ★
R ★ ★ ★ ★ ★ ★ ★ ★	T ★ ★ ★ ★ ★ ★ ★ ★

The Phantom of the Opera (1911)

C ★ ★ ★ ★ ★	P ★ ★ ★ ★ ★ ★ ★
R ★ ★ ★ ★ ★ ★ ★ ★ ★	T ★ ★ ★ ★ ★ ★ ★ ★

Ira Levin

LEVIN, Ira (1929) American mystery writer. Levin became a boy wonder of mystery with his first novel, *A Kiss before Dying*, written when he was in his early twenties. It was an instant success and was awarded Best First Novel Edgar in its year. Later his non-mystery novel, *Rosemary's Baby*, received equal acclaim and opened up the field of horror to bandwagon followers. However, Levin's chief interest is in playwriting. After enormous success with his adaptation of *No Time for Sergeants* in the mid-fifties, he made several attempts at Broadway success before writing *Death Trap*, a long-running, prize-

C = Characterization   P = Plot

winning mystery play. His books have been highly successful motion pictures.

A Kiss before Dying (1953)

C ★★★★★★★	P ★★★★★★★★
R ★★★★★★★	T ★★★★★★★★

Rosemary's Baby (1967)

C ★★★★★★★	P ★★★★★★★★
R ★★★★★★★★	T ★★★★★★★★★

The Boys from Brazil (1976)

C ★★★★★★★	P ★★★★★★★
R ★★★★★★★	T ★★★★★★★★

LEWIN, Michael Z. (1942) American detective novelist, resident in England and basketball columnist of the Somerset Standard. He writes classic private-eye stories, generally featuring impecunious Albert Samson of Indianapolis, whom he has described, well, as "soft-boiled but still an egg."

The Silent Salesman (1978)

C ★★★★★★★★	P ★★★★★★★
R ★★★★★★★★	T ★★★★★★★

LEWIS, Roy (1933) British detective novelist, educationalist and writer on business law. His earlier books had a predominantly legal flavour. Latterly he has concentrated with good effect on locale, catching not merely the look but the life of areas of Britain he knows well. Occasionally he uses as hero the cadaverous Inspector Crow. At his best a strong theme gives his books a slow but powerful impetus.

A Distant Banner (1976)

C ★★★★★★★★	P ★★★★★★★★
R ★★★★★★★	T ★★★★★

A Certain Blindness (1980)

C ★★★★★★★★	P ★★★★★★★★
R ★★★★★★★★	T ★★★★★★

LEWIS, Roy Harley British bookseller and detective novelist. His occasional crime novels, as might be expected, are set in the world of bookselling, which he manages to embroil reasonably credibly with

crime. The chief pleasure to be got from them is in the bookish facts and suppositions that are popped in like raisins in a cake.

A Cracking of Spines (1980)

C ★★★★★★	P ★★★★★★★
R ★★★★★★★★	T ★★★★★

LININGTON, Elizabeth (1921) American mystery writer. Elizabeth Linington under her own name and her better-known pseudonyms, (Dell Shannon, Lesley Egan, Egan O'Neill, Anne Blaisdell), is the most prolific American woman writer of the day. She was the first woman in today's mystery field to make the police story her own, a field which had previously been allotted to male writers. She has received Edgar scrolls for *Nightmare* in 1961 and *Knave of Hearts* in 1963. Her first mystery, *Case Pending* (1960) remains outstanding among her works, her knowledge of social work giving it a special authenticity.

A Case for Appeal (1961)

C ★★★★★★	P ★★★★★★★
R ★★★★★★★	T ★★★★★★

Against the Evidence (1963)

C ★★★★★★	P ★★★★★★★
R ★★★★★★★	T ★★★★★

Greenmask (1965)

C ★★★★★★	P ★★★★★★★
R ★★★★★★★	T ★★★★★★

LITTELL, Robert (1939) American espionage novelist, novelist, and former *Newsweek* general editor in Europe and Russia. His first novel. *The Defection of A. J. Lewinter*, about an American scientist whom ironically neither side knows the value of, won the Gold Dagger of the Crime Writers Association and reviewers' plaudits on both sides of the Atlantic. His work is marked by writing that is accurate, vivid, funny, compassionate and illuminating, if sometimes disconcertingly whimsical. He has the gift of being able to

R = Readability   T = Tension

Robert Littell

use humour to illuminate themes of great seriousness and has made of the spy tale novels that create worlds of their own, stamped with an idiosyncratic outlook yet commenting truly on the shifts and ideals of the world we live in.

The Defection of A. J. Lewinter (1973)

C ★ ★ ★ ★ ★ ★ ★ ★		P ★ ★ ★ ★ ★ ★ ★	
R ★ ★ ★ ★ ★ ★ ★ ★		T ★ ★ ★ ★ ★ ★ ★ ★	

The Debriefing (1979)

C ★ ★ ★ ★ ★ ★ ★ ★		P ★ ★ ★ ★ ★ ★ ★ ★ ★	
R ★ ★ ★ ★ ★ ★ ★ ★ ★		T ★ ★ ★ ★ ★ ★ ★ ★	

The Amateur (1981)

C ★ ★ ★ ★ ★ ★ ★ ★ ★		P ★ ★ ★ ★ ★ ★ ★ ★ ★	
R ★ ★ ★ ★ ★ ★ ★ ★ ★		T ★ ★ ★ ★ ★ ★ ★ ★ ★	

LITVINOV, Ivy (?-1977) British-born wife of Maxim Litvinov, Commissar for Foreign Affairs and Soviet Ambassador in Washington. She wrote one detective story only, but it is decidedly interesting on two counts. First, it gives a vivid, accurate and charming picture of Moscow life in the 1920s. Second, it was written as the result of hypnotic instruction by a distinguished German specialist visiting Moscow to examine the brain of the recently dead Lenin.

His Master's Voice (1930)

C ★ ★ ★ ★ ★ ★ ★ ★ ★		P ★ ★ ★ ★ ★ ★ ★	
R ★ ★ ★ ★ ★ ★ ★ ★		T ★ ★ ★ ★ ★ ★	

LOCKRIDGE, Richard (1898) and **Frances** (?-1963) American mystery writers. The Lockridges, both Missourians with Missouri newspaper backgrounds before moving on to New York, created one of the most enjoyable detecting teams of the forties and following decades in their characters Mr and Mrs North, who were featured in more than 25 books. They were also happily translated to the screen, and to radio and television. A second series, also highly successful, featured the compassionate police officer, Captain Heimrich. The New York background of the Norths is portrayed with exceptional verisimilitude. Since the death of his wife, Frances, Richard Lockridge has written little.

The Norths Meet Murder (1936)

C ★ ★ ★ ★ ★ ★ ★		P ★ ★ ★ ★ ★ ★	
R ★ ★ ★ ★ ★ ★ ★		T ★ ★ ★ ★ ★ ★	

Foggy, Foggy Death (1950)

C ★ ★ ★ ★ ★ ★ ★		P ★ ★ ★ ★ ★ ★	
R ★ ★ ★ ★ ★ ★		T ★ ★ ★ ★ ★ ★	

The Long Skeleton (1958)

C ★ ★ ★ ★ ★ ★ ★		P ★ ★ ★ ★ ★ ★	
R ★ ★ ★ ★ ★ ★		T ★ ★ ★ ★ ★ ★	

LORAINE, Philip British thriller writer, and under his real name, Robin Estridge, novelist and screenwriter. A much-travelled man, his books reflect this with above average atmosphere as well as intricate plotting and characters of some depth.

Lions' Ransom (1980)

C ★ ★ ★ ★ ★ ★ ★		P ★ ★ ★ ★ ★ ★ ★ ★ ★	
R ★ ★ ★ ★ ★ ★ ★ ★		T ★ ★ ★ ★ ★ ★ ★	

LORAC, E. C. R. (1894-1958) British detective novelist, who wrote almost as prolifically as Carol Carnac (q.v.). The 48 Lorac books, typical examples of British Golden Age work, almost all feature Inspector MacDonald of Scotland Yard, much given to exclaiming "Losh" in moments of excitement. His creator, whose real name was Edith Caroline

Rivett, has a stitched tunicle on display in Westminster Abbey.

The Dog It Was That Died (1952)

C ★★★★★★	P ★★★★★★★★
R ★★★★★★★	T ★★

LORD, Graham (1943) British suspense writer and books columnist, born in Rhodesia. He began writing crime in response to a competition organized by a British and an American publisher, and his entry, *Marshmallow Pie,* was one of two runners-up. Since, at longish intervals, he has added to that good start with books plainly written by someone who can use the language to fine effect and is willing to comment sharply on contemporary life.

Marshmallow Pie (1970)

C ★★★★★★★	P ★★★★★★★
R ★★★★★★★★	T ★★★★★★

The Nostradamus Horoscope (1981)

C ★★★★★★★★	P ★★★★★★★
R ★★★★★★★★	T ★★★★★★★★

LOVESEY, Peter (1936) British detective novelist. He won an international contest for a new crime story in 1970 with *Wobble to Death,* a tale of the Victorian walking races

known as wobbles. (Athletics and its history are his hobby). There followed an increasingly assured flow of Victorian police procedural novels featuring Sergeant Cribb and his assistant, Constable Thackeray, notable for the research put into them and unostentatiously used. As Peter Lear he wrote the bestselling *Golden Girl,* about an Olympics entrant. In more recent times he has moved to crime in the 1930s.

Wobble to Death (1970)

C ★★★★★★	P ★★★★★★★
R ★★★★★★★★	T ★★★★★★★

Swing, Swing Together (1976)

C ★★★★★★★★	P ★★★★★★★
R ★★★★★★★★	T ★★★★★★★

Waxwork (1978)

C ★★★★★★★★	P ★★★★★★★★★
R ★★★★★★★★★	T ★★★★★★★★★

LOWDEN, Desmond (1937) British thriller writer. Formerly a film technician and then author of TV plays, Lowden has written a handful of thrillers that generate more than average excitement as much from a certain oddity as from anything else.

Boudapesti 3 (1979)

C ★★★★★★★	P ★★★★★★★★
R ★★★★★★★★	T ★★★★★★★

LOWNDES, Mrs Belloc (1868-1947) British mystery and historical novelist. Hilaire Belloc's sister, she wrote in *The Lodger* (1913) a fictionalized account, not without merit as a suspense story – it was praised by Hemingway – of the Jack the Ripper murders. Among her nearly fifty titles she evolved a character, Hercules Popeau, retired from the Paris Sûrété, but if Agatha Christie had ever read about him she had forgotten.

The Lodger (1913)

C ★★★★★	P ★★★★★★★
R ★★★★★★	T ★★★★★★★★

Peter Lovesey

R = Readability   T = Tension

LUARD, Nicholas (1938) British espionage novelist, co-founder of *Private Eye* magazine. Educated at the Sorbonne, Cambridge and the University of Pennsylvania, he was a Coldstream Guards officer with a N.A.T.O. forward Intelligence unit. His books are memorable for the confident authenticity of their locales (which are apt to be places not frequently penetrated) and the seriousness of their telling. They are reputed occasionally to upset the C.I.A.

The Robespierre Serial (1975)

C ★ ★ ★ ★ ★ ★ ★	P ★ ★ ★ ★ ★ ★ ★ ★
R ★ ★ ★ ★ ★ ★ ★ ★	T ★ ★ ★ ★ ★ ★ ★ ★

The Dirty Area (1979)

C ★ ★ ★ ★ ★ ★ ★ ★	P ★ ★ ★ ★ ★ ★ ★ ★
R ★ ★ ★ ★ ★ ★ ★ ★	T ★ ★ ★ ★ ★ ★ ★ ★

LUCE, Helen (1934) British crime novelist and in private life a consultant pathologist. *In the Midst of Death* is a good whodunit with a juicy hospital background, both in blood and house politics. She tells a good story.

In the Midst of Death (1980)

C ★ ★ ★ ★ ★ ★ ★ ★	P ★ ★ ★ ★ ★ ★ ★
R ★ ★ ★ ★ ★ ★ ★ ★	T ★ ★ ★ ★ ★ ★

LUDLUM, Robert (1927) American thriller writer, who also writes as Jonathan Ryder and Michael Shepherd. Ludlum was an actor and producer before he turned to writing. His novels usually have their roots in the contemporary American political scene, but his writing talents are flexible enough to encompass wider themes as in his imaginative and exciting "religious" thriller, *The Gemini Contenders*.

The Gemini Contenders (1976)

C ★ ★ ★ ★ ★ ★ ★	P ★ ★ ★ ★ ★ ★ ★ ★ ★
R ★ ★ ★ ★ ★ ★ ★ ★	T ★ ★ ★ ★ ★ ★ ★ ★

The Parsifal Mosaic (1982)

C ★ ★ ★ ★ ★ ★ ★	P ★ ★ ★ ★ ★ ★ ★ ★ ★
R ★ ★ ★ ★ ★ ★ ★	T ★ ★ ★ ★ ★ ★ ★ ★

LUTZ, John (1939) American mystery writer. Primarily a short story writer with more than 100 to his published credit, Lutz is widely anthologized. As yet he has written but a few novels.

Bonegrinder (1980)

C ★ ★ ★ ★ ★	P ★ ★ ★ ★ ★ ★
R ★ ★ ★ ★ ★	T ★ ★ ★ ★ ★

Gavin Lyall

LYALL, Gavin (1932) British thriller/adventure novelist. A former R.A.F. pilot and Air Correspondent

Robert Ludlum

C = Characterization   P = Plot

of *The Observer,* he began with books in which flying, vividly described, played a large part. But an almost equal part was played by the dialogue of his heroes, a pure British equivalent, and of its time too, to the wisecracking dialogue of Hammett (q.v.) and Chandler (q.v.). It is, of course, talk that reflects the man. Lyall's heroes have the independence and not unthoughtful toughness of the best 1930s private eyes. Later he sometimes abandoned flying in favour of the complexities of espionage as the excitement factor. In this he is equally successful. He is, sadly, by no means a prolific writer, with only eight titles in twenty years of writing.

Ed McBain

The Wrong Side of the Sky (1961)

C ★ ★ ★ ★ ★ ★ ★ ★	P ★ ★ ★ ★ ★ ★ ★
R ★ ★ ★ ★ ★ ★ ★ ★	T ★ ★ ★ ★ ★ ★ ★

Judas Country (1975)

C ★ ★ ★ ★ ★ ★ ★	P ★ ★ ★ ★ ★ ★ ★ ★ ★
R ★ ★ ★ ★ ★ ★ ★ ★ ★	T ★ ★ ★ ★ ★ ★ ★ ★

The Secret Servant (1980)

C ★ ★ ★ ★ ★ ★ ★	P ★ ★ ★ ★ ★ ★ ★ ★ ★
R ★ ★ ★ ★ ★ ★ ★ ★	T ★ ★ ★ ★ ★ ★ ★ ★

McBAIN, Ed (1926) American mystery writer, pseudonym of Evan Hunter. Ed McBain is the most successful of Evan Hunter's pseudonyms. McBain is known world-wide for his 87th Precinct (New York City) police procedural series. It was introduced in 1956 with *Cop Hater* and *The Mugger.* The characters of the 87th Precinct have been popular screen and television characters for many years. In his own name, Evan Hunter has written many crime novels, the best known being *The Blackboard Jungle* (1954), the first detailed story of violence in city

schools and a classic of its times.

Killer's Choice (1957)

C ★ ★ ★ ★ ★	P ★ ★ ★ ★ ★ ★ ★
R ★ ★ ★ ★ ★ ★ ★	T ★ ★ ★ ★ ★

Killer's Wedge (1959)

C ★ ★ ★ ★ ★ ★	P ★ ★ ★ ★ ★ ★ ★
R ★ ★ ★ ★ ★ ★ ★ ★	T ★ ★ ★ ★ ★

Doll (1965)

C ★ ★ ★ ★ ★ ★ ★	P ★ ★ ★ ★ ★ ★ ★
R ★ ★ ★ ★ ★ ★ ★ ★	T ★ ★ ★ ★ ★ ★

McCARRY, Charles (1929) American espionage novelist, sometime speech writer for President Eisenhower and C.I.A. agent. He writes seldom, but he writes at a high level indeed. His first novel, *The Miernik Dossier,* was written in just that form, the dossier, a procedure asking for trouble and boredom. But instead of merely ladling out pretend facts it told a compelling story and a poignant one. *The Tears of Autumn,* his next work, was not much less affecting, though the fact was perhaps disguised by the sensationalism of reviewers who thought its story of why Kennedy was assassinated was inside dope. *The Secret Lovers,* his third book, lived up to the promise of its wonderfully ambiguous title, drawing a subtle parallel between the shifts of illicit love and the compli-

R = Readability   T = Tension

cations of the agent's existence. The fourth book, *The Better Angels* (1979), tackled a major theme, whether man is essentially a possible being of goodness or is inevitably flawed, through a major story of a U.S. Presidential election. It did not perhaps quite succeed, but if it failed it failed greatly.

The Miernik Dossier (1973)

C ★ ★ ★ ★ ★ ★	P ★ ★ ★ ★ ★ ★ ★
R ★ ★ ★ ★ ★ ★	T ★ ★ ★ ★ ★ ★ ★

The Tears of Autumn (1975)

C ★ ★ ★ ★ ★ ★ ★	P ★ ★ ★ ★ ★ ★ ★
R ★ ★ ★ ★ ★ ★ ★	T ★ ★ ★ ★ ★ ★

The Secret Lovers (1977)

C ★ ★ ★ ★ ★ ★ ★	P ★ ★ ★ ★ ★ ★
R ★ ★ ★ ★ ★ ★ ★	T ★ ★ ★ ★ ★ ★

before psychiatry became a household world.

Panic (1944)

C ★ ★ ★ ★ ★ ★	P ★ ★ ★ ★ ★
R ★ ★ ★ ★ ★ ★	T ★ ★ ★ ★ ★ ★

Through A Glass Darkly (1950)

C ★ ★ ★ ★ ★ ★	P ★ ★ ★ ★ ★ ★
R ★ ★ ★ ★ ★ ★	T ★ ★ ★ ★ ★ ★

The Sleepwalker (1974)

C ★ ★ ★ ★ ★ ★	P ★ ★ ★ ★ ★
R ★ ★ ★ ★ ★ ★	T ★ ★ ★ ★ ★ ★

McCLURE, James (1939) South African crime novelist, of British stock, now resident in Britain. He writes most often mystery stories featuring Lieutenant Tromp Kramer, South African detective,

Charles McCarry (left)

James McClure

McCLOY, Helen (1904) American mystery writer. From her entrance into mystery with *Dance of Death* (1938), the literary quality of Helen McCloy's writing and her understated aura of terror, have lifted her books above the norm. The detective featured in most of her work is Dr Basil Willing, psychiatrist and medical assistant to New York's district attorney. Helen McCloy introduced Dr Willing to readers long and his Zulu sidekick, Sergeant Zondi, and is remarkable for the manner in which he is able to sympathize with people of all races and conditions on either side of the great divide in South African society. This was evident from his first book, *The Steam Pig* (1971), winner of the Gold Dagger of the Crime Writers Association in Britain. At one level this was simply a clever and well-written murder mystery, but the

C = Characterization   P = Plot

crime hinged ingeniously on the concealed racial origin of the girl Coloured victim and, as the investigation proceeded, layer after layer of South African society was revealed with insight and sympathy, all the more telling since Lieutenant Kramer is by no means a simple crusading liberal for all his liking of his Bantu assistant. McClure's passionate concern with Africa was shown yet more clearly in the adventure novel he wrote in 1976, *Rogue Eagle*. A large-scale piece of writing, it successfully mingles the facts of history and geography with a grippingly exciting story. It well deserved its Crime Writers Association Silver Dagger award. He has also written major factual studies of police work both in Britain and America.

Rogue Eagle (1976)

C ★ ★ ★ ★ ★ ★ ★ ★	P ★ ★ ★ ★ ★ ★ ★
R ★ ★ ★ ★ ★ ★ ★ ★ ★	T ★ ★ ★ ★ ★ ★ ★ ★

The Sunday Hangman (1977)

C ★ ★ ★ ★ ★ ★ ★ ★	P ★ ★ ★ ★ ★ ★ ★
R ★ ★ ★ ★ ★ ★ ★	T ★ ★ ★ ★ ★ ★ ★

The Blood of An Englishman (1980)

C ★ ★ ★ ★ ★ ★ ★ ★	P ★ ★ ★ ★ ★ ★ ★ ★
R ★ ★ ★ ★ ★ ★ ★	T ★ ★ ★ ★ ★ ★ ★

McCUTCHAN, Philip (1927)

British suspense writer, and writer of sea stories. He is one of the mass-producers. Not content with 42 novels under his own name in 22 years, he also writes as T. I. G. Wigg, as Robert Conington Galway and as Duncan MacNeil. In his own name he produces a Commander Shaw series of hectic spy tales and a Simon Shard series of equally incident-packed detective stories. Action is his byword.

A Very Big Bang (1975)

C ★ ★ ★ ★ ★	P ★ ★ ★ ★ ★ ★
R ★ ★ ★ ★ ★ ★ ★	T ★ ★ ★ ★ ★

Werewolf (1982)

C ★ ★ ★ ★ ★	P ★ ★ ★ ★ ★
R ★ ★ ★ ★ ★ ★ ★	T ★ ★ ★ ★ ★

MCDONALD, Gregory (1937)

American crime novelist, and former award-winning journalist. He writes books, each one of which is apt to do something unattempted yet in the mystery novel, featuring either Fletch, a drop-outish journalist, or Flynn, a highly unconventional policeman, or both. The books are remarkable for their wit and their (partly concealed) high intelligence (McDonald studied at Harvard under the theologian Paul Tillich), but by no means neglect to tell gripping stories and to posit highly intriguing situations. *Fletch* and *Confess, Fletch* won Edgars from the Mystery Writers of America.

Fletch (1974)

C ★ ★ ★ ★ ★ ★ ★ ★	P ★ ★ ★ ★ ★ ★ ★
R ★ ★ ★ ★ ★ ★ ★ ★	T ★ ★ ★ ★ ★ ★ ★

Confess, Fletch (1976)

C ★ ★ ★ ★ ★ ★ ★ ★	P ★ ★ ★ ★ ★ ★ ★ ★
R ★ ★ ★ ★ ★ ★ ★ ★	T ★ ★ ★ ★ ★ ★ ★

Fletch and the Widow Bradley (1981)

C ★ ★ ★ ★ ★ ★ ★ ★	P ★ ★ ★ ★ ★ ★ ★ ★
R ★ ★ ★ ★ ★ ★ ★ ★	T ★ ★ ★ ★ ★ ★ ★ ★

MacDONALD, John D. (1916)

American mystery writer. One of the most popular of American mystery writers, a multi-million copy best-seller, John D. Mac-

John D. MacDonald

R = Readability   T = Tension

Donald has accomplished it in unusual fashion, his books first appearing as original paperbacks. His best known character is Travis McGee, a hard-hitting but not gritty private eye. Travis lives aboard his boat, "The Busted Flush", in Florida waters. He has been filmed but never with the special appeal which MacDonald generates for him. Travis is MacDonald's mouthpiece, and as tough mentally as physically, striking out verbally even against popular injustices. The titles of most of the McGee books are in colour, borrowed perhaps subliminally from Frances Crane's earlier colour books. Among his honours, MacDonald received the Ben Franklin Best Short Story award in 1955, the Grand Prix de Litterature Policière of France in 1964, and the Grand Master Edgar from Mystery Writers of America in 1971.

The Deep Blue Goodbye (1964)

C ★ ★ ★ ★ ★	P ★ ★ ★ ★ ★
R ★ ★ ★ ★ ★ ★ ★	T ★ ★ ★ ★ ★ ★ ★

A Purple Place for Dying (1964)

C ★ ★ ★ ★ ★	P ★ ★ ★ ★ ★
R ★ ★ ★ ★ ★ ★ ★	T ★ ★ ★ ★ ★ ★ ★

Darker than Amber (1966)

C ★ ★ ★ ★ ★	P ★ ★ ★ ★ ★ ★
R ★ ★ ★ ★ ★ ★ ★	T ★ ★ ★ ★ ★ ★ ★

Ross Macdonald

MacDONALD, Philip (1899) British detective novelist and Hollywood screenwriter, who also wrote as Oliver Fleming, Anthony Lawless and Martin Porlock. Many of his books featured Colonel Anthony Gethryn, logical tracker down of inconsistencies and oddities. The books were in the full tradition of the Golden Age detective story, and some are among its best examples. John Dickson Carr (q.v.) singled out *Murder Gone Mad*, a *tour de force* among *tours de force*, as one of the ten best detective novels.

The Rasp (1924)

C ★ ★ ★ ★ ★ ★	P ★ ★ ★ ★ ★ ★ ★ ★ ★
R ★ ★ ★ ★ ★ ★ ★ ★	T ★ ★ ★ ★ ★ ★ ★

Murder Gone Mad (1931)

C ★ ★ ★ ★ ★ ★	P ★ ★ ★ ★ ★ ★ ★ ★ ★ ★
R ★ ★ ★ ★ ★ ★ ★ ★	T ★ ★ ★ ★ ★ ★ ★

The Maze (1932)
(*Persons Unknown* in U.S.)

C ★ ★ ★ ★ ★ ★	P ★ ★ ★ ★ ★ ★ ★ ★ ★
R ★ ★ ★ ★ ★ ★ ★	T ★ ★ ★ ★ ★ ★

MACDONALD, Ross (1915) American mystery novelist, some of whose titles have appeared as by John Macdonald or John Ross Macdonald, and whose early books came out under his own name, Kenneth Millar (he is married to Margaret Millar (q.v.)). He is the acknowledged heir to Hammett (q.v.) and Chandler (q.v.), a writer of private-eye novels set in corrupt, sun-blest, ocean-kissed California. His detective is Lew Archer, perennially and classically working out of a small, sad office, familiar (a little disconcertingly) with good modern painting and authors, and, in his creator's own words, "the classless, restless man of American democracy". Macdonald has all Chandler's gift for the vivid phrase, and then some. Perhaps sometimes too much. But his sudden flares of illumination tend to be in his descriptive writing rather than in a detective's wisecrack comments. But they make the stories immensely sharp to the reader's eye and give Macdonald opportunities for the keen social comment that plainly fires him, and which has led critics to say that he is not only a major American crime novelist but a major American novelist.

The Galton Case (1959)

C ★★★★★★★★	P ★★★★★★★★
R ★★★★★★★★★	T ★★★★★★★★

The Far Side of the Dollar (1965)

C ★★★★★★★★★★	P ★★★★★★★★★★
R ★★★★★★★★★★	T ★★★★★★★★★★

Sleeping Beauty (1973)

C ★★★★★★★★★	P ★★★★★★★★
R ★★★★★★★★★	T ★★★★★★★★

McGERR, Patricia (1917) American mystery writer. Patricia McGerr is known for being one of the few writers, man or woman, who has created a woman protagonist without womanly frills. A prolific short story writer as well as novelist, a number of her works have appeared on screen and on television. Among her many honours, Miss McGerr is one of the few Americans to be honoured with the Grand Prix de Litterature Policière of France.

Catch Me If You Can (1948)

C ★★★★★★★	P ★★★★★★
R ★★★★★★★	T ★★★★★

Follow as the Night (1950)

C ★★★★★★★	P ★★★★★★★
R ★★★★★★★	T ★★★★★

Death in A Million Living Rooms (1951)

C ★★★★★★★	P ★★★★★★
R ★★★★★★★	T ★★★★★★

McGIVERN, William P. (1927) American mystery writer. A newspaperman turned successful crime writer in 1948 and screenwriter in the sixties, William (Bill) McGivern has had nine of his novels translated into major motion pictures. He has also written many short stories for both pulp magazines and slicks such as the *Saturday Evening Post*. He is a craftsman as well as a natural news writer, the combination producing some excellent tight writing. His earlier works centred on corruption in metropolitan police activity but his more recent novels have been concerned with espionage in foreign locations.

The Big Heat (1953)

C ★★★★★★	P ★★★★★★★
R ★★★★★★★	T ★★★★★★★

Rogue Cop (1954)

C ★★★★★★	P ★★★★★★★
R ★★★★★★★	T ★★★★★★★★

The Caper of the Golden Bulls (1966)

C ★★★★★	P ★★★★★★★
R ★★★★★★★	T ★★★★★★★

MacINNES, Helen (1907) American mystery-suspense author. Scots born, Helen MacInnes began her writing career after coming to the United States in 1937 and thus is claimed as an American writer. She is one of the topmost names in the suspense field, always a best seller, with more than 20 million copies sold in the United States alone. Her books are concerned with espionage and international politics with global background material. Miss MacInnes has researched her backgrounds, with one exception, in person, and has as carefully researched her themes. Many of her novels have become major motion pictures.

Above Suspicion (1941)

C ★★★★★★★	P ★★★★★★★★★
R ★★★★★★★	T ★★★★★★★

Neither Five Nor Three (1951)

C ★★★★★★	P ★★★★★★★★
R ★★★★★★★	T ★★★★★★★

Decision at Delphi (1960)

C ★★★★★	P ★★★★★★★
R ★★★★★★★	T ★★★★★★★

MacKENZIE, Donald (1918) Canadian suspense novelist. One of

R = Readability   T = Tension

the specialists in literary suspense-espionage books. Born in Canada, he now makes his home in England and Europe. His books are high on authenticity, particularly the European backgrounds.

The Quiet Killer (1968)

C ★ ★ ★ ★ ★ ★	P ★ ★ ★ ★ ★ ★
R ★ ★ ★ ★ ★ ★ ★	T ★ ★ ★ ★ ★ ★

Raven's Revenge (1982)

C ★ ★ ★ ★ ★ ★	P ★ ★ ★ ★ ★ ★
R ★ ★ ★ ★ ★ ★ ★	T ★ ★ ★ ★ ★

MACLEAN, Alistair (1922) British thriller writer. His naval war service is reflected in his first book, *HMS Ulysses* (1955) written when he was working as a Glasgow schoolteacher. His output since then has covered the fields of espionage and fairly straight crime, but it is as a writer of compelling action adventures that he has excelled, though sadly there has been some falling off in terms of characterization and depth since his beginnings.

HMS Ulysses (1955)

C ★ ★ ★ ★ ★ ★ ★	P ★ ★ ★ ★ ★ ★ ★
R ★ ★ ★ ★ ★ ★ ★ ★	T ★ ★ ★ ★ ★ ★ ★ ★

The Guns of Navarone (1957)

C ★ ★ ★ ★ ★ ★	P ★ ★ ★ ★ ★ ★ ★
R ★ ★ ★ ★ ★ ★ ★ ★	T ★ ★ ★ ★ ★ ★ ★ ★

McLEOD, Charlotte (1922) American mystery novelist. She uses as background sometimes rural America, itself pleasantly unusual, and sometimes swanky Boston, and she fills her books with nice people (the murderers are perhaps too easy to spot, but not to pin down). She shows that warm sentiment has its place in crime writing.

The Luck Runs Out (1981)

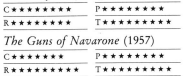

C ★ ★ ★ ★ ★ ★	P ★ ★ ★ ★ ★ ★ ★
R ★ ★ ★ ★ ★ ★	T ★ ★ ★

McMULLEN, Mary (1920) American mystery writer. Like Ursula Curtiss (q.v.), a talented writing daughter of Helen Reilly, an important crime writer in her lifetime.

Alistair Maclean

Mary McMullen received the Best First Novel Edgar in 1951 for *Stranglehold* (*Death of Miss X* in U.K.). Having proved to her mother and her sister that she too could write a mystery, she returned to her career in fashion design for the next twenty years. In 1974 she reappeared with *The Doom Campaign* and has published at least one mystery a year since.

A Country Kind of Death (1975)

C ★ ★ ★ ★ ★	P ★ ★ ★ ★ ★ ★
R ★ ★ ★ ★ ★ ★	T ★ ★ ★ ★ ★

The Other Shoe (1981)

C ★ ★ ★ ★ ★	P ★ ★ ★ ★ ★
R ★ ★ ★ ★ ★ ★	T ★ ★ ★ ★ ★

MALING, Arthur (1923) American mystery writer. A businessman who is a "born writer", Arthur Maling was recognized as one of the best of the new mystery writers with his first, *Decoy*, and he has never failed in subsequent books to live up to that ranking. Most of his plots have to do with business affairs, although recently he has set his intrigues outside America with considerable success. He received the

Edgar for Best Novel in 1980 for *The Rhinegold Route*.

Decoy (1969)

C ★ ★ ★ ★ ★ ★	P ★ ★ ★ ★ ★ ★ ★
R ★ ★ ★ ★ ★ ★ ★	T ★ ★ ★ ★ ★ ★

The Koberg Link (1979)

C ★ ★ ★ ★ ★ ★	P ★ ★ ★ ★ ★ ★
R ★ ★ ★ ★ ★ ★ ★	T ★ ★ ★ ★ ★

The Rhinegold Route (1979)

C ★ ★ ★ ★ ★ ★	P ★ ★ ★ ★ ★ ★ ★ ★
R ★ ★ ★ ★ ★ ★ ★ ★	T ★ ★ ★ ★ ★ ★ ★

MANN, Jessica (1937) British crime novelist. She has neither a permanent detective nor any continuity of setting. Instead she ranges with a novelist's sharp eye over selected areas of contemporary British life involving the people she finds there in some crime that adds the element of suspense to her stories. Her main interest, clearly, is the people she writes about and she shows them to her readers with a considerable perception that has given her a high place among British crime novelists of the 1970s and 1980s.

The Eighth Deadly Sin (1976)

C ★ ★ ★ ★ ★ ★ ★ ★	P ★ ★ ★ ★ ★ ★ ★
R ★ ★ ★ ★ ★ ★	T ★ ★ ★ ★ ★

The Sting of Death (1978)

C ★ ★ ★ ★ ★ ★ ★ ★	P ★ ★ ★ ★ ★ ★ ★
R ★ ★ ★ ★ ★ ★ ★	T ★ ★ ★ ★ ★

Funeral Sites (1981)

C ★ ★ ★ ★ ★ ★ ★ ★	P ★ ★ ★ ★ ★ ★ ★ ★
R ★ ★ ★ ★ ★ ★ ★ ★	T ★ ★ ★ ★ ★ ★ ★ ★

MARKHAM, Robert see AMIS, Kingsley

MARKSTEIN, George (1929) British espionage novelist, television and screenwriter (of among others the award-winning *Robbery*). A background in Intelligence enables him to bring the ring of authenticity to fast-moving, well written books, strongly linked to events in the real world (*Ultimate Issue* (1981) put forward a theory that the West con-

Jessica Mann

nived at the building of the Berlin Wall).

The Man from Yesterday (1976)

C ★ ★ ★ ★ ★ ★ ★ ★	P ★ ★ ★ ★ ★ ★ ★ ★ ★
R ★ ★ ★ ★ ★ ★ ★ ★ ★	T ★ ★ ★ ★ ★ ★ ★ ★

MARLOWE, Dan J. (1914) American mystery writer. A successful business man turned full-time writer in 1937, Dan Marlowe is one of the few American mystery writers whose books appear first as paperback originals. His series character, Johnny Killain, a New York detective, was introduced in 1959 in *Doorway to Death*, and has appeared in many books since. Through *The Name of the Game Is Death* in 1962, narrated by a fictional bank robber, Marlowe became a sponsor of an actual bank robber serving a term in prison, who has now become a writer. The Mystery Writers of America first original paperback award went to Marlowe in 1970 for *Flashpoint*, later retitled *Operation Flashpoint*.

Doorway to Death (1959)

C ★ ★ ★ ★ ★ ★	P ★ ★ ★ ★ ★ ★
R ★ ★ ★ ★ ★ ★ ★ ★	T ★ ★ ★ ★ ★ ★ ★

Operation Flashpoint (1970)

C ★ ★ ★ ★ ★ ★	P ★ ★ ★ ★ ★ ★ ★
R ★ ★ ★ ★ ★ ★ ★ ★	T ★ ★ ★ ★ ★ ★ ★ ★

MARLOWE, Derek (1938) British novelist. Marlowe's thrillers are only a part of his writing output. They are

R = Readability   T = Tension

notable for their ingenuity of plot and elegance of style, but he has yet to improve upon his first, *A Dandy In Aspic,* in terms of involving the reader in a fascinating and truly "thrilling" story.

A Dandy in Aspic (1966)

C ★ ★ ★ ★ ★ ★ ★	P ★ ★ ★ ★ ★ ★ ★ ★
R ★ ★ ★ ★ ★ ★ ★ ★	T ★ ★ ★ ★ ★ ★ ★

MARQUAND, John P. (1893-1960)

American author. Marquand, one of the foremost American novelists, was also a detective story writer. In 1935 he introduced the delightful Japanese detective, Mr. Moto, in *No Hero.* Although obviously indebted to Earl Derr Biggers' Chinese detective, Charlie Chan, for the concept of Mr Moto, Marquand put his own craftsman's mark on his Japanese detective. The Mr Moto series was a notable success, each one serialized in the *Saturday Evening Post* to a large audience before appearing in book form. The books are still popular, the entire series being reprinted in paperback in 1977. Although Marquand is best known in literary circles for *The Late George Apley,* the novel for which he won the Pulitzer Prize in 1937, to readers at large he will always be thought of as the creator of Mr Moto.

Last Laugh, Mr Moto (1942)

C ★ ★ ★ ★ ★ ★ ★ ★	P ★ ★ ★ ★ ★ ★ ★
R ★ ★ ★ ★ ★ ★ ★	T ★ ★ ★ ★ ★ ★ ★

MARRIC, J. J.

Pseudonym of John Creasey (q.v.) when writing his Commander Gideon books. These are police-procedurals, notable for the attractive and comforting character of their protagonist (who works his way up from Chief-Inspector to Commander during the 21 books of the series), and for the impression of documentary accuracy they give.

Gideon's Day (1955)

C ★ ★ ★ ★ ★	P ★ ★ ★ ★ ★ ★
R ★ ★ ★ ★ ★ ★ ★	T ★ ★ ★ ★ ★ ★

MARSH, Ngaio (1899-1982)

New Zealand detective novelist and theatre director (for services to which she became Dame Ngaio in 1966). Starting in 1942 she wrote more than 30 distinguished detective novels, most of them featuring Roderick Alleyn, a decidedly gentlemanly Scotland Yard officer rising steadily to the heights of his profession and marrying in the course of time Agatha Troy, celebrated portrait painter. Dame Ngaio's great strength lies in her characterization (plot sometimes gets a mite perfunctory, and even story is occasionally in the 'Then-Alleyn-interviewed-him-and-then-her' mode). She can depict for our delight people who are at the same time seemingly real and often splendidly larger than life. In some of her books she frees herself from the straitjacket of a puzzle plot by writing the pure thriller (*Spinsters in Jeopardy*). The theatre, the world of art and New Zealand have been her main backgrounds, but she has written interestingly of places as diverse as Britain's East Anglia (*Clutch of Constables,* 1969) and Rome (*When in Rome,* 1970) and whatever she writes and wherever it is set there is always the elegant prose and a fine sprinkling of apt literary quotation to give added pleasure. She has written a charming autobiography, *Black Beech and Honeydew* (revised edition 1982), which gives an illuminating insight into the mind of a master storyteller.

Surfeit of Lampreys (1940)
(Death of A Peer in U.S.)

C ★ ★ ★ ★ ★ ★ ★ ★	P ★ ★ ★ ★ ★ ★ ★
R ★ ★ ★ ★ ★ ★ ★ ★	T ★ ★ ★ ★ ★ ★

Final Curtain (1947)

C ★ ★ ★ ★ ★ ★ ★	P ★ ★ ★ ★ ★ ★ ★
R ★ ★ ★ ★ ★ ★ ★ ★	T ★ ★ ★ ★ ★ ★

Spinsters in Jeopardy (1953)
(The Brides of Death in U.S.)

C ★ ★ ★ ★ ★ ★ ★ ★	P ★ ★ ★ ★ ★ ★ ★ ★
R ★ ★ ★ ★ ★ ★ ★ ★	T ★ ★ ★ ★ ★ ★ ★

MARSHALL, William (1944) Australian police procedural writer, now resident in Ireland. He writes a series set in Hong Kong and featuring the detectives of the Yellowthread Street police station, a fictitious building but close to truth in its details. A fascination with the extraordinary in crime, amounting sometimes to the ridiculous, is one of his hallmarks. Another is his gift for rumbustious humour.

Perfect End (1981)

C ★ ★ ★ ★ ★ ★	P ★ ★ ★ ★ ★ ★ ★
R ★ ★ ★ ★ ★ ★ ★ ★	T ★ ★ ★ ★ ★ ★ ★ ★

MASON, A. E. W. (1865-1948) British novelist and playwright. Classical scholar, Naval Intelligence agent, actor and Liberal M.P., Mason also found time for a prolific literary output. His dozen crime novels, including the five which feature his Sûreté detective, Inspector Hanaud, are eventful, colourful and atmospheric and in addition often display a keen awareness of the quirks of the human mind. *Fire Over England* (1936) is a spy story with British agent Robin Aubrey, but set rumbustiously in Elizabeth I's days.

At The Villa Rose (1910)

C ★ ★ ★ ★ ★ ★ ★ ★	P ★ ★ ★ ★ ★ ★ ★ ★
R ★ ★ ★ ★ ★ ★ ★ ★	T ★ ★ ★ ★ ★ ★

The House of The Arrow (1924)

C ★ ★ ★ ★ ★ ★ ★ ★	P ★ ★ ★ ★ ★ ★ ★ ★ ★
R ★ ★ ★ ★ ★ ★ ★ ★ ★	T ★ ★ ★ ★ ★ ★ ★ ★ ★

MASON, F. Van Wyck (1901-78) American mystery writer. Mason had simultaneously two successful writing careers, that of an historical novelist and that of a mystery novelist. The mystery novels were principally of political intrigue with the knowledgeable Colonel North as chief character. Mason's own record in World War II was extraordinary. He was chief historian at Supreme Headquarters American Expeditionary Force, a recipient of the Croix de Guerre (two palms), and named an officer of the French Legion of Honour.

Seeds of Murder (1930)

C ★ ★ ★ ★ ★	P ★ ★ ★ ★ ★ ★ ★
R ★ ★ ★ ★ ★ ★ ★ ★	T ★ ★ ★ ★ ★ ★

Trouble in Burma (1962)

C ★ ★ ★ ★ ★	P ★ ★ ★ ★ ★ ★ ★
R ★ ★ ★ ★ ★ ★ ★	T ★ ★ ★ ★ ★ ★

MASUR, Harold Q. (1909) American mystery writer, who also uses the pseudonyms Guy Fleming and Edward James. A full time attorney-at-law, a part-time writing instructor in New York colleges, a magazine editor, a consultant for the Joint Chiefs of Staff, Department of Defense, and a multi-officer for Mystery Writers of America, Hal Masur has also found time to write some of the most entertaining mysteries, featuring Scott Jordan, like Masur himself, a lawyer. Jordon, in Perry Mason fashion, acts as a detective in defence of his clients.

Make A Killing (1964)

C ★ ★ ★ ★ ★ ★	P ★ ★ ★ ★ ★ ★ ★
R ★ ★ ★ ★ ★ ★ ★	T ★ ★ ★ ★ ★ ★

MATHER, Berkely British thriller writer. Mather became a full-time writer after a long career as a professional soldier. His thrillers, set for the most part in India with forays into neighbouring territories, are fast-moving, action-packed tales of espionage, written with style and panache and a tremendous sense of the subcontinent's moods and backgrounds.

The Pass beyond Kashmir

C ★ ★ ★ ★ ★ ★ ★ ★	P ★ ★ ★ ★ ★ ★ ★
R ★ ★ ★ ★ ★ ★ ★ ★	T ★ ★ ★ ★ ★ ★ ★

The Break in the Line (1970)

C ★ ★ ★ ★ ★ ★ ★ ★	P ★ ★ ★ ★ ★ ★ ★ ★
R ★ ★ ★ ★ ★ ★ ★ ★	T ★ ★ ★ ★ ★ ★ ★ ★

MAUGHAM, W. Somerset (1874-1965) British novelist and playwright, who wrote a single book of short stories about espionage, based

R = Readability   T = Tension

Somerset Maugham

to some extent on his own experiences as a British agent in Switzerland and Russia during the 1914-18 War. The book is claimed as the first fiction to show what spying really implied, the unpleasant betrayals, the long fruitless hours, the worries over routine, the absurd but tragic mistakes. It makes fascinating reading.

Ashenden (1928)

C ★ ★ ★ ★ ★ ★ ★ ★ ★	P ★ ★ ★ ★ ★ ★
R ★ ★ ★ ★ ★ ★ ★ ★	T ★ ★ ★ ★ ★ ★ ★

MAY, Peter (1951) British journalist and crime novelist. His *Hidden Faces*, which could have been a routine tough journalist story set amid corruption in Brussels, has more than its due quota of atmosphere and an underlying moral concern which lift it high.

Hidden Faces (1981)

C ★ ★ ★ ★ ★ ★ ★	P ★ ★ ★ ★ ★ ★ ★
R ★ ★ ★ ★ ★ ★ ★	T ★ ★ ★ ★ ★ ★ ★

MAYO, James (1914) Pseudonym of Stephen Coulter (q.v.). His thrillers, mostly featuring art dealer and Intelligence man Charles Hood, are among the host of Ian Fleming (q.v.) imitations and, indeed, among the most effective. All the ingredients are there – manly and sophisticated

hero, perverted master criminals, plenty of sex and sadism – but without Fleming's panache.

Hammerhead (1964)

C ★ ★ ★ ★ ★	P ★ ★ ★ ★ ★ ★ ★
R ★ ★ ★ ★ ★ ★ ★ ★	T ★ ★ ★ ★ ★ ★ ★

Once in a Lifetime (1968)
(*Sergeant Death* in U.S.)

C ★ ★ ★ ★ ★ ★	P ★ ★ ★ ★ ★ ★ ★
R ★ ★ ★ ★ ★ ★ ★ ★	T ★ ★ ★ ★ ★ ★ ★ ★

MEGGS, Brown (1930) American mystery writer. Before publication of his first mystery novel, Brown Meggs had been a story analyst for Warner Brothers Pictures, seemingly his only connection with writing and writers. From work in pictures, he moved on to become an executive with Capitol Records in Hollywood, and was a vice-president there when *Saturday Games,* his first novel, appeared. The story is a memorable one in the mystery genre. It was honoured with an Edgar scroll in 1974. Meggs has written only one mystery since, *The Matter of Paradise,* a beautifully crafted novel of the reunion of a number of preparatory students after ten years apart. For mystery at its finest, someone should isolate Meggs on a desert isle for a season or so with plenty of paper and pens.

Saturday Games (1973)

C ★ ★ ★ ★ ★ ★ ★	P ★ ★ ★ ★ ★ ★ ★
R ★ ★ ★ ★ ★ ★ ★	T ★ ★ ★ ★ ★ ★ ★ ★

The Matter of Paradise (1975)

C ★ ★ ★ ★ ★ ★ ★	P ★ ★ ★ ★ ★ ★ ★ ★
R ★ ★ ★ ★ ★ ★ ★	T ★ ★ ★ ★ ★ ★ ★

MELVILLE, James British detective novelist. Under a well-preserved pseudonym, a lecturer in Japan for the British Council writes crime novels about Superintendent Otani, a middle-aged thoughtful Japanese detective, whose cases seem often to involve foreigners who are (to him) incomprehensible. Written with humour, the books convey a great

C = Characterization   P = Plot

deal about contemporary Japan and Japanese attitudes.

A Sort of Samurai (1981)

C ★★★★★★★★	P ★★★★★★
R ★★★★★	T ★★★★★★

MELVILLE, Jennie (1922) British suspense novelist. The name is a pseudonym for Gwendoline Butler (q.v.) but generally speaking the Melville books differ markedly from the Butlers, though they themselves divide into two distinct categories. One is police procedurals, somewhat more fantastic than the classic prototype with a joky tone that is subtly disturbing. They feature Inspector Charmian Daniels. The other sort are modern-day gothics, sometimes with an interesting industrial archaeology background.

Raven's Forge (1975)

C ★★★★★★★	P ★★★★★★★
R ★★★★★★★★	T ★★★★★★★★★

Murder Has A Pretty Face (1981)

C ★★★★★★★	P ★★★★★★
R ★★★★★★★★	T ★★★★★★★

Nicholas Meyer

MEYER, Nicholas (1945) American mystery writer. Nicholas Meyer while yet in his twenties leapt to the pinnacle of American mystery in 1973 with *The Seven-Per-Cent Solution,* a Sherlock Holmes pastiche. It was an immediate best-seller and one of the most popular of the Literary Guild selections of that year. Almost simultaneously, Meyer published his mystery, *Target Practice,* which was honoured by an Edgar scroll as one of the Best First Novels. Being in constant demand as a screenwriter, Meyer has published few mysteries since, to the regret of his multitude of admirers.

Target Practice (1973)

C ★★★★★★★	P ★★★★★★★★
R ★★★★★★★★	T ★★★★★★

The Seven-Per-Cent Solution (1973)

C ★★★★★★	P ★★★★★★★★
R ★★★★★★★★	T ★★★★★★

MEYNELL, Laurence (1899) British detective novelist, children's writer and novelist (sometimes as Robert Eton). His crime writing career began in 1928 and continued at a book a year at least up to the 1980s. His early work is almost entirely forgotten, but in later days he has had two interesting phases. First, he wrote, starting from about 1970, novels with some highly unusual circumstance as their mainspring. Then he began a series featuring the engaging man-about-bars Hooky Hefferman, private detective with a dragon aunt.

The Curious Crime of Miss Julia Blossom (1970)

C ★★★★★★★	P ★★★★★★★★
R ★★★★★★★★	T ★★★★

Hooky and the Villainous Chauffeur (1979)

C ★★★★★★★	P ★★★★★★★
R ★★★★★★★★	T ★★★★★★

MICHAELS, Barbara see PETERS, Elizabeth.

MILLAR, Margaret (1915) American mystery novelist. No woman in twentieth-century American mystery writing is more important than Margaret Millar, Canadian born, American adopted. The finest of craftsmanship distinguishes all of

R = Readability T = Tension

her novels. In all she also reflects the social mores of her times. Although a Santa Barbara resident, she was named A Woman of the Year in 1965 by the *Los Angeles Times.* The Edgar for Best Novel was awarded her in 1955 for her mystery, *The Beast in View.* Margaret Millar is married to mystery novelist, Kenneth Millar, who writes as Ross Macdonald.

The Iron Gates (1945)

C ★ ★ ★ ★ ★ ★					P ★ ★ ★ ★ ★						
R ★ ★ ★ ★ ★ ★					T ★ ★ ★ ★ ★						

Beyond This Point Are Monsters (1970)

C ★ ★ ★ ★ ★ ★ ★					P ★ ★ ★ ★ ★ ★						
R ★ ★ ★ ★ ★ ★ ★					T ★ ★ ★ ★ ★ ★						

Mermaid (1982)

C ★ ★ ★ ★ ★ ★					P ★ ★ ★ ★ ★ ★						
R ★ ★ ★ ★ ★ ★ ★					T ★ ★ ★ ★ ★ ★						

MITCHELL, Gladys (1901) British detective novelist. Her first detective story came out in the heyday of the art in 1929 and introduced to the world Mrs (later Dame) Beatrice Lestrange Bradley, psychiatric ad-

Gladys Mitchell

viser to the Home Office, one of the enduring Great Detectives. The books are marked by the gusto of their writing, by a very well-stocked store of literary quotations, often by an interest in witchcraft, by good plotting, by naughty but endearing

digressions. They have appeared at the rate of one a year, always featuring Dame Beatrice, for more than half a century. Miss Mitchell received in 1975 a Special Award from the Crime Writers Association for "fifty distinguished books".

Faintley Speaking (1954)

C ★ ★ ★ ★ ★ ★					P ★ ★ ★ ★ ★ ★ ★						
R ★ ★ ★ ★ ★ ★					T ★ ★ ★ ★						

Late, Late in the Evening (1976)

C ★ ★ ★ ★ ★ ★ ★					P ★ ★ ★ ★ ★ ★						
R ★ ★ ★ ★ ★ ★ ★					T ★ ★ ★ ★ ★ ★						

Here Lies Gloria Mundy (1982)

C ★ ★ ★ ★ ★ ★					P ★ ★ ★ ★ ★ ★						
R ★ ★ ★ ★ ★ ★ ★					T ★ ★ ★ ★ ★						

MOFFAT, Gwen (1924) British crime novelist. Gwen Moffat's career as a mountain guide and contributor to newspapers and radio on related matters is reflected both in her frequent choice of wild and remote settings and in the mountaineering interests of her series character, Miss Melinda Pink, Justice of the Peace. An easy style, clever puzzles and evocative backgrounds are the hallmarks of Gwen Moffat's work.

Persons Unknown (1978)

C ★ ★ ★ ★ ★ ★					P ★ ★ ★ ★ ★ ★						
R ★ ★ ★ ★ ★ ★ ★					T ★ ★ ★ ★ ★ ★						

MORICE, Anne (1918) British suspense writer. From a theatrical background herself, she has produced a regular series featuring Tessa Crichton, theatre star married to a Scotland Yard detective. The books are light-hearted and in the good old tradition of such writers as the early Ngaio Marsh (q.v.), murder for puzzle's sake.

Death in the Round (1980)

C ★ ★ ★ ★ ★ ★					P ★ ★ ★ ★ ★ ★ ★						
R ★ ★ ★ ★ ★ ★					T ★ ★						

Hollow Vengeance (1982)

C ★ ★ ★ ★ ★ ★					P ★ ★ ★ ★ ★ ★						
R ★ ★ ★ ★ ★ ★ ★					T ★ ★ ★						

C = Characterization   P = Plot

MOYES, Patricia (1923) British crime writer. Patricia Moyes had worked as Peter Ustinov's secretary and assistant editor of *Vogue* before her first novel appeared in 1959. Since then she has written more than a dozen, all featuring Scotland Yard detective, Henry Tibbett. Their plots hang together well, their puzzles tease, their overall tone is pleasant, even charming, their settings varied and well observed.

Season of Snows and Sins (1971)

C ★★★★★★	P ★★★★★★★
R ★★★★★★	T ★★★★★★

NEBEL, Frederick American "hardboiled" novelist and short-story writer. He wrote two hardboiled novels in the thirties and a handful of short stories of the same sort in the fifties. But they hit the target, as not all of his fellow workers in this sub-genre truly did. Nebel, however, knew how to make his heroes credibly tough and their humour equally tough and credible.

Fifty Roads to Town (1936)

C ★★★★★★	P ★★★★★★★
R ★★★★★★★★	T ★★★★★★★

Six Deadly Dunes (stories, 1950)

C ★★★★★★★★	P ★★★★★★★
R ★★★★★★★★	T ★★★★★★★★

NEWMAN, Bernard (1897-1968) British espionage writer and travel writer (and author of *How to Run An Amateur Concert Party*, 1925), who also wrote as Don Betteridge, mostly also in the spy vein. Between 1934 and 1968 he produced 33 crime novels, some of them murder stories, many with Papa Pontivy as hero. Though he put in a solid background of fact, he saw his stories, and life too

perhaps, through a thick romantic haze.

The Double Menace (1955)

C ★★★★★★	P ★★★★★★★
R ★★★★★★★★	T ★★★★★★★

NEWMAN, G. F. (1935) British police novelist and television writer. He is rare, perhaps unique, among crime writers in that what motivates him is a desire to show the police "as they really are", that is as much more corrupt than is generally admitted, especially by police procedural novelists in Britain. His most successful venture, or at least most notorious, was the television series *Law and Order*, subsequently made into three novels. His interest in the police, and their reverse the criminals, began when two of his school friends joined the force, and others joined the criminal ranks. He believes his work in crime fiction has had some effect on attitudes within British society. But police corruption is not his only concern in fiction; he has written about a corrupt, paedophiliac politician (based, he says, on truth) in *The Obsession* and about American crime and corruption, seemingly authentically, in *The List*.

A Villain's Tale (1978)

C ★★★★★★★	P ★★★★★★★
R ★★★★★★★★★	T ★★★★★★★★

The List (1979)

C ★★★★★★	P ★★★★★★★
R ★★★★★★★★★	T ★★★★★★★★★

The Obsession (1980)

C ★★★★★★★	P ★★★★★★★
R ★★★★★★★★	T ★★★★★★★

NIELSEN, Helen (1918) American mystery writer. An unlikely combination of talents distinguishes Helen Nielsen, who is also an important aeronautical draftsman. Miss Nielsen was a newspaper and commercial artist before World War II which introduced her to aeronautics. She is not only a novelist but

R = Readability   T = Tension

also a short story and television drama writer. Her mysteries are noted for good writing as well as for her story-telling ability.

Verdict Suspended (1964)

C ★ ★ ★ ★ ★ ★ ★	P ★ ★ ★ ★ ★ ★
R ★ ★ ★ ★ ★ ★ ★	T ★ ★ ★ ★ ★ ★

NORTH, Gil (1916) British crime novelist and under his own name, Geoffrey Horne, novelist. Between 1960 and 1972 he wrote ten novels and one volume of novellas about Sergeant Cluff, policeman of the little town of Gunnarshaw, Yorkshire, a detective in the Maigret tradition. The writing is curiously involved, but the character comes over well as does his simple, everyday setting.

Sergeant Cluff Rings True (1972)

C ★ ★ ★ ★ ★ ★ ★ ★	P ★ ★ ★ ★ ★ ★
R ★ ★ ★ ★ ★ ★	T ★ ★ ★ ★

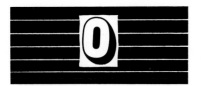

O'DONNELL, Lillian American mystery writer, who was formerly an actress, she became the first woman stage director of the New York theatre, taking on the position for the Shuberts in 1940. Her mysteries more often than not concern the theatre, with a verisimilitude only a professional can bring to this background. She has also received special praise for her woman police detective, Norah Mulcahaney, called by critics "the best woman cop" in mystery.

Death Blanks the Screen (1960)

C ★ ★ ★ ★ ★ ★	P ★ ★ ★ ★ ★ ★ ★
R ★ ★ ★ ★ ★ ★ ★	T ★ ★ ★ ★ ★ ★

Falling Star (1979)

C ★ ★ ★ ★ ★ ★	P ★ ★ ★ ★ ★ ★ ★
R ★ ★ ★ ★ ★ ★ ★ ★	T ★ ★ ★ ★ ★ ★ ★

O'DONNELL, Peter (1920) British suspense writer and strip cartoon author. His heroine, the tough, clean-cut, beautiful orphan refugee Modesty Blaise began in a strip, drawn by Jim Holdaway. She moved on to short stories and finally to adventure novels, as in fiction she moved on from the wrong side of the law to the right. All the while she gathered for herself a popular myth quality.

The Impossible Virgin (1971)

C ★ ★ ★ ★	P ★ ★ ★ ★ ★ ★ ★ ★
R ★ ★ ★ ★ ★ ★ ★ ★ ★	T ★ ★ ★ ★ ★ ★ ★ ★

O'HARA, Kenneth (1924) British detective novelist and under her own name, Jean Morris, talented novelist. At rare intervals she has produced extraordinary crime books, lively as jumping jacks, stuffed with out-of-the-way knowledge, with an undertow of the eerie. *The Times* review of one of them began "Oysters! Caviare! . . ."

The Company of St George (1972)

C ★ ★ ★ ★ ★ ★ ★ ★	P ★ ★ ★ ★ ★ ★ ★ ★
R ★ ★ ★ ★ ★ ★ ★ ★	T ★ ★ ★ ★ ★ ★

The Searchers of the Dead (1979)

C ★ ★ ★ ★ ★ ★ ★ ★	P ★ ★ ★ ★ ★ ★ ★
R ★ ★ ★ ★ ★ ★ ★ ★ ★	T ★ ★ ★ ★ ★ ★ ★

O'HARA, Kevin (1892-1972) British thriller writer under this pseudonym, and detective novelist under his own name, Marten Cumberland (q.v.). The O'Hara books, stuffed with action, going at a rip and full of snappy dialogue, featured Chico Brett, a half-Irish Argentinian or half-Argentine Irishman, a London hardboiled private-eye.

It's Your Funeral (1966)

C ★ ★ ★ ★ ★	P ★ ★ ★ ★ ★ ★ ★
R ★ ★ ★ ★ ★ ★ ★	T ★ ★ ★ ★ ★ ★

OLBRICH, Freny British police procedural novelist, born in London of Parsi parents, educated in Bombay where she eventually came to lecture in English literature, married to a German and settled in Scotland. She writes a series featuring Chief Inspector Desouza of the Bombay CID, notable for the portrayal of a richly different background (set somewhere in the slightly distant past).

Desouza in Stardust (1980)

C ★ ★ ★ ★ ★ ★ ★ ★	P ★ ★ ★ ★ ★ ★
R ★ ★ ★ ★ ★ ★ ★ ★ ★	T ★ ★ ★ ★ ★ ★

ORCZY, Baroness Emma Magdalena Rosalia Maria Josefa Barbara (1865-1947) British espionage adventure novelist and crime short-story writer, of Hungarian origin and French education. Her great success was in the creation of the aristocrat agent of the days of the French Revolution, the Scarlet Pimpernel (q.v.). But she also wrote a number of series of crime short stories, of which the best are those featuring The Old Man in the Corner, precursor of a hundred armchair detectives, who operated from an A.B.C. teashop where he met a young girl journalist. But she also created Lady Molly of Scotland Yard considered by chiefs and men alike the greatest authority among them on criminal investigation, and secretly married to Captain Hubert de Mazareen who is in prison!

The Scarlet Pimpernel (1905)

C ★ ★ ★ ★ ★ ★	P ★ ★ ★ ★ ★ ★ ★ ★
R ★ ★ ★ ★ ★ ★ ★ ★ ★ ★	T ★ ★ ★ ★ ★ ★ ★ ★

The Old Man in the Corner (stories, 1909) (*The Man in the Corner* in U.S.)

C ★ ★ ★ ★ ★	P ★ ★ ★ ★ ★ ★ ★
R ★ ★ ★ ★ ★ ★ ★	T ★

OSMOND, Andrew (1928) British political crime novelist in collaboration with Douglas Hurd (q.v.). He contributed to their books experience gained in the Foreign Service from 1962 to 1967. He was also a founder of the magazine, *Private Eye*. Later he wrote thrillers, again

Andrew Osmond

with a large political content, on his own account. Buchanish (see BUCHAN, John) is the word.

Saladin! (1975)

C ★ ★ ★ ★ ★ ★	P ★ ★ ★ ★ ★ ★ ★
R ★ ★ ★ ★ ★ ★ ★ ★	T ★ ★ ★ ★ ★ ★ ★ ★

PAGE, Emma British detective novelist. Her books appear rarely but she has established something of a corner of her own in the crime field with cunningly plotted, highly domestic murders in accurate, local settings of the contemporary British scene.

Every Second Thursday (1981)

C ★ ★ ★ ★ ★ ★ ★ ★	P ★ ★ ★ ★ ★ ★ ★ ★ ★
R ★ ★ ★ ★ ★ ★	T ★ ★ ★ ★

PALMER, Stuart (1905-68) American mystery novelist and screenwriter, formerly an iceman, an apple-picker, a reporter, a poet and a ghost-writer, among other things. He began with something of a false start, a book called *Ace of Jades*

R = Readability   T = Tension

(1931), but that same year saw him get into his stride with his first Hildegarde Withers (q.v.) mystery, *The Penguin Pool Murder.* Thereafter almost all his books featured her, until towards the end he introduced Howie Rook, a woman-hating newsman. He brought to murder a nicely light approach.

The Penguin Pool Murder (1931)

| C ★ ★ ★ ★ ★ | P ★ ★ ★ ★ ★ ★ ★ |
| R ★ ★ ★ ★ ★ ★ ★ | T ★ ★ ★ ★ ★ |

PARKER, Robert B. (1932) American private-eye novelist and former professor at Northeastern University, Boston. His doctoral dissertation was on the traditional private-eye novel and he later created Spenser, a wisecracking Boston P.I. (and dedicated gourmet) named after the sixteenth-century English poet. His 1976 book, *Promised Land,* won the Mystery Writers of America Edgar.

The Godwulf Manuscript (1973)

| C ★ ★ ★ ★ ★ ★ ★ | P ★ ★ ★ ★ ★ ★ ★ |
| R ★ ★ ★ ★ ★ ★ ★ | T ★ ★ ★ ★ ★ ★ ★ |

Promised Land (1976)

| C ★ ★ ★ ★ ★ ★ ★ | P ★ ★ ★ ★ ★ ★ ★ ★ |
| R ★ ★ ★ ★ ★ ★ ★ | T ★ ★ ★ ★ ★ ★ ★ |

Robert B. Parker

PARRISH, Frank Pseudonym, jealously guarded, of a British author producing under this name detective novels featuring Dan Mallett, poacher, and remarkable for their evocation of the underside of rural Britain, both in its petty crime and its wildlife aspect. Mallett is a remarkable creation, credibly intelligent, sharply contemptuous of false values, real.

Fire in the Barley (1977)

| C ★ ★ ★ ★ ★ ★ ★ ★ | P ★ ★ ★ ★ ★ ★ |
| R ★ ★ ★ ★ ★ ★ ★ | T ★ ★ ★ ★ ★ ★ ★ ★ |

Snare in the Dark (1982)

| C ★ ★ ★ ★ ★ ★ ★ ★ | P ★ ★ ★ ★ ★ ★ ★ |
| R ★ ★ ★ ★ ★ ★ ★ | T ★ ★ ★ ★ ★ ★ ★ ★ ★ |

PATTERSON, Harry (1929) British thriller writer who also writes as Martin Fallon; James Graham; Jack Higgins (q.v.); and Hugh Marlowe. For many years Patterson combined his career as a teacher and lecturer with his fiction writing. His prolific output includes some straight mystery stories, but his greatest talent is for fast moving adventure and suspense novels.

The Valhalla Exchange (1976)

| C ★ ★ ★ ★ ★ | P ★ ★ ★ ★ ★ ★ |
| R ★ ★ ★ ★ ★ ★ ★ | T ★ ★ ★ ★ ★ ★ ★ ★ |

PAYNE, Laurence (1919) British actor and humorous crime novelist. He produced in the years after 1951 a handful of books, crime stories with a light, even frivolous, touch, marked by that ease in dialogue which many actor-writers seem to achieve. They gained a select circle of enthusiastic admirers.

The Nose on My Face (1961)

| C ★ ★ ★ ★ ★ ★ | P ★ ★ ★ ★ ★ ★ |
| R ★ ★ ★ ★ ★ ★ ★ ★ | T ★ ★ ★ ★ ★ |

PENDLETON, Don (1927) American crime writer, who also writes as Dan Britain and Stephen Gregory. After a career in engineering management for Aerospace, Pendleton turned to writing in the sixties. He is known for science fiction as well as for the hardboiled mysteries of his Executioner series. He also writes sexuality non-fiction.

Hawaian Hellground (1975)

| C ★ ★ ★ ★ | P ★ ★ ★ ★ ★ |
| R ★ ★ ★ ★ | T ★ ★ ★ ★ |

PENTECOST, Hugh (1903) American mystery writer, pseudonym of Judson Philips. Most of his books are under the Pentecost pseudonym but he also published as Judson Philips. First published in 1925 when in college, Pentecost is a notably prolific writer both in novel and short story. His first mystery novel, *Cancelled in Red,* was winner of the Dodd Mead mystery competition in 1939. Best known of his characters is Pierre Chambrun, who manages New York's classic prestige hotel, given another name, but scarcely distinguishable from the Plaza. Philips also finds time to be an active producer and director of the Sharon (Connecticut) Playhouse which he founded in 1950. In 1973, he was honoured by the Mystery Writers of America with the Grand Master Edgar.

I'll Sing at Your Funeral (1942)

| C ★ ★ ★ ★ ★ | P ★ ★ ★ ★ ★ |
| R ★ ★ ★ ★ ★ | T ★ ★ ★ ★ |

The Homicide Horse (1979)

| C ★ ★ ★ ★ ★ | P ★ ★ ★ ★ ★ |
| R ★ ★ ★ ★ ★ | T ★ ★ ★ ★ ★ |

PEROWNE, Barry (1908) British pasticheur and under his real name, Philip Atkey, mystery novelist. He took up the Raffles of E. W. Hornung (q.v.) and added to the saga some 22 volumes, novels and short-story collections. Most pastiches of crime heroes (especially of Sherlock Holmes) fail pretty horribly. Perowne's do not, despite his eventually bringing Hornung's anti-hero into the mid-twentieth century and his making his crimes less heinous.

Raffles of the Albany (1976)

| C ★ ★ ★ ★ ★ ★ | P ★ ★ ★ ★ ★ ★ |
| R ★ ★ ★ ★ ★ ★ | T ★ ★ ★ ★ ★ |

PERRY, Ritchie (1942) British thriller writer. His hero is a British agent, one Philis, sub-Deightonish, somewhat cowardly, more than somewhat amorous, hating Pawson, his superior in mysterious SR2. The books are written in a rather off-the-cuff manner which is often engaging.

Grand Slam (1980)

| C ★ ★ ★ ★ | P ★ ★ ★ ★ ★ ★ |
| R ★ ★ ★ ★ ★ ★ | T ★ ★ ★ ★ ★ |

PETERS, Elizabeth (1927) American mystery writer. Under her own name, Barbara Mertz she was a non-fiction writer with such published works as *Temples, Tombs and Hierglyphics* (1964), and *Red Man, Black Land* (1966), a study of daily life in Egypt. She has a doctorate from the University of Chicago in archaeology, specializing in Egyptology, and she spent enough time in Egypt, she says, "to have my backgrounds established", before she took the name of Elizabeth Peters and produced *Crocodiles on the Sandbank* in 1975. It is a Victorian period piece introducing a charming and amusing young couple who are Egyptologists. In her second tale of their archaeological work, she introduced their incredible son, Rameses, even more of an original than his parents, and one of the high comic characters of the decade. Before the Peters books, she established herself under the name Barbara Michaels as one of the leading writers of romantic mysteries.

The Camelot Caper (as Michaels, 1969)

| C ★ ★ ★ ★ ★ ★ | P ★ ★ ★ ★ ★ ★ |
| R ★ ★ ★ ★ ★ ★ | T ★ ★ ★ ★ ★ ★ |

The Curse of the Pharoahs (1981)

| C ★ ★ ★ ★ ★ ★ | P ★ ★ ★ ★ ★ ★ |
| R ★ ★ ★ ★ ★ ★ | T ★ ★ ★ ★ ★ ★ |

R = Readability   T = Tension

PETERS, Ellis (1913) British detective novelist and under her own name, Edith Pargeter, historical novelist. She has had a varied career as a crime writer, beginning with a series about various members of the Felse family, father a provincial CID man, young Dominic a teenager involved in crime. The stories ranged in setting from Cornwall to Delhi. Music often entered in. *Death and the Joyful Woman*, a case in point, won a Mystery Writers of America Edgar in 1962. Latterly Miss Peters turned to eleventh-century Britain and a monk-sleuth Brother Cadfael. His 1980 adventure, *Monk's Hood* – it is stuffed with historical detail – won the Crime Writers Association Silver Dagger.

Death and the Joyful Woman (1961)

| C ★★★★★★★★ | P ★★★★★★★ |
| R ★★★★★★★★★ | T ★★★★★★★★ |

A Morbid Taste for Bones (1977)

| C ★★★★★★★ | P ★★★★★★★ |
| R ★★★★★★★★ | T ★★★★★★ |

Monk's Hood (1980)

| C ★★★★★★★★ | P ★★★★★★★ |
| R ★★★★★★★★ | T ★★★★★★ |

PINCHER, Chapman (1914) British journalist and author of spy exposés, and crime novelist. Chiefly he has written spy novels that give the impression of saying things that just cannot be said in a non-fiction book, including delectable Whitehall gossip. But he has written also in a purer crime style with some success.

The Penthouse Conspirators (1970)

| C ★★★★★★ | P ★★★★★★★ |
| R ★★★★★★★★ | T ★★★★★★★ |

The Four Horses (1978)

| C ★★★★★★★★ | P ★★★★★★★★★ |
| R ★★★★★★★★ | T ★★★★★★★★ |

PLAYER, Robert B. (1905-78) British detective novelist and architect (Hoffman Wood Professor of Architecture, University of Leeds). He wrote as a hobby and produced over a period of thirty years only five books. But they are packed with delights. They have a magnificent bravura to them, not hesitating joyfully to involve such august institutions as the Papal throne and the British Royal Family.

The Ingenious Mr Stone (1945)

| C ★★★★★★★★ | P ★★★★★★★★ |
| R ★★★★★★★★★ | T ★★★★★★★★ |

Oh! Where Are Bloody Mary's Earrings? (1972)

| C ★★★★★★★★ | P ★★★★★★★★ |
| R ★★★★★★★★★ | T ★★★★★★★ |

Let's Talk of Graves, of Worms and Epitaphs (1975)

| C ★★★★★★★★ | P ★★★★★★★★★ |
| R ★★★★★★★★★ | T ★★★★★★★★ |

Chapman
Pincher

POE, Edgar Allan (1804-49) American short story writer and poet, who in fewer than half a dozen stories laid down (though without immediate followers) most of the ground rules of detective fiction. In just the three tales about Le Chevalier C. Auguste Dupin he created the Great Detective, together with his innocent, admiring narrator friend, his Dr Watson, and together too with the stupid police detective, here Monsieur G----, forerunner of Inspector Lestrade and many another. In the first of these three tales, "The Murders in the Rue Morgue", Poe adumbrated the locked-room impossible mystery. In "The Mystery of Marie Roget" he postulated armchair detection (what at a long future date Agatha Christie's Hercule Poirot (q.v.) was to call using "the little grey cells"). In the third story, "The Purloined Letter", he set out the device used in ten thousand variations by a thousand followers, concealment by the most obvious place. That story, too, may be seen as the prototype of the modern spy tale. For these stories he invented as well the word that may be said to lie at the heart of the detective novel: "ratiocination". In one other tale, "The Gold Bug", he produced a cryptogram that had to be deciphered, and in "Thou Art the Man", despite its melodramatic climax, he set two precedents, false clues left by the guilty man to implicate an innocent and the least likely person turning out to be the murderer. But the important thing is that all these stories were written with such power that they live and will continue to live, to excite, to mystify and to grip the imagination.

Tales of Mystery and Imagination (1852)

C ★ ★ ★ ★ ★ ★ ★	P ★ ★ ★ ★ ★ ★ ★ ★ ★
R ★ ★ ★ ★ ★ ★ ★ ★ ★	T ★ ★ ★ ★ ★ ★ ★ ★ ★

PORTER, Joyce (1924) British farce crime writer. She practises a difficult art, treading the tightrope between deflating comedy and intriguing puzzle. Not always is she successful, but when she is she is very successful. The majority of her books feature Inspector Wilfred Dover, fat, greedy, lazy, rude, and the chief pleasure of them is his appallingly gross behaviour (though he has somehow to pull in the murderer). Perhaps even more successful as a character is her female lead in other books, the Hon. Con (Constance Ethel Morrison-Burke), steamroller semi-aristocrat locked into bungalow life.

Dead Easy for Dover (1978)

C ★ ★ ★ ★ ★ ★ ★	P ★ ★ ★ ★ ★ ★ ★ ★
R ★ ★ ★ ★ ★ ★ ★ ★	T ★ ★ ★ ★

The Cart Before the Horse (1979)

C ★ ★ ★ ★ ★ ★ ★	P ★ ★ ★ ★ ★ ★ ★ ★
R ★ ★ ★ ★ ★ ★ ★ ★	T ★ ★ ★ ★

POST, Melville Davisson (1871-1930) American mystery writer. Melville Davisson Post, one of the pioneers of American crime literature, took his law degree in 1892 and practiced for eleven years before becoming a full-time writer. His first book was a collection of his short stories about a lawyer, *The Strange Schemes of Randolph Mason*. Lawyer Mason circumvented the law in his defence of criminals. This led to such a furore among readers, on the grounds that the author was helping wrongdoers escape just due, that Mason subsequently changed his character into a staunch defender of the law. Post wrote no novels, all of his mysteries being short stories, and all being published in magazines before they were collected within book covers. He was and is still considered a master of detective plot, yet it was for character and historical scene that he is best remembered. His most noted character, Uncle Abner, was a Virginia squire of the early nineteenth century. The first Uncle Abner stories appeared in 1911, and were collected some years

R = Readability   T = Tension

later in the volume, *Uncle Abner: Master of Mysteries*. In the more than sixty years since its appearance, this book has never been out of print. Critics have said of Uncle Abner that he is the most important contribution to American detective fiction from Auguste Dupin to Philo Vance. As with the other early writers, it is impossible to evaluate their qualities by today's standards; one must depend on the evaluation of their times.

The Complete Uncle Abner (1977)

C ★★★★★★★	P ★★★★★★★
R ★★★★★★★	T ★★★★★★

POTTS, Jean (1910) American

mystery writer. The novels of Jean Potts have a depth beyond most mysteries of her time. *Go, Lovely Rose* received the Edgar in 1954 for Best First mystery. Miss Potts is also a leading mystery short-story writer.

Death of a Stray Cat (1955)

C ★★★★★★	P ★★★★★
R ★★★★★★	T ★★★★★

The Trash Stealer (1967)

C ★★★★★★	P ★★★★★
R ★★★★★★★	T ★★★★★★

POWELL, James (1932) Canadian

crime short-story writer. He has been called the S. J. Perelman of the mystery story, chiefly for his tales of the bungling Acting Sergeant Bullock of the Mounties and also for his invented European mini-country, San Sebastiano of the quaint customs. There are, too, stories of detection in fairy-tale settings, again where humour is not unabsent. There is no collection, but the Ellery Queen anthologies often contain his work.

POYER, Joe (1939) American

espionage novelist. His fast-moving, adventure-filled stories are notable, too, for the amount of careful research that goes into them. He was one of the first to move the spy set-up from Russia to China.

The Chinese Agenda (1972)

C ★★★★★★	P ★★★★★★★
R ★★★★★★★	T ★★★★★★★

PRICE, Anthony (1928) British

espionage novelist and newspaper editor. Price is a suspense novelist with a passion for history, and he has ingeniously made even the English Civil War underlie a contemporary espionage story (*War Game*, 1976). He produces characters that are delightfully unstereotyped and almost always dauntingly intelligent. (He is a master of the remark that says one thing and means another, and we readers generally catch on long after his characters). His plots abound with subtlety; his pages pullulate with sharp little jokes. Many of his books have chronicled the adventures of the British agent, Colonel David Audley, the later ones even going back to his days as a Second World War green, but bright, lieutenant (*The '44 Vintage*, 1978). *Other Paths to Glory* won the Crime Writers Association Gold Dagger in Britain in 1974.

The Labyrinth Makers (1970)

C ★★★★★★★	P ★★★★★★★★
R ★★★★★★★	T ★★★★★★

Other Paths to Glory (1974)

C ★★★★★★★	P ★★★★★★★★
R ★★★★★★★	T ★★★★★★★★

Soldier No More (1981)

C ★★★★★★★★	P ★★★★★★★★
R ★★★★★★★★	T ★★★★★★★★

PROCTER, Maurice (1906-73)

British crime writer. A soldier, then a police-constable until 1946, Procter uses his knowledge of the police world well in his novels, though curiously he had been writing for some years before he moved away from the fictional idea of the police detective to the police-procedural form. His northern English settings

C = Characterization   P = Plot

are well observed.

Man in Ambush (1958)

Hideaway (1968)

QUEEN, Ellery Pseudonym adopted by Frederic Dannay (1905) and Manfred B. Lee (1905-71),

Frederic Dannay

Manfred B. Lee

American mystery writers and magazine editors. The Brooklyn cousins, Frederic Dannay and Manfred Lee, became Ellery Queen when they were in their early twenties. Collaborating, they wrote their first mystery novel, submitted it to a contest jointly sponsored by *McClure's* magazine and Frederick Stokes, publisher. They won, but they didn't win, as *McClure's* was sold in those months to *Smart Set*, whose editor proceeded to choose another manuscript for the prize. Stokes, however, published the Queen entry, *The Roman Hat Mystery*, and history was made. The year was 1929. Ellery Queen, one of the most successful collaborations in the annals of mystery writing, had been launched. Awards are too many to mention in a brief biography; they take up a full column of fine print. After numerous previous Edgars, Ellery Queen was honoured in 1960 by the Mystery Writers of America with their Grand Master Edgar. As important as are the Ellery Queen novels, perhaps he is even more important as an editor, founding *Ellery Queen's Mystery Magazine* in 1941. With *EQMM* (it is best known by its initials), the Queen co-editors revitalized the mystery short story and developed an innumerable number of today's mystery novelists. The Queen cousins also published a few novels under the pseudonym Barnaby Ross, notably *The Tragedy of X* and *Drury Lane's Last Case*. And only recently has Fred Dannay revealed that his name is also a pseudonym, his real name being Daniel Nathan. (Dannay is made up of "Dan" adding the phonetic "Na" of his surname.) With all their awards and honours and with all of their contributions to the genre, the devotion of true and lasting Queen followers is for the novels. Ellery Queen was never satisfied to write "just another mystery". The Queen books have literary quality as well as the shrewd

R = Readability   T = Tension

devisings of two shrewd minds.

The Dutch Shoe Mystery (1931)

C ★★★★★★	P ★★★★★★★★
R ★★★★★★★	T ★★★★★★

Calamity Town (1942)

C ★★★★★★★	P ★★★★★★★
R ★★★★★★★	T ★★★★★★

And On the Eighth Day (1965)

C ★★★★★★★	P ★★★★★★★
R ★★★★★★★★	T ★★★★★★

QUENTIN, Patrick. American-English mystery writers, who also wrote as Q. Patrick and Jonathan Stagge. Unravelling the Patrick Quentin pseudonym is a mystery writer's game. It begins with Richard Wilson Webb and his Peter Duluth series. He collaborated, with Mary Louise Aswell, literary editor of *Harper's Bazaar*, on *S.S. Murder* (1933). In 1934 Hugh Callingham Wheeler (1912), English-born, as was Webb, came to the United States and they became not only Q. Patrick but Patrick Quentin and occasionally Jonathan Stagge. Webb left the series in the 1950s and Wheeler carried on alone until the 1960s. At that time he turned to playwriting and has received the Tony theatrical award and the New York Drama Critics Circle award for the book of Stephen Sondheim's *A Little Night Music* (1972), for the revival of *Irene* (1973) and *Candide* (1974). The Quentin books had charm and sophistication. The Stagge series was darker, with hints of the supernatural.

Puzzle for Fools (1936)

C ★★★★★★	P ★★★★★★
R ★★★★★★	T ★★★★★

Black Widow (1952)

C ★★★★★★	P ★★★★★★
R ★★★★★★	T ★★★★★★

QUINNELL, A. J. American suspense novelist. The name is a highly protected pseudonym. Frenzied readability appears to be his hall-mark, but his characters have some depth despite the glossy trimmings and the amount of blood that flows.

Man on Fire (1981)

C ★★★★★★★	P ★★★★★★
R ★★★★★★★★	T ★★★★★★★★

RADLEY, Sheila British detective novelist. A newcomer to the crime-writing ranks, she writes with some distinction traditional mysteries set in an East Anglian town. Her detective is the likeable, domestic Chief Inspector Quantrill.

Death and the Maiden (1978)

C ★★★★★★★	P ★★★★★
R ★★★★★★	T ★★★★★

RAE, Hugh C. (1935) Scottish crime novelist and, as Robert Crawford, thriller writer. Markedly tough in a particularly Scottish way, he sets his books firmly in Scottish surroundings, whether the romantic but storm-battered Hebrides or the slums (or suburbs) of Glasgow. His characterization, too, may be thought of as Scottish, going deep and in no way meretricious.

The Shooting Gallery (1972)

C ★★★★★★★	P ★★★★★★
R ★★★★★★★	T ★★★★★★★

RAMSAY, Diana American mystery novelist. She writes pleasantly. There is a mystery to puzzle out. There is the attraction between members of the opposite sex. There are nicely interesting backgrounds, and Lieutenant Mike Meredith, of the New York Police Department, is not immune to Cupid's weapon.

You Can't Call It Murder (1977)

C ★★★★★★	P ★★★★★★
R ★★★★★★★★	T ★★★★★

C = Characterization   P = Plot

Ruth Rendell

RATHBONE, Julian (1935) British suspense novelist and novelist. Exotic locales and a high degree of tension mark out the crime novels of Julian Rathbone. They are also well written (his mainstream novel *King Fisher Lives* was nominated for the prestigious Booker Prize in 1976).

A Raving Monarchist (1978)

| C ★ ★ ★ ★ ★ ★ ★ ★ | P ★ ★ ★ ★ ★ ★ ★ |
| R ★ ★ ★ ★ ★ ★ ★ ★ | T ★ ★ ★ ★ ★ ★ ★ ★ ★ |

Base Case (1981)

| C ★ ★ ★ ★ ★ ★ ★ | P ★ ★ ★ ★ ★ ★ ★ |
| R ★ ★ ★ ★ ★ ★ ★ ★ | T ★ ★ ★ ★ ★ ★ ★ ★ ★ |

REEVE, Arthur B. (1880-1936) American mystery writer. A Princeton University graduate, Reeve took a postgraduate degree in law at New York Law School. However, he never practised law, his interest was writing and he went into magazine work. In 1910 in *Cosmopolitan* magazine, he introduced Craig Kennedy, "scientific detective", who became an instant success and who popularized science through his exploits. Reeve's first book, *The Poisoned Pen*, was published in 1911. Although the material is melodramatic by current standards, Reeve became the foremost mystery writer of his day. His imagination was also in demand for the serials of the early days of motion pictures.

The Poisoned Pen (1911)

| C ★ ★ ★ ★ | P ★ ★ ★ ★ ★ ★ ★ |
| R ★ ★ ★ ★ ★ ★ ★ | T ★ ★ ★ ★ ★ ★ ★ |

The Clutching Hand (1934)

| C ★ ★ ★ ★ | P ★ ★ ★ ★ ★ ★ ★ |
| R ★ ★ ★ ★ ★ ★ ★ | T ★ ★ ★ ★ ★ ★ |

RENDELL, Ruth (1930) British crime novelist. She occupies a leading place among contemporary British crime writers and was awarded the Gold Dagger of the Crime Writers Association in 1976 for *A Demon in My View*. She has also gained an Edgar from the Mystery Writers of America for a short story.

She writes two sorts of crime novel, a fairly conventional detective series featuring Chief Inspector Wexford, a policeman in a country town not too far from London, and one-off suspense novels marked by a strong and curious imagination. Wexford is a detective in the unostentatious mould and the main interest in the books that feature him is in the ingenuity of plot, though the characters, both police and suspects, are by no means cardboard. The suspense novels concentrate on character, though often of a distinctly outré sort, and are remarkable for their willingness to handle the toughest of subjects.

A Judgment in Stone (1977)

| C ★ ★ ★ ★ ★ ★ ★ ★ ★ | P ★ ★ ★ ★ ★ ★ ★ ★ |
| R ★ ★ ★ ★ ★ ★ ★ ★ ★ ★ | T ★ ★ ★ ★ ★ ★ ★ ★ ★ ★ |

Put on by Cunning (1981)

| C ★ ★ ★ ★ ★ ★ ★ | P ★ ★ ★ ★ ★ ★ ★ ★ ★ ★ |
| R ★ ★ ★ ★ ★ ★ ★ | T ★ ★ ★ ★ ★ |

Master of the Moor (1982)

| C ★ ★ ★ ★ ★ ★ ★ ★ | P ★ ★ ★ ★ ★ ★ ★ ★ |
| R ★ ★ ★ ★ ★ ★ ★ ★ ★ | T ★ ★ ★ ★ ★ ★ ★ ★ |

RHODE, John (1884-1965) British detective story writer. He is one of the sturdy steadies of the Golden Age of the detective story, writing 76 books mostly the cases of Dr Priestley, a somewhat sub-Thorndyke (see

R = Readability   T = Tension

FREEMAN, R. Austin) figure between 1924 and 1961. They have all the characteristics of the middle-ranking books of the period, ingenuity of plot, carboardity of character, chunter of story. He was also Miles Burton (q.v.). He took a leading part in the Detection Club and its multi-authored *The Floating Admiral* (1931).

Death at Breakfast (1936)

C ★ ★ ★ ★	P ★ ★ ★ ★ ★ ★ ★ ★
R ★ ★ ★ ★ ★ ★ ★	T ★ ★ ★ ★ ★

RICE, Craig (1908-57) American

mystery writer. Georgiana Ann Randolph, Chicago newswoman, took her pseudonym, Rice, from the aunt who raised her, and Craig from another family branch. Her own life was a mystery novel in itself but she did not write in that tenor. The chief ingredient of her best-selling mysteries was humour. John J. Malone, a drinking Chicago lawyer, and his pals, a bright young couple, Jake Justice and Helene Brand, were her most popular characters. She wrote serious mysteries under the pseudonyms Daphne Sanders and Michael Venner but they did not measure up in importance to the Rice books. Craig Rice was in demand as a screenwriter, forming a writing team with Stuart Palmer (q.v.), creator of Hildegarde Withers. She also ghosted delightful mysteries for actor George Sanders and for the strip-tease actress, Gypsy Rose Lee. The popularity of Craig Rice was such that she appeared on the cover of *Time* magazine in 1946. Best remembered of her many books is *Home Sweet Homicide* which featured her own three children under fictional names.

Eight Faces at Three (1930)

C ★ ★ ★ ★ ★	P ★ ★ ★ ★ ★ ★ ★
R ★ ★ ★ ★ ★ ★ ★ ★	T ★ ★ ★ ★ ★

Home Sweet Homicide (1944)

C ★ ★ ★ ★ ★ ★	P ★ ★ ★ ★ ★ ★ ★
R ★ ★ ★ ★ ★ ★ ★ ★	T ★ ★ ★ ★ ★

RINEHART, Mary Roberts (1876-

1958) American mystery writer. The most important American woman mystery writer has been and continues to be Mary Roberts Rinehart. No other has made such a contribution to the mystery novel, changing its then conventional detective formula to a fully-fleshed novel of people and place, reflecting the modes and manners of their time. Mary Roberts graduated from nursing school in Pittsburgh, Pennsylvania, in 1896 at the age of nineteen. Three days later she married young Dr Stanley Rinehart. Three sons were born within the next five years: Stanley who became the Rinehart of Farrar and Rinehart, publishers; Frederick who also became a publisher; and Alan who became a writer. The stock market crash of 1903 left the Rineharts heavily in debt and to help with family expenses, Mrs Rinehart wrote her first story. It sold immediately to *Munsey's*, a leading magazine of the day, and she was paid $34. She proceeded to write and sell 45 more stories that year, earning $1842.50, a fair sum at that time. It was *Munsey's* who suggested she write a full-length mystery which they would serialize before book publication. She wrote two, *The Circular Staircase*, published in 1908, and *The Man in Lower Ten* in 1909, which was also serialized before publication. Both manuscripts she sent to Bobbs-Merrill, publishers, and they immediately sent a representative to sign her to their list. Both were best-selling books and are still kept in print. After *Munsey's* faded, all the Rinehart stories, mystery and non-mystery, were serialized in the *Saturday Evening Post*. Many of her books became successful plays on Broadway, the first being *The Bat*, adapted from *the Circular Staircase*. It still plays in repertory. Later many of her books became motion pictures. Mrs Rinehart's mysteries had plenty of murders but there was always humour to leaven the violence. The catch phrase "Had-I-but-known", later applied to her works, quite obviously came from those who had never read her. She was a fine writer and all that implies, a craftsman, a creator of memorable characters, and a wily plotmaster. In 1953 the Mystery Writers of America honoured her with a Special Edgar in recognition of her contribution to the mystery genre.

The Circular Staircase (1908)

C ★★★★★★★★	P ★★★★★★★★
R ★★★★★★★★★★	T ★★★★★★★★

The Wall (1938)

C ★★★★★★★★	P ★★★★★★★
R ★★★★★★★★★	T ★★★★★★★

The Yellow Room (1945)

C ★★★★★★★★	P ★★★★★★★★
R ★★★★★★★★★	T ★★★★★★★

RITCHIE, Jack (1922) American crime short-story writer. Whimsy marks out the clever stories of Jack Ritchie, though he can also write in a serious vein. But inept detectives are more apt to play their part, a butler has been know to do it and a bath-tub to get full of jello. His work has frequently appeared in the *American Best Detective Stories of the Year* series.

A New Leaf and Other Stories (1971)

C ★★★★★★★	P ★★★★★★★★★
R ★★★★★★★★★	T ★★★★★★

ROBERTS, James Hall (1927) American thriller novelist, who also wrote as Robert L. Duncan (His real name). He has written little, but has earned great praise. There are three Roberts novels, produced between 1964 and 1967, and between 1970 and 1979 there were four Duncans. He succeeded in combining the thriller form with that of a quest of a quite different sort, the search for faith. The books are very much of their time, the last tortured quarter

of the twentieth century. But, although they are concerned with such matters as authenticating a manuscript which may have been written by Jesus himself (the intricacies made marvellously clear), they never in any way approach the pietistic but are completely suspenseful. He has been spoken of as an American Graham Greene.

The Q Document (1964)

C ★★★★★★★★★	P ★★★★★★★★
R ★★★★★★★★	T ★★★★★★★★

The Burning Sky (1966)

C ★★★★★★★★★	P ★★★★★★★★
R ★★★★★★★★	T ★★★★★★★★

The February Plan (1967)

C ★★★★★★★★	P ★★★★★★★★★
R ★★★★★★★★	T ★★★★★★★

ROBESON, Kenneth see DENT, Lester

ROFFMAN, Jan British gothic suspense novelist. Under this name Margaret Summerton (q.v.) wrote as many novels as under her own name. Like the Summerton books they have a distinctly feminine approach (but that's one that many male readers enjoy) and they are notable, too, for the ingenuity combined with the oddity of her stories. For a British writer she had the curious, if hardly enviable, distinction of having many of her books published only in the United States.

Grave of Green Water (1968)

C ★★★★★★★	P ★★★★★★★★
R ★★★★★★★★	T ★★★★★★★★

ROHMER, Sax (1883-1959) British thriller writer of immense popularity in his time through his creation, the evil Dr Fu Manchu. Yet he never saved the large sums he was paid and ended his days in an unheated apartment in New York, where his wife used to provoke him deliberately into the state of fury in which he wrote best his tales of the malevolent

R = Readability   T = Tension

and would then lock him in one room until he had produced. His obsessive interest in the occult (he was at one time a fellow society member of the notorious Aleister Crowley) give his books a certain wild power and a wealth of quite accurate detail.

The Mystery of Dr Fu Manchu (1913)

C ★ ★ ★ ★	P ★ ★ ★ ★ ★ ★ ★
R ★ ★ ★ ★ ★ ★ ★ ★ ★	T ★ ★ ★ ★ ★ ★ ★

ROSS, Angus (1927) British espionage writer. He writes a series of fast-paced spy thrillers with a tough, if somewhat reluctant, agent hero, Marcus Farrow, much concerned with good and plentiful grub. A good many of the books are distinguished by being set in unusual British provincial cities.

The Aberdeen Conundrum (1977)

C ★ ★ ★ ★ ★ ★	P ★ ★ ★ ★ ★ ★
R ★ ★ ★ ★ ★ ★ ★	T ★ ★ ★ ★ ★ ★ ★

ROSS, Frank Pseudonymous British thriller writer. The pen-name belongs to two journalists who worked as a team for three books but subsequently each used the name independently. Much the same spirit, however, marks all the Frank Ross books, notably a belting pace, plenty of factual detail and giant-sized plots.

The Shining Day (1981)

C ★ ★ ★ ★ ★	P ★ ★ ★ ★ ★ ★
R ★ ★ ★ ★ ★ ★ ★	T ★ ★ ★ ★ ★ ★ ★ ★

ROSS, Jonathan (1916) British police procedural novelist and former Detective Chief Superintendent John Rossiter (q.v.). He has written from 1968 onwards an increasingly adept series of linked police novels with a number of running characters, notably Detective Superintendent George Rogers, set in an unnamed provincial city. He never hesitates to show the grim and bloody side of police work, but the skill of the writing, sinewy and

direct, particularly latterly, takes away from any mere shock factor. His people, police, villains and bystanders, are notably real and seen in depth. He also writes as John Rossiter (q.v.).

The Burning of Billy Toober (1974)

C ★ ★ ★ ★ ★ ★ ★ ★	P ★ ★ ★ ★ ★ ★ ★
R ★ ★ ★ ★ ★ ★ ★ ★	T ★ ★ ★ ★ ★ ★ ★ ★

A Rattling of Old Bones (1979)

C ★ ★ ★ ★ ★ ★ ★ ★	P ★ ★ ★ ★ ★ ★ ★
R ★ ★ ★ ★ ★ ★ ★	T ★ ★ ★ ★ ★ ★ ★ ★

Dark Blue and Dangerous (1981)

C ★ ★ ★ ★ ★ ★ ★ ★	P ★ ★ ★ ★ ★ ★ ★
R ★ ★ ★ ★ ★ ★ ★ ★ ★	T ★ ★ ★ ★ ★ ★ ★

ROSSITER, John (1916) British thriller writer. This is the real name of the pseudonymous Jonathan Ross (q.v.) and under it he has written a number of novels featuring Roger Tallis, British agent, carrying a more than usual element of detection. They are pacily written and very readable.

The Golden Virgin (1975)
(*The Deadly Gold* in U.S.)

C ★ ★ ★ ★ ★ ★	P ★ ★ ★ ★ ★ ★ ★
R ★ ★ ★ ★ ★ ★ ★ ★	T ★ ★ ★ ★ ★ ★ ★

ROYCE, Kenneth (1920) British thriller writer, who has also written in the same vein using the name Oliver Jacks. He is notable for no-nonsense straightforward accounts of adventures, intricately plotted and often set against exotic backgrounds, visited by the author. He gained wide popularity with a series featuring Spider Scott, the XYY man (possessed of a genetic inheritance predisposing him to crime) and based on a man he met when a Prison Visitor.

The XYY Man (1970)

C ★ ★ ★ ★ ★ ★ ★	P ★ ★ ★ ★ ★ ★ ★ ★
R ★ ★ ★ ★ ★ ★ ★ ★	T ★ ★ ★ ★ ★ ★ ★ ★

10,000 Days (1981)

C ★ ★ ★ ★ ★ ★	P ★ ★ ★ ★ ★ ★ ★
R ★ ★ ★ ★ ★ ★ ★	T ★ ★ ★ ★ ★ ★ ★

RUELL, Patrick (1936) British detective novelist, better known as Reginald Hill (q.v.). He has written a handful of books under the Ruell name, presumably to avoid flooding the market as Hill. But they are by no means second-rank stuff, being marked by much joyous ingenuity in the Michael Innes (q.v.) tradition and a touch of underpinning seriousness.

Red Christmas (1972)

| C ★ ★ ★ ★ ★ ★ | P ★ ★ ★ ★ ★ ★ ★ |
| R ★ ★ ★ ★ ★ ★ ★ | T ★ ★ ★ ★ ★ ★ ★ |

Urn Burial (1975)

| C ★ ★ ★ ★ ★ ★ | P ★ ★ ★ ★ ★ ★ ★ |
| R ★ ★ ★ ★ ★ ★ ★ | T ★ ★ ★ ★ ★ ★ |

RUSSELL, A. J. American suspense novelist and television writer (Emmy award winner). He came late to the crime novel, but came with a fair bang in *The Devalino Caper*, the story of a million dollar theft in Indiana, notable for its moment-by-moment description, its sharp dialogue and a hero who is shrewd yet sympathetic.

The Devalino Caper (1975)

| C ★ ★ ★ ★ ★ ★ ★ | P ★ ★ ★ ★ ★ ★ ★ ★ |
| R ★ ★ ★ ★ ★ ★ ★ | T ★ ★ ★ ★ ★ ★ ★ |

Pour the Hemlock (1979)

| C ★ ★ ★ ★ ★ ★ ★ | P ★ ★ ★ ★ ★ ★ ★ |
| R ★ ★ ★ ★ ★ ★ ★ | T ★ ★ ★ ★ ★ ★ |

RUSSELL, Martin (1934) British suspense novelist. The plots, the surprises, the cunning complications and, above all, intriguingness of situation are the distinguishing marks of this author. A number of his books have featured a provincial reporter, Jim Larkin, but he is used mainly as a convenient viewpoint.

Double Deal (1976)

| C ★ ★ ★ ★ ★ | P ★ ★ ★ ★ ★ ★ ★ |
| R ★ ★ ★ ★ ★ ★ | T ★ ★ ★ ★ ★ ★ ★ |

Rainblast (1982)

| C ★ ★ ★ ★ ★ | P ★ ★ ★ ★ ★ ★ ★ |
| R ★ ★ ★ ★ ★ ★ | T ★ ★ ★ ★ ★ ★ ★ |

Douglas Rutherford

RUTHERFORD, Douglas (1915) British suspense writer, and for seventeen years a master at Eton. Besides collaborating with Francis Durbridge (q.v.) on a couple of novels, he has produced a long series of thrillers almost all with a background of fast driving of one sort or another. His handling of this theme is expert.

Porcupine Basin (1981)

| C ★ ★ ★ ★ ★ | P ★ ★ ★ ★ ★ ★ |
| R ★ ★ ★ ★ ★ ★ ★ | T ★ ★ ★ ★ ★ ★ |

S

ST JAMES, Ian (1936) British crime novelist, resident in Ireland, and a millionaire by the age of 30, when the merchant bank backing his business enterprise collapsed. His first book, *The Money Stones*, used his experience, however, to good effect. It made financial wheeling and dealing comprehensible as well as exciting.

The Money Stones (1980)

| C ★ ★ ★ ★ ★ ★ ★ | P ★ ★ ★ ★ ★ ★ ★ ★ |
| R ★ ★ ★ ★ ★ ★ ★ ★ | T ★ ★ ★ ★ ★ ★ ★ |

R = Readability T = Tension

SANDERS, Lawrence (1920)

American mystery novelist. Sanders wrote his first novel when he was 50 years old. However, he had served a long apprenticeship as an editor, and, as he relates it, finally said to himself, "I could write the stuff better myself." He could and did with the immediate success of his first book, *The Anderson Tapes*. He is an excellent writer who well deserves his best-selling position in the medium.

The Anderson Tapes (1970)

C ★ ★ ★ ★ ★ ★	P ★ ★ ★ ★ ★ ★
R ★ ★ ★ ★ ★ ★	T ★ ★ ★ ★ ★

The First Deadly Sin (1973)

C ★ ★ ★ ★ ★ ★	P ★ ★ ★ ★ ★ ★
R ★ ★ ★ ★ ★ ★ ★	T ★ ★ ★ ★ ★ ★

The Tangent Objective (1976)

C ★ ★ ★ ★ ★	P ★ ★ ★ ★ ★ ★
R ★ ★ ★ ★ ★ ★	T ★ ★ ★ ★ ★

SAPPER (1888-1937) Pseudonym

for Herman Cyril McNeile, British thriller writer. A career soldier, McNeile began writing soon after World War I and his main character, Bulldog Drummond, reacts both to the dullness of peace and the continued but now subversive threat from Britain's enemies. Simplistic, jingoistic, racist, sexist, and occasionally sadistic, the books are nevertheless rattling good yarns.

Bulldog Drummond At Bay (1935)

C ★ ★ ★ ★ ★	P ★ ★ ★ ★ ★ ★
R ★ ★ ★ ★ ★ ★ ★	T ★ ★ ★ ★ ★

SAYERS, Dorothy L. (1893-1957)

British detective novelist, playwright and amateur theologian. Her thirteen detective novels were immensely popular in the years between 1923 and 1937 when they were written: they were also savagely unpopular, both then and yet more so later. To her devotees charges of snobbery, arrogance, condescension and even unreadability seem altogether irrelevant.

Her virtues, they say, far outweigh any blemishes. They relish her originality, her cunning with plot, her intelligence, her wit and the energy of her characterization. But most of all they adore Lord Peter Wimsey, a deliberately contrived figure to appeal to a readership below his social class. In earlier books he was more than half P. G. Wodehouse's Bertie Wooster (right down to the omniscient manservant, Jeeves modulated into Bunter); in later books he became the sort of person his creator could see herself being in love with, "an eighteenth century Whig gentleman born a little out of his time". Always, too, he was something of Baroness Orczy's (q.v.) Scarlet Pimpernel, the dilettante with the spine of steel. If Wimsey developed towards an inner seriousness, so did the books. Miss Sayers eventually saw that what had

Sapper

been mere playthings, brightly garnished puzzle toys, could be made into novels of manners with the extra tug of a mystery to be solved, even something more, commentaries on aspects of life using the powerful tool of symbolism to achieve their aim. Yet at the same time she had begun to lose interest in the whodunit as such. Her religious preoccupations loomed larger and larger and at last Wimsey was aban-

C = Characterization   P = Plot

doned, not sent to death over some Reichenbach Falls like Sherlock Holmes but married and done for.

The Documents in the Case (1930)

C ★★★★★★★	P ★★★★★★★★★
R ★★★★★★★★	T ★★★★★★★

The Nine Tailors (1934)

C ★★★★★★★	P ★★★★★★★★★
R ★★★★★★★★	T ★★★★★★★

Gaudy Night (1935)

C ★★★★★★★★★	P ★★★★★★★★
R ★★★★★★★★★	T ★★★★★★★★

SCHERF, Margaret (1908) American crime writer. After working in publishing for some years, Margaret Scherf became a full-time writer in 1939, since when she has written some two dozen crime novels, marked by good characterization, reasonable ingenuity and a pleasing sense of humour.

The Corpse in the Flannel Nightgown (1966)

C ★★★★★★★	P ★★★★★★★
R ★★★★★★★★	T ★★★★★★

SCOTT, Jack (1922) British crime novelist, novelist under real name, Jonathan Escott, former dance band crooner and Silver Johnny Gray, Singing Cowboy. His police novels have become increasingly skilled and are remarkable for the strongly flavoured style they achieve, gamy as a well-hung pheasant.

A Distant View of Death (1981)

C ★★★★★★★	P ★★★★★★★★
R ★★★★★★★★	T ★★★★★★★

An Uprush of Mayhem (1982)

C ★★★★★★★★	P ★★★★★★★
R ★★★★★★★★	T ★★★★★★★

SEELEY, Mabel (1903) American mystery writer. She was the leading writer reviving the Mary Roberts Rinehart (q.v.) tradition in the 1930s. She had literary style and the gift of creating shivers of suspense. She began to write straight novels in

the 1950s and has not published mysteries since.

The Crying Sister (1939)

C ★★★★★★★	P ★★★★★★★
R ★★★★★★★★	T ★★★★★★★★

Stranger Beside Me (1951)

C ★★★★★★★	P ★★★★★★
R ★★★★★★★★	T ★★★★★★★

SELWYN, Francis (1936) British historical crime novelist, and under his own name, a wellguarded secret, writer on criminal and military history. His novels are the adventures in Victorian England of Sergeant Verity, of the Plain-clothes Detail at Scotland Yard. Verity is stolid, genial and something of a puritan; his cases invariably take him into the sexual underside of Victorian society.

Sergeant Verity and the Swell Mob (1981)

C ★★★★★★★	P ★★★★★★★
R ★★★★★★★★	T ★★★★★★

SETON, Anya (1916) British novelist, born in New York. Some of her books rank as gothics for their colourful and romantic settings, though many are historical biographies. Passionate heroines are her big thing, and she sends them into action with splendid fervour.

Dragonwyck (1945)

C ★★★★★★★	P ★★★★★★★★
R ★★★★★★★★★★	T ★★★★★★★★

SEYMOUR, Gerald (1941) British thriller novelist and former television news reporter. Writing novels seems to be a hazard of British television reporting (John Simpson, Sandy Gall, Gordon Honeycombe) but Seymour had writing in his bloodstream with a father, William Kean Seymour, poet and novelist, a mother, Rosalind Wade, prolific novelist, let alone James Hilton (q.v.) and James Hanley as godfathers. His own books spring from his reporting experiences, in Ulster,

R = Readability   T = Tension

Italy, Israel. They are packed with authentic detail, excitingly told and not without feeling.

Harry's Game (1979)

C ★ ★ ★ ★ ★ ★ ★	P ★ ★ ★ ★ ★ ★ ★
R ★ ★ ★ ★ ★ ★ ★	T ★ ★ ★ ★ ★ ★ ★ ★

Red Fox (1979)

C ★ ★ ★ ★ ★ ★	P ★ ★ ★ ★ ★ ★ ★
R ★ ★ ★ ★ ★ ★ ★ ★	T ★ ★ ★ ★ ★ ★ ★

SHANNON, Dell see LINING-TON, Elizabeth.

SHEARING, Joseph (1866-1952) Pseudonym for Gabrielle Margaret Vere Campbell, British novelist who also wrote as Marjorie Bowen and George Preedy. This hugely prolific author is at her best in crime writing when she uses Victorian settings, frequently reconstructing and re-working famous mysteries of the period. Depth of research and richly detailed descriptions compensate for occasional lack of narrative momentum, and her portrayals of Victorian female life are always fascinating.

For Her to See (1947)
(So Evil My Love in U.S.)

C ★ ★ ★ ★ ★ ★ ★	P ★ ★ ★ ★ ★
R ★ ★ ★ ★ ★ ★	T ★ ★ ★ ★ ★

SIMENON, Georges (1903) French crime novelist, all of whose major works have been translated into English, some excellently, a few not so well. His books, of which there are many indeed, divide into two categories, perhaps three. First there are the dozens, all pretty short, written between 1933 and 1973, featuring Inspector Maigret. Then there are the crime novels, as many, as good, that have no particular hero and are often studies in psychological disintegration. To these can be added the novels that escape being crime but have all the intensity of those that are. All of them give us writing of the highest kind. Simenon is so skilled (such a genius) that he

Georges Simenon

can make even a simple description of Maigret riding to work on a Paris bus as gripping as the climax of many an adventure novel. Maigret is the detective as author. He solves his cases in the same way that Simenon writes, by absorbing himself in the particular situation that he has chosen to investigate until it is clear to him down to the very bottom, the least detail. "She's all yours . . ." he says as the last words of the last book about Maigret (he announced his retirement from fiction on 7 Feb 1973, and stuck to it) and this is precisely it: the character we have been investigating is, when it comes to the final pages, all ours. He saw Maigret's function and his own as being one and the same: to discover, to understand, to enlarge the known world. And in performing this task again and again he gave us, too, a huge panorama of twentieth-century life, chiefly of life in Paris, but also in many parts of France, in France overseas and even in America. He was doing, in the Maigret books and in the others, what Balzac was doing in presenting us with the *Comédie Humaine,* darting a bright light on to the lives of dozens and dozens of ordinary people who, like all of us potentially, are at the same time extraordinary.

The Simenon Omnibuses

SIMON, Roger L. (1943) American novelist. Roger L. Simon has chosen in his crime-writing to work in the hard-nosed private-eye tradition. He has updated his detective, ex-Berkeley radical Moses Wine, while retaining much of the old, well-tried apparatus of the genre, a compromise which has met with some success and promises more.

The Big Fix (1973)

C ★ ★ ★ ★ ★ ★	P ★ ★ ★ ★ ★ ★
R ★ ★ ★ ★ ★ ★ ★	T ★ ★ ★ ★ ★ ★

SIMPSON, Dorothy (1933) British detective novelist. "Pleasant" is the word for this new author of domestic detective stories featuring Inspector Thanet and set in Kent. The exploration of murky pasts is gently done.

The Night She Died (1980)

C ★ ★ ★ ★ ★ ★ ★	P ★ ★ ★ ★ ★ ★ ★
R ★ ★ ★ ★ ★ ★ ★ ★	T ★ ★ ★ ★ ★ ★

SIMPSON, John (1944) Former BBC television political editor and news presenter who has turned to espionage fiction, with marked success. *Moscow Requiem,* his first novel, showed high intelligence, width of intellectual background and strong, clear narration.

Moscow Requiem (1981)

SIMS, George (1923) British suspense novelist. An uneven writer, apt to defy the canons of his art, at his best he is extraordinarily good, able to describe a love affair in a truly affecting way, able to describe a fist-fight so that you know who hit who and where, able within a crime story to show a character maturing. His books are full of nut-crunchy facts (sometimes too full). He can evoke a landscape (particularly a London one) brilliantly. But sometimes he writes himself into the ground.

The Last Best Friend (1967)

C ★ ★ ★ ★ ★ ★ ★ ★	P ★ ★ ★ ★ ★ ★ ★
R ★ ★ ★ ★ ★ ★ ★	T ★ ★ ★ ★ ★ ★ ★ ★

Deadhand (1971)

C ★ ★ ★ ★ ★ ★ ★	P ★ ★ ★ ★ ★
R ★ ★ ★ ★ ★ ★ ★	T ★ ★ ★ ★ ★ ★ ★

Who Is Cato? (1981)

C ★ ★ ★ ★ ★ ★ ★	P ★ ★ ★ ★ ★ ★ ★ ★
R ★ ★ ★ ★ ★ ★ ★ ★	T ★ ★ ★ ★ ★ ★ ★ ★

SINCLAIR, Michael (1938) British espionage novelist, real name Michael Shea, Press Secretary to Her Majesty the Queen. His books, infrequent and plainly the products of a hobby, are filled with the results of painstaking research, presented with every appearance of ease. They have, too, a flavour always of oddity.

The Masterplayers (1978)

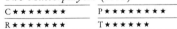

SMITH, Martin Cruz (1942) American mystery writer, who uses the pseudonym Simon Quinn for paperback series. Bill Smith, as he is known to his friends, wrote his first mystery novel, *Gypsy in Amber* in 1970; he followed it with *Canto for A Gypsy* in 1971, both of these under his name, Martin Smith. Both received Edgar scrolls, Best First and Best Novel. In 1977, his novel *Nightwing* also received Best Novel honours. For this he used the name by which he is now known worldwide, Martin Cruz Smith. "Cruz" is a name commonly given to boys of the Northern Pueblos of New Mexico, and his mother is a Northern Pueblo Indian. For the eight years in which he was writing these

R = Readability   T = Tension

C. P. Snow

other books, he was also working on his novel, *Gorky Park*, one of the foremost mysteries of the twentieth century. *Gorky Park* was published in 1981 to unparalleled success.

Gypsy in Amber (1970)

C ★ ★ ★ ★ ★ ★ ★	P ★ ★ ★ ★ ★ ★ ★
R ★ ★ ★ ★ ★ ★ ★	T ★ ★ ★ ★ ★ ★ ★

Nightwing (1976)

C ★ ★ ★ ★ ★ ★ ★	P ★ ★ ★ ★ ★ ★ ★
R ★ ★ ★ ★ ★ ★ ★	T ★ ★ ★ ★ ★ ★ ★

Gorky Park (1981)

C ★ ★ ★ ★ ★ ★ ★	P ★ ★ ★ ★ ★ ★ ★
R ★ ★ ★ ★ ★ ★ ★ ★	T ★ ★ ★ ★ ★ ★ ★ ★

SMITH, Shelley (1912) British detective novelist. At intervals in the years 1942-78 she has written fourteen crime novels, initially classic-type whodunits, latterly psychological suspense stories, though she hardly sticks to any sort of formula. At her best she achieves a very high level of writing, and she can produce a plot of enormous ingenuity. The lonely attract her and the way that a minor criminal act can lead inexorably to the greatest one of all.

An Afternoon to Kill (1953)

C ★ ★ ★ ★ ★ ★ ★	P ★ ★ ★ ★ ★ ★ ★ ★ ★
R ★ ★ ★ ★ ★ ★ ★	T ★ ★ ★ ★ ★ ★ ★

The Ballad of the Running Man (1961)

C ★ ★ ★ ★ ★ ★ ★	P ★ ★ ★ ★ ★ ★
R ★ ★ ★ ★ ★ ★ ★	T ★ ★ ★ ★ ★

SNOW, C.P. (1905-80) Otherwise Lord Snow, senior civil servant, novelist, scientist, philosopher of science. But his first work of fiction was a whodunit, *Death Under Sail*, and his last was a detective novel with philosophical overtones, *A Coat of Varnish*. He wrote nothing else in the crime field.

Death Under Sail (1932)

C ★ ★ ★ ★ ★	P ★ ★ ★ ★ ★ ★ ★
R ★ ★ ★ ★ ★ ★	T ★ ★ ★ ★

A Coat of Varnish (1979)

C ★ ★ ★ ★ ★ ★ ★ ★	P ★ ★ ★ ★ ★ ★ ★
R ★ ★ ★ ★ ★ ★ ★	T ★ ★ ★ ★ ★

SPILLANE, Mickey (1918) American thriller writer, best known for his creation Mike Hammer, though some of his books feature Tiger Mann. He was the most popular American novelist, in any field, in the 1950s when his unabashed mixture of sex and violence most appealed. After seven books with sales in the five or six million bracket he abruptly retired in 1952 for nearly ten years. He then wrote again for some seven years from 1961, retired again and had a third short burst of writing in the early 1970s. In these later periods he tended to reproduce effects and successes from early days, but those first books have a crude vigour and a lack of inhibition that make them stand out. He once said: "You don't read a book to get to the middle: you read it to get to the end."

I, the Jury (1947)

C ★ ★ ★ ★ ★	P ★ ★ ★ ★ ★ ★ ★
R ★ ★ ★ ★ ★ ★ ★ ★	T ★ ★ ★ ★ ★ ★ ★ ★

Kiss Me, Deadly (1952)

C ★ ★ ★ ★	P ★ ★ ★ ★ ★ ★ ★
R ★ ★ ★ ★ ★ ★ ★ ★	T ★ ★ ★ ★ ★ ★ ★ ★

STARK, Richard (1933) American suspense writer, otherwise Donald E. Westlake (q.v.). Under the Stark label he produced a paperback series (hardbacked in Britain) about Parker, a professional thief, notable for his cold-blooded attitude. The first of them, *The Hunter*, became the film, *Point Blank*. The Parker stories are harsh and written with terse economy. There was a spin-off from them, some books about Alan Grofield, bank robber and actor, somewhat lighter in tone.

The Hunter (1962)
(*Point Blank* in U.K.)

C ★ ★ ★ ★ ★	P ★ ★ ★ ★ ★ ★ ★
R ★ ★ ★ ★ ★ ★	T ★ ★ ★ ★ ★ ★

STEIN, Aaron Marc (1906) American mystery writer. One of the most prolific of mystery writers, New York born and bred, Aaron Marc Stein published his first novel in 1930 on graduation from Princeton. With the exception of the three years he served in the Army in World War II, he has published several mysteries every year since under his own name and his pseudonyms. All of his books are smart and sound, the kind of good mystery writing which has made the genre the most popular form of recreational reading in the United States. As Stein, he features a young archaeological pair and also a hard-hitting engineer, Matt Erridge, in each series using overseas backgrounds. Stein was honoured with a Grand Master Edgar by the Mystery Writers of America in 1978.

Death Takes A Paying Guest (1947)

C ★ ★ ★ ★ ★	P ★ ★ ★ ★ ★ ★
R ★ ★ ★ ★ ★	T ★ ★ ★ ★ ★

Death Meets 400 Rabbits (1953)

C ★ ★ ★ ★ ★	P ★ ★ ★ ★ ★ ★
R ★ ★ ★ ★ ★ ★	T ★ ★ ★ ★ ★

I Fear The Greeks (1966)

C ★ ★ ★ ★ ★ ★	P ★ ★ ★ ★ ★ ★
R ★ ★ ★ ★ ★ ★	T ★ ★ ★ ★ ★ ★

STERN, Richard Martin (1915) American suspense novelist and mainstream novelist. He won with his first novel, *The Bright Road to Fear*, an Edgar from the Mystery Writers of America, and in the books

Mary Stewart

Aaron Marc Stein

he has written since he has kept up a high standard, in good, intelligent English, evincing always a sharp curiosity about what makes things happen, giving his readers a wide variety of well-pictured backgrounds. In 1973 he produced what he considered a mainstream novel, *The Tower*, a book that started a whole sub-sub-genre of disaster stories.

The Bright Road to Fear (1958)

C ★ ★ ★ ★ ★ ★	P ★ ★ ★ ★ ★ ★
R ★ ★ ★ ★ ★ ★	T ★ ★ ★ ★ ★ ★ ★

The Tower (1973)

C ★ ★ ★ ★ ★	P ★ ★ ★ ★ ★ ★
R ★ ★ ★ ★ ★ ★	T ★ ★ ★ ★ ★ ★ ★ ★

R = Readability T = Tension

STEWART, Mary (1916) British romantic suspense writer. After a highly successful career in secondary and higher education, Mary Stewart has made herself undisputed mistress of the modern gothic genre while generally managing to avoid being mastered by its cliches. Her secret is sympathetic and believable characters, beautifully realized settings, and highly literate writing.

Nine Coaches Waiting (1958)

C ★ ★ ★ ★ ★ ★ ★	P ★ ★ ★ ★ ★ ★ ★ ★
R ★ ★ ★ ★ ★ ★ ★	T ★ ★ ★ ★ ★ ★ ★

This Rough Magic (1964)

C ★ ★ ★ ★ ★ ★ ★ ★ ★	P ★ ★ ★ ★ ★ ★ ★ ★
R ★ ★ ★ ★ ★ ★ ★ ★	T ★ ★ ★ ★ ★ ★ ★

Airs Above the Ground (1965)

C ★ ★ ★ ★ ★ ★ ★	P ★ ★ ★ ★ ★ ★ ★
R ★ ★ ★ ★ ★ ★ ★ ★	T ★ ★ ★ ★ ★ ★ ★

STONE, Hampton (1906) (Pseudonym of Aaron Marc Stein, q.v.), American mystery writer. Hampton Stone was considered the best writer of the Stein triad, the author here permitting his literary qualifications to shine through. The books featured New York Assistant District Attorney Gibson and were published under the prestige Inner Sanctum colophon of Simon and Schuster, presided over by Lee Wright, one of the leading mystery editors of the publishing world. The Stone titles are almost as titillating as reading the stories in their endless ingenuity and merry quippishness.

The Girl with the Hole in Her Head (1949)

C ★ ★ ★ ★ ★ ★	P ★ ★ ★ ★ ★ ★ ★
R ★ ★ ★ ★ ★ ★ ★	T ★ ★ ★ ★ ★ ★

The Man Who Was Three Jumps Ahead (1959)

C ★ ★ ★ ★ ★	P ★ ★ ★ ★ ★ ★ ★
R ★ ★ ★ ★ ★ ★ ★ ★	T ★ ★ ★ ★ ★ ★

STOUT, Rex (1886-1975) American mystery writer. After a successful business career of many years duration, Rex Stout created the

Rex Stout

popular detecting team of Nero Wolfe and Archie Goodwin in *Fer-de-Lance* (1934) and was launched on an even more prestigious career. Nero Wolfe is of the Sherlock Holmes tradition of eccentrics, a sedentary fat man rather than a peripatetic lean one, devoted to fine food rather than to his pipe, and with a fetish for orchids rather than opium. Archie is a street-wise young fellow who acts as Wolfe's leg man. Their relationship was never spelled out. Archie lived with Wolfe, and why not?, free gourmet board and a free room in an all-male household. Although Archie was always eyeing the girls, he scarcely had an opportunity to be with one, being at Wolfe's beck and call night and day, and having to account for his time when out of the house. There was more than a sprinkling of Rex Stout in Nero Wolfe. Physically Stout was small and lively, but Wolfe was a curmudgeon after Stout's own heart and both gloried in it. Besides being one of the most prolific of twentieth-century mystery writers, Stout was an active worker for writers' rights throughout his life. At various times he headed the Author's Guild, the Author's League and the Mystery Writers of America. As so many of America's foremost mystery writers, Stout was never an Edgar

C = Characterization   P = Plot

winner for novel, but in 1958 he was honoured as a Grand Master of M.W.A. With Ellery Queen and Erle Stanley Gardner, Stout was one of the three mystery greats in America from the thirties into the seventies.

League of Frightened Men (1935)

C ★ ★ ★ ★ ★ ★	P ★ ★ ★ ★ ★ ★
R ★ ★ ★ ★ ★ ★ ★	T ★ ★ ★ ★ ★ ★

Too Many Cooks (1938)

C ★ ★ ★ ★ ★ ★	P ★ ★ ★ ★ ★
R ★ ★ ★ ★ ★ ★ ★	T ★ ★ ★ ★ ★

Please Pass the Guilt (1973)

C ★ ★ ★ ★ ★ ★ ★	P ★ ★ ★ ★ ★ ★
R ★ ★ ★ ★ ★ ★ ★	T ★ ★ ★ ★ ★ ★

STUART, Ian (1927) British crime writer, not to be confused with 'Ian Stuart', a pseudonym used by Alastair MacLean (q.v.). Out of his experience in light engineering he has written chiefly murder mysteries with a background of the workings of industry as they actually happen in Britain. Shop-steward negotiations, small-scale take-over bids, obtaining orders, marketing a new product: all are interesting grist to his mill.

The Renshaw Strike (1980)

C ★ ★ ★ ★ ★ ★	P ★ ★ ★ ★ ★ ★
R ★ ★ ★ ★ ★ ★ ★	T ★ ★ ★ ★ ★

STUBBS, Jean (1926) British crime novelist and historical novelist. Reading an old account of the trial of Mary Blandy in 1752 started Jean Stubbs as a crime writer with what she called "a crime documentary", *My Grand Enemy* (1967). Later she branched into Victorian-Edwardian crime with the imaginary cases of Inspector Lintott before abandoning the genre (alas) in favour of historical sagas. In both these and in crime she tells a corking good story.

Dear Laura (1973)

C ★ ★ ★ ★ ★ ★	P ★ ★ ★ ★ ★ ★
R ★ ★ ★ ★ ★ ★ ★	T ★ ★ ★ ★ ★ ★ ★

SUMMERTON, Margaret British gothic suspense writer, who also wrote as Jan Roffman (q.v.). In the twenty years from 1957 she wrote fourteen novels mostly with a touch of the eerie in them, appealing perhaps chiefly to women. Of her best books it can be said, "Once read, not easily forgotten."

A Memory of Darkness (1967)

C ★ ★ ★ ★ ★ ★	P ★ ★ ★ ★ ★ ★
R ★ ★ ★ ★ ★ ★ ★	T ★ ★ ★ ★ ★ ★ ★

Julian Symons, drawing by Wyndham Lewis

SYMONS, Julian (1912) British man of letters. Julian Symons has much claim to be the high priest of British crime-writing. Poet, critic, social historian, he must, though he was never at a university, at one stage have appeared to be a type of that once widespread species, the British academic who takes to detective fiction, usually pseudonymously, as a relaxation from the intellectual rigours of his discipline. But that stage is long past and after more than twenty novels and a great deal of critical writing, including *Bloody Murder* (1972) (*Mortal Consequences* in U.S.) which is currently the best history of the genre, Symons has moved crime-writing to the centre of his creative life just as surely as he has moved to its own

R = Readability   T = Tension

centre. As crime stories, his novels sometimes suffer from a certain slackness of structure, perhaps because his mind is more closely concerned with the social content of crime than with its detection, though when he wishes to puzzle, as in *The Players and The Game* (1972) and *A Three-Pipe Problem* (1975), he displays a ready talent. But basically his books are studies of flawed characters in a flawed society and their appeal and interest are general rather than generic.

The Colour of Murder (1957)

| C ★ ★ ★ ★ ★ ★ ★ ★ | P ★ ★ ★ ★ ★ ★ ★ |
| R ★ ★ ★ ★ ★ ★ ★ | T ★ ★ ★ ★ ★ ★ ★ |

The End of Solomon Grundy (1964)

| C ★ ★ ★ ★ ★ ★ ★ ★ | P ★ ★ ★ ★ ★ ★ ★ ★ |
| R ★ ★ ★ ★ ★ ★ ★ | T ★ ★ ★ ★ ★ ★ ★ |

The Players and the Game (1972)

| C ★ ★ ★ ★ ★ ★ ★ ★ | P ★ ★ ★ ★ ★ ★ ★ ★ |
| R ★ ★ ★ ★ ★ ★ ★ ★ | T ★ ★ ★ ★ ★ ★ ★ ★ |

TAYLOR, Phoebe Atwood (1909-76) American mystery writer. Phoebe Atwood Taylor published her first mystery when she was only 22 years old, the year after her graduation from Barnard College. It introduced Asey Mayo, the Cape Cod detective whose dry humour was a part of his New England shrewdness. As Alice Tilton she wrote of Leonidas Witherall, a suburban Bostonian, also with the humour and a keen eye for Boston social customs. Both characters were neighbour folk, she lived near Boston in winter and on the Cape in summer.

The Cape Cod Mystery (1931)

| C ★ ★ ★ ★ ★ ★ ★ | P ★ ★ ★ ★ ★ ★ ★ |
| R ★ ★ ★ ★ ★ ★ ★ | T ★ ★ ★ ★ ★ |

TEY, Josephine (1897-1952) British detective novelist and, as Gordon Daviot, noted playwright. She is one of the perennials of the crime scene with three books at least that are reprinted time and again in a total output of only eight. Of the three (listed below) curiously only one, *The Daughter of Time*, features her regular hero, Inspector Alan Grant, a quiet gentlemanly Scot at Scotland Yard, and this is an offbeat case in which, lying in hospital, he speculates about the murder of the Princes in the Tower in 1480 and finds wicked King Richard III innocent. The continued interest in her books springs from her quiet creation of credible people who have relationships a good deal more complicated, and likely, than in all but a few of her Golden Age contemporaries (and indeed in the bulk of her successors).

The Franchise Affair (1948)

| C ★ ★ ★ ★ ★ ★ ★ ★ | P ★ ★ ★ ★ ★ ★ ★ |
| R ★ ★ ★ ★ ★ ★ ★ | T ★ ★ ★ ★ ★ ★ |

Brat Farrar (1949)
(*Come and Be Killed* in U.S. hardback)

| C ★ ★ ★ ★ ★ ★ ★ ★ | P ★ ★ ★ ★ ★ ★ |
| R ★ ★ ★ ★ ★ ★ ★ | T ★ ★ ★ ★ ★ |

The Daughter of Time (1951)

| C ★ ★ ★ ★ ★ ★ ★ | P ★ ★ ★ ★ ★ ★ |
| R ★ ★ ★ ★ ★ ★ ★ | T ★ ★ ★ ★ ★ |

THAYER, Lee (1874-1973) Artist and writer. Although primarily a designer and decorator (when she was in her teens her paintings were shown at the 1893 Chicago World's Fair), she was one of the most prolific writers of her time, her mysteries featuring Peter Clancy, red-haired detective. She was also the oldest writer to write a mystery when in 1966, at the age of 92, she published *Dusty Death*.

Guilt-Edged (1950)
(*Guilt-Edged Murder* in U.K.)

| C ★ ★ ★ ★ ★ | P ★ ★ ★ ★ ★ |
| R ★ ★ ★ ★ ★ | T ★ ★ ★ ★ ★ |

Leslie Thomas

both in the United States and in Europe, Africa and elsewhere, before becoming a writer. Thomas bites hard on today's problems but as he is as great a humorist as he is a crusader, all of his books are excellent entertainment. Under the pseudonym Oliver Bleeck he has also written a number of best of breed since the beginning of the line in 1969 with *The Brass Go-Between*. Thomas also writes for the screen and a number of his novels have become successful motion pictures.

The Seersucker Whipsaw (1967)

C ★ ★ ★ ★ ★ ★	P ★ ★ ★ ★ ★ ★ ★
R ★ ★ ★ ★ ★ ★ ★	T ★ ★ ★ ★ ★ ★

The Fools in Town Are on Our Side (1970)

C ★ ★ ★ ★ ★ ★	P ★ ★ ★ ★ ★ ★ ★
R ★ ★ ★ ★ ★ ★ ★	T ★ ★ ★ ★ ★

Chinaman's Chance (1978)

C ★ ★ ★ ★ ★ ★	P ★ ★ ★ ★ ★ ★ ★
R ★ ★ ★ ★ ★ ★ ★	T ★ ★ ★ ★ ★ ★

THOMAS, Leslie (1931) British novelist and occasional crime novelist. This bestselling author (*The Virgin Soldiers*) has at least twice written books that come into the crime field, with *Dangerous Davies*, a touching police procedural about a no-good detective, and with *Ormerod's Landing*, an extremely effective and moving espionage novel set in the 1939-45 War.

Dangerous Davies (1976)

C ★ ★ ★ ★ ★ ★ ★	P ★ ★ ★ ★ ★ ★
R ★ ★ ★ ★ ★ ★ ★	T ★ ★ ★ ★ ★ ★

Ormerod's Landing (1978)

C ★ ★ ★ ★ ★ ★ ★ ★	P ★ ★ ★ ★ ★ ★ ★
R ★ ★ ★ ★ ★ ★ ★	T ★ ★ ★ ★ ★ ★ ★

THOMAS, Ross (1926) American mystery writer. In 1966 with the publication of *The Cold War Swap*, Thomas took the Mystery Writers of America Edgar for Best First Novel. Born in Oklahoma, he was a newspaperman and a public relations man

June Thomson

THOMSON, June (1930) British detective novelist. With books that on the face of it seem to be no more

R = Readability   T = Tension

than quiet, ordinary examples of the classic detective story, chronicling the cases of Inspector Finch (Inspector Rudd in U.S.), she has reached an extraordinarily high level of achievement, standing perhaps second only to P.D. James (q.v.) in the art of combining the puzzle story and the novel of character. She is remarkable for her precise observation, both of people and the countryside she sets her stories in, for her sympathetic portrayal of the lone and the lonely, for her moral undertow.

A Question of Identity (1977)

C ★ ★ ★ ★ ★ ★ ★ ★ ★	P ★ ★ ★ ★ ★ ★
R ★ ★ ★ ★ ★ ★ ★ ★	T ★ ★ ★ ★ ★ ★ ★

Alibi in Time (1980)

C ★ ★ ★ ★ ★ ★ ★ ★ ★	P ★ ★ ★ ★ ★ ★
R ★ ★ ★ ★ ★ ★ ★ ★ ★	T ★ ★ ★ ★ ★ ★ ★

Shadow of A Doubt (1981)

C ★ ★ ★ ★ ★ ★ ★ ★ ★	P ★ ★ ★ ★ ★ ★ ★ ★
R ★ ★ ★ ★ ★ ★ ★ ★ ★	T ★ ★ ★ ★ ★ ★ ★ ★

TREAT, Lawrence (1903) American mystery writer. Lawrence Treat legally changed his real name of Lawrence Arthur Goldstone to his pseudonym in the forties. He is more noted today for short story, having published more than 100, than for novels. In 1964 he received the Mystery Writers of America Edgar for Best Short Story. However, he was a leading mystery novelist in the forties with his "alphabet" series beginning with *B as in Banshee*.

D as in Dead (1941)

C ★ ★ ★ ★ ★ ★	P ★ ★ ★ ★ ★ ★ ★
R ★ ★ ★ ★ ★ ★ ★	T ★ ★ ★ ★ ★ ★

Q as in Quicksand (1947)

C ★ ★ ★ ★ ★ ★	P ★ ★ ★ ★ ★ ★
R ★ ★ ★ ★ ★ ★	T ★ ★ ★ ★ ★ ★

TREVANIAN (1925) American crime novelist. Pseudonym of Rodney Whitaker, former Professor at the University of Texas. A curious writer with under his belt *Shibumi* (1979), a big bestseller, two highly stylish, very sharp comedy espionage stories featuring Jonathan Hemlock, art historian, mountain climber, ineffable snob and assassin, and a fine, thoughtful police novel set in Canada, *The Main*.

The Eiger Sanction (1972)

C ★ ★ ★ ★ ★ ★ ★	P ★ ★ ★ ★ ★ ★ ★ ★
R ★ ★ ★ ★ ★ ★ ★ ★ ★	T ★ ★ ★ ★ ★ ★ ★ ★

The Main (1976)

C ★ ★ ★ ★ ★ ★ ★ ★ ★	P ★ ★ ★ ★ ★ ★ ★
R ★ ★ ★ ★ ★ ★ ★ ★ ★	T ★ ★ ★ ★ ★ ★ ★ ★ ★

TREVOR, Elleston (1920) British suspense novelist who also has the pen-names of Adam Hall (q.v.), Mansell Black, Trevor Burgess, T. Dudley-Smith, Roger Fitzalan, Howard North and Simon Rattray. By which it may be seen how prolific he is. Besides the titles under other names there were between 1946 and 1979 a total of 32 Trevor books, among them more than one fact-buttressed, fast-moving bestseller (below).

The Flight of the Phoenix (1964)

C ★ ★ ★ ★ ★ ★ ★	P ★ ★ ★ ★ ★ ★ ★ ★ ★
R ★ ★ ★ ★ ★ ★ ★ ★ ★	T ★ ★ ★ ★ ★ ★ ★ ★ ★

TRIPP, Miles (1923) British suspense novelist and Charity Commission official. Oddness is perhaps the die-stamp of Miles Tripp. Almost every one of a score of books is marked by a curious idea or a main character on the edge of the unlikely. And who else would produce a crime novel entitled *Malice and the Maternal Instinct* (1969)? Sometimes the oddness goes too far for most palates, but at his best he achieves a compulsion few can match.

One Is One (1968)

C ★ ★ ★ ★ ★ ★ ★ ★	P ★ ★ ★ ★ ★ ★ ★
R ★ ★ ★ ★ ★ ★ ★ ★	T ★ ★ ★ ★ ★ ★ ★ ★

A Woman at Risk (1974)

C ★ ★ ★ ★ ★ ★ ★ ★ ★	P ★ ★ ★ ★ ★ ★ ★
R ★ ★ ★ ★ ★ ★ ★ ★ ★	T ★ ★ ★ ★ ★ ★ ★ ★

C = Characterization   P = Plot

TWAIN, Mark (1835-1910) Major American novelist, pseudonym of Samuel Langhorne Clemens. Among his output are more than a few pieces in which detection, often of a humorous sort, plays a major part. Indeed, *Life on the Mississippi* (1883) incorporates the first story to use a thumb print as identification, a device later much expanded in *Pudd'nhead Wilson*. *Simon Wheeler, Detective* (1903) was his last, never finished work.

Pudd'nhead Wilson (1894)

C ★ ★ ★ ★ ★ ★ ★	P ★ ★ ★ ★ ★ ★ ★
R ★ ★ ★ ★ ★ ★ ★ ★	T ★ ★ ★ ★ ★ ★

Mark Twain

TWOHY, Robert American crime short-story writer, full time. He can produce the straightforward detective tale, the serious study of crime and, equally, something as zany as they come. A cab driver for ten years, he frequently sets stories in that world, but he also writes light-heartedly about Hollywood greats. In general his stories reflect a strong lack of interest in the pretences of society. They are uncollected.

UHNAK, Dorothy (1933) American mystery writer. A policewoman for fourteen years before launching into her career as a writer, Dorothy Uhnak is one of the genuine new stars of the late twentieth century. *Policewoman*, called a semi-autobiography, was her first book, written while she was still active on the New York Police force. Although praised always for her authenticity, this accounts for only a part of her success. Her works are crime novels rather than mysteries and she writes them with as much drive and force as the best male writers in the field. In 1968 the Mystery Writers of America made a dual award for Best First Novel, Mrs Uhnak's *The Bait* sharing the honour. Two of her novels have been Literary Guild selections, *Law and Order* (1973) and *The Investigation* (1977).

The Ledger (1970)

C ★ ★ ★ ★ ★ ★	P ★ ★ ★ ★ ★ ★ ★
R ★ ★ ★ ★ ★ ★ ★	T ★ ★ ★ ★ ★ ★

False Witness (1981)

C ★ ★ ★ ★ ★ ★	P ★ ★ ★ ★ ★ ★
R ★ ★ ★ ★ ★ ★ ★	T ★ ★ ★ ★ ★ ★

UNDERWOOD, Michael (1916) British mystery writer. An Oxford graduate and barrister, he served for twenty-five years in the office of the Director of Public Prosecutions. He carried on his writing career simultaneously with his government work after the appearance of his first book, *Murder on Trial* in 1954. His books are distinguished by his presentation of problems connected with British legal procedures. They have been published in translation in all West-

R = Readability T = Tension

ern European countries and have a wide audience in the United States.

Death on Remand (1956)

C ★ ★ ★ ★ ★ ★	P ★ ★ ★ ★ ★ ★ ★
R ★ ★ ★ ★ ★ ★ ★	T ★ ★ ★ ★ ★

Double Jeopardy (1981)

C ★ ★ ★ ★ ★ ★ ★	P ★ ★ ★ ★ ★ ★ ★ ★
R ★ ★ ★ ★ ★ ★ ★	T ★ ★ ★ ★ ★ ★

The Hand of Fate (1981)

C ★ ★ ★ ★ ★ ★ ★ ★	P ★ ★ ★ ★ ★ ★ ★ ★ ★
R ★ ★ ★ ★ ★ ★ ★ ★	T ★ ★ ★ ★ ★ ★ ★

UPFIELD, Arthur W. (1888-1964) Australian crime novelist. Born in England, Upfield's early antipodean background as trapper, miner, cook and boundary rider thoroughly Australianized him. His books, many of which feature his attractive half-caste detective "Bony" (Detective Inspector Napoleon Bonaparte of the Queensland Police), are well plotted, exciting as well as puzzling, and filled with beautifully observed pictures of the land and the people.

Murder Must Wait (1953)

C ★ ★ ★ ★ ★ ★ ★ ★	P ★ ★ ★ ★ ★ ★ ★
R ★ ★ ★ ★ ★ ★ ★ ★ ★	T ★ ★ ★ ★ ★ ★ ★

Bony and the Black Virgin (1959)

C ★ ★ ★ ★ ★ ★ ★ ★	P ★ ★ ★ ★ ★ ★ ★
R ★ ★ ★ ★ ★ ★ ★ ★	T ★ ★ ★ ★ ★ ★ ★ ★ ★

VALIN, Jonathan (1948) American mystery novelist. He writes private-eye novels (Harry Stoner is his hero), set unusually and interestingly in Cincinnati, Ohio, where he was born though he now teaches creative writing at the University of Washington. He is married to the poet, Katherine Valin. The books are noticeably well written, underpinned by a wealth of allusion, and with good stories in the traditional private-eye hunt style.

Final Notice (1981)

C ★ ★ ★ ★ ★ ★ ★ ★	P ★ ★ ★ ★ ★ ★ ★
R ★ ★ ★ ★ ★ ★ ★ ★	T ★ ★ ★ ★ ★ ★ ★

VAN DE WETERING, Janwillem (1931) Dutch-born police procedural novelist, now resident in America, who writes in English. He studied philosophy in London and Buddhism under a Zen master in Japan. He then became a member of the Amsterdam Municipal Police. His ten novels have featured Adjutant Grijpstra of the Amsterdam police, his sergeant and superiors, even once taking them to America. They are curious books, mazy in direction, full of fine insights, gently mad even.

The Corpse on the Dike (1977)

C ★ ★ ★ ★ ★ ★ ★ ★	P ★ ★ ★ ★ ★
R ★ ★ ★ ★ ★ ★ ★	T ★ ★ ★ ★

The Mind Murders (1981)

C ★ ★ ★ ★ ★ ★ ★ ★	P ★ ★ ★ ★ ★
R ★ ★ ★ ★ ★ ★ ★ ★	T ★ ★ ★ ★ ★

VAN DINE, S. S. (1888-1939) American mystery writer. Willard Huntington Wright, artist and art critic, journalist and literary critic, under the pseudonym of S. S. Van Dine became one of the most important of all American mystery writers. He had turned to mystery when convalescing from a serious breakdown in health. He gathered together some 2000 books of detection, seventy-five years worth, and from his reading in them decided to write a mystery of his own. He wrote 30,000 words synopsizing his plans for three novels. All were immediately accepted by Scribner's. The first, *The Benson Murder Case*, based on an actual New York murder, was published in 1926. Philo Vance, his detective, based to quite an extent on Lord Peter Wimsey, was an amusing and brilliant dilettante as well as a smart deductive detective. From all

S. S. van Dine

accounts, Van Dine had as many eccentricities as his character. The pen name S.S. Van Dine was from a family name, Van Dyne, with the S.S. simply for ships, the author being a frequent traveller to and fro across the Atlantic. A pen-name was chosen because Wright believed he was stepping down from his high position in literature and art by writing mysteries. However, the mysteries he wrote changed the face of mystery writing in the 1920s, from the formalized story to an intimate picture of New York life, close to *romans à clef*.

The Canary Murder Case (1927)

| C ★ ★ ★ ★ ★ ★ | P ★ ★ ★ ★ ★ ★ ★ |
| R ★ ★ ★ ★ ★ ★ ★ | T ★ ★ ★ ★ ★ ★ |

The Greene Murder Case (1928)

| C ★ ★ ★ ★ ★ ★ | P ★ ★ ★ ★ ★ ★ ★ |
| R ★ ★ ★ ★ ★ ★ ★ | T ★ ★ ★ ★ ★ ★ |

The Bishop Murder Case (1929)

| C ★ ★ ★ ★ ★ ★ | P ★ ★ ★ ★ ★ ★ ★ |
| R ★ ★ ★ ★ ★ ★ ★ | T ★ ★ ★ ★ ★ ★ ★ |

VAN GREENAWAY, Peter (1929) British crime novelist. From *Judas!* in 1972 through a dozen successors

Van Greenaway has done odd and extraordinary things with the crime novel, probably not to everyone's taste but savoursome to those in tune with him. *The Destiny Man*, for example, doesn't hesitate to put words on to the pen of Shakespeare (lost diary) while *A Man Called Scavener* is a cathedral town whodunit that might have been written by the eccentric Ronald Firbank.

The Destiny Man (1977)

| C ★ ★ ★ ★ ★ ★ ★ | P ★ ★ ★ ★ ★ ★ ★ |
| R ★ ★ ★ ★ ★ ★ ★ | T ★ ★ ★ ★ ★ |

A Man Called Scavener (1978)

| C ★ ★ ★ ★ ★ ★ ★ | P ★ ★ ★ ★ ★ ★ |
| R ★ ★ ★ ★ ★ ★ ★ | T ★ ★ ★ ★ ★ |

VAN GULIK, Robert (1910-67) Dutch detective novelist, writing in English. A former Dutch ambassador to Japan, he began by translating a traditional Chinese story dating from the Tang dynasty (750 AD) about the crime-solving Judge Dee. From this he went on to invent Judge Dee stories, taking care always to keep well within authentic Chinese customs. The books made good stories, unimpeded by too much tushery.

Necklace and Calabash (1967)

| C ★ ★ ★ ★ ★ | P ★ ★ ★ ★ ★ ★ |
| R ★ ★ ★ ★ ★ ★ ★ | T ★ ★ ★ ★ |

WADE, Henry (1887-1969) Pseudonym for Sir Henry Lancelot Aubrey-Fletcher, British crime novelist. Henry Wade's writing career stretched from the so-called Golden Age to the late fifties. From start to finish he took a long hard look at the British legal system, and he maintained the highest standards of plotting and characterization

R = Readability   T = Tension

throughout his books which range in form from classic detective stories to detailed anatomies of crime.

The Duke of York's Steps (1929)

C ★★★★★★★★★	P ★★★★★★★
R ★★★★★★★	T ★★★★★★★

A Dying Fall (1955)

C ★★★★★★★★★	P ★★★★★★★★
R ★★★★★★★★	T ★★★★★★★

WAHLÖÖ, Per (1926-75) and **SJÖWALL, Maj** (1935) Swedish husband-and-wife crime novelists. They wrote ten novels about the work of the Stockholm police, having decided at the outset that this was enough. Outwardly police procedurals, with the customary concomitant of side-looks into the lives of the dependants of their selected police figures, the books in fact do a good deal more than merely tell stories explaining what it is like to work as a police detective. Chiefly through their main protagonist, Martin Beck, a modern anti-hero, they give readers novels of strong social comment, focussed naturally on Sweden but not without relevance for all Western capitalist democracies. And, if this sounds lugubrious (which occasionally perhaps it is), it should be noted that they also hit at times on a splendid vein of farcical humour. Julian Symons, the British critic, has said of these books that "they are among the most original of modern crime stories, and that they often succeeded in doing with the crime story something no other writers . . . even attempted."

Roseanna (1967)

C ★★★★★★★★★	P ★★★★★★★
R ★★★★★★★★	T ★★★★★★★★

The Laughing Policeman (1970)

C ★★★★★★★★★	P ★★★★★★
R ★★★★★★★★	T ★★★★★★★

The Terrorist (1977)

C ★★★★★★★★★	P ★★★★★★★
R ★★★★★★★★	T ★★★★★★★★

WAINWRIGHT, John (1921) British crime novelist. Notably prolific, sometimes producing four or even six books in a year, and able to write in a variety of sub-genres, Wainwright nevertheless achieves, especially in his later books, an extraordinarily high standard. He has been nominated more than once for the Crime Writers Association awards. Perhaps one strain can be picked out as threading through many of his police procedurals, through his successful attempt at a Christie-like whodunit (*High-class Kill*, 1973), even through spy tales, this is his Yorkshire background. The writing has the blunt directness of the Yorkshireman, and something of his contempt for the soft and the southern. Yet Wainwright is not without compassion, as the occasional homosexual in his stories will show, or his accounts of the appalling lot of the disliked prisoner. All in all he is a natural fiction writer, able to convert into story almost anything that comes his way.

The Eye of the Beholder (1980)

C ★★★★★★★	P ★★★★★★★★★
R ★★★★★★★★	T ★★★★★★★

Man of Law (1980)

C ★★★★★★★	P ★★★★★★★★★
R ★★★★★★★★	T ★★★★★★★

An Urge for Justice (1981)

C ★★★★★★★★★	P ★★★★★★★★
R ★★★★★★★★★	T ★★★★★★★

WALLACE, Edgar (1875-1932) British crime writer, dramatist and journalist. By any standards a remarkable man. Illegitimate son of an actress, he was brought up by a Billingsgate fish-porter but rose to be an author so popular that at one time every fourth book sold in Britain was one of his. After success in the Boer War as a Reuter's correspondent he began to write thrillers. His method was to seize on an idea, tell it as vividly as possible and then trust to luck to get the girl out of the gas-

C = Characterization　P = Plot

Edgar Wallace

Joseph Wambaugh

filled pit or whatever peril else he had hit on. Mysteries abound. No one but hero and heroine is what they seem. We move in a flash from one dire situation to another. It's all go. And it was all written at top speed (a 75,000-word book over a weekend; 36 hours non-stop production). So the books are generally careless, and breathless. But some rise above the self-imposed handicaps, almost at random in either the crime tales of Socrates Smith or those of Derrick Yale, "the psychometrical detective", or the Turf tales of Educated Evans or the stories of Mr J. G. Reeder of the Public Prosecutor's office.

The Four Just Men (1906)

C ★ ★ ★ ★	P ★ ★ ★ ★ ★ ★ ★ ★
R ★ ★ ★ ★ ★ ★ ★ ★	T ★ ★ ★ ★ ★ ★ ★

The Mind of Mr J. G. Reeder (1925)

C ★ ★ ★ ★ ★ ★	P ★ ★ ★ ★ ★ ★ ★ ★
R ★ ★ ★ ★ ★ ★ ★ ★	T ★ ★ ★ ★ ★ ★ ★ ★

The Squeaker (1927)
(*The Squealer* in U.S.)

C ★ ★ ★ ★	P ★ ★ ★ ★ ★ ★ ★ ★
R ★ ★ ★ ★ ★ ★ ★ ★ ★	T ★ ★ ★ ★ ★ ★ ★ ★ ★

WAMBAUGH, Joseph (1937) American police procedural novelist

and former detective sergeant in the Los Angeles Police Department. His realistic, if slightly overheated, portrayals of police life, its humour, its sex, its degradations, are bestsellers. But they are more than mere bestsellers: they strive to say something not only about police life but about life as a whole. The writing pours on in a compulsive flow, which sometimes disguises arrant digressions.

The New Centurions (1970)

C ★ ★ ★ ★ ★ ★ ★	P ★ ★ ★ ★ ★ ★
R ★ ★ ★ ★ ★ ★ ★ ★	T ★ ★ ★ ★ ★ ★ ★ ★ ★

The Onion Field (1973)

C ★ ★ ★ ★ ★ ★ ★	P ★ ★ ★ ★ ★ ★
R ★ ★ ★ ★ ★ ★ ★ ★ ★	T ★ ★ ★ ★ ★ ★ ★ ★ ★

The Glitter Dome (1981)

C ★ ★ ★ ★ ★ ★ ★	P ★ ★ ★ ★ ★ ★
R ★ ★ ★ ★ ★ ★ ★ ★ ★	T ★ ★ ★ ★ ★ ★ ★

WATSON, Clarissa American mystery novelist and also art gallery owner. She writes, briskly and with sophistication and not a few jokes, about the art world of East Coast America, displaying much erudition with the lightest of touches. The touch indeed is perhaps too light when it comes to plot construction

R = Readability   T = Tension

and circumspect clueing.

The Bishop in the Back Seat (1981)

C ★ ★ ★ ★ ★ ★	P ★ ★ ★ ★ ★
R ★ ★ ★ ★ ★ ★ ★	T ★ ★ ★ ★ ★

WATSON, Colin (1920) British humorous crime writer. In the imaginary, but not altogether unreal, Midlands town of Flaxborough corruption is endemically rife, sexuality is more or less unbridled and modest Inspector Purbright tries to cope. Watson has the rare gift of combining a mystery, or a spy story (*Hopjoy Was Here*, 1962) with deflating farce, and to it he adds an acidic touch of satire. The result rates high. He is also the author of *Snobbery With Violence*, a much-quoted study of the audience for British crime novels, in which he coined the enormously useful expression "Mayhem Parva".

Coffin, Scarcely Used (1958)

C ★ ★ ★ ★ ★ ★ ★	P ★ ★ ★ ★ ★ ★ ★
R ★ ★ ★ ★ ★ ★ ★	T ★ ★ ★ ★ ★

Blue Murder (1979)

C ★ ★ ★ ★ ★ ★ ★	P ★ ★ ★ ★ ★ ★ ★ ★
R ★ ★ ★ ★ ★ ★ ★	T ★ ★ ★ ★ ★

Plaster Sinners (1980)

C ★ ★ ★ ★ ★ ★ ★	P ★ ★ ★ ★ ★ ★ ★
R ★ ★ ★ ★ ★ ★ ★	T ★ ★ ★ ★ ★

WAUGH, Hillary (1920) American mystery writer, who also writes as H. Baldwin Taylor and as Harry Walker. Hillary Waugh wrote three mysteries in the late 1940s before his classic *Last Seen Wearing* was published in 1952. This story of a girl's death in a New England small town is as detailed as a police casebook, translated into a fictional story by a fine craftsman. Waugh is not only an important crime writer of police cases, he is also one of the main strengths of the Mystery Writers of America which he has served in every executive position and at one time or another as chairman of every committee in the organization. He

received a Grand Masters Award from the Swedish Academy of Crime Writers in Stockholm in 1981.

Madame Will Not Dine Tonight (1947)

C ★ ★ ★ ★ ★ ★	P ★ ★ ★ ★ ★ ★ ★
R ★ ★ ★ ★ ★ ★ ★	T ★ ★ ★ ★ ★ ★

Last Seen Wearing (1952)

C ★ ★ ★ ★ ★ ★ ★	P ★ ★ ★ ★ ★ ★ ★
R ★ ★ ★ ★ ★ ★ ★	T ★ ★ ★ ★ ★ ★ ★

Madman at My Door (1978)

C ★ ★ ★ ★ ★ ★	P ★ ★ ★ ★ ★ ★
R ★ ★ ★ ★ ★ ★ ★	T ★ ★ ★ ★ ★ ★

Colin Watson

Hillary Waugh

C = Characterization   P = Plot

Donald E. Westlake

WELLS, Carolyn (1869-1942) American mystery writer. Carolyn Wells was the author of more than 170 books of which more than 75 were detective novels. Her detective was Fleming Stone, and she followed a schedule of writing three books featuring him each year. She was more noted for her children's books and for her anthologies of humour which are still standard works in America. She also wrote *The Technique of the Mystery Story* in 1913 (revised in 1927).

The Fleming Stone Omnibus (1933)

C ★ ★ ★	P ★ ★ ★ ★ ★ ★ ★
R ★ ★ ★ ★ ★ ★ ★	T ★ ★ ★ ★ ★

WENTWORTH, Patricia (1878-1961) British detective story writer. She was the creator of Miss Silver, literary cousin to Agatha Christie's (q.v.) Miss Marple, though created in the same year, 1928, so neither derives from the other. Miss Silver features in many of the 65 novels written between 1923 and 1961, popular in paperback twenty years after their author's death. Generally they mix adroitly romance and crime, with a good old haunted house liable to play a part and young love being as satisfactorily brought to a conclusion as Miss Silver's handling of the case.

Pilgrim's Rest (1946)

C ★ ★ ★ ★ ★	P ★ ★ ★ ★ ★ ★ ★
R ★ ★ ★ ★ ★ ★ ★	T ★ ★ ★ ★ ★ ★ ★

WESTLAKE, Donald E. (1933) American mystery writer. Although Donald Westlake first wrote in traditional hard-boiled mystery style, he turned to humorous cases with *The Fugitive Pigeon* (1965) and became one of the success stories of the day. He gives to his bungling characters a warmth which sets them above just funny men. He also writes books featuring an ex-policeman, under the pen name Tucker and about a professional thief as Richard Stark. Westlake received the Edgar

for Best Novel in 1967 for *God Save The Mark*. A number of his books have been successful on the screen.

The Spy in the Ointment (1966)

C ★ ★ ★ ★ ★ ★ ★	P ★ ★ ★ ★ ★ ★ ★
R ★ ★ ★ ★ ★ ★ ★ ★	T ★ ★ ★ ★ ★ ★

The Hot Rock (1970)

C ★ ★ ★ ★ ★ ★ ★ ★	P ★ ★ ★ ★ ★ ★ ★ ★
R ★ ★ ★ ★ ★ ★ ★ ★ ★	T ★ ★ ★ ★ ★ ★ ★

Castle in the Air (1980)

C ★ ★ ★ ★ ★ ★ ★	P ★ ★ ★ ★ ★ ★ ★
R ★ ★ ★ ★ ★ ★ ★ ★ ★	T ★ ★ ★ ★ ★ ★

Dennis Wheatley

WHEATLEY, Dennis (1897-1977) British crime writer. Dennis Wheatley's writing career, preceded by several years in the family wine

R = Readability   T = Tension

business, produced more than sixty novels covering a wide range from straight detection to supernatural fantasy. Despite their often stiff characterization and stiffer style, the books struck a vein of taste for the strange, the exotic and the aristocratic patriotic which made many of them best-sellers.

The Devil Rides Out (1934)

C ★ ★ ★ ★	P ★ ★ ★ ★ ★ ★
R ★ ★ ★ ★ ★ ★	T ★ ★ ★ ★ ★ ★ ★ ★

The Black Baroness (1940)

C ★ ★ ★ ★ ★	P ★ ★ ★ ★ ★ ★
R ★ ★ ★ ★ ★ ★	T ★ ★ ★ ★ ★ ★ ★

They Used Dark Forces (1964)

C ★ ★ ★ ★ ★	P ★ ★ ★ ★ ★ ★ ★
R ★ ★ ★ ★ ★ ★	T ★ ★ ★ ★ ★ ★ ★

WHITFIELD, Raoul (1897-1945) American pulp short-story writer and novelist. He produced only three novels but dozens of stories for *Black Mask*, some under the penname Ramon Decolta with a hero Jo Gar, a Filipino private eye, which are among his best. He specialized in the action stories beloved of *Black Mask*'s editor, Captain Shaw.

Green Ice (1930)

C ★ ★ ★ ★ ★ ★	P ★ ★ ★ ★ ★ ★ ★ ★
R ★ ★ ★ ★ ★ ★ ★ ★ ★	T ★ ★ ★ ★ ★ ★ ★ ★ ★

WHITNEY, Phyllis (1903) American mystery writer. Phyllis Whitney is best known for her books for young people, although she also writes adult mysteries. In 1960 she received the first Edgar award given for a Juvenile Novel with *The Mystery of the Haunted Pool*. In 1963 she again received an Edgar for Best Juvenile, with *Mystery of the Hidden Hand*.

Seven Tears for Apollo (1963)

C ★ ★ ★ ★ ★ ★ ★	P ★ ★ ★ ★ ★ ★
R ★ ★ ★ ★ ★ ★ ★	T ★ ★ ★ ★ ★ ★

WILCOX, Collin (1924) American mystery writer, who also writes as Carter Wick. Former businessman

Collin Wilcox approached the business of writing with a clear-cut strategy, to create a detective hero around whom he could build a successful series. After a boss shot with Stephen Drake, a clairvoyant journalist, Wilcox has succeeded with Lieutenant Frank Hastings, of San Francisco Homicide, and is now firmly established in the top group of police procedural writers.

The Lonely Hunter (1969)

C ★ ★ ★ ★ ★ ★ ★ ★	P ★ ★ ★ ★ ★ ★ ★
R ★ ★ ★ ★ ★ ★ ★	T ★ ★ ★ ★ ★ ★ ★ ★

Doctor, Lawyer . . . (1977)

C ★ ★ ★ ★ ★ ★ ★	P ★ ★ ★ ★ ★ ★ ★ ★
R ★ ★ ★ ★ ★ ★ ★ ★	T ★ ★ ★ ★ ★ ★ ★ ★ ★

WILES, Domini (1943) British suspense novelist and Yorkshire dialect poet. She daringly, and not unsuccessfully, set her first novel, *Death Flight*, in America. Tension is its keynote in situation after situation. It is a mode she has followed subsequently.

Death Flight (1977)

C ★ ★ ★ ★ ★ ★ ★	P ★ ★ ★ ★ ★ ★ ★
R ★ ★ ★ ★ ★ ★ ★ ★	T ★ ★ ★ ★ ★ ★ ★ ★ ★

Pay-off (1982)

C ★ ★ ★ ★ ★	P ★ ★ ★ ★ ★ ★ ★
R ★ ★ ★ ★ ★ ★ ★ ★	T ★ ★ ★ ★ ★ ★ ★ ★ ★

WILLIAMS, Alan (1935) British thriller writer. Williams' experiences as a correspondent in Algeria, Vietnam, Czechoslovakia and Ulster obviously helped provide the authentic feel of his varied backgrounds. His spy novels are all based on historical fact, in their occasions if not their details, but their pacy excitement derives from their author's writing skill.

The Beria Papers (1973)

C ★ ★ ★ ★ ★ ★ ★	P ★ ★ ★ ★ ★ ★ ★ ★ ★
R ★ ★ ★ ★ ★ ★ ★ ★ ★	T ★ ★ ★ ★ ★ ★ ★ ★

Gentleman Traitor (1975)

C ★ ★ ★ ★ ★ ★ ★ ★	P ★ ★ ★ ★ ★ ★ ★
R ★ ★ ★ ★ ★ ★ ★ ★ ★	T ★ ★ ★ ★ ★ ★ ★

C = Characterization   P = Plot

WILLIAMS, David (1926) British detective novelist and chairman of an advertising and public relations firm. He began writing late in life pleasant stories about one Mark Treasure, wealthy businessman involved by chance in crime. But the stories developed and improved book by book until his hilarious 1980 novel was short-listed, deservedly, for the Crime Writers Association Gold Dagger.

Murder for Treasure (1980)

C ★ ★ ★ ★ ★ ★ ★ ★	P ★ ★ ★ ★ ★ ★ ★ ★
R ★ ★ ★ ★ ★ ★ ★ ★	T ★ ★ ★ ★ ★ ★ ★

Ted Willis

WILLIS, Ted (1918) British crime writer, television writer, playwright and since 1963 Life Peer as Baron Willis of Chiselhurst. He was the creator of that nicest of policemen, Dixon of Dock Green, who, though originally a stage character, later in a film and as a long-running hero/ narrator of a television series, also appeared between hard covers in *The Blue Lamp* (1950) and others. But late in a busy writing career Ted Willis took to the crime novel directly with *Death May Surprise Us* (1974) (*Westminster One* in U.S.), a suspense story that used his knowledge of Parliament gained through much work in the House of Lords.

Other suspense stories, increasingly successful, followed.

Man-Eater (1976)

C ★ ★ ★ ★ ★ ★ ★	P ★ ★ ★ ★ ★ ★ ★ ★
R ★ ★ ★ ★ ★ ★ ★ ★	T ★ ★ ★ ★ ★ ★ ★ ★

The Buckingham Palace Connection (1978)

C ★ ★ ★ ★ ★ ★ ★	P ★ ★ ★ ★ ★ ★ ★
R ★ ★ ★ ★ ★ ★ ★	T ★ ★ ★ ★ ★ ★ ★

WILSON, Colin (1931) British philosopher, writer on the paranormal, novelist, historian of murder, visiting professor in the United States and crime writer. He has written five crime novels, each marked in a different way by the philosophical and the horrible. *Ritual in the Dark* is a study of a modern Jack the Ripper, exploring murder as creation. In *The Schoolgirl Murder Case* the detective mixes mysticism with clue-hunting.

Ritual in the Dark (1960)

C ★ ★ ★ ★ ★ ★ ★	P ★ ★ ★ ★ ★ ★ ★
R ★ ★ ★ ★ ★ ★ ★	T ★ ★ ★ ★ ★ ★ ★ ★

The Schoolgirl Murder Case (1974)

C ★ ★ ★ ★ ★ ★	P ★ ★ ★ ★ ★ ★
R ★ ★ ★ ★ ★ ★ ★	T ★ ★ ★ ★ ★ ★ ★

WILSON, Jacqueline (1945) British suspense novelist. She uses settings of an ordinary domestic kind and fits into them situations that grip, true and human. Added to these qualities is an ability to write about intimate sex without hesitation or exaggeration. Her stories are told in highly readable, unpretentiously accurate English that converts what could have been twaddle into truth.

Snap (1974)

C ★ ★ ★ ★ ★ ★ ★ ★	P ★ ★ ★ ★ ★ ★ ★ ★
R ★ ★ ★ ★ ★ ★ ★ ★	T ★ ★ ★ ★ ★ ★ ★ ★

WILSON, Steve (1943) British thriller novelist. After leaving Oxford University he travelled by motor-cycle widely in Europe and at length in South America and the U.S. He uses his experiences of the

R = Readability   T = Tension

drug scene and the world of wandering youth to excellent effect in fast-moving books which yet find time for dense (if never thickety) description, aware of the past as well as the present. His hero is Jack, known as the Dealer.

Dealer's Wheels (1982)

| C ★ ★ ★ ★ ★ ★ ★ ★ | P ★ ★ ★ ★ ★ ★ ★ ★ |
| R ★ ★ ★ ★ ★ ★ ★ ★ | T ★ ★ ★ ★ ★ ★ ★ ★ |

WOOD, Christopher (1935) British adventure suspense novelist and screenwriter (for two Bond films, *The Spy Who Loved Me* and *Moonraker*). He believes in catching the reader in the midriff, for example with a full-out description of snake-gutting as the opening of *Taiwan*. After that the pages packed with action follow bam-bam-bam through to the end.

Taiwan (1981)

| C ★ ★ ★ ★ ★ ★ | P ★ ★ ★ ★ ★ ★ ★ |
| R ★ ★ ★ ★ ★ ★ ★ ★ | T ★ ★ ★ ★ ★ ★ ★ |

WOODHOUSE, Martin (1932) British scientist and suspense novelist. His first novel was *Tree Frog* (1966) and like its successors it stood out for an individual wit. He is notably aware and a decidedly civilized writer.

Mama Doll (1972)

| C ★ ★ ★ ★ ★ ★ ★ ★ | P ★ ★ ★ ★ ★ ★ ★ ★ |
| R ★ ★ ★ ★ ★ ★ ★ ★ ★ | T ★ ★ ★ ★ ★ ★ ★ ★ |

WOODS, Sara (1922) British detective novelist, resident in Canada. She began in 1962 a regular series – two a year – of whodunits with strong legal backgrounds, featuring Antony Maitland, barrister, and gradually introducing his family and friends, who have become very real characters while still not bulking overlarge in the stories they inhabit. The stories are told in admirable clear-running prose. Frequently, but not always, Ms Woods hits on a fine, intriguing plot. Almost always there is a courtroom finale, tense but devoid of Perry Mason conjuring.

They Stay for Death (1980)

| C ★ ★ ★ ★ ★ ★ ★ ★ | P ★ ★ ★ ★ ★ ★ ★ ★ |
| R ★ ★ ★ ★ ★ ★ ★ ★ | T ★ ★ ★ ★ ★ ★ |

Dearest Enemy (1981)

| C ★ ★ ★ ★ ★ ★ ★ ★ | P ★ ★ ★ ★ ★ ★ ★ ★ |
| R ★ ★ ★ ★ ★ ★ ★ ★ | T ★ ★ ★ ★ ★ |

Enter a Gentlewoman (1982)

| C ★ ★ ★ ★ ★ ★ ★ ★ | P ★ ★ ★ ★ ★ ★ ★ ★ |
| R ★ ★ ★ ★ ★ ★ ★ ★ | T ★ ★ ★ ★ ★ ★ |

WOOLRICH, Cornell (1903-68) American mystery writer who also wrote as William Irish. Cornell George Hopley-Woolrich was a New York near-recluse but a writer of high estate. His awards are many, from his first prize-winning novel *Children of the Ritz* (1927), a non-mystery, to his Edgars for novel and screen, and his many short-story awards including the French Mystery Prize for short story. His first mystery was *The Bride Wore Black* (1940), a particular success, and as William Irish he added to his successes with *The Phantom Lady* in 1942. He was an inventive writer whose stories more often than not were set on the seamy side of New York.

The Black Curtain (1941)

| C ★ ★ ★ ★ | P ★ ★ ★ ★ ★ ★ |
| R ★ ★ ★ ★ ★ ★ | T ★ ★ ★ ★ ★ ★ ★ |

The Black Angel (1943)

| C ★ ★ ★ ★ ★ | P ★ ★ ★ ★ ★ ★ |
| R ★ ★ ★ ★ ★ ★ | T ★ ★ ★ ★ ★ ★ ★ |

The Black Path of Fear (1944)

| C ★ ★ ★ ★ ★ | P ★ ★ ★ ★ ★ ★ |
| R ★ ★ ★ ★ ★ ★ ★ | T ★ ★ ★ ★ ★ ★ ★ |

YATES, Dornford (1885-1960) British adventure novelist, pseudonym for Major Cecil Mercer.

C = Characterization   P = Plot   R = Readability   T = Tension

"Sometimes," wrote Cyril Connolly, distinguished critic, "at great garden parties, literary luncheons, or in the quiet of an exclusive gunroom, a laugh rings out . . . admirers of Dornford Yates . . . have found out each other." They are admiring the racist, sexist, imperialist adventures of the well-off Berry and Co, Major Pleydell of White Ladies, and his friends. But told with huge zest and considerable wit, from 1907 to 1954.

Berry and Co (1920)

C ★ ★ ★ ★ ★	P ★ ★ ★ ★ ★ ★ ★
R ★ ★ ★ ★ ★ ★ ★ ★ ★	T ★ ★ ★ ★ ★ ★ ★

YORK, Andrew (1930) Pseudonym of Christopher Robin Nicole, British novelist, who also writes as Robin Cade; Peter Grange; Mark Logan; and Christina Nicolson. Nine years of working in a West Indian bank can hardly have prepared Andrew York to write his fast moving, violently melodramatic thrillers featuring Jonas Wilde, the Eliminator, a secret agent licensed to kill. Different from, and more promising than, the Wilde books are those recounting Police Chief Munroe Tallant's investigations on a West Indian island.

The Eliminator (1966)

C ★ ★ ★ ★ ★ ★	P ★ ★ ★ ★ ★ ★
R ★ ★ ★ ★ ★	T ★ ★ ★ ★ ★ ★ ★

Tallant for Trouble (1977)

C ★ ★ ★ ★ ★ ★ ★	P ★ ★ ★ ★ ★ ★ ★
R ★ ★ ★ ★ ★ ★ ★	T ★ ★ ★ ★ ★ ★ ★ ★ ★

YORKE, Margaret (1924) British suspense novelist. She began in 1970 with a series about Patrick Grant, don detective, but in 1974 with *No Medals for the Major* started combining crime with studies of psychology, whydunits. She is distinctly a woman writer with all the sympathy that implies, especially for the hapless victims of events, with all the penetration of often contradictory motives and with that toughly practical handling of problems that is a particular female gift (as in her story of rape, *The Hand of Death*). Sensitivity is her hallmark.

No Medals for the Major (1974)

C ★ ★ ★ ★ ★ ★ ★	P ★ ★ ★ ★ ★ ★
R ★ ★ ★ ★ ★ ★ ★	T ★ ★ ★ ★ ★

The Cost of Silence (1977)

C ★ ★ ★ ★ ★ ★ ★	P ★ ★ ★ ★ ★ ★ ★
R ★ ★ ★ ★ ★ ★ ★	T ★ ★ ★ ★ ★ ★ ★

The Hand of Death (1981)

C ★ ★ ★ ★ ★ ★ ★	P ★ ★ ★ ★ ★ ★ ★
R ★ ★ ★ ★ ★ ★ ★	T ★ ★ ★ ★ ★

YUILL, P. B. British crime novelist, pseudonym of Gordon Williams (1939), novelist, and Terry Venables (1943), football club manager. The first book under this name was by Gordon Williams alone, an excellent creepy, *The Bornless Keeper*. Thereafter the two collaborated on the adventures of James Hazell, London private detective, East Ender, tough, warm. The books portray excellently contemporary London and often the parts other writers do not reach, the ordinary working-class tower blocks, for instance. But they are also notable for their undertow of moral comment.

The Bornless Keeper (1974)

C ★ ★ ★ ★ ★ ★ ★	P ★ ★ ★ ★ ★ ★ ★ ★
R ★ ★ ★ ★ ★ ★ ★	T ★ ★ ★ ★ ★ ★ ★ ★ ★

Hazell and the Menacing Jester (1976)

C ★ ★ ★ ★ ★ ★ ★	P ★ ★ ★ ★ ★ ★
R ★ ★ ★ ★ ★ ★ ★ ★ ★	T ★ ★ ★ ★ ★ ★ ★

"P. B. Yuill" (Gordon Williams and Terry Venables)

THE PEOPLE OF CRIME FICTION

The People of Crime Fiction
H. R. F. Keating

ABNER
Uncle

Uncle Abner is a mighty figure. He solved the mysteries that confronted him in a backwoods Virginia community, of which he was squire, in the first years of the nineteenth century before the infant American nation had any proper police system. He had two great attributes for his self-imposed task: a profound knowledge and love of the Bible, and keen observation of human actions (as when he showed that a deaf man could not have written a certain document because a word in it was mis-spelt phonetically). There never has been a detective of fiction with the tremendous moral power of this simple, strong and sane American.
Creator: Melville Davisson Post

ALLEYN
Det. Supt. Roderick

Roderick Alleyn is a gentleman. He is also a Scotland Yard policeman. And he has few, if any, of the mannerisms of the Great Detectives of the days that preceded him. He carries himself with an accidental elegance, learnt perhaps in his Eton schooldays, under which compassion lies. And toughness. With the passing years from his first appearance in 1934, as he rose from Inspector to Superintendent, he betrayed more and more human feelings. They led him eventually to court and marry Agatha Troy, painter, and to suffer a wartime separation from her and feel the awkwardness of coming together again after years apart. The popular Press called him "the handsome detective", but the soubriquet that pleased him (or his pencil-wielding alter ego) was "that nice chap, Alleyn". And you should pronounce it "Allen".
Creator: Ngaio Marsh

The illustrations of The People of Crime Fiction come from a variety of sources: film and television stills; book and magazine illustrations; postage stamps; and in two cases the creators of the characters have themselves drawn portraits for use in this book. Several illustrations have been specially commissioned.

APPLEBY
Sir John

Appleby equals erudition. "The Deipnosophists," he murmurs in mid-investigation in an Oxford college study (Where else?), "Schweighauser's edition . . . Dindorf's compacter". Decently concerned with putting the bracelets on a murderer, he is as much, or more, concerned to put a ready and urbanely witty reply to an interlocutor (for the better amusement of those who happen to be reading about him). He began as a humble – well, humblish – Inspector; he ended as Commissioner of the Metropolitan Police and the recipient of a knighthood. Yet even in retirement he solved a case or two, sometimes in the country gentry world of his sculptress wife's deliciously eccentric family, the Ravens. If your murder's committed in a great house with top people as suspects, Appleby's your man.
Creator: Michael Innes

ARCHER
Lew

He is a private investigator. Private, so that we don't ever know too much about him (a divorce; a career in the police ended when he refused to condone corruption; a liking for the works of the Japanese artist Kuniyoshi). An investigator, in that what makes him tick is finding out why, going deep – almost always into a wealthy California family where a father has alienated children. He has opted for the shadows, not the sunlight. He is an underground man. He might almost be a writer. And like a mole he throws up to the surface every now and again what lies underneath our complexities and complacencies.
Creator: Ross Macdonald

AUDLEY
Dr. David

He works for one of those mysterious, more or less unnamed British Intelligence outfits, and he considers himself (He is formidably intelligent) "not a field man, never had been and never wanted to be". But the Unseen Hand deals with that from time to time. As the years have gone by, we have dug further and further into his history. We know now, we who at the beginning had only a bare name, Audley, and his observant, thoughtful eyes, we know a good deal now of his earliest life, his 1939-45 War career as a young lieutenant soon caught up in great matters, a rebellious period when he tried hard to be a minor historian, an ancient family house, a strained relationship with the man he called his father. At his peak he has perhaps the subtlest mind ever to have pitted wits in the shifting world of spying and counter-spying, and he is very much an upper-class Englishman, reticent, honourable, past-imbued.
Creator: Anthony Price

BECK
Martin

Walter Matthau in
The Laughing Policeman

He is Swedish. Strong-jawed. Laconic. With stomach pains. Out of love with an ever-plumper wife. And senior man in the Stockholm Homicide Squad. Unusually for a fictional detective, he changed a good deal during his recorded life, growing older, growing wiser, at one time trying to take all the guilt for wrongful police action on to his thin shoulders, later taking a new view of the work he has to do. If the picture seems dreary, it sometimes is, though the dreariness is toughened by strong views on the failings of society and, thank goodness, swept away by the moments of wild farce that are apt to befall him.
Creators: Maj Sjowall and Per Wahloo.

BLAISE
Modesty

A Neville Colvin drawing from the long-running strip cartoon in *The Evening Standard* (now *The New Standard*)

THEY'RE JUST HAMMERS FOR THE LOCAL CRIME BOSS—I *KEPT* TELLING THEM I'M NOT HERE ON BUSINESS BUT THEY WOULDN'T BELIEVE ME

A female James Bond, so she perhaps began. But, in comic strip and in book and, straying rather under the hands of Joseph Losey, on film, she has developed into a lady with her own views of the world and how to get through it. She started on the wrong side of the law – as a refugee from some Levant back-alley, given that forename because she had none of it, at least in her hunger for knowledge – and she has ended, aided and abetted but never bedded by the Cockney tearaway Willie Garvin, as a goodie. But still a toughie.

Creator: Peter O'Donnell

BLAKE
Sexton

Illustration by E. E. Briscoe from *The Union Jack* magazine (Nov 1911)

From ephemeral hero of a story for British boys in *The Halfpenny Marvel* in 1893 to a figure of myth: that's the career of Sexton Blake, detective. Some 200 authors are reputed to have stirred the brew from time to time, as well as film scriptwriters and television serial merchants (he was played by Laurence Payne, on the side a detective novelist). He began life as a sub-Sherlock Holmes figure, with a Baker Street flat and Tinker, a more active page-boy than Holmes's Billy, and went on to be an all-purpose hero, British to the core. *Creator:* Harry Blyth

BOLAN
Mack

Otherwise The Executioner, hero of
a long series of American
paperbacks, and, if we want to be
sociological, harbinger of the
America of President Reagan and the
Moral Majority. Carrying with him
the aura of Vietnam, it is his mission
to wipe out in military style Mafia
hoods and the like as he travels from
city to city in the U.S.A. under the
motto "Live large and stay hard".
He has been called the Everyman of
the 1970s, committed to lone
vengeance against a corrupt society.
Creator: Don Pendleton

BONAPARTE
Det. Insp. Napoleon

Known as Bony. Found as a baby
beneath a tree in Queensland,
Australia, son of an Aborigine
mother and a white father, he was
taken to an orphanage where, seen
by the matron trying to eat a
biography of the great French
emperor, he was given his names. He
proved highly intelligent, graduated
from Brisbane University and then
joined the police. He owes his chief
characteristic, his ability to read "the
book of the bush" to one Tracker
Leon, a half-caste employee of the
Queensland Police encountered by
his creator during years of
wandering over Australia's wide
spaces. Bony is tenacious and
boastful, and charming. But his
boast of never having been defeated

over a case was always made good,
even when in *An Author Bites the
Dust* (1948) he had to investigate
within the urban confines of
Melbourne.
Creator: Arthur W. Upfield

BOND
James

Agent 007, licensed to kill. He liked his martinis "shaken, not stirred", and he had much the same aim vis-à-vis women, whom he preferred "well-scrubbed". Many and varied and extraordinarily named were those who yielded to his charm, though his affairs never lasted long. Even when he married the less exotically named Tracy, fate (or fiction's imperious demands) brought about her death at an assassin's hand that very day. What precisely about him it was that attracted these butterfly swarms it is hard to say. It may have been the three-inch scar that showed "whitely down the sunburned skin of his right cheek" and the comma of black hair dangling above it. It may have been his immaculate, British gentlemanly appearance in general. His black knitted tie could have wreaked devastation with some. Or perhaps his athletic powers were the irresistible attraction: he fought best at odds of three to one, with both judo and karate (but never kung-fu) at his command, plus an extraordinary skill in knife-throwing. Or his warranted proof against the utmost refinements of torture, especially with priapic overtones, may have been what lay beneath so many easy liaisons. But perhaps it was no more than his golf, played always for money. Or his equally cool prowess at the gambling tables. Then again a gun has notorious phallic connotations, and Bond carried a 0.25 Beretta in a holster under his left arm and was a superb marksman. Or could it have been his cherished 1933 four-and-a-half litre Bentley, with extra accessories? Or that his expertise at the restaurant table paralleled that on the twisting roads? And, finally, was that rigorous breakfast of orange-juice, scrambled eggs and bacon the put-off that brought so many promising erotic sagas to early conclusions, his stern Scottish father (surrogated by the ever-paternal M) correcting the morning after the excesses that a Swiss mother had begun to bring about the night before?

Creator: Ian Fleming, succeeded by Robert Markham, John Gardner and others

Sean Connery in *Goldfinger* (1964),

George Lazenby in
On Her Majesty's Secret Service (1969)

BRADLEY
Dame Beatrice

In more than 50 books the career of Beatrice Adela Lestrange Bradley, psychiatric adviser to the Home Office, has been faithfully chronicled. Twice married, possibly even three times, though for many years without the encumbrance of any spouse (A faithful secretary, Laura, conveniently wife of a Scotland Yard detective, does much of the husband donkey-work), she has solved numerous complex crimes, often by ladling out vigorous common sense coupled with curiously whimsical humour, just occasionally by committing a justified murder of her own. She was early made a Dame Commander of the Order of the British Empire. Dame Beatrice has stayed middle-aged, and infinitely old and wise – as a holder of honorary degrees from every university except Tokyo ought to be – through some 50 years' adventuring. She has retained, too, the looks that have caused her to be described as "a benign lizard" or "not unlike a witch" (one of whom she believed to be an ancestress of her own) and, be it noted, handsome.

Creator: Gladys Mitchell

BRANDSTETTER
Dave

Insurance investigator and homosexual. His father, with whom he had a complex relationship and who dies in the course of the recorded career, was head of a big California insurance company, for which Brandstetter works because, like the classic private eyes before him, investigation is what he wants to do. And a classic private eye Brandstetter is, ever pursuing the truths he suspects lie behind the facades put in front of him. In so far as he is this, it is irrelevant that he happens to be homosexual. The statutory blondes the private eye meets are in his case attractive young men whom he takes to bed for longer or shorter times. And that is all. It makes heterosexual readers think, and perhaps widens their sympathies. But it almost always so happens that Brandstetter's cases take him into the various gay worlds of California and so, though we thus see exotic locales, perhaps the universality of his adventures is the less.

Creator: Joseph Hansen

BROWN
Father

His achievement in the matter of the Moonshine Murder was considered by some "the most remarkable triumph in the history of detective science". But he was a man remarkable for not being remarkable, round of face and body, black of garments, which looked both commonplace and jaunty, so gently genial that he is very shrewd; he had difficulty always in rolling his old umbrella with its knob like a club, or indeed in keeping it off the floor. He worked by trying to get inside possible suspects "and when I'm quite sure that I feel like a murderer, of course I know who he is". He knew who they were; we know almost nothing about him, beyond that his first name began with a J and that he popped up during a long priesthood in an extraordinary variety of places, Chicago, Paris, Hartlepool (County Durham), Cobhole (Essex), Scarborough (Yorkshire), the London borough of Camberwell, Latin America, Scotland, Norfolk, Italy, Exmoor, Cornwall, Oxford, Boston (Mass.), Spain. *Creator:* G. K. Chesterton.

BUNTER
Former Sergeant

Glyn Houston in BBC Television's *The Nine Tailors* (1974)

He was in Lord Peter Wimsey's company in the Army in France during the 1914-18 War and afterwards became his servant, making himself, too, an expert forensic photographer. He is the epitome of 1920s manservantness, even to speaking on the telephone with "that throttled stridency peculiar to well-trained persons" and to greeting the grisliest crimes with the expression "very gratifying". He was meticulous as a valet. Lord Peter's dress-shirts were always in the second drawer of the wardrobe, his silk socks in the tray on the right-hand side and the dress-ties just above them.
Creator: Dorothy L. Sayers

CADFAEL
Brother

He lived in the eleventh century and was the monk in charge of the herb garden in the abbey at Shrewsbury, a Welshman half at home, half not, among the Englishmen in this thriving border town. He was half at home, half not, too, among the religious brethren since, although he had an unshakeable vocation, earlier in life he had been a soldier and had wandered the world, not altogether innocently. This gave him understanding of a wide variety of human beings, which, coupled with keen observation and strong powers of deduction, made him a considerable detective long before any such had been thought of.
Creator: Ellis Peters

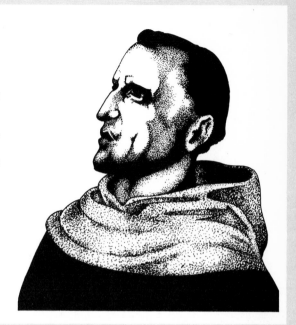

CAMPION
Mr. Albert

Under this mildly good name hid one Rudolph, a royal, and hidden he stayed till the end. But of the person who at first hid behind owlish spectacles and a silly ass manner – *a.k.a.* "Tootles Ash", he said – something more did through the years and the books emerge. Seriousness showed through and people came to turn to him as a "universal uncle". After mysterious and unrecorded work during World War II he found "the great carpet of his half-finished private life hung on a shadowy loom before him, the threads tangled and dusty, the pattern but half-remembered". But both that life and criminal investigation were resumed until at last the fair hair had turned a distinguished white and the puzzling and light-hearted cases of old became affairs of state.
Creator: Margery Allingham

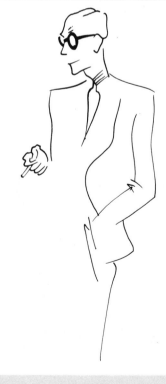

CARELLA
Det., 2nd Grade,
Stephen Louis

of the 87th Police Precinct in an imaginary city.

Known as Steve. "They keep telling me Carella is the hero of the series," moans Ed McBain, author of the many books about that collective hero, the detective squad of the 87th Precinct in a place called Isola (and they keep telling him that's Manhattan, too). Carella was even killed in the third original paperback of the series in the general interest. But there is a good precedent for detective revival. So beyond saying that Carella's wife is Teddy, who is beautiful and a deaf-mute, let us mention some other members of the squad. There is the somewhat paternal Lieutenant Byrnes. There is Detective Meyer Meyer (he of the joky father), patient as an older brother. There is Detective Bert Kling, youngish and learning. There is Detective Cotton Hawes, redheaded with a streak of white. There is Detective Arthur Brown, huge and black. And there is even a bad apple in the barrel, Detective Andy Parker. And there are more. When McBain sets out to have a collective hero, he collects.

Creator: Ed McBain

Burt Reynolds in *Fuzz* (1972)

CARTER
Nick

From the cover of
*Nick Carter Detective
Library* (1891)

The year 1886 saw Nick Carter spring to life in the evanescent pages of the *New York Weekly*, written, under orders, by one John R. Coryell. Since then many another scribe has scribbled, one of them, Frederic van Rensselaer Dey, to the extent of more than 1000 stories. Carter himself was, at least in his beginnings, on a similar heroic scale, able to fell an ox with one biff from "his small, compact fist" as well as having been trained by his Dad to observe the minutest detail and to produce voices ranging from an old woman's squeak to the basso of "a burly ruffian". From this to sophisticated secret agent operating in 1980s paperbacks is a long journey. Nick Carter made it. *Creator:* Ormond G. Smith, magazine proprietor.

CHAMBRUN
Pierre

Manager of New York's "finest luxury hotel", the Beaumont, where rather more mysteries are apt to happen than real life perhaps provides. But worry not. Pierre Chambrun, in between smoking Egyptian cigarettes, rejecting lunch because that's when the Beaumont is busiest and drinking quantities of Turkish coffee, sees to the bottom of each one as it comes up, with some assistance from his PR man. His chief attribute is "some kind of magical radar system behind his bright black eyes" that enables him to "sense a malfunction in the Swiss-watch operation of the world over which he presides". With those eyes that can also show compassion or be as severe as those of a hanging judge he would plainly make out as a detective almost anywhere. *Creator:* Hugh Pentecost

CHAN
Charlie

A detective of the Honolulu Police,
of Chinese descent, father of eleven
children beginning with "No. 1
Son", chubby and charming Chan is
a great hand with the apt aphorism
("The fool in a hurry drinks his tea
with the fork") and was created with
the laudable intention of providing
some positive discrimination after
many a year of wicked Chinese. He
featured in only six novels, but all
but one were filmed and there were
many later cinema spin-offs in most
of which Chan was played by a
Swede, Warner Oland.
Creator: Earl Derr Biggers

Warner Oland in *Charlie Chan at the Opera* (1936)

Alastair Sim in *Green for Danger* (1946)

COCKRILL
Inspector

A little man (several inches too short
to be a British police officer, except
when the gangling Alastair Sim is
playing him in that perennial thriller
movie, *Green for Danger*), Cockie
might well be called The Case of the
Vari-coloured Hair, sometimes
white, sometimes grey. Yet he is
always himself, chirpy, apt to be
waspish, a great picker and stealer of
miscellaneous hats, but no fool. He
was somewhat disadvantaged by
having been created an officer of the
Kent police and thus in principle
confined to that county. But his
begetter was well capable of creating
a whole fictional island, San Juan el
Pirata, on which he could be
involved in murder while
holidaying. And he believes in the
truth of things.
Creator: Christianna Brand

CONTINENTAL OP
The

He has no other name but that. 'Op' is for 'operative' and 'Continental' is the Continental Detective Agency, an organization modelled very closely on Pinkerton's for which the Op's onlie begetter worked. Hammett has said that he knew many operatives much like his man, unromantic, fat, middle-aged. But the Op, like them, is as well tough, tough, tough. Yet, real person though he is, he is also paradoxically the eyes of a writer, a writer of the best sort of fiction, stories that take the false fronts we all present to the world and "stir things up" (the Op's own description of his method of work) till one by one those fronts are knocked away and the true state of things is clearly seen.

Creator: Dashiell Hammett

From *Black Mask* magazine

COOL
Mrs Bertha

She is huge, fuelled often by triple helpings of pecan waffles. She is irascible. She ran a California private detective agency from 1936 onwards when she became a widow (or from 1939 till 1970 to go by the 29 books). She had a partner, a tiny disbarred lawyer, Donald Lam, who once described her as resembling "a cylinder of currant jelly". More comprehensively she has been called "profane, massive, belligerent and bulldog". She was, however, more than capable of using such language and worse on her own behalf. Her tough talk and tough mind always belied a grandmother's twinkling looks.

Creator: A. A. Fair

CRIBB
Sergeant

Alan Dobie as
Sergeant Cribb in the
Granada television series

Scotland Yard detective officer of the 1880s who, in profile, reminds young ladies of active imagination of the map of Portugal, sharp featured and with an imperfect nose. His staccato manner of speech conceals a kindly soul, and his invariable bowler hat hides a shrewd mind that is very seldom tricked by the many pretences of Victorian life. He is however too cunning not to give all such their outward due, especially when they emanate from his superior officer as they frequently do.

Creator: Peter Lovesey

CUFF
Sergeant

He was said to be the finest police detective in England at the time of the mysterious affair of the Moonstone diamond at Lady Verinder's house in Yorkshire in the year 1848, a business which after his retirement to devote himself to his hobby of rose-growing he was able to see to a satisfactory conclusion, despite an early false start. Gabriel Betteridge, Lady Verinder's house-steward, described him thus: "A grizzled, elderly man, so miserably lean that he looked as though he had not got an ounce of flesh on his bones in any part of him. He was dressed all in decent black, with a white cravat round his neck. His face was as sharp as a hatchet, and the skin of it was as yellow and dry and withered as an autumn leaf. His eyes, of a steely light grey, had a very disconcerting trick, when they encountered your eyes, of looking as if they expected something more from you than you were aware of yourself."
Creator: Wilkie Collins

DALGLEISH
Commander Adam

Poet. A widower – his wife died in childbirth as did the baby – he is sometimes, despairing of love affairs in which he and his partner are "groomed for pleasure like a couple of sleek cats", as much preoccupied with remarriage as with murder. Quite rightly. But he is a good Scotland Yard man, solving the mysteries that confront him in the way mysteries are best solved, by the use of sympathetic imagination. Still, his flat in Queenhithe, a significantly unresidential city area of London distinguishedly bordering the Thames, remains unshared, with its fifteenth-century lectern among the furniture, and he is able to drive his sporty Cooper Bristol untamed. He is and always will be, whatever may befall him, essentially self-sufficient, even to forcing on himself a certain callousness, wary of "susceptibilities to which he, Dalgleish, had no right." And however much, bit by bit, we get to know about him he remains a very private person.
Creator: P. D. James

DALZIEL
Det. Supt. Andrew

and PASCOE
Det. Insp. Peter
of some provincial city.

Detective-Superintendent Andrew Dalziel

Drawing by creator

The Laurel and Hardy of detection? Well, no. Perhaps the Hardy (fat) and Laurel (slight), but as apt to be serious as humorous (and blackishly humorous when they are funny). But it's a splendid combination: the late middle-aged, lifetime-a-copper, gross, earthily commonsensical Dalziel (and you're supposed to pronounce it Dayell) and the youngish, head-in-air, sociology graduate, liberal-minded Pascoe, advancing from sergeant to inspector and losing a few illusions on the way. They complement each other. They score off each other. They, grudgingly, have come to respect each other. They even Watson and Holmes each other, and Holmes and Watson.
Creator: Reginald Hill

DA SILVA
Capt. José Maria Carvalho Santos

Zé to his friends. A detective of the Rio de Janeiro police, he is tall and athletic but his face is pock-marked and he wears a brigand moustache, "almost as a challenge". It is a challenge that appeals to many, many women. Son of a rich family, he became interested in criminology while studying in the States and he has refused promotion in order to stay as an investigator. He hates airplanes, snakes and fat women in trousers and he has a terrible temper. In short, he's human. As he should be, being closely based on a real-life Brazilian police officer.
Creator: Robert L. Fish

DEE
Judge Jen-djieh

He lived in China between 630 and 700 A.D. and, though his cases are fictional, he was a real magistrate, exercising the functions at times of an investigator, and eventually rising to be Premier to the Empress Wu. Like oriental potentates in other cultures or the Latin and Greek gods, he often put himself into disguise and mingled with the

common folk in order to glean information. Often, too, he found himself dealing with three cases at once: it was a traditional Chinese way of going about detection in fiction. But, sitting in silence, stroking his long beard, with his three wives keeping discreetly out of the way, invariably he reached a solution, or rather three.
Creator: Robert Van Gulik

DOVER
Chief Insp. Wilfred

Illustration by Keith Jones
from the jackets of the Dover
series (Weidenfeld & Nicolson)

"And I'll tell you something else for free," he growls, speaking straight from the stomach. "I can do without looking at nasty messes like this right after my lunch." The local police, at whom he has growled, are somewhat surprised to hear this from a member of the famed Scotland Yard Murder Squad, but Dover bluntly adds "I could throw up right now." This is his style, except that it doesn't perhaps convey the full extent of his laziness which must be added to his much spoken of dentures and digestive processes and his crude contempt for all around him, mitigated only by gross flattery to anyone likely to provide food and drink. He got into the Murder Squad simply because no one else would have him, but safely there he makes sure he looks after Number One. Luck, taking advantage of others and an occasional sudden access of shrewdness solve his cases for him. *Creator:* Joyce Porter

DRUMMOND
Bulldog

Otherwise Captain Hugh Drummond, *D.S.O.*, *M.C.*, of 60a Half Moon Street, London W.1., formerly of the Royal Loamshire Regiment where he was worshipped by the men, a cousin of Lord Staveley, *a.k.a.* Old Turnip-Top. Hearty blows, preferably directed at foreigners, beer by the tankard, a Sports Bentley, only one light to shoot out in the luxurious salons into which, a captive disguised as a typical somebody in the lower orders, he is so often brought: this is the world of Bulldog Drummond. Phyllis is his wife ("By God, the swine, they've got Phyllis") and Carl Peterson, often vanquished, as often popping up pristine for the next round or fielding his mistress, Irma, as a substitute, is his perennial enemy.

Drummond himself is yet more perennial. He may have faded away but, surviving two or more authors, he never died, despite his occasional fears that This is The End ("Good-bye, chaps, and all that sort of rot"). *Creator:* Sapper and later Gerard Fairlie, and Henry Reymond in books-of-the-films

Illustration by Howard K. Elcock for *The Pipes of Death* (1921)

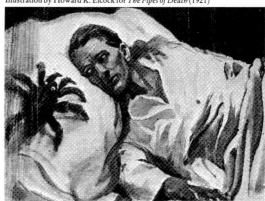

DUPIN
Le Chevalier C. Auguste

There was residing in Paris in the year 18-- a young gentleman of excellent, even illustrious, family reduced by a variety of untoward events to poverty. Meeting an American of similar interests, he agreed to share with him a time-eaten and grotesque mansion at No 33 Rue Dunot in the Faubourg St Germain. There, plunged into perpetual Night, they lived shuttered in and only when the sable divinity permitted wandered the streets. Dupin, his friend hazarded, was a Bi-Part Soul, part creative, part "resolvent". Le Chevalier proved, however, a dab hand at solving the odd mystery, some murders in the Rue Morgue, the death of the

unfortunate Marie Roget (in circumstances curiously parallel to the demise of a Mary Rogers in the vicinity of New York), an affair of a purloined letter in which his services were so earnestly sought by Monsieur G----.
Creator: Edgar Allan Poe

FELL
Dr. Gideon

He weighed a huge amount. He looked much like the great G. K. Chesterton, and often behaved in much the same eccentric fashion, "wearing a box-pleated cape as big as a tent" with spectacles "set precariously on a pink nose", their black ribbon blowing wide "with each vast puff of breath which rumbled up from under his three chins and agitated his bandit's moustache". Meeting him was said to be like encountering Old King Cole or Father Christmas. The sort of mysteries he enjoyed solving – and "enjoyed" is the word – are those that are "impossible" or those that seem to have a snicker of the supernatural about them. He solved them in some 23 novels and a good many short stories between 1933 and 1967, and they can still give a lot of pleasure. In one of the 23, *The Hollow Man* (*The Three Coffins* in the U.S., 1935), he delivers what has been held to be the classic discourse on locked-room murders.
Creator: John Dickson Carr

FELLOWS
Chief Fred C.

He is chief of police for the little Connecticut town of Stockford, a place ordinary as peanuts except that it does have rather a lot of mysterious murders. It is not for nothing that Chief Fellows' creator was First Selectman (in England it would be mayor) of the Connecticut town of Guilford and before that editor of the weekly newspaper in a similar nearby community. Fellows himself chews tobacco, tells corny but pointed stories and worries about his waistline. But he is au fait with current forensic science, for all that his approach is often decidedly informal and his headquarters in the Town Hall basement, and he can always keep smartypants Lieutenant Biloxi of the State Troopers from muscling in.
Creator: Hillary Waugh

Drawing by creator

FEN
Professor Gervase

Professor of English Language and Literature at the University of Oxford, and, self-proclaimed, "the only literary critic turned detective in the whole of fiction". He frequently moaned about the lack of really puzzling cases, but he moaned exuberantly, as he did everything else. Even when confronted on arrival in Sanford Angelorum (*Buried for Pleasure*, 1949) with a station platform of singular dinginess he only "repined briefly" before setting out for adventure like a modernized unruly knight, a variety of hats classified as "extraordinary" in place of helmet and plumes. This immoderate enthusiasm landed him over the years in a variety of situations of the utmost farcicality.
Creator: Edmund Crispin

FRENCH
Inspector

He is the Mr Plod of fictional sleuths, working his way with equal solidity through false alibis (very apt to depend on railway timetables) and statutory meals. Is there a new development in a case? What is French's immediate reaction? "Come and have a bite of breakfast and then let's hear the great news" (*Sir John Magill's Last Journey*, 1930), or with an alibi on the point of being broken "French was impatient to get to his calculations, but it was so nearly supper time that he had to wait till the meal was over" (*Anything to Declare*, 1957). Yet his cases still fascinate from the sheer methodicalness of their solutions.
Creator: Freeman Wills Crofts

FU MANCHU
Dr.

His originator speaks (in a 1934 broadcast) about prowling London's Limehouse area in the early years of the twentieth century: "One night, and appropriately enough it was a foggy night, I saw a tall and very dignified Chinaman alight from a car. He was accompanied by an Arab girl, or she may have been Egyptian, and as I saw the pair enter a mean-looking house, and as the fog drew a curtain over the scene, I conceived the character of Dr Fu Manchu." He saw him as a personality "exceeding the normal" who could be "a force which could upset Governments and perhaps change the course of civilization." Thank goodness Sir Denis Nayland Smith was there to protect us all.
Creator: Sax Rohmer

GAMADGE
Henry

He was Agatha Christie's chosen favourite among American fictional sleuths, as might be expected a cultured and gentle New Yorker. Bibliophile, consultant on autographs and inks, his cases often, but not always, required his specialist knowledge. But he was younger than this image might suggest, somewhere in his thirties and with an attractive habit of twisting his mouth in a smile. But he was no womanizer (He had both wife and young son, not to speak of the cat, Martin).
Creator: Elizabeth Daly

GENTLY
Det. Supt.

Once described by the American critic Anthony Boucher as "probably the best interrogator in the business", Gently also makes a point of being a benign observer of the contemporary British (and occasionally French) scene. Race prejudice, Zen, capital punishment, lesbianism, violence: you name it, Gently has pondered it. Beneath a somewhat neutral surface he displays a calm intelligence coupled with a solid determination.
Creator: Alan Hunter

GHOTE
Insp. Ganesh Vinayak

of the Bombay CID.

Ghote (You pronounce it *Go-tay*, aspirating the G if you want to be really ethnic) is the great put-upon of crime literature. His superiors generally despise him and drop him in awkward situations with terrible regularity. But the criminals he has to deal with are equally hard on him, whether they be street urchins or extraordinarily rich and influential (Dread word) businessmen. Yet he always gets his man, despite his huge diffidence and a not small capacity for making mistakes. Which means he walks a twisted tightrope. He has contrived to do so, however, in a manner which the critics have described as 'endearing, enchanting, engaging.'

Creator: H. R. F. Keating

Zia Mohyeddin in BBC Television's *Hunt the Peacock* (1969)

GIDEON
Commander George

Known as "GG". He is the epitome of the good British policeman. Slow to anger, but implacable when he meets crimes of cruelty or encounters a "rotten apple" in the force. Indeed, he sometimes seems to live up to the Biblical connotations of his name and it has been said that, give him a gown and a flowing beard, and he would look pretty much the Old Testament prophet. This makes him occasionally ponder conscientiously whether he achieves full communication with his underlings at Scotland Yard. He has a sterling home life, too, married to nice Kate and with young adult children who give him decent worries to push aside when crime imperiously calls.
Creator: J. J. Marric, and after his death William Vivian Butler

GOODWIN
Archie

He is legman to the great Nero Wolfe (*qv*), one of the most demanding jobs in detective fiction, something that causes him to drink a great deal of milk. But milksop he is not. Typist, on the other hand, he was, and Wolfe's cases needed at times a great deal of typing. But since Wolfe boasted (not always truthfully) that he never left his house on business, Archie did get out a good deal to question suspects and, thanks to a faultless memory, report back verbatim. He also had a girlfriend, Lily Rowan, for whom he must have had to abandon the brownstone at times too, since Wolfe considered women "astounding . . . animals". Yet the Goodwin heart always gave an extra thump when his boss pronounced the magic words "Satisfactory, Archie."
Creator: Rex Stout

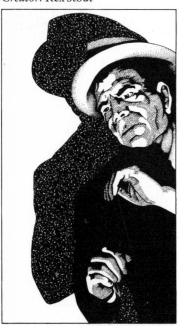

HAMMER
Mike

He was perhaps the nastiest hardboiled dick ever to stalk the pages, a great kicker in the groin, shooter in the belly, breaker of bones, gouger-out of eyes and burner-up of baddies in general. On the other hand, it can be said of him that he is actually more intelligent than many reviewers portrayed him. And he was, after all, patriotic. And actually brave. On his first appearance, too, in *I, The Spy* (1947) he sold six million copies.
Creator: Mickey Spillane

Biff Elliott in *I, The Jury* (1953)

HANNAY
Major-General Sir Richard, *K.C.B., D.S.O., Légion d'Honneur, Justice of the Peace.*

Amateur British agent from early 1914, when aged 37, till past the age of 50. He was missing the top of his left thumb (shot off by wicked Dominick Medina in *The Three Hostages*, 1924) but otherwise was exceptionally clean-limbed. He needed to be fit: much of his time adventuring was spent being chased (in *The Thirty-nine Steps*, 1915, *Greenmantle*, 1916, *Mr Standfast*, 1919). He might seem to have avoided the pursuing enemies only when he exploited his talent for disguise, as a milkman, a chauffeur, a roadmender, an American (Heavens!), as a religious publisher's representative, as a film producer and, worse, as a pacifist. He could do the "old Mashona trick" of catching a thrown knife in his mouth, something he learnt as a puir Scot making enough money in South Africa to set up as a landed gent in England and join a lot of decent clubs. He was a terribly good sport, praising most of his enemies and frequently belittling his own courage. He wasn't awfully good with women. He knew, he would say, as much about them "as I know about the Chinese language". But he did have good German, French, Shangaan and Sesutu.
Creator: John Buchan

Robert Donat
in *The Thirty-nine Steps* (1935)

HELM
Matt

He was America's answer to James Bond (*qv*), like him outmanoeuvring the wicked Russians aided, and sometimes nearly subverted, by a wide variety of delicious ladies. But six-foot four he-man American to Bond's suave Brit, he drives not a Bentley but a pick-up, takes his martinis as they come without insisting on three measures of Gordon's gin to one of vodka and a half of Kina Lillet, takes his orders from 'Mac' not snooty old 'M', was a wildlife photographer rather than a casino expert. Like his creator he also wrote Westerns till duty called (and was an American of Scandinavian origin). But once duty did call he fought hard, stuck his neck out whenever it was called for, and sometimes when it hardly was, but was a nice guy throughout even when killing people.
Creator: Donald Hamilton

Dean Martin in
The Silencers (1966)

HOLMES
Sherlock

Why is Sherlock Holmes such a towering figure in crime fiction? Not because he was the first scientific detective, although that played its part in securing his first popularity. Not because he was a pioneer "series character" with the stories running in the *Strand* magazine, though this too helped largely with the initial necessary take-off. Not because his creator hit on the splendid device of Dr Watson, though here again was something that helped enormously in the beginning. No, Holmes lives because he was a "real" person, and this is not because he was modelled on Dr Joseph Bell, though he was. But such a lift from life is always only a starting-off point for the imaginative writer. Nor even does Holmes live because he "was" Arthur Conan Doyle, although he does indeed have as his basis the curious and powerful contradictions that lay underneath the outwardly stolid, Dr Watsony exterior of his originator. But there have been countless authors who have put themselves-plus into fiction and have failed to produce very memorable characters. No, Holmes truly lives because Doyle on this base of himself and his contradictions was able, from the workings of intuition, to portray a person with a full, human existence of his own, with the contradictions of real life at once typical of his exact era and strongly individual. So we get Holmes the athletic, the master of the singlestick, and also the effete violin-player. We get Holmes the finest example of the "gentleman" (his greatest condemnation was "How an English gentleman could behave in such a manner is beyond my comprehension") and Holmes the victim of "drug mania". We get the Holmes of "red-Indian composure" who was yet restless, nervy and excitable. We get Holmes hating publicity and yet egging on Watson to recount his exploits. We get Holmes the Darwinian scientist, ever looking forward to more and better progress, and we get Holmes the introspective music-lover, the man who could talk about "those unusual and outré features which are . . . dear to me". We get Holmes the woman hater who yet showed "a remarkable gentleness and courtesy" to them. A bundle of contradictions. But a bundle. Something single and united. A human being.

Creator: Arthur Conan Doyle

JONES
Grave Digger

(Not to mention **JOHNSON, Coffin Ed**).
They were black detectives operating in the horrifyingly violent and macabrely comic world of New York's Harlem and were as tough and violent on occasion as the soul brothers they warred against, thinking nothing, for instance, of shooting away a car's mirror as a warning not to hog the road. They were at first marked by compassion amid the hellishness, but with time each found grimly that even compassion could die and its place be taken by cynicism. They were physically all they needed to be, looking like a pair of "big shouldered plowhands in Sunday suits at a Saturday night jamboree". And when they wanted a little jamboree of their own they went to places like a pork store to eat hot chicken feetsy against a decor so bilious-looking that "only the adhesive consistency of Mammy Louise's Geechy stews could hold the food in the stomach."
Creator: Chester Himes

Godfrey Cambridge and Raymond St. Jacques in *Cotton Comes to Harlem*

LOVEJOY
Mr

Antiques dealer and amorist, called just Lovejoy by one and all. "Women and antiques are very similar," he says with his habitual brash cheekiness. "They come either in epidemics or not at all." So, scouring the East Anglian countryside knocking at doors, quite often he is out of luck and stony broke, sometimes he is in luck and chasing some priceless object – he has the gift, not unknown elsewhere, of being able to tell by touch whether anything old is genuine – while simultaneously trying to keep several willing females from finding out about each other. He does it all with a zest, and a knockabout way with the English language, that is hard to resist, especially as his reflections abound with highly knowledgeable tips about collecting.
Creator: Jonathan Gash

LUGG
Magersfontein

Valet to Mr Albert Campion (*qv*), old lag (i.e. former convicted prisoner). He had a magnificent crudity in his dealings with life ("Not 'arf a funny bloke outside," he said in a hoarse whisper. "A foreigner. Shall I chuck a brick at 'im?"). He was large and he was lugubrious, "a hillock of a man, with a big pallid face which reminded one irresistibly of a bull terrier. He was practically bald, but by far the most outstanding thing about him was the all-pervading impression of melancholy which he conveyed." (*Mystery Mile*, 1930). Born doubtless in 1899, year of the Boer War battle at Magersfontein, he hardly changed over the years, thank goodness, and Mr Campion with his fancy notions was ever his despair.
Creator: Margery Allingham

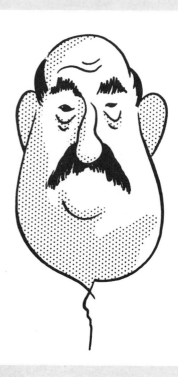

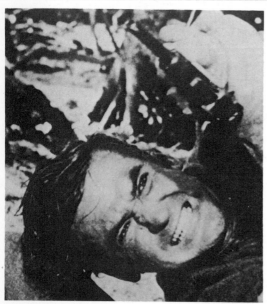

Rod Taylor in *Darker than Amber* (1970)

McGEE
Travis

Like many a distinguished predecessor (Robin Hood, Jonathan Wild the receiver-thief taker, Vidocq founder of the Paris Sûreté) Travis McGee is a baddie (with a good streak) turned goodie. He began as a recoverer of stolen goods, often by direct action from the thieves – "salvage operations" he called them – and has ended as pretty much a straight private eye helping those in distress (frequently feminine) from his boat in Florida, *The Busted Flush*, won at cards. He is aided in his role as twentieth-century knight-errant by being six-foot four and a former football professional and also by being extremely handsome and, one gathers, rather therapeutic in bed.
Creator: John D. MacDonald.

MAIGRET
Jules

Commissaire (eventually) at the Quai des Orfèvres, the Paris police headquarters. He is, in fact, the writer as investigator. Investigator of human beings in all their surprising variety. He brings his inquiries to success by reaching, through intuition largely (on one notable occasion solving the case by burying himself under bedclothes with a fearsome cold), an understanding of the murderer he is investigating. He speaks of "a kind of intimacy" he achieves with them. From his very first case he had in mind a childhood conception, the existence of a "repairer of destinies", a doctor-cum-priest figure "able to live the lives of every sort of man". Maigret himself had wanted to become a doctor but was unable to because of lack of family funds. He joined the police instead, pounded a beat, worked in the vice squad – he always had great sympathy for prostitutes as "victims" – and then as a detective rose to the top. As a person he is the soul of the bourgeois, happily married, never moving till retirement from his comfortable old flat in the Boulevard Richard Lenoir, pipe smoking – fifteen in the rack on his desk – drinking with keen appreciation, eating good peasanty food with yet more appreciation, patient and quiet.
Creator: Simenon

Rupert Davies as Maigret in
BBC Television's long-running series

MAITLAND
Antony, Q.C.

There cannot ever have been an English barrister who has got more involved in crime before it reaches the stage of advocacy than Antony Maitland. Yet he is a stickler for correctness in court, where his manoeuvres are fascinatingly authentic, and only perhaps once in more than 30 adventures does he allow himself a touch of the Perry Masons (*qv*) (*Cry Guilty*, 1981). Indeed, he usually makes efforts not to become entangled in any extra-mural activities, though when he feels that justice will not be done he plunges in, much to the anxiety of his wife, Jenny, and the somewhat lofty disapproval of his uncle, Sir Nicholas Harding Q.C., whose house in Kempenfeldt Square he has a share of. His domestic life is, in fact, almost as interesting and as cosily comforting as are his legal and detective successes.
Creator: Sara Woods

MARLOWE
Philip

Los Angeles private eye, named romantically for the sixteenth-century English dramatist. In the last letter his creator wrote he spoke of him as "a lonely man, a poor man, a dangerous man, and yet a sympathetic man", one who was always to have a rather shabby office and never to have a permanent lover (though in the book left unfinished, *The Poodle Springs Mystery*, Marlowe is married to a millionairess, if still clinging to that shabby office). If there is an unreconciled clash here, it reflects itself in Marlowe. He is the "hardboiled tec": but he has had two years at college and will praise Flaubert's writing and play enough chess to study it on his own. Ross Macdonald, whose Lew Archer (*qv*) is in many ways Marlowe's heir, has commented that "It is Marlowe's doubleness that makes him interesting: the hard-boiled mask half-concealing Chandler's poetic and satiric mind". Perhaps in one way that poetic mind expressed itself successfully, not in any of the somewhat high-faluting phraseology that Chandler could produce ("Down these mean streets a man must go," as he wrote of the classic private eye, "who is not himself mean, who is neither tarnished nor afraid"), but in the wisecrack and the flipped-in description, those succinct and witty expressions of a whole philosophy of life. There is Marlowe's description of the huge Moose Malloy in *Farewell, My Lovely* as "about as inconspicuous as a tarantula on a slice of angel food". There is his comment on the overblown Grayle house in the same book that it "probably had fewer windows than the Chrysler building". There is that moment in

The Big Sleep when he says "Neither of the two people in the room paid any attention to the way I came in, although only one of them was dead." There is his late lament for an altered Los Angeles in *The Little Sister:* "It had no more personality than a paper cup." Marlowe's greatness lies in the way he sees the world he walks through.
Creator: Raymond Chandler

Six faces of Marlowe on film *(from top)*: Robert Montgomery, Dick Powell, Robert Mitchum, Humphrey Bogart, Elliott Gould, James Garner

MARPLE
Miss

Actress and crime writer
Dulcie Gray as Miss Marple

A tall thin old lady (not like Margaret Rutherford in the films) with white hair, a pink-and-white face and an expression of great gentleness in china blue eyes, aged 74 when she began in 1928 and used to wear black mittens, more up-to-date at the time of her last case in 1938 or 1939 (though *Sleeping Murder* was published only posthumously in 1976). But shrewd. And with a nose for evil, an intuitive faculty quite different from Hercule Poirot's busy little grey cells. She had a tart appreciation of the importance of gossip, however, "how often is tittle-tattle, as you call it, true!". In fact, all innocence as she seems, she is a thorough-going cynic, "it is really very dangerous to believe people. I never have for years." It is as well that she did not, or the many murderers in the neighbourhood of the quiet village of St Mary Mead, and those encountered in occasional holidays in the Caribbean or at Bertram's Hotel in London, would never have been brought to book, having been compared to their downfall with a delinquent butcher's boy or a housemaid who, although she always turned the mattresses every day, "except Fridays of course", proved to be her master's kept woman.

Creator: Agatha Christie

MASON
Perry

Los Angeles trial lawyer and, in preparing his defences, a detective who boldly adopted extra-legal procedures to get evidence. His speciality was courtroom fireworks (Many of the gimmicks he used were used before him by his creator) and they were so successful that in the 82 cases he fought prosecuting District Attorney Hamilton Burger never won once. Mason was a great fighter for truth, and regularly accepted clients who could not pay. But, unlike many real-life lawyers who are practised in turning a blind eye to the obvious guilt of the people they are defending, Mason used to say boldly "I never take a case unless I am convinced my client was incapable of committing the crime." If there might seem to be a certain predictability in his career, it is offset by the corkscrew complexity of most the cases he triumphed in, a twistiness that kept readers by the million devotedly hooked.
Creator: Erle Stanley Gardner

Left to right: Della Street, Perry Mason, Hamilton Burger from *The Saturday Evening Post* (1961)

MENDOZA
Lieut. Luis Rodolfo Vincente

of the Bureau of Robbery-Homicide, Los Angeles Police Department.
Cardplayer. As a boy in the east L.A. slums, indeed, he was in danger of becoming a cardsharp but, hooked on justice, he joined the police and now uses a deck principally because he "thinks better with the cards in his hands". In the police he rose steadily, something that enabled him, coupled with an inheritance, to indulge a taste for expensive tailoring and led him eventually to a fine house, a pretty wife and lots and lots of domesticity, right down to cats, assorted, and a Scottish housekeeper, forthright. As a detective, he relies heavily on intuition but knows that it must be backed by the hard work of a constant group of dedicated (and domestic, too) assistants.
Creator: Dell Shannon

MORIARTY
Professor James

The Napoleon of crime. He was, to quote Sherlock Holmes, his opponent in a titans' struggle between good and evil, "a man of good birth and excellent education, endowed by Nature with a phenomenal mathematical faculty", but "a criminal strain ran in his blood". Holmes first clashed with him at arm's length in the Valley of Fear case (he was unknown to the public until Dr Watson wrote of him) but it was in 1891 that he entered the Baker Street rooms and addressed Holmes as follows: "You crossed my path on the 4th of January. On the 23rd you incommoded me; by the middle of February I was seriously inconvenienced by you; at the end of March I was absolutely hampered in my plans." A terrible battle soon followed ending, apparently, only when both men plunged to death at the Reichenbach Falls. Moriarty's similarity to the German superman philosopher Nietzsche has been noted.
Creator: Arthur Conan Doyle, with uncanonical additions by John Gardner.

Illustration by Sidney Paget from The Strand Magazine (Dec 1893)

MOTO
Mr. I.O.

Peter Lorre (left) in *Think Fast Mr Moto* (1939)

Japanese secret agent, whose much lauded career, begun in 1935 with *Ming Yellow*, ceased abuptly to be reported shortly after Pearl Harbour (though it was briefly resumed in 1957 in *Stopover: Tokyo*). An aristocrat with a whole bundle of talents at his fingertips, "I can do many, many things . . . mix drinks and wait on tables . . . manage small boats . . . carpentry and surveying and five Chinese dialects" and also a fine chauffeur and excellent shot, he was especially adept at rescuing weak young Americans in trouble in exotic locales. Nevertheless his novelist originator said of him: "I wrote about him to get shoes for the baby."
Creator: John P. Marquand

NORTH
Mr. and Mrs.
(Jerry and Pam)

They sprang to life in a series of humorous sketches in the *New Yorker* and were then lent by Richard Lockridge to his wife, Frances, for mystery novels. Pam North, in fact, got her forename in such a marital exchange. For some time Richard, in writing the mysteries, had contrived to call her only "Mrs North", but then an occasion arose when Mr North had to attract her attention. "Hey, Fran" was typed. Then in proof this was thought too near the wifely knuckle, the available spaces were counted and "Pam" inserted. (The North came from the Bridge columns). Mr North was a publisher. Mrs North, to quote Otto Penzler, was "as exasperating as a real-life woman" and was Mr North's cat-caring, body-discovering, otherwise unengaged helpmeet.
Creators: Frances and Richard Lockridge

Gracie Allen (pointing) in *Mr and Mrs North* (1942)

OAKES
Boysie

We met him first dead scared in dangerous war's end Berlin, wrongly taken for a cool killer. We said goodbye to him after a trip into space which was not without sexual connotations. He was born of anti-Bondism (Ironical in view of his begetter's later re-begetting), on the wrong side of 40, fearful of violence, air-sickness victim and afflicted with heights phobia. Gardner said of him he was "what most of us are like – luxury-loving, lecherous and a mass of neuroses". He managed to achieve some luxury (and more lechery) while keeping the neuroses at bay by sub-contracting his hit-man tasks to a Soho crook, and in the course of his career he grew up a little to the point where he could say "Don't you see there are no such things as goodies and baddies any more, only just people standing in the dusk of history?"
Creator: John Gardner

Rod Taylor in *The Liquidator* (1965)

PALMER
Harry

Otherwise "Anonymous". In the films of the Deighton books he bears this name; in the books, cunningly, it is never stated that he is each time the same individual ("I heard a soft voice say 'Hallo, Harry.' Now my name isn't Harry, but in this business it's hard to remember." – *The Ipcress File,* 1962.) In this way he can be stretched over an inordinate length of contemporary history. But, whoever he is and whatever his name may be, he has always had that splendidly insolent wit, the attack-defence of the working-class lad of high intelligence finding himself (as did his creator once) working in the world of the Old Boy network. Harry Palmer is very much a real agent, preoccupied with his expenses, working in the very places that real-life spies work and seeing such places as they do, using the same highly sophisticated devices and with every sign of intimate knowledge. And he's charming, a delight to be alongside in whatever adventure.
Creator: Len Deighton

Michael Caine in *The Ipcress File* (1965)

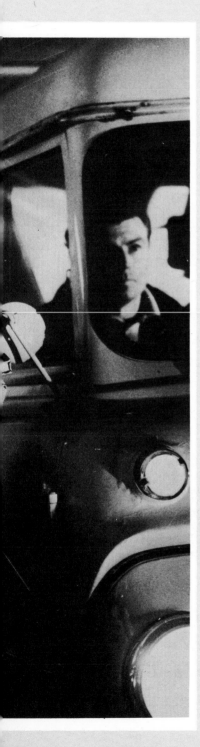

PIBBLE
Det. Supt. James
retired.

He was born in 1915. He was educated at lower middle-class Clapham Academy, topped up by Hendon Police College (for the picked-out flyers). But, despite his early promise and his considerable intelligence, despite being "a copper's copper" even, he was somehow doomed. He got given the jobs that were bound to bring not kudos but condemnation, if not contempt, whatever success in them he had. He was yet another crime hero to start out in reaction to James Bond (*qv*); he had to be unsexy, fallible, no asserter of his rights. And, as such, he came together as a remarkably true portrait of a man.
Creator: Peter Dickinson

POIROT
Hercule

Late of the Belgian Sûreté. Very late. It has been argued, notably by Julian Symons (*qv*), that he did not die at the ripe old age of 135. But the evidence, though as is the way of these things it is somewhat obfuscated, certainly states once clearly that he retired from the Belgian police in 1904 and as so many of his cases refer to events of the time, and occasionally to actual dates, going on into the 1970s, he can be made out to be ordinarily elderly only by a good deal of contriving.

And Poirot was not ordinary. He was shorter than the ordinary. He was much more meticulously dressed. He was cleverer. His little grey cells, so often boasted of, churned faster than the ordinary by a good many revolutions. And his moustaches . . . It would be a bold man who dared describe that work-of-art as ordinary. His detestations were not ordinary either. There was the sea, so unruly that it prevented him ever triumphing, as he surely would have done, in America. There

was lack of symmetry, a thing that so enraged him that he lived for a long time in a London flat (Whitehaven Mansions, or perhaps Whitehouse, or perhaps perhaps Whitefriar) that was a paragon of parallelisms. There was "your English poison", tea, to which he utterly preferred a tisane or a cup of thick sweet chocolate, thereby making himself at one bound the detective all Englishmen loved to hate. And this was the secret of his success: he was, more or less of course omniscient (only once does he say of himself that he has been thirty-six times imbecile, and even then he triumphed eventually), but omniscience is unpleasing. However, make him a fearful foreigner doing all the wrong things and then he can be cheerfully despised – even as he beats the reader hollow in unravelling the case in front of them both.

Creator: Agatha Christie

QUEEN
Ellery and
QUEEN
Inspector Richard

Ellery, the elegant, the extra bright, is clearly the Holmes of this duo, for all that he is the mystery-writer narrator of most of the books. But the man whom in the early cases he called "Pater", despite an honest American upbringing, is only half a Dr Watson, a person of decided astuteness for all that he is described as "a small, withered, rather mild-appearing old gentleman". The Queens' 221b Baker Street is a brownstone on New York's West 87th Street, and its most significant feature is, not "VR" for Victoria Regina picked out in bullet pocks on the wall, but three volumes of the Arabian Nights. Because the Queens live and work, really, in a wonderland where crimes are marvellously complex and mysteries are always at last made clear, where the bizarre is the everyday, where Dashiell Hammett (*qv*) could ask their creator to "explain your famous character's sex life, if any". But time passed. Ellery Queen dropped both his pince-nez and his equally irritating polysyllables and moved into a more realistic world. Here he did fall in love (*Calamity Town*, 1942) and real people were killed for real reasons and were awarded in the end revulsion mixed with compassion. The progress is not very satisfactory for the sketcher of a biography, but it provided countless readers over a span of more than forty years with two very different, but equally appetizing, kinds of crime novel.

Creator: Ellery Queen

William Gargan (second left) in *A Desperate Chance for Ellery Queen* (1942)

QUILLER

George Segal in *The Quiller Memorandum* (1966)

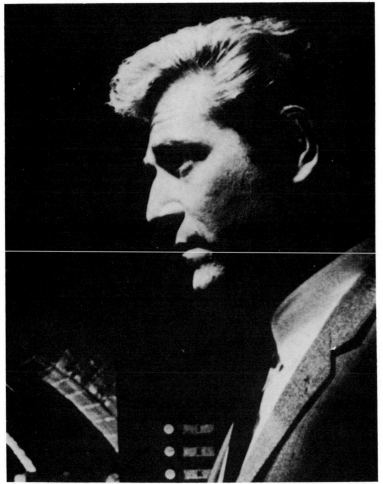

That's not, of course, his name. Just the code identification for the best agent working in London for the Bureau, which is an almost equally nameless organization that does the things M.I.5 and D.I.6 can't or won't. And Quiller also has the suffix '9', which means he can stand any amount of torture up to unconsciousness or mental breakdown. So we're in the world of the super-tough, and Quiller is as super-tough as they come, able to drive at super-top speeds (all the while thinking away about torque and things like that), able to fight with super-fast reflexes (all the while thinking about the circulation of the blood). He's a super-loner, too (Last Testament: "Nothing of value, no dependants, next-of-kin unknown"), and he doesn't drink or smoke (those reflexes, man, those reflexes) and he goes with wolverine women only.

Creator: Adam Hall

RAFFLES
A.J.

Amateur cricketer, "a dangerous bat, a brilliant field, and perhaps the very finest slow bowler of his decade" (which was the 1890s), and amateur cracksman. Raffles was the first, and is perhaps the greatest, of the crime anti-heroes. He was, above all, a gentleman. His rooms in Albany, that exclusive block of apartments in the heart of London's West End, were arranged "with the right amount of negligence and the right amount of taste". His manners were faultless; his consideration for others consistent. He smoked only the rarest Sullivan cigarettes; he quoted Keats. And he awoke adoration in Bunny, the man who had been his fag (no! it's a schoolboy servant) and whom he later rescued from the utter disgrace of unpaid card debts by initiating him into the sport that excelled even cricket, burgling. Raffles died heroically fighting for England in South Africa. But. Let his begetter speak: "Raffles was a villain when all was written; it is no service to his memory to gloze the fact."

Creator: E. W. Hornung. With uncanonical additions by Barry Perowne

RIPLEY
Tom

He is a lie preferrer, a compulsive impersonator, a murderer, sometimes for no good reason. He is a risk taker. When we first met him in New York in 1955 he gave someone a false name and then almost immediately changed it, just to see if he could get away with it. He did. He gets away with a hell of a lot. And we, most of us, love him for it. Partly this is because he has charm, a charm reinforced in the later books by his straightforward love and affection for his beautiful French wife and for his beautiful French house with its much worked garden. For, in short, his true contact with such roots of life as still exist in a rootless world. And we follow him, too, because he tells us something about that late twentieth-century existence. He is the embodiment of the modern theologians' Situation Ethics. The man he is going to murder in *Ripley Under Ground* (1970) exclaims exasperatedly "I cannot understand your total disconnection with the truth of things". But Tom is telling us that that old concept has gone. We live in an all-fluid world. He is our guide.
Creator: Patricia Highsmith

Dennis Hopper in *The American Friend* (1980)

RUSSELL
Colonel Charles

Head of the Security Service in Britain, latterly retired. He is unchippably Establishment, a top dog without the possibility of ever letting himself down. He is a person above any mere temporary prime minister in guarding his country's interests, and a person, too, above all ordinary conventions. *Realpolitik* is what he practises, perfectly ready, when it suits, to talk as man to man, spymaster to spymaster, with the Russian top dog or, even, the American. Or to go yet higher ("he hadn't expected God would be a fool. He'd be a senior administrator"). His other talents include swimming, "it was one of the things, with golf and fishing, which for a man of his age he did better than most". He measures exactly six foot one, the one inch representing surely his being one up on your ordinary tall man but never wanting to go beyond a decent gentlemanly height.
Creator: William Haggard

SAINT
The

Otherwise Simon Templar. He was the prophet of danger. His creed was that danger makes you feel most intensely alive. So, while he was when the chips were down on the side of the good, he was a great breaker of the law. His creator said in a broadcast about him in 1934 that he saw the police as "excellent fellows for keeping an eye on pedestrian crossings and closing down night-clubs and preventing people having a drink at the wrong time . . . and generally adding to the perpetual hilarity of English life". But the Saint, he said, wanted "something more elementary and honest – battle, murder and sudden death, with plenty of good beer and damsels in distress and a complete callousness about blipping the ungodly over the beezer". And when he blips, in London or New York, he leaves his calling card, a stick figure with a halo. But, tremendous success that he was, he lived on and on, from his first adventure in 1928 to 1970 at least, and later in other hands. So he moved with the times. Beer and damsels (as such) went; martinis and girls arrived.
Creator: Leslie Charteris

SCARLET PIMPERNEL The

Nom de guerre (the pimpernel is a little red flower which he used sometimes as a code signal) of a daring and much disguised rescuer of noble aristos from under the very blade of Madame Guillotine, who hid behind the effete persona of Sir Percy Blakeney, fop. "They seek him here, They seek him there, Those Frenchies seek him everywhere. Is he in heaven? Is he in hell? That demn'd elusive Pimpernel." It may well be said that his creator, taking hints from various distinguished figures in literature, Shakespeare (Prince Hal) and Jane Austen (Frank Churchill in *Emma*) among them, stamped out once and for all this archetypal figure, since imitated over and over again, notably in crime fiction by Margery Allingham with her Mr Campion (*qv*), by Dorothy L. Sayers with Lord Peter Wimsey (*qv*) and in dozens of spy stories.
Creator: Baroness Orczy

Leslie Howard with Merle Oberon in *The Scarlet Pimpernel* (1934)

SCHMIDT
Inspector

Chief of Homicide, New York City Police Department. Since 1935 when he first appeared till into the 1980s he has not changed nor aged a wink. His feet were hurting him when Hitler was coming to power; he takes his shoes off whenever he can in the age of the laser. A native of Manhattan, he has all the gift of the inner-city New Yorker for insult (affectionate for friends) and all the acquired distrust that a sidewalks upbringing implants. But he lacks, or lost long ago, the New Yorker's irascibility. Schmitty is the soul of patience as time and again he tracks down his man.

Creator: George Bagby

SHAYNE
Mike

He's the nice private eye. In 71 novels and some short stories he used his fists time and again but very seldom used a gun. He is, in his originator's words, "an ordinary guy like the reader himself". He had a wife at one time, but she died young, causing him to leave his Miami stamping-ground for New Orleans for a while. It was in New Orleans in fact that his creator saw for only the second brief time the man who, when he wanted to write a private-eye novel, leapt at once into his mind. He had encountered him first in Tampico, Mexico, when as a young sailor in a bar brawl he was rescued by a quiet but big-fisted red-headed man who had been sitting alone drinking brandy from a shot glass with iced water as a chaser. He never learnt his name, but years later recognized him in a French Quarter bar in New Orleans, only to see him, hardly had they met, marched away by two mysterious men, a look of chill on his face.

Creator: Brett Halliday

Lloyd Nolan in *Michael Shayne, Private Detective* (1940)

SMALL
Rabbi

from Barnard's Crossing, Mass.
As much, or more, concerned with the religious life of the Jewish community in his town than with murder, David Small, of the rabbinical stoop and spectacles and of the typical absent-mindedness, despite his comparative youth, became involved with crime on seven occasions, one for each day of the week. For such a successful, if thoroughly amateur and armchair, detective it is curious that he seemed to be in constant danger of not having his contract renewed by his congregation. His unshakeable honesty would appear to have been the stumbling-block.

Creator: Harry Kemelman

SMILEY
George

Head of "The Circus" as British Intelligence is called (at least in book pages), latterly retired. He first appeared, modestly, in *Call for the Dead* (1961), vaguely liberal and matched against an old anti-Nazi comrade, the Jewish communist, Dieter Frey. He then made a digression into detection when asked as a friend to investigate murder at a classy British school. He played peripheral parts in two more espionage affairs before coming into his own as a towering figure in the trilogy that began with *Tinker, Tailor, Soldier, Spy* (1974) in which, apparently retired, he seeks out a mole in the very heart of his own old organization. His apotheosis, rightly called *Smiley's People* (1980), sees him sombre even in ultimate victory over his long-time Russian opponent, Karla. Smiley is the reflective spymaster par excellence, always aware of all the implications of his actions, yet carrying them through even when they hurt his profoundest convictions. He is a fictional creation who, ultimately, came to stand for a whole tradition in Western life and thought – and was yet a recognizable person. *Creator:* John Le Carré

Alec Guinness in BBC Television's
Tinker, Tailor, Soldier, Spy (1979)

SPADE
Sam

"Samuel Spade's jaw was long and bony, his chin a jutting v under the more flexible v of his mouth . . ." So begins *The Maltese Falcon* (1930), Spade's single appearance in print. The paragraph, which goes onto describe the v motif running through his whole face, ends "he looked rather pleasantly like a blond Satan." So we know he is tough, "hardboiled" as it was then, and we know, too, that he is, though nearly indistinguishable from the criminals he hunts, on the side of the good. "Don't be too sure I'm as crooked as I'm meant to be," he says, with that deeper and deeper ambiguity that makes him the fascinating figure he is. His gift is that he sees things plain, all things even himself. So, though he knows at the end of the book that "all of me wants to – wants to say to hell with the consequences" and succumb to the beautiful killer Brigid O'Shaughnessy, he rejects this unreality. He does it for all of us.
Creator: Dashiell Hammett

Humphrey Bogart in *The Maltese Falcon* (1941)

STRANGEWAYS
Nigel

Amateur detective, and nephew, conveniently, of Sir John Strangeways, an assistant commissioner at Scotland Yard. He was, on his first appearance, almost to the life his poet begetter's friend and mentor, W. H. Auden; he became with time and maturity very much his begetter himself. He was clever and literary as could be, sent down from Oxford for answering exam questions with limericks ("very good answers") and ever after apt with the right quotation. Because he came to be so closely modelled on his creator Nigel altered slowly over the years of his career until at last in *The Morning After Death* (1966), set in an American university and with a line from Emily Dickinson as the title, he announced "the private investigator is *out*."
Creator: Nicholas Blake

THATCHER
John Putnam

Banker. He is senior vice-president of the Sloan Guaranty Trust Company of Wall Street, an occupation that enables him fairly plausibly to present himself at the scene of various interesting activities around America and even elsewhere, though the way mysterious deaths occur where Thatcher is must be seen as a concession, and a delightful one, to fiction. It is his urbane, rueful, shrewd judgment of people rather than any expert knowledge of stocks and bonds, let alone of fingerprints and other fal-lals, that enables him always to triumph over both the mysteries he meets and the vagaries of his colleagues at the Sloan, about which he can be very funny though generally keeping his sharper thoughts inside his own head.
Creator: Emma Lathen

THORNDYKE
Dr.

He was conceived out of an interest in medical jurisprudence some time in the 1880s when his creator was a student, though he lay quietly germinating in the unconscious mind for twenty years after that till, stirred by the success of Sherlock Holmes, he rose into life. Unlike Holmes, however, Thorndyke was not modelled on any respected teacher (much less on the author himself), but was an idealized construction and deliberately made an ideal human being with a symmetrical face of the classical type and a Grecian nose, as his begetter described him. Indeed, Thorndyke goes further in superiority, being not a detective (Pah!) but "an investigator of crime", a scientist pure and simple (armed with "the inevitable green case" of instruments) and pretty god-like.
Creator: R. Austin Freeman

Drawing by H. M. Brock from *Pearson's Magazine*

TIBBETT
Henry

He is Mr. Ordinary as Scotland Yard detective, his features unmemorable, his hair an undistinguished sandy colour. He is conscientious and occasionally intuitive in a nice, ordinary sort of way ("My nose tells me"). He is apt to speak "thoughtfully" and to gaze at things "long and earnestly". It is his lot, however, to be given by providence or his superiors cases in a variety of exotic locales from ski-resorts in

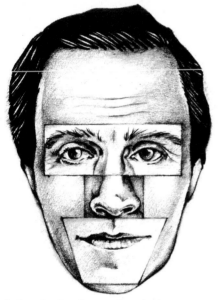

Switzerland to the sun-drenched Caribbean. But he and his wife, Emmy, who is nice too, have a continuing home life, with a ramifying family and hobbies and known preferences in food and drink.
Creator: Patricia Moyes

TIBBS
Virgil

He is a black detective ("despite his dark complexion his features were aquiline") of the Pasadena Police Department in California, though the case that brought him to prominence, *In the Heat of the Night* (1965), took place when he was sent to America's Deep South and encountered race prejudice at its simplest and most hateful, reacting to it with quiet dignity ("They call me *Mister* Tibbs"). His subsequent cases on his home territory have been designed, in his creator's words, "to help explain the police function to the citizenry at large and to show how modern, enlightened police departments function". He is modest to a fault about the part he plays in this.
Creator: John Ball

Sidney Poitier in *In the Heat of the Night* (1967)

TRENT
Philip

His last case was his first, and nearly his only. After that debut book in 1913 the waiting world had to remain waiting until in 1926 came *Trent's Own Case*, to be followed by some short stories, *Trent Intervenes*, in 1938. And that was all. Yet he is important. He was, arguably, the first of the ungreat detectives, the human ones. Dorothy L. Sayers (*qv*), for instance, acknowledged that her "poor Peter" owed a great deal to Trent besides the habit of quotation. Certainly he is remembered as "one of the most attractive sleuths of all time", friendly, tactful, quietly humorous ("Oh, to be in England now that April's there, and whoever wakes in England is entirely unaware whether it's going to rain cats and dogs or be gay with sunshine, birds and blossoms") and very much the human being rather than the master detective. He was an artist by profession.
Creator: E. C. Bentley

Illustration by Jack Faulks from *The Strand Magazine* (June 1938)

VANCE
Philo

Almost the only reason for including this venerable, half-forgotten figure from the early Golden Age of detective fiction in this list is to be able to quote the immortal lines of Ogden Nash: "Philo Vance/Needs a kick in the pance". He did. He was insufferable. A blithering Englishman transformed, and made more blithering, into an American "young social aristocrat" and aesthete. He dropped his every final g; he smoked Régie cigarettes; and he was a Nietzschean superman as well, quite prepared to commit his own murders. Yet he was the most popular fictional detective of his day and his cases were of a logical complexity that has its mad charm.
Creator: S. S. Van Dine

William Powell (left) in *The Kennel Murder Case* (1933)

VAN DER VALK
Inspector Piet

Barry Foster in Thames Television's *Van der Valk*

He was born out of a notion, itself a misconception, that all fictional detectives were boring platitudes, either "mannerisms-and-manservants" or "the beat-up Cal-Flor eye". He died by his author's hand, in mid-book, out of a belief, misconceived too, that because occasional detectives are shot in real life a fictional detective who was, as Van der Valk certainly was, a "real" human being, must get shot too. However, he left behind him ten books that show him as a rounded, complex and contradictory person. A Dutchman, with much Dutch coarseness, yet sensitive. Honest, in that he was incorrupt; yet prepared to be dishonest to secure a conviction. A peasant (if such crude typology must be used); but proud of being an Amsterdamer. Bored by his job; yet wholly interested in his cases. A believer in feminism; yet his wife, Arlette, took pride, until after his death, in being only a housewife. An idealist; yet convinced that ideals for a policeman are a luxury. But all the contradictions did hang together.

Creator: Nicolas Freeling

WATSON
Dr. John *sometimes called James.*

If Conan Doyle had not invented Sherlock Holmes, Dr Watson would be his outstanding contribution to the art of crime fiction. He solved the whole problem of having a Great Detective who in a trice can see to the depths of the matter but who yet must hold off with his revelation till the end of the tale. So, by seeing through Watson's eyes, we readers can learn just enough at just the right times. Yet Doyle was cleverer than this: Watson is not precisely us, our presence in the story. He is stupider, just a little, than us. So we both stay with him and by-pass him to be with Holmes himself in part. Watson, too, enabled Doyle to produce stories in a series, all the same, each different. We owe him a great debt. What of the man himself? He possessed not a few of the characteristics of his creator, "If I have one quality upon earth it is common sense." He was, above all, decent and straightforward in the central tradition of British life at that time. "Watson," cried Holmes, "you are a British jury." And, though often left groping by Holmes and often teased by him, he was courageous without blemish when courage was called for (so we put ourselves eagerly into his shoes) and he could on occasion hit back at his hero and ours. He was no two-dimensional device, useful as a device though he was, but a truly human figure.

Creator: Arthur Conan Doyle

WEXFORD
Chief Insp. Reginald

of the Kingsmarkham police, Sussex.
He is staid, middle-aged, highly
moral, yet tolerant and
paradoxically almost as ready with a
quotation as the mercurial don
detectives themselves (but where are
the ranked books in his ordinary
home?). His best quality, both as
someone to read about and as
someone detecting, is his interest in
people, their quirks, their foibles,
their weaknesses, the reasons they
commit murder. He is, too,
intensely domestic, retreating often
to the comfort of his home
surroundings and Dora, his wife,
watching with concern the progress
of his grown-up daughters, one of
whom is a well-known television
actress.
Creator: Ruth Rendell

WIMSEY
Lord Peter

If you love a lord, you'll love Peter
Death Bredon Wimsey, second son
of the Duke of Denver. There are
those that don't. He was created to
make money for his author
(satisfyingly but reticently rich
himself), and he came to birth
originally in a never-finished Sexton
Blake (*qv*) story some five years
before his first seeing the light of
day. Something of a caricature in the
beginning, part Scarlet Pimpernel
(*qv*), part P. G. Wodehouse's Bertie
Wooster, he grew into humanity,
especially in his long and tortuous
courtship of Harriet Vane, and
perhaps degenerated into yukkiness
in the last short stories when the
super-eligible bachelor of yore (It is
discreetly indicated that he is a
considerate tiger in bed) has become
an all-wise father. Yet, springing as
he did in one bound out of his
creator's mind, he had in him always
what he was later to become. In the
first book about him he has
nightmares from his 1914-18 War
experiences; in the last full-length
story he is prey to fierce depression
when he knows that through him a
man will be hanged. And if in the
early days he whistled in an unlikely
way a whole Bach fugue, later he
showed real appreciation of music.
He is a person one can thoroughly
believe in, li!.e, even love as many
women readers do, or hate, as some
male readers do. He remains one of
the immortals of the genre.
Creator: Dorothy L. Sayers

Ian Carmichael in BBC Television's *The Nine Tailors* (1974)

WITHERS
Miss Hildegarde

The schoolmarm sleuth of New York, with her dog, Talleyrand, an apricot-coloured poodle. Snoopy is what she is, so much so that Inspector Piper, whom she regularly insists on assisting – she listens to the police radio and sells charity tickets around police headquarters – once spoke of this little old spinster as "hurling a monkeywrench into the machine". She, on the other hand, can be equally tart about him. Her taste in hats is horrendous, and she wafts round her a perfume of mingled soap and chalk dust (the latter despite being long retired from teaching).
Creator: Stuart Palmer

Edna May Oliver, with James Gleason as Inspector Piper, in *The Penguin Pool Murder* (1932)

WOLFE
Nero

We know a lot about Nero Wolfe, the man often looked on, especially in Britain, as the American Sherlock Holmes. Dozens of short stories, novellas and novels have made him, his brownstone on New York's West 35th Street, his eccentricities and his entourage wonderfully familiar. He was, if we are to believe W. S. Baring-Gould's 1969 biography of him – and on the whole we shouldn't; "Pfui" Wolfe would have said – a twin illegitimate son of Sherlock Holmes and Irene Adler. But what is fact, or fiction-fact at least, is that he weighed one-seventh of a ton, that he was a gourmet's gourmand, that he possessed some 10,000 orchids, that he spoke seven languages including Bari and Albanian, that he hated all things mechanical and most especially the automobile, that he laughed perhaps once a year and then snortingly, that only on his last appearance, in *A Family Affair* (1975), did he venture on such an oath as "By God" or be as directly rude as to say to Inspector Cramer "Shut up" or find himself at a loss for words. Words, oratorically delivered and precise, were his means of living. And he used them often to devastating effect. "I am congenitally tart and thorny," he said. It was no word of a lie.
Creator: Rex Stout

NERO WOLFE

1.50

SAN MARINO

Why People Read Crime Fiction

Professor
Philip Graham

IT SEEMS REASONABLY certain that reading about crime has little to do with committing crime, for the crimes one reads about in fiction are not those that criminals usually perpetrate. This seems particularly true of murder, especially the type of premeditated murder which forms the substance of many detective stories.

In the United Kingdom murder is an uncommon crime, and of the 200 or so committed each year, a sizeable number are unpremeditated assaults involving family members, often occurring at or before breakfast. Such connubial carnage over the cornflakes forms, it will surely be agreed, a relatively small part of the subject matter of crime fiction. In the United States murder is much more common. But the robbery with violence which leads to murder and which represents by far the commonest form of murder in the U.S., is also little portrayed in crime fiction.

Perhaps the main reason why crime has so little to do with crime fiction lies in the fact that most criminal activity is boring and straightforward, and requires little detective ability to resolve. The angry, depressed housewife who stabs her violent, alcoholic husband to death and then wanders into the neighbour's house in a dazed state carrying a bread-knife dripping with blood, hardly calls for the skill of a Poirot. The youth who habitually carries a gun when he plunders apartment houses and shoots to kill when he is surprised, might earn a moment's brief observation from Philip Marlowe, but will never have a whole book dedicated to him.

In some ways, the neglect of common crime as less than fascinating by crime fiction writers is undeserved. The dramatic interaction in a marriage which eventually leads to the ultimate form of violence, and the subtle ways in which emotional deprivation and poverty can lead to violent crime could well form the subject matter of many a modern "psychological" novel of the type that Zola once wrote so well. But most serious crime is brief, sordid and uninteresting; most criminals in real life are less complex than their counterparts in fiction, and the factors that go to make people commit crimes are very different from those which motivate people to read about them.

Psychoanalysts of a previous generation tried to explain the compulsively gripping quality of the detective story by pointing to particular conflicts which the reader had experienced in childhood. In particular, Pedersen-Krag, a psychoanalyst writing over 30 years ago, suggested that the crime-fiction addict was motivated by curiosity over the "primal scene" – parental sexual intercourse. She proposed that "the reader addicted to mystery stories tries actively to relive and master traumatic infantile experiences he once had to endure passively. Becoming the detective, he gratifies his infantile curiosity with impunity, redressing completely the helpless inadequacy and anxious guilt unconsciously remembered from childhood." A little later Charles Rycroft, a British analyst, considered Wilkie Collins' *The Moonstone,* the great nineteenth-century detective story, in greater depth with this theory in mind. He saw the jewel referred to in the title as a symbol of the virginity of the heroine.

This theory does not sound very convincing today. The notion that in adult life we remain preoccupied with our parents' intercourse does not correspond with our own experience, nor with the observations that, as parents, we make of our children. Of course, children are curious once they learn the facts of life about their parents' behaviour in this respect, but the evidence that the questions they ask themselves and the anxiety they experience lie buried in their minds like a ticking time bomb into adult life rests largely on the distorted memories of a small number of psychoanalyzed neurotic patients.

The human brain thrives on stimulation, and normal people will seek excitement if it is lacking in their everyday lives. The slogan "Horler for Excitement" sold a lot of Sydney Horler's thrillers in the 1930s.

All the same, there is a compulsive fascination with crime and its detection which often does persist from childhood. Stories with a detective component, like Enid Blyton's *The Secret Seven* or Carolyn Keene's Nancy Drew mysteries, are very popular even in early childhood, and many adults who are hooked on crime fiction, first began to read about crime at least as early as their mid-adolescent years. So the notion that early experience is important in understanding why people read crime fiction is far from ridiculous, even though we may need to look elsewhere than parental intercourse if we wish to discover the reasons for people's fascination with the genre.

The first mysterious problem to be tackled concerns the reasons why some people seem to enjoy being frightened. No very convincing explanations have ever been produced as to why men will put their lives at peril climbing mountains or driving racing cars when, on their own admission, they find these activities frightening. Why do otherwise sensible, middle-aged women pay good money to expose themselves to horror films which make them scream with terror, or indeed why does a large section of the population buy or borrow books which give them nightmares and worsen the insomnia from which many of them are already suffering?

Explanations drawn from our understanding of the physiology of the brain take us some way. Several years ago it was discovered that an important function of the central part of the brain was to maintain "arousal" – the level of alertness or somnolence which an individual showed at any one time. Stimulating this part of the brain electrically increased alertness in a general way. It was also demonstrated in both humans and other animals that if an individual was bombarded with sensations it would try to avoid further stimulation, and if subjected to unvarying monotonous input, the individual would seek out more sources of stimulation.

There is some evidence that too much or too little stimulation can be positively harmful to brain function. For example in children with epilepsy, it has been demonstrated that, if one gives them mental arithmetic tasks, both extremely difficult and very easy sums seem to bring out epileptic activity. Tasks which are within the ability of the child but which require some effort damp down abnormal epileptic activity. The process of seeking an optimal level of stimulation has been called "sensoristasis", the term implying that there is a physiological regulation of behaviour to ensure that the level of sensory stimulation is kept reasonably steady, at least during waking hours.

This may help us to understand why man is a problem-producing as well as a problem-solving animal. Much effort has gone into explaining how man tackles tasks with which he is faced. Behaviourist psychologists for example, have spent years of their lives studying how rats will run mazes in order to avoid punishment or gain rewards. The concept of "sensoristasis" explains to some degree why, when there are no problems to be solved, man will create them for himself. The commuter faced with an hour's train journey will tackle a crossword puzzle. Men and women bored with their marriages will create problems for themselves in other relationships. The millionaire who need never earn another penny for the rest of his life will start reinvesting his fortune merely for the sake of exercising his mind by playing the market.

This may take us some way to understanding why people seek stimulation when it is lacking, but why should they seek to become frightened as a means of achieving such stimulation? Here one needs to draw on ideas which point to the way in which people will seek out relief of tension for its own sake. There is something enormously rewarding and pleasurable in stopping a painful activity. Indeed for some of us the real reward for taking vigorous physical exercise is that we feel so much better when we stop.

The same may be said of the reduction of fear. It seems that for some people, the reward obtained by the cessation of fear is considerably greater thn the mental pain produced by the fear itself. If this is so, one would expect that individuals would obtain this type of pleasure only from genuinely experienced, unpleasant fear, and this certainly seems to be the case. The child on the roller coaster is certainly genuinely frightened at the time he is on the machine, even if he begs for another turn when he is safely back with his parents. Of course, if the fear is very intense and so unpleasant that its memory persists in vivid form after the experience, then the child will want to avoid a repetition.

Detective and even thriller writers seem to take pretty good care this will not happen. Inevitably they rely on the reader identifying personally with the characters in their books, but usually however realistically physical the descriptions of violence may be, there is rather little attention given to the emotional reactions of the protagonist. There is little harping on the fear and pain suffered by the victim, or the terror of detection experienced by the criminal. The reader is thereby protected from too painful an identification which might prevent him from reading on.

So we have some idea why people enjoy problem-solving exercises and why they might choose fear-inducing experiences for this purpose. But why should so many of them choose to read crime fiction as a means to this end? Here it may be useful to examine perhaps the most popular current theory of emotional development in childhood, that body of ideas which concerns itself with the way babies and their parents become emotionally and physically *attached* to each other, to see whether this can shed light on the problem.

John Bowlby, the psychiatrist most responsible for developing ideas in this area, has pointed out that attachment is biologically necessary for the young to survive. A species in which the young wandered off into danger would rapidly die out.

Behaviour which is important for attachment shows itself in a variety of ways. For example a toddler will travel only a certain distance from its mother (or whoever is its main attachment figure) without looking to check where she is. If she is out of sight, he will rapidly return. In order to achieve successful attachment, babies and toddlers have to be able to recognize their own mothers correctly, and differentiate them from other people. It has now been shown that even in the first few weeks of life, babies can do this by smell and hearing.

Linked to attachment to parents is the child's fear of strangers – an emotion which all normal children begin to show round about the age of six months to one year. When someone unfamiliar to the child comes on the scene (and this of course holds as much for fond grandmothers who have not seen the baby for some time as for unrelated strangers) the baby will cling to its mother for comfort and to reduce anxiety. These forms of behaviour arise at least partly because of in-built mechanisms which are inherited by both child and mother. The infant's smile which releases fond feelings in the mother initially is a genetically-determined response. The mother's concern for her toddler when it is out of sight arises both as a result of experience learned in her own childhood and because she has been genetically programmed to behave in this way.

Now parents and children develop types of attachment behaviour which characterize their interaction in a particular way. Just as mothers and children vary in their personality (some, for example being warm and exuberantly affectionate, while others are more restrained) so they vary in the way they interact together. For the child, this interaction is his first relationship, and its characteristics are likely to set the pattern for later relationships. Thus, for example, children whose links with their mothers are permeated by what Bowlby calls "insecure anxiety" – uncertainty and lack of confidence in their mother's whereabouts and love, will in later life, often have a need to test out the affection of those to whom they are close.

It should be stressed that, even for the most secure child, attachment is always threatened to some degree. Indeed if the child thinks it is not, it is growing up in an unreal world. The child's attachment is bound to be put in jeopardy by a host of other relationships in which both mother and child are involved. It is in the context of the jealousies and rivalries which these other relationships stimulate, and of the threat that they pose to the security of his attachment, that suspicion and fascination with the possibility of violence is first experienced by the child.

In the family dramas played out in the lives of young children they act at different times as victims, criminals and detectives. The precious jewel which is at risk of theft and for which murder may be committed has however usually very little to do with parental intercourse, though certainly rivalry with one or other parent may be a factor. Instead it has to do with the perfect relationship – with the mother, with both parents, or with whoever the child has his most important attachments – which the child imagines to be his but which in fact can never be attained. For the mother will always want, if she is sensible and normal, to give attention to other children, her husband and her friends.

The child is faced with these imperfections in his relationships. He may develop murderous feelings towards a younger brother, for example, but these will be unacceptable to his parents and even, because of his fondness for his brother in other ways, unacceptable to himself. So they are repressed. He cannot understand why he should feel threatened, and therefore he becomes suspicious. At times he feels he has been robbed. His unacceptable feelings rise to the surface and he feels himself a murderer. At other times he acts the detective, trying to work out who can have taken from him what is most precious, but he is always barred from finding a solution because the criminal will always be himself or someone else of whom he is fond.

The Mysterious Bookshop *on New York's West 56th Street sells nothing but crime and suspense fiction, and, although the city has numerous general bookstores* *with crime fiction on their shelves, New York has another specialist store, Murder Inc on West 87th Street.*

In the later adolescent and adult life of the individual his anxiety will be stirred by situations which approximate to those which produce these early unacceptable feelings in childhood. It is not surprising then that detective fiction with its emphasis on murder and theft contains such fascination for all of us. As children we have had to deal with what we have felt to be the unlawful removal of the affection of those to whom we have been attached and our own murderous feelings towards those we have suspected of perpetrating such crime.

In reading such stories, as Rycroft has earlier suggested, we are attempting to resolve the unresolvable, to find the solution to the perfect crime – that in which the detective, the criminal and the victim are one and the same person, namely ourselves. In *The Murder of Roger Ackroyd* and *Ten Little Niggers* Agatha Christie came close in different ways to achieving the creation of these insoluble crimes and the popularity of these books owes something to the degree to which they recreate the childhood situation I have described.

The denouement of many detective stories seems designed to release the tension of those whose childhood fantasies have been activated in this way. The suspects are brought together in one room (a family reunion), the detective puts them one by one in the position of the accused (paternal interrogations of the family to detect the wrongdoer) and finally the culprit is identified and those readers (surely the majority) who have identified with the attractive characters, can usually enjoy a sense of relief that they have escaped punishment.

But why is it that some of us are so much more fascinated than others by this genre of fiction? If we have all, in our childhood, had to deal with these conflicts, why do they sometimes, but by no means always persist in this form?

It is here that personality, inherited or moulded by learning in other ways, may be important. For it is, in particular, those of us who show compulsive tendencies to check, to keep things in good order, to strive towards perfection who are most affected. Pierre Janet, the nineteenth-century French neurologist and psychiatrist, described this personality well. Amongst the characteristics of those he described was a tendency to experience constantly a "sentiment d'incompletude" – a feeling that something remains to be done, a preoccupation with perfection and imperfection. Of course in our daily lives the tendency to experience this feeling may be most helpful, when it is appropriately experienced (checking often discovers mistakes), but if an individual is constantly haunted by it, then he becomes oppressed and disturbed.

The compulsive personality must surely be particularly absorbed by crime fiction. A mass of detail is usually provided by the author, of which the reader can hope to retain only a fraction. The sense of imperfection is constantly disturbed, but the reader can go on, knowing if he persists to the end that finally the criminal will be apprehended and justice will be done. In real life the reader who is a compulsive personality is usually left still doubting; but in the fantasy of the detective story tension is reduced as all doubts and uncertainties are resolved for him – at least until he starts the next book.

Compulsive people are therefore more likely to need to walk over the battlefields of their childhood again and again, checking for clues as to why the outcome sometimes went against them, who it was who conspired for their defeat. Their capacity to identify with protagonists will reactivate their earlier feelings in a way which they find irresistible.

But there is a further type of identification which may be important for them – that in which the reader puts himself in the position of author. For perhaps in no other form of fiction does the reader so frequently stop to consider why the author has developed the story in the way he has. Why is this particular detail regarding the whereabouts of the characters inserted with such completeness? Why does the detective make a visit to this particular suspect before the others? In asking these questions of the author, the reader both cuts himself off from the story in a way which protects him from becoming too involved, and also achieves a feeling of omnipotence. As someone, so to speak, able to get inside the author's mind he can share the feeling of creation and control over the unfolding of the story – a feeling which may enable him to achieve at last a sense of mastery over those childhood situations in which he was helpless and adults seemed to hold all the power.

Philip Graham is Professor of Child Psychiatry at The Institute of Child Health, London, and Consultant Psychiatrist at the Hospital for Sick Children, Great Ormond Street.

Index